PERSPECTIVES ON CORPORATE CITIZENSHIP

Edited by Jörg Andriof and Malcolm McIntosh

Perspectives on Corporate Citizenship

EDITED BY
JÖRG ANDRIOF AND
MALCOLM McINTOSH

Greenleaf
PUBLISHING
2001

© 2001 Greenleaf Publishing Limited

Published by Greenleaf Publishing Limited
Aizlewood's Mill
Nursery Street
Sheffield S3 8GG
UK

Typeset by Greenleaf Publishing.
Printed and bound, using acid-free paper from managed forests, by
Creative Print & Design (Wales), Ebbw Vale.

British Library Cataloguing in Publication Data:

1. Social responsibility of business
I. Andriof, Jorg   II. McIntosh, Malcolm
658.4'08

ISBN 187471939X

CONTENTS

FOREWORD

Professor Dr André Habisch,
Catholic University of Eichstätt and
Managing Director, Center for Corporate Citizenship

Corporate citizenship is certainly one of the big issues of the 21st century. All over the Western world, the importance of an increased co-operation between business and society is acknowledged not only by politicians and academics but also by a growing number of business leaders. Empirical research shows: networks of co-operations are 'social capital' in order to overcome the downsides of globalisation such as social exclusion, ecological problems and mutual distrust between actors from different social and cultural backgrounds.

In the industrial society of the 19th century, physical capital was the key factor of growth and development. In the second half of the 20th century, human capital gained more and more relevance. Within the globalised information society of the 21st century, however, social capital is the driver of organisational and societal improvements: As Robert D. Putnam has shown in his recent volume, *Bowling Alone*,[1] with social capital, economic as well as political and cultural life is stimulated. Therefore, business learns to invest in social capital as it invested in physical and human capital.

In the US during the late 1980s President George Bush initiated a process of cultural change within the business world. The Reagan years with their simplified shareholder orientation had opened up large differences between business élites and other groups in society. Founding new intermediary institutions and starting a long-term communication programme, President Bush tried to overcome dilemmas of mutual distrust. The Clinton administration continued these efforts. Ten years later 'corporate citizenship' is a well-developed issue among US corporations even from different industrial sectors and sizes. The cultural change between business and society is an important companion of the long-lasting success of the American economy.

1 Robert D. Putnam, *Bowling Alone: The Collapse and Revival of American Community* (Simon & Schuster, 2000).

In Europe, a comparable process is emerging in the last couple of years. The foundation of the Prince of Wales Business Leaders Forum in 1992, the European Business Network for Social Cohesion in 1995, the Copenhagen Centre in 1997, the Enquête Commission of the German Bundestag in 1999—these are all are signs of a new orientation of politics and business. However, in every European country special cultural and social traditions also add special aspects to the common frame of corporate citizenship. Thus, at the beginning of the discussion, a brainstorming from different disciplines and national cultural perspectives is important. But we also need a global dialogue between politicians, business and research institutions about 'best practice' and ways to enhance and effectively co-ordinate 'corporate citizenship' activities.

The global problems of the 21st century are in no way easy to tackle. Ecological crisis, organised crime, international justice—these cannot be resolved by any 'global administration' to provide an institutional framework as we know it from the national context. Rather, what we need are networks of co-operation between responsible leaders in different branches of society. We have to understand 'corporate citizenship' not as a mere public relations activity, but as an important device of new governance structures on an international and global level. It is not about nice shop-window activity but about acting co-responsively for the urgent problems humankind will face in the 21st century. This volume, along with (hopefully) many others that follow, may open up new theoretical perspectives in order to lead the way in that direction.

INTRODUCTION

Jörg Andriof and Malcolm McIntosh

**Corporate Citizenship Unit,
Warwick Business School, UK**

◢ What is corporate citizenship?

Many still argue that corporate citizenship is not a proper concern of business, following Milton Friedman's (1970) line that the business of business is business and the sole social responsibility of a company is to maximise profits for its shareholders. Getting involved with wider societal issues takes a company's eye 'off the ball' and risks a drop in productivity. Companies are ill suited to such work and there is no legal or democratic basis for it. Social investment is a misuse of shareholders' money, which should instead be returned to them for their use as they see fit. This was all part of the 1980s shareholder value debate, which succeeded in increasing the focus in many companies on their core business activities, including aligning social investment much more closely with business strategy. The idea that business has a broader 'societal responsibility' or 'citizenship' role is strengthening with the development of the global economy. The enhanced legitimacy and liberation of private enterprise in the late 1980s and early 1990s coupled with exponential growth in enabling global networking technology have led to the dominance of what can be called 'global informational capitalism'.

A glance at Table 1 of selected highlights of critical incidents, new standards, initiatives and institutions associated with the role of big business in society should serve to establish that something important is going on. The critical incidents show that the wider role of business in an increasingly global ecological and social environment clearly matters, and the new standards, initiatives and institutions show that business is increasingly involved in addressing the relevant issues. Table 1 also shows that, while ecological issues predominated

	Phase I: 1960–83 Awakening	Phase II: 1984–94 Engaging	Phase III: 1995–present Networking
Critical incidents	► Nestlé Baby Food, 1970 ► Seveso Disaster, 1974 ► Amoco Cadiz Oil, 1978 ► Ford Pinto, 1978	► Bhopal, 1984 ► Chernobyl, 1986 ► Chico Mendes, 1988 ► Exxon Valdez, 1989	► Shell, Brent Spar, 1995 ► Saro-Wiwa Execution, 1995 ► Nike child labour, 1996 ► Asian financial crisis, 1997
New standards and initiatives	► US Environmental Protection Act, 1969 ► Club of Rome, 1972 ► Brandt Report, 1980 ► Global 2000 Report, 1980	► Responsible Care, 1985 ► Brundtland Report, 1987 ► UN Summit for Children, 1990 ► Rio Earth Summit, 1992	► Apparel Industry Partnership, 1996 ► ISO 14000 series, 1996 ► SA 8000 series, 1997 ► Triple bottom line concept, 1998
New institutions	► Council on Economic Priorities, 1969 ► Greenpeace, 1972 ► United Nations Environment Programme, 1973 ► World Resources Institute, 1983	► Third World Network, 1985 ► Caux Round Table, 1986 ► SustainAbility, 1987 ► PWBLF, 1990 ► Amnesty Business Group, 1991 ► World Business Council for Sustainable Development, 1991	► EBNSC, 1995 ► Corporate Citizenship Unit, 1996 ► Ethical Trading Initiative, 1997 ► Business Partners for Development, 1997 ► CEPAA, 1998

CEPAA = Council on Economic Priorities Accreditation Agency
EBNSC = European Business Network for Social Cohesion
PWBLF = Prince of Wales Business Leaders Forum

Table 1 **Corporate citizenship: from awakening to networking**

Source: Andriof and Marsden 1999

early on, issues concerning human rights and social exclusion have assumed equal importance and all of them are now being approached in a more holistic way under the general heading of 'sustainability'.

Citizenship is defined as the rights and duties of a member of a country. Companies, as independent legal entities, are members of countries and can be thought of as corporate citizens with legal rights and duties. All companies, therefore, are corporate citizens, but their citizenship performance varies just as it does for any individual citizen. As Peter Drucker (1993) says, citizenship is more than just a legal term, it is a political term: 'As a political term citizenship means active commitment. It means responsibility. It means making a difference in one's community, one's society, and one's country.' Drucker might have added, in today's global economy, 'one's world'.

Good corporate citizenship, therefore, can be defined as understanding and managing a company's wider influences on society for the benefit of the company and society as a whole (Marsden and Andriof 1998). It is becoming closely associated with the idea of 'sustainability'. It is also synonymous with the concept of 'corporate societal responsibility'. The new word *societal* is used to avoid the limited interpretation of the term 'social responsibility', when translated into Continental European cultures and languages, as applying to social welfare issues only. The term 'societal responsibility' covers all dimensions of a company's impacts on, relationships with and responsibilities to society as a whole.

These impacts, which have a ripple effect on society, like a stone being thrown into a pond, can be divided into three broad, overlapping areas—economic, environmental and social—as summarised in Figure 1.

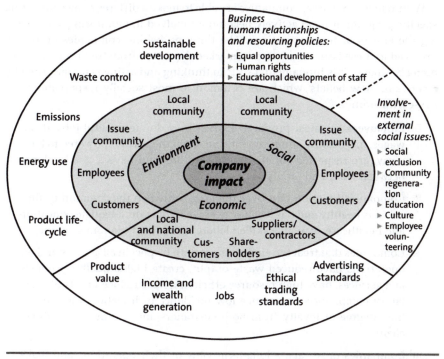

Figure 1 **A company's ripple effect**

◢ What are firms responsible for?

So what is corporate social responsibility, and what are the implications for business operations as we near the new millennium? Corporate social responsibility (CSR) is not 'chequebook philanthropy', nor is it limited to the study of business ethics. It arises from a deeply held vision by corporate leaders that business can and should play a role beyond just making money. It embraces an understanding that everything a company does has some flow-on effect either inside or outside the company, from customers and employees to communities and the natural environment. In a nutshell, therefore, CSR encompasses four distinct areas:

- The environment
- The workplace
- The community
- The marketplace

Within these four areas companies are able to make a difference by conducting specific programmes and actively becoming involved in monitoring and changing the effects of their operations. The thinking behind companies becoming involved in these issues represents a marked departure from traditional ways of doing business. This fundamental shift in thinking and acting is underscored by a series of 'new beliefs' which are common to most socially responsible businesses, including:

- Employees are most productive when they do meaningful jobs at fair wages, in a healthy environment, and when they are empowered to have a say, are respected for their contributions and have a good balance between work and family life.

- Companies function best over the long run when the community they are in is healthy and has a below-average crime rate, adequate education and healthcare, available skilled labour and robust economic activity.

- Companies that treat the environment with respect in all aspects of their operations have reduced waste output, create higher-quality products and services, have high resource efficiency, have reduced costs of regulatory compliance, experience low incidence of litigation and enjoy a high degree of loyalty from both customers and business-to-business clients.

- Companies must take a long-term view of their operations and make decisions that consider a more holistic view of the world; sometimes this means forgoing short-term profits in favour of long-term benefits.

- A company's reputation is becoming more and more important as consumers and investors consider reputation and performance as being as important as price when making purchasing decisions.

Some of these beliefs may be considered to be a little 'new age' and, as mentioned above, may seem to be at odds with more traditional beliefs, so it should be noted now that one of the most important socially responsible things a business can do is be profitable. By being profitable a business can provide sustainable jobs for its employees, good returns for investors and prosperity for the communities in which it operates.

◢ What are the forces for change?

Why now? Why bother with all these socially responsible concerns if profitability provides jobs and prosperity anyway? Several separate but interlinked forces have been combining over recent years to bring business to where it is now.

- **Deregulation and globalisation.** These have provided business with many opportunities previously denied to it. Among these opportunities has been the ability to compete in most of the world's markets, the ability to raise funds from numerous different and competing sources and the opportunity to buy supplies from anywhere in the world. The effects of these changes have included an increase in competitive local markets and the squeezing out of the 'little man', cross-cultural business investments and transactions and, in many cases, the location of factories so as to make use of cheap foreign labour.

- **Rapid advances in communication technology.** These have allowed information to be relayed around the globe almost instantaneously and with minimal costs. There are few areas of our (Western) society that have not been affected by the truly incredible changes that have occurred in communication technology and by those technologies that are still developing (e.g. the Internet).

- **The rise in the power of the consumer.** The combination of deregulation, globalisation and advances in communications technology, described above, has resulted in what many have termed 'the information age'. With access to instant, free information from a variety of sources, to a multitude of service and product providers and to a multitude of global investment opportunities and with the unopposed spread of capitalism as the dominant economic structure the rise in the power of the consumer has been unrestrained.

The net outcome is that we now live in a world where corporations are oriented very much towards the consumer and employee because these people hold the ultimate power in the system. So, the answer to the question of 'Why social responsibility now?' is that consumers and employees are now well informed about the challenges facing the world, they have little faith in governments' ability to change things, they acknowledge the corporation as the most powerful social construct of the present era and, most importantly, they are willing to reward corporations who are responsive to their concerns.

Furthermore, it is worth noting that many large firms who are 'converts' to this new way of thinking are requiring their suppliers to provide details of their policies on social responsibility (particularly from an environmental perspective). This is probably the most powerful force for change, as it is these actions by large corporations that can effectively exclude suppliers from the marketplace if they are not socially responsible. The use of child labour and the protection of social diversity are important issues within this context.

Regardless of which view about the importance and the impact of social responsibility may be correct, the fact remains that corporate citizenship is most likely to become a more significant issue as we move into the next millennium. The ramifications of not addressing best practice in the four areas of environment, workplace, marketplace and community range from poor media coverage to exclusion from some marketplaces altogether. In summary, therefore, it is an area that corporations will ignore at their peril.

What are the perspectives on corporate citizenship?

The chapters of this book are organised into three sections. Each of the sections contains a mixture of chapters: some develop the conceptual ideas and frameworks of corporate citizenship; others describe broad empirical research findings or particular country, industry or company practice. The collection of chapters in Part 1—'Evolution, Context and Concepts of Corporate Citizenship'—explores the development of the ideas and the elements that describe what is meant by corporate citizenship. In Part 2—'Governance and Leadership of Corporate Citizens'—the theme of corporate citizenship is continued, but in terms of the focus on the management aspects considering corporations as citizens. Finally, the chapters in Part 3—'Stakeholder Engagement and Social Accountability'—address the fact that corporations are surrounded by stakeholders with whom they have to engage to fulfil their business objectives and to whom they therefore are accountable. All are part of the continuous critical debate within corporate citizenship.

Part 1: Evolution, Context and Concepts of Corporate Citizenship

Chapter 1 focuses on the foundations of corporate citizenship. Developing good corporate citizenship in the dynamic complexity of the new economy means that companies need to develop and sustain relationships with key stakeholders. Waddock argues that there are two foundational ingredients of corporate citizenship: integrity and mindfulness. Integrity means honesty, and includes firm adherence to a code as well as soundness and 'wholeness', indicating the need for an integral vision of the firm as a corporate citizen. Mindfulness means that corporate leaders, increasingly, will need wisdom, which demands that they achieve relatively high cognitive, moral and emotional levels of development. She defines citizenship as relationships with key stakeholders, requiring an integral vision for the firm, a vision based not only on the objective but also on the subjective elements important to integrity. Only by building in reflection and learning capabilities aimed at enhancing leadership capacity for integrity and mindfulness can companies meet the growing demands for corporate citizenship.

Windsor's chapter evaluates the corporate citizenship notion and movement, which although a relatively recent practitioner development involves some old issues. Social responsibility, social performance and corporate citizenship are equally diffuse conceptions. Windsor states that corporate citizenship reflects some specific developments concerning corporate compliance and altruism that shape business conduct toward a strictly strategic evaluation of all functions and activities. The corporate citizenship notion comes with two difficulties that should be considered more carefully. The notion implicitly limits responsibility to that of the ordinary individual citizen; and global corporations may prove to be footloose, without real attachment to communities. Windsor proposes an alternative theory of progressive responsibilities that increase with wealth and power. The theory is akin to progressive taxation, the basic principle for which was articulated in Adam Smith's *The Wealth of Nations* (Smith 1976). This alternative theory is proposed in order to help evaluate the conventional interpretation of corporate citizenship.

Birch titles his chapter 'Corporate citizenship: rethinking business beyond corporate social responsibility'. He states that the literature on corporate social responsibility is extensive, running into thousands of titles and extending back for at least 60 years. Many of the themes and issues raised in this literature are as relevant today as they were when first written. However, increasingly, Birch argues, the concept of corporate social responsibility has restricted companies and other organisations in their development of corporate citizenship as they have focused on programmes of activities, generally external to the company, and not on systemic and holistic cultural change within the company itself. Effective corporate citizenship, he argues, is possible only if business rethinks itself beyond the externalities of corporate social responsibility towards a more systemic, holistic, acceptance of corporate citizenship principles at every level, for every policy and in all operations of the company. This is a hard task, and Birch concludes his chapter with an account of the way in which BP Amoco in Australia has begun the process of positioning itself as a corporate citizen by going beyond the externalities of corporate social responsibility.

'Global corporate citizenship in a dot.com world: the role of organisational identity' is the theme of Post and Berman's chapter. In their view, global corporate citizenship involves aligning a company's civic role with its business purpose. Most corporations remain far from achieving their potential for integrating community involvement with business practice, yet the promise is surely there. Post and Berman propose that the drivers of change—intense competition, new technologies, globalisation, a concern for ethics and values, ecological issues and the changing role of government—will continue to prod companies and managers to reinvent their businesses and expand their civic role. As companies and managers do so, their relationships with all stakeholders will change. Reputation, image and corporate identity are of growing importance as price and product quality become less differentiating in a world of abundance. When customers have many choices, companies cannot assume that customers will do business with firms that ignore their responsibilities as corporate citizens. Post and Berman examine models of global corporate citizenship, with a special focus on how the Internet is influencing business responses.

In their chapter, Wood and Logsdon theorise 'business citizenship'. As corporate citizenship replaces the concept of 'corporate social responsibility', they are concerned that the core content of social responsibility may be lost in favour of a narrow, voluntaristic concept of community service. They argue that the broad ethics-based norms of social responsibility must be integrated into corporate citizenship. They suggest that the term 'business citizenship' may better incorporate the broader perspective on business rights and duties, stakeholder relationships, opportunities and challenges that accompany the current global socioeconomy. To develop a working theory of business citizenship, Wood and Logsdon first extract key ideas about individual citizenship and apply them to business organisations. This step requires an analysis of two perspectives on individuals, organisations and states: the minimalist and the communitarian views. Next, they transpose the concept of business citizenship from a single community perspective to a global perspective by comparing the communitarian view of citizenship with the universal rights view. This allows a view of business citizenship that accommodates strong moral guidance, structural and institutional realities and essential flexibility.

The chapter by Swanson and Niehoff blends research on corporate social responsibility and employee citizenship to propose a framework for the integration of these concepts. This integrated perspective, referred to as 'business citizenship', calls for the executive stewardship of citizenship within business organisations so that such organisations can function as good citizens in society.

◢ Part 2: Governance and Leadership of Corporate Citizens

Corporate citizenship generally implies the existence of core organisational values, which have a direct bearing on integrity values and relational values. Through a content analysis of corporate codes of ethics, Dion shows how such codes are very often more 'legalistic' than truly 'ethical'. The more that corporate codes of ethics are legalistic, the less they reflect a wide concept of corporate citizenship. Corporate citizenship should aim at internalising an 'ethic of care' and adopt a cross-cultural and/or inter-religious approach to ethical issues in international business. International corporate citizenship implies a struggle for co-operation (working together: openness to others), a search for mutual understanding (hoping together: cross-cultural and/or inter-religious dialogue, a capacity to question our own assumptions) and a respect for basic human rights (living together).

Corporate citizenship presupposes a culture of 'togetherness', which is grounded in caring for others, as manifested through an ethical, visionary and globalising leadership of business chief executive officers.

The 'moral leader' is at the centre of Carroll's chapter as an essential ingredient for successful corporate citizenship. He proposes that for successful corporate citizenship it is necessary to have a robust understanding of the concept and to fully appreciate how moral leadership fits in with that concept. In his chapter he argues that corporate citizenship builds on its 'four faces': economic, legal, ethical and philanthropic. Each must be understood for effective corporate citizenship to be exercised. The most challenging 'face' of corporate citizenship pertains to ethical or moral leadership. Following a discussion differentiating management from leadership, it is maintained that moral leadership can be usefully compared with immoral and amoral leadership and that it has its own distinctive characteristics. Some of these characteristics build on the moral management model previously postulated by Carroll. Further, moral leadership is characterised by at least seven 'habits' that moral leaders need to possess. It is reasoned that moral leadership is necessary to sufficiently implement effective corporate citizenship.

Glazebrook analyses how Australia's top 500 companies are becoming corporate citizens. Since the mid-1990s, Australia, like many other countries, has engaged in a vigorous debate about the emerging field of corporate citizenship and, in particular, about how business demonstrates this in practice. This debate, however, has unfolded in a very selective and divisive manner within Australia, often raising only those issues that serve to advance a particularly narrow perspective rather than being grounded in the broader debate happening across the country. There has also been a failure to take account of the significant interpretations being made in practice about corporate citizenship by many of the nation's major institutions. Glazebrook uses recent research into Australia's top 500 companies and key developments emerging from the parliament, media and judiciary to form the basis of his chapter in order to develop a much more comprehensive analysis of corporate citizenship from an Australian perspective than currently exists. He bases his discussion on the key themes of public policy, governance, the law and incentives.

In the past, nation-states were concerned above all with sovereignty and security. Nowadays, states are expected to fulfil a pre-eminently welfare-based role. Formerly, multinational corporations (MNCs) were concerned almost exclusively with productivity and profits for shareholders. Presently, stakeholders require that MNCs also deliver products and services in an ecologically sustainable and socially responsible way. In his chapter, Sison describes how a transformationalist view of globalisation allows us to understand these changes in the nature of MNCs and governments taken in parallel. Particularly, Mobil advertorials provide an excellent example of how an MNC lives up to its social responsibility by the standards of the Organisation for Economic Co-operation and Development (OECD). MNC participation in global governance may be legitimated and enhanced not only by its efficient provision of welfare but also by its recognition of stakeholder rights and commitment to stakeholder democracy.

Cohen focuses his chapter on the globalisation of corporate citizenship and the United Nations (UN). In less than a decade this most comprehensive, global, inter-governmental organisation has transformed itself from being wary of business to establishing dramatic numbers of partnerships throughout its system of 30 agencies and over 50,000 employees. Business has worked with the UN since its inception, but primarily in sectors where common international standards were needed. The new UN–business relationship is oriented toward fulfilling the UN's mandate to reduce poverty and promote sustainable development. However, the UN will need to form partnerships with business carefully in order not to jeopardise its credibility or to 'bluewash' bad corporate reputations. Non-govern-mental organisations fear that business will have an ever-greater say at the UN to the detriment of its mission. With safeguards, such as uniform agency guidelines and training of UN staff for business partnerships, the UN has the potential to formalise stakeholder partnerships on an unprecedented global scale.

◢ Part 3: Stakeholder Engagement and Social Accountability

Partnerships between business, civil society organisations and the state are emerging as key mechanisms for addressing social and environmental challenges. Their effectiveness is a function of their ability to build up the individual and collective institutional enablers of their members, their ability to generate vitality and innovation, their impact on knowledge creation and its management, and on their accountability mechanisms in terms of form and legitimacy. Ultimately, they will form an increasingly important element of an organic civil governance process in the 'new economy'. In his chapter Zadek outlines some of the key concepts and tools with which the effectiveness and role of such partnerships might be assessed and calls it 'partnership alchemy'.

In the chapter by Andriof four different patterns of stakeholder partnership building are described, derived from four different analysed stakeholder partner-ships. Empirical and theoretical reasoning leads to a logical judgement on the basis of circumstantial evidence and prior conclusions rather than on the basis of direct observations. Furthermore, four patterns of stakeholder partnership build-ing are extracted, rather than focusing on the underlying theory. Proposed defining elements of partnerships are transformed into four 'Ps' for stakeholder partner-ship building: purposes, pacts, power relationships and processes of stakeholder partnership developments. These four elements are explored as part of an emerg-ing paradigm of social innovations. Each analysed stakeholder partnership repre-sents a diverse purpose, pact, power relationship and process of partnership development. For each element, five descriptive variables are identified that enable similarities and differences between the various elements to be analysed.

In their chapter, Gao and Zhang propose that social auditing has attracted an unprecedented level of both practical and academic interests since the 1990s. By comparing social auditing processes and reports from five different organisations they investigate how organisations engage stakeholders in social auditing. Social auditing is generally a process that an organisation undertakes when assessing and reporting on its social performance, focusing on stakeholder involvement and accountability. While social auditing is generally an organisation-based process, Gao and Zhang have found that the organisations they studied followed more or less the same social auditing process and adopted similar approaches to engage stakeholders in social auditing. The whole process of social auditing has been driven predominantly by the management of the organisations. Very limited meaningful engagement, defined in AA 1000 (AccountAbility Standard 1000; ISEA 1999), exists in these organisations.

What gets recorded and what gets rewarded are the two issues Davenport and Lewellyn focus on. In their chapter they report on an initial effort to build a bridge between theory and practice via a large-scale study of citizenship media reports (the records) and citizenship awards (the rewards). Using Davenport's 20 principles of corporate citizenship as the framework, they conducted a comparative content analysis of ten years of citizenship-related awards and 5 years of media stories of corporate citizenship. Among the results Davenport and Lewellyn found that 2 of the 20 principles (responsible human resource management and a family-friendly work environment) were the 'most rewarded'. Responsible human resource management was also the most frequently 'rewarded' behaviour. An intriguing finding is the discovery that a group of companies having numerous media reports were almost never 'awarded'. They also found another group composed of frequent award-winners who almost never receive positive press for their citizenship efforts. The results provide an initial barometer of how corporate citizenship is actually being practised among US companies. Davenport and Lewellyn conclude with recommendations for future research to continue bridging the gap between theory and practice in corporate citizenship.

Corporate citizenship demands that businesses strive to be more accountable for their actions. Holland and Gibbon therefore focus their chapter on processes in social and ethical accountability, especially external reporting mechanisms. They consider that the challenge is to locate the most appropriate mechanisms for delivering accountability. Calls from stakeholders for greater accountability from business organisations continue to grow, and many companies are attempting to respond by developing reporting frameworks in which their performance in the environmental, social and ethical spheres can be accounted for. At the same time, there has been an increase in the development of standards and guidelines designed to improve the quality, quantity and usefulness of the reported information. However, there is the potential for a mismatch between the mechanism a company chooses to frame its report and the requirements of the stakeholders. Although there is guidance as to how to report in a subject-specific way, there is less guidance in a context-specific direction. Holland and Gibbon provide a review of four of the latest guidelines that offer some assistance to organisations seeking to report social and environmental issues in selecting the most appropriate mechanism for them.

If this book has a message it is that corporate citizenship matters and that organisations are heterogeneous and that these two factors are intimately related. The book has been designed to stimulate the imagination and to inform the judgement of all those engaged in corporate citizenship, either currently or in the future, as it is assumed that the quality of their judgement matters. All of the contributions in their separate ways challenge corporate citizenship thinking. This book is a collection that provides an overview of where corporate citizenship is going and what the emerging issues are for corporate citizenship thinking for the next decade. Corporate citizenship in the future must be able to deal with complexity, learning and flexibility. Managers must be prepared and able to change their thinking and aspiration accordingly: 'if the times and conditions change, he will be ruined because he does not change his methods of procedure . . . because he cannot be persuaded to depart from a path, having always prospered by following it' (Machiavelli 1513).

The book has been designed to present both the past and the future of corporate citizenship. It does this by selecting topics that, in the view of the editors, are substantive rather than merely fashionable or transitory and from which the reader should emerge with an excitement about what it means when we call something 'corporate citizenship'.

Part 1
EVOLUTION, CONTEXT AND CONCEPTS OF CORPORATE CITIZENSHIP

INTEGRITY AND MINDFULNESS
Foundations of corporate citizenship*

Sandra Waddock
Boston College, Carroll School of Management, USA

Debate rages about whether there is a 'new' economy and, if so, what the implications are for the corporate citizenship of large corporations. The 'new economy'
is technologically sophisticated (and technologically driven), entrepreneurial,
incredibly fast-paced, and global. It demands integration internally and externally, through electronic technology as well as organisationally in terms of internal systems, and across organisational and industry boundaries. Potentially, this
new economy outdates traditional views of the dynamics of the business cycle
(e.g. Greenspan 1998; Hamel 1998; *Economist* 1999e; D'Andrea Tyson 1999; Sahlman 1999). Some have characterised the current business climate as hyper-
turbulent (D'Aveni 1994), while others claim that only world-class organisations
can succeed (Kanter 1995) in such highly competitive and dynamic contexts.

Whether or not the new economy actually exists, what is clear is that current
economic and industry conditions certainly demand new and different ways for
companies to relate to their stakeholders if they hope to succeed. Issues of ecological sustainability, transparency and accountability, human rights and labour
relations (especially in sourcing from less developed areas of the world), and
corruption are topics that face global companies and their leaders on a daily basis.
Stakeholders representing these and other varied interests, particularly the interests of primary stakeholders such as owners, employees, customers and suppliers,
frequently seek interaction with—and action from—company leaders regarding
their specific issues.

Most corporate leaders today would probably attest to emerging dynamics of
change and integration that focus ever-greater attention on company activities

---

* Many of the ideas in this chapter are derived from my forthcoming book, *Leading
Corporate Citizens: Meeting the Business in Society Challenge* (McGraw–Hill, 2001).

that have traditionally been conducted behind closed doors. Externally, demands for greater accountability, transparency and dialogue with stakeholders in multiple arenas are mounting. Information on corporations' stakeholder-related and citizenship practices has become increasingly available to interested parties, through rating systems developed by social investors and activists, as well as governmental release of ecological information, such as the Toxic Release Inventory, not to mention the attention of the broadcast and print media.

As the 1999 World Trade Organisation controversy in Seattle aptly illustrates, activists have learned how to use the Internet as an informational and organising tool to focus attention on labour, human rights and environmental practices that they find troublesome. These tools and analyses mean that information about company practices is easy to disseminate to interested audiences. Interested stakeholders can readily find out about many corporate practices—accurately or not—that were once (and sometimes still are) well behind the corporate veil. It also means that establishing sound relationships between companies and their primary and critical secondary stakeholders, i.e. those groups that constitute the company and have the power to affect its operations, are under a spotlight as never before.

The rapid pace of technological change combines with the growing activism and sophistication of some external stakeholders with whom companies might once have had little contact. For example, activists in Seattle did much of their organising using electronic communication; these activists included human rights activists, labour groups and environmentalists, among others interested in corporate (and country) accountability. Similarly, new organisations focused on improving country and corporate practices and decreasing corruption, such as Transparency International, now demand greater transparency and openness with respect to corporate practices in the global arena.

Other organisations regularly rate aspects of corporate citizenship (traditionally called corporate social responsibility). Such organisations include the Council on Economic Priorities, Kinder, Lydenberg, Domini, ethical/social investors, investment firms such as Calvert and Trillium, and other parties, such as the Social Investment Forum, an association of social investors. Similarly, the Reputation Management research group at New York University, headed by scholar Charles Fombrun, is finding new ways to assess corporate reputation and link reputation to financial performance. In the UK, organisations such as Sustain-Ability, AccountAbility, the New Economics Foundation and Business in the Community focus on improving what has come to be called the 'triple bottom line' of corporate financial, ecological and social performance.

What does all of this attention to corporate citizenship mean for companies and those who lead them? Arguably, the implications are significant. In what follows, I will argue that leading corporate citizens need new levels of mindfulness and integrity at the individual and organisational levels if they are to be able to develop constructive relationships with key stakeholders. Relationships with stakeholders constitute the essence of corporate citizenship. Simultaneously, integrity and mindfulness are problematic in that they pose significantly new demands for developing both individual leaders and companies. The reasoning behind these ideas is laid out below.

◢ Operating with integrity

A foundational argument in this chapter is that integrity—in the full sense of the word—is at the core of good corporate citizenship. The primary synonym for integrity is honesty, according to Webster's dictionary. Honesty means honesty with both self and the other stakeholders with which the company deals. Being honest with oneself means exploring what the realities are, knowing who or what one is, and acting forthrightly, consistent with that knowledge. Integrity, at its most basic level, therefore, means living up to a set of standards and principles, which implies a deep respect for others, that is, for the stakeholders who are affected by the corporation's actions (or, alternatively, who can affect the corporation) (Freeman 1984).

Webster's offers three definitions of integrity, which are relevant to the present discussion. One definition is 'firm adherence to a code, especially of moral or artistic values', with the synonym of incorruptibility. Second is soundness or an unimpaired condition. Third, and directly related to the second, is that integrity relates to the state of being complete or undivided, that is, to wholeness. The next sections will elaborate on these definitions as they apply to corporate citizenship.

Firm adherence to a code

Adherence to a code suggests a values-driven basis for corporations attempting to act with integrity. Corporate citizenship is, if nothing else, based on a combination of standards and what I have elsewhere termed 'constructive values', that is, positive values that guide behaviour. This adherence to a set of values is at the centre of the definition of corporate citizenship used here. It suggests that developing corporate citizenship is more art than science (and is, as well, artistic) in that it needs to be fundamentally values-driven, but in a constructive or positive way.

What types of value can be considered 'constructive'? For an answer to this question, we turn to the seminal work on leadership by James McGregor Burns (1978). Burns says that values can be end values and modal values. The sorts of value that are 'constructive', that is, positive guides for behaviour, are, by Burns's definition, end values in that they describe desirable end states, collective goals or explicit purposes that help to establish standards for making choices among a set of alternatives. Notice that the term 'end values' combines identifying an explicit goal that defines core purpose with the standards (the code) that must be lived up to so that goal can be attained.

The work of James Collins and Jerry Porras in their book *Built to Last* provides some insight into the content of end values that may be appropriate in developing corporate citizenship (although these authors state that the types of value companies have do not matter, I will here respectfully disagree). Collins and Porras (1997) studied what they called 'visionary' companies to determine on what basis their long-term success was built. Consistent with the view of corporate citizenship in this chapter, the researchers found that visionary companies succeeded far beyond the also very successful comparison companies. Visionary companies, Collins and Porras found, developed 'core ideologies', consisting of clearly identified vision or purpose and the set of core values that sustains and supports the vision over a relatively long time-period. They were also guided in the shorter term by BHAGs, that is, big hairy audacious goals.

End values are deeply felt core values, which inspire the human spirit. It is exactly this type of value that appears in the visionary companies studied by Collins and Porras. For example, American Express's core ideology involves 'heroic customer service, worldwide reliability of services and encouragement of individual initiative', while Marriott's focuses on friendly service and excellent value, treating people with respect, hard work combined with fun, continual self-improvement and overcoming adversity. Similar end values are evident in all of the visionary companies studied by Collins and Porras (1995: 68-71). Clearly, the values articulated and implemented by these companies have intrinsic merit and are of a nature that many, if not most, people (whatever their cultural, ethnic or religious heritage) can agree serve as inspirational bases for guiding behaviour.

Core ideology serves the purpose of guiding a firm, as the definition 'adherence to a code' proposes. Specifically, end values help companies to operationalise their values in their day-to-day practices by providing the 'how we do things around here' set of standards needed to determine what is and what is not appropriate in a given situation or with respect to a particular stakeholder. Freeman and Gilbert (1988) have called such a guiding set of values an enterprise strategy and suggested that the key question 'What do we stand for?' should be asked along with the fundamental strategic question 'What business are we in?' Asking, answering and implementing the enterprise strategy question would arguably go a long way towards developing integrity, defined as adherence to a code, in corporate citizens.

Soundness and wholeness

These two definitions of integrity are discussed together because they are closely related. Integrity with respect to a corporate citizen indicates soundness, in the sense that an organisation's condition is unimpaired and healthy. To the extent that the organisation has integrity, it is complete, not fragmented, whole in and of itself. It is, in short, integrated, which implies that its systems work together towards the common purpose identified by the vision and end (core) values of the core ideology.

Sound organisations, then, are healthy, meaning that all aspects are working well—and to the extent they are actually integrated, they are working together systemically. Soundness, in this sense, implies fiscal stability as well as, for private-sector organisations, profitability. Additionally, soundness implies the solidity or security that is provided by having internal practices that respect the stakeholders affected by those practices, that do not permit corruption to enter into the system, similar to the notion of adherence to a code or set of principles, discussed above.

Systems, notably, are wholes. More accurately, as Ken Wilber (1996) points out, they are, in Arthur Koestler's word, holons. Holons are simultaneously both wholes and parts. Corporate citizens—all organisations, for that matter—are also holons, in the sense that they are whole systems, have integrity, in and of themselves. But, simultaneously, they are inextricably embedded as parts of a broader system, i.e. of an industry in which they are in competition with other similar organisations, which is itself part of a broader economic system. More to the point, as holons, corporate citizens recognise their status not only as integral wholes (consisting of other holons such as strategic business units, divisions, plants or other facilities, departments, teams and individuals, and so on), but also as parts of society, inextricably wedded to the whole.

This embeddedness, in which one 'whole/part', as Wilber (1996) terms them, is also a part of something bigger and more complex than itself—and also contains 'whole/parts' (holons) less complex than itself—means that what happens to one holon affects what happens to other holons within the system. Such relatedness is, of course, the fundamental insight of stakeholder theory (e.g. Freeman 1984; Freeman and Gilbert 1988; Evan and Freeman 1988; Donaldson and Preston 1995; Clarkson 1995). Relationship is also the basis of the present definition of corporate citizenship. Thus, the definition and the systems perspective are fundamentally relational, in that they demand attention to—or, alternatively, as will be discussed below, mindfulness of—the ways in which one's own practices and behaviours impact others.

Considered as wholes, companies are complete systems, all of whose parts are interdependent and interrelated. Fragmentation or inconsistency, particularly with respect to the 'code' or set of principles that constitutes the vision and values discussed above, become problematic for companies because they can readily lead to treatment of stakeholders that is inconsistent with the inspirational end values associated with good corporate citizenship. Considered as parts, corporate citizens recognise their own interdependence and interrelationship with other elements of human civilisation, which constitute society. They also recognise that they are deeply dependent on a healthy ecological environment, of which they are a more complex and therefore more 'developed' part, and without which they cannot survive (see Wilber 1995, 1996).

Recognising these relationships and interdependences, which are ultimately their primary and secondary stakeholder relationships, good corporate citizens know that they need to develop internal practices to deal with their stakeholders that are based on the set of values they articulated as part of their core ideology.

Values-based practices—policies, procedures and processes—are, when based on integrity, ones that respect the fundamental worth and dignity of these stakeholders as well as of the natural environment on which the corporation depends.

The integral perspective

There is another important meaning to the wholeness associated with operating with integrity and that is developing what Wilber (1995) terms an 'integral perspective'. Wilber studied numerous literatures and came to a fascinating insight: most of the time, writers addressed or took a position with respect to only one of four possible ways of viewing a given situation. A typical and, in the Western world, dominant perspective is the traditional 'scientific' or objective perspective. From this perspective, one can study things or understand a situation from an objective perspective, based on what can be observed and classified as data. This objective perspective is typically external to the observer and can focus its attention on either individual phenomena or collective (i.e. inter-objective or observable social) phenomena.

Equally important, although frequently overlooked or lacking credibility particularly in the Western tradition, are subjective and inter-subjective phenomena. Subjective phenomena by their nature cannot be empirically observed. Instead, they must be articulated through conversation so that the subject gives his or her meaning to the phenomenon. Subject phenomena include ideas, respect, emotions, inspirations, spirituality and artistry or aesthetics. Similarly, abstract collective concepts, such as moral or ethical beliefs, religious systems and culture, fall into what Wilber terms the inter-subjective or collective realm.

The key to understanding anything fully, according to Wilber (1996), is to understand not just one of these four perspectives but, simultaneously, all four, which are present in every situation. Indeed, as with developing the relationships between a company and its stakeholders, understanding aspects of the subjective and inter-subjective realms requires that we ask what has been experienced by the other person or persons. In short, the subjective or inter-subjective (what Wilber terms the 'left-hand' side of his two-by-two matrix) demands conversation—dialogue—if it is to be understood, because it is fundamentally not measurable empirically.

Understanding the subjective and inter-subjective aspects of being a corporate citizen operating with integrity, it follows, means that corporate leaders will increasingly need dialogic and relationship-building skills. These skills are key to what strategy scholar Jim Waters (Bird and Waters 1989) termed 'good conversations', that is, dialogue between leaders within companies and their stakeholders. Entering into productive dialogues with stakeholders means that leaders need to be able to understand or 'take' the perspective of those stakeholders—the other—into account. Clear understanding is needed between company and stakeholder, not only of each other's point of view, but also of what it is the stakeholder(s) are experiencing as a result of the corporation's practices (and vice versa). This conversation needs to be dialogic rather than argumentative or discussion-based (see Senge 1990).

Operating with integrity also means that leaders need to understand how the company's actions affect relevant stakeholders in any given situation. That is, they need to be able to think through the full system and integral (emotional, aesthetic, cultural) consequences of their activities and practices. We shall call this combination of skill and insights 'mindfulness'. And mindfulness, it will be argued below, demands relatively high levels of cognitive, moral and emotional functioning from leaders and managers, levels that not all readily attain without significant work.

◢ Operating mindfully

Wisdom, management scholar Russell Ackoff (1999: 14) says, 'is the ability to perceive and evaluate the long-run consequences of behaviour'. This capacity of what we shall call 'mindfulness', following Karl Weick (1999), is 'associated with a willingness to make short-run sacrifices for long-term gains' (Ackoff 1999: 14). The notorious short-sightedness, not to mention the sorry state of relationships that many companies have with some of their stakeholders, suggests that mindfulness may be in woefully short supply among corporate leaders.

Certainly, mindfulness—wisdom—requires a degree of maturity and insight that not every leader finds easy to attain. Being mindful arguably demands that individual decision-makers acting on a company's behalf function at relatively high developmental levels, not only cognitively, but also morally and emotionally. In particular, if corporate citizenship demands building relationships with stakeholders, it also demands insightful understanding of these stakeholders' perspectives, and doing that requires a fairly high cognitive capacity as a starting point.

Seeing the consequences and implications of actions, one of the requisites of integrity as described above, marries cognitive with moral development, also at a relatively high level. Not only does thinking through consequences demand systemic thinking, but it also means leaders have to be well aware of the ways that others stakeholders will perceive and understand their actions and practices. Additionally, they have to be willing to reflect honestly about their understanding, about their relationship with other stakeholders, and about their own roles within the company.

Developing this level of understanding and reflection means that leaders not only need the cognitive capacity to 'perspective-take', but also the moral capacity to understand how their decisions affect others (which is the essence, after all, of ethics). Further, because sound relationships are key to the stakeholder-based definition of corporate citizenship, leaders also need emotional maturity sufficient to build lasting relationships with critical stakeholders. Emotional maturity means that leaders can engage in 'good conversations' or dialogue with stakeholders, and take actions that respect and are sensitive to stakeholders' interests, while still achieving their own interests.

A short review of major cognitive, moral and emotional developmental theories, all of which would appear requisite to mindfulness in corporate citizenship, may shed some light on the developmental attributes needed for corporate citizenship. Perhaps it will also help to determine what qualities and attributes might be developed in leaders if their companies are to operate with integrity.

Cognitive development

Self-awareness, consciousness, is the essence of being human, according to biologists Maturana and Varela (1998) and de Waal (1996). Biologists such as Maturana and de Waal closely link the development of language and self-consciousness, suggesting that human beings are inherently social creatures, living (and working) in communities that have shared purposes. Cognitive development is particularly important in developing corporate citizenship today because of the difficulties involved in working in networked, dynamic and complex environments, which exist both inside and outside the corporation. Because I have suggested that the basis of corporate citizenship is creating relationships with key stakeholders, the capacity to understand those stakeholders—others—is an important key to corporate citizenship. And that capacity comes, at least initially, with cognitive development. To understand this point more fully we need to explore, briefly, some of the major theories of cognitive development.

Although the cognitive domain is only one of multiple arenas in which adults continue to mature and develop (e.g. Gardner 1983; Wilber 1995), it is a critically important one with respect to corporate citizenship. Developmental theorists, such as Piaget (1969), Kegan (1982, 1994), Kohlberg (1976, who studied moral development, and will be discussed in greater detail below) and Wilber (1995, 1996), typically suggest that individuals go through three major developmental stages. These stages are generically known as pre-conventional, conventional and post-conventional.[1] Although these stages are associated with cognitive development, they have analogues in other domains of development where stage (or, better, nesting) theories exist: for example, moral development.

Individuals at the pre-conventional stages of development generally do not yet understand society's expectations or system, but rather reason from a fear of being punished or from self-interest. They find it difficult to separate themselves from others. Individuals at the conventional stages focus on conforming to society's rules, because these are the 'conventions' that dictate norms and expectations. Individuals at this developmental stage are firmly embedded within their reference groups, recognising others and relying on external reference groups or

---

1 Wilber suggests that there is also a post-post-conventional stage which he associates predominantly with spiritual development; this will not be addressed here.

society for expectations they should try to meet. Post-conventional reasoning allows individuals to understand and accept that there are rules and expectations in society, but also become aware that there are general principles underlying these rules and expectations that can shift as the situation changes. Self and others are clearly differentiated at this stage of cognitive development.

Empirical research suggests that most adults progress little beyond the conventional stages of development. The problem is that, as developmental theorist Robert Kegan (1994) says, the demands of modern society mean that many people are 'in over [their] heads' (to paraphrase the name of his book) in terms of their ability to cope with modern societal, business and life demands. Applied to corporate citizenship, which demands building stakeholder relationships, it is clear that the demands on cognitive capacity are significant and equally likely that many corporate managers and leaders are also 'in over their heads'. For example, research by Torbert (1991) and Fisher and Torbert (1995) suggests that few managers ever reach the 'strategist' (a post-conventional) stage of development or beyond.

Cognitive maturity, then, means that leaders are able to really see or hear other stakeholders' point of view and to understand the system in which they are embedded. This capacity, of course, is fundamental to developing corporate citizenship through building constructive stakeholder relationships. Yet, apparently, cognitive development at the necessary post-conventional stage is in short supply among people in general as well as in managers more particularly. And, as will be discussed in the next section, cognitive development alone is unlikely to be a sufficient developmental grounding for managers attempting to build excellence in corporate citizenship.

Moral development

Not only do individuals go through pre-conventional, conventional and post-conventional stages of cognitive development, but these cognitive stages are tracked, at least to some extent (Kohlberg 1976), by moral development, with cognitive development apparently an important precondition for later stages of moral development. Indeed, Kohlberg notes that individuals cannot reason morally at stages higher than they have achieved cognitively, which makes moral development to some extent interrelated with (albeit lagging behind) cognitive development. And it follows that, if few individuals achieve the higher stages of cognitive development, even fewer achieve the necessary post-conventional levels of moral development associated with principled reasoning.

Like cognitive developmental theorists, Kohlberg (as well as Gilligan 1982) asserts that there are three major developmental stages associated with moral development, which are the same as those associated with cognitive development. Pre-conventional-stage individuals reason that they should do right to avoid punishment or to further their own self-interest. Individuals at the conventional stage of moral development reason that they need to conform to their peer group's expectations or, more generally, to the rules of society in order to do good.

Post-conventional moral reasoning, on the other hand, focuses on doing things ethically because these individuals value the integrity of the system as a whole and because they are reasoning from what they perceive to be universal moral principles (often following self-chosen guidelines).

Further, Kohlberg (1976) notes that social interaction, the opportunity for dialogue and exchange (i.e. with stakeholders), which I have defined as the basis of corporate citizenship, is one key means of making progress in terms of moral development, as it enhances insight into the perspective of others. This type of 'role-taking' (Kohlberg), which is an important key to stakeholder relationships, can only be done at higher stages of moral development.

Carol Gilligan (1982), who studied moral development in women, also discovered the same three generic stages of moral development. Gilligan claims that women's moral development is more relational than that of men. In what she terms an 'ethic of care', Gilligan says that women move from caring for self at pre-conventional stages, to caring for self and other at the conventional stages. The post-conventional stage involves moral reasoning about the dynamics of the relationship, including the interconnectedness of self and other. Other researchers suggest that, overall, women may be reasoning at higher, i.e. more relational and systemically oriented, levels than men (Bebeau and Brabeck 1987; Sweeney 1995; Cohen *et al.* 1998).

In the post-conventional stage of development, individuals can 'hold' multiple perspectives simultaneously, can understand interconnectedness and system implications of actions and decisions, and can operate from a set of principles, whether an ethic of care or principles of rights and justice. These mental and moral qualities are exactly the ones needed by leaders of organisations attempting to operate with integrity with respect to their stakeholders, yet they appear to be in short supply. To add to the complexity, arguably, functioning at these two developmental levels needs to be complemented by a third type of development, which Daniel Goleman (1995) terms 'emotional intelligence', because corporate citizenship is defined by the quality of relationships.

Emotional intelligence

Goleman (1995, 1998) documents that individuals mature emotionally as they age, though he does not present evidence of the types of stages of development proposed by other developmental theorists. Still, emotional development (which Goleman calls 'emotional intelligence') is a key to gaining a realistic perspective on the self as well as working with others successfully.

According to Goleman (1995), emotional intelligence consists of several capabilities or skills, including knowing one's emotions or self-awareness, managing emotions (building on self-awareness) and self-motivation. The other two attributes are a capacity to recognise emotions in others, frequently called empathy, and the ability to handle relationships. As we have noted above, these attributes are exactly the ones needed in developing long-term stakeholder relationships.

Awareness and self-knowledge allow for the development of vision and meaning within organisations, a key to tapping into the subjective and inter-subjective aspects of organisational life and corporate citizenship. Since corporate citizenship is all about developing relationships, clearly the capacity for managing one's emotions (which is included in what Senge [1990] terms 'self-mastery') and empathy for others (which requires the cognitive and perhaps moral capacity for perspective-taking) will influence a leader/manager's capacity to work successfully with stakeholders.

Goleman (1995) also highlights four emotional competences clearly relevant to building and sustaining long-term systemically oriented stakeholder relationships: organising groups, negotiating, developing personal connections and social analysis. Thinking from the integral perspective discussed above, leaders need to be able to 'manage with heart', as Goleman puts it, with respect to primary stakeholders such as customers, employees, suppliers and owners. In particular, as stakeholders frequently have conflicting goals and agendas, the key to successful corporate citizenship is managing difficult interactions in an emotionally mature way.

◢ 'Good conversation': dialogue as stakeholder practice

Dialogic processes may well form a necessary basis for developing constructive relationships with stakeholders in the turbulent conditions of the new economy because conditions are rapidly changing and managers need to be constantly aware of what is going on with both internal and external stakeholders. To develop such relationships successfully, managers and leaders need entirely new levels of awareness: what we have termed 'mindfulness' (Weick 1999). Arguably, leaders need to be able to develop companies that have the inherent integrity of intent and action needed in an era that demands ever-greater corporate transparency and accountability for stakeholder-related practices, as well as the relationship capabilities needed to sustain constructive stakeholder interaction.

Corporate integrity means that companies have and maintain strong adherence to constructive core values that inspire value-driven behaviours with respect to stakeholders, and high principles and standards. Stakeholders in the new economy will probably continue to gain the power to demand transparency and increased accountability for corporate actions, putting ever-increasing pressures on the capacities of managers to meet those demands. Without attention to the subtle, non-observable aspects of corporate citizenship, aspects that draw out aesthetic qualities, meanings, emotional impacts, as well as the observable and quantifiable aspects of performance, companies may well be in serious trouble with stakeholders.

Such demands will call for levels of what we have termed 'mindfulness' in corporate leaders that have not been necessary in the past, when connectedness was perhaps less obvious than in this dynamic, technologically connected and resource-constrained age. It may well be that stakeholder demands and the attendant need for perspective-taking were less vociferous in the 'old' than the 'new' economy. Mindfulness implies the systems-thinking capacity to make connections, not only among ideas, products and services but also with respect to the needs and interests of key stakeholders. Key stakeholders are the primary stakeholders that constitute the company (owners, employees, customers and suppliers) as well as critical secondary stakeholders on whom the company depends for infrastructure—communities and governments. Further, the success of the entire system depends, ultimately (and too frequently this point is unrecognised), on a long-term healthy natural environment that supports human civilisation (Maturana and Varela 1998).

Mindfulness also means that corporate decisions are made with wisdom. Achieving wisdom, however, requires emotional maturity that permits attention to aspects of organisational life for which the fast-paced, competitive and complex economy appears to leave few resources, especially of time. Ironically, only by slowing the pace to build in reflective practices (Argyris and Schön 1974; Schön 1983), to develop learning organisations (Senge 1990), and by paying attention to the subjective and inter-subjective elements of corporate citizenship can company leaders actually develop the necessary cognitive, moral and emotional capacities they need. And, arguably, they will also be more productive economically by enhancing their stakeholder relationships (Waddock and Graves 1997a, 1997b).

Corporate integrity means that stakeholders are dealt with holistically and honestly, with their needs and interests fully taken into consideration. Taking stakeholders into consideration does not necessarily mean that their needs and interests are always accommodated, rather that they are fully understood and that *mutual* accommodation can be achieved, with multiple sets of needs and interests understood and considered. Achieving this level of stakeholder interaction means that leaders (and stakeholder leaders, presumably) have the necessary capacities for perspective-taking, understanding the perspectives of others, which are achieved in the post-conventional stages of cognitive and moral development, as well as high levels of emotional intelligence. Such mindfulness—wisdom— brings with it the other important aspect of integrity—honesty—that is needed for successful corporate citizenship.

Corporate citizenship operationalised through stakeholder relationships is holistic, or integral. It demands qualities in individual and organisation development beyond the traditional or readily measured (financially or in productivity terms). Citizenship demands responsible use of the power and resources that companies and their leaders command, and it demands relationship-building *with* stakeholders, not 'management' of them. These relationships, viewed holistically, mean paying attention to things typically somewhat neglected in corporate life. For example, companies would also need to consider the aesthetic implications of decisions, the meaning of decisions to stakeholders, the emotional impact of decisions, and even (as the spirituality in business movements suggests) the spiritual implications of corporate actions with respect to stakeholders.

Arguably, understanding stakeholders holistically is best accomplished through a dialogic process, through conversations, which is exactly what is needed to develop the very cognitive, moral and emotional capacities needed (Kohlberg 1976). Attempts to engage with others are the developmental exercises needed to enhance mutual understanding and push the limits of cognitive, moral and emotional development. Not all efforts will succeed, of course, but, without those efforts, parties are left apart, not integrated and warring, not in collaboration.

There is significant evidence from the work of Argyris and Schön (1974) and Argyris (1993, 2000) that what we have here termed 'mindfulness' can, with difficulty, be enhanced. Doing so requires significant investment, not in speeding up corporate activities but rather in slowing them down, in providing time for reflection (Schön 1983; Argyris 1993, 2000; Raelin 2000), for dialogue and development of understanding, and for mutual problem-solving through collaboration around important issues. Finding ways to build in reflection on learning (Senge 1990) and develop communities of practice around important issues (Wenger 1998) can be other ways to develop what Senge (1990) calls a 'learning organisation'. And learning may be the necessary foundation for the mindfulness and integrity needed for corporate citizenship as we have defined it. In this sense mindfulness means that neither leaders nor their enterprises can ever stop learning or developing.

New-economy organisations, today, provide few safe havens for these forms of reflection, learning and individual and organisational growth towards mindfulness and integrity. Yet, only by engaging with stakeholders holistically, by integrating not only the quantifiable and measurable aspects of their demands but also the spiritual, emotional and aesthetic, can true corporate citizenship actually be achieved.

CORPORATE CITIZENSHIP
Evolution and interpretation

Duane Windsor
Rice University, USA

Corporate citizenship has become an important practitioner-based movement in recent years, and various recognition awards are given. The underlying notion argues essentially that successful companies voluntarily tend (empirically) and all companies should (prescriptively) behave as (or at least 'as if they were') virtuous citizens and good neighbours. The two terms are intertwined: citizenship conveys a sense of responsibility for social impacts, neighbourliness a sense of responsibility for local community impacts. The argument holds, as a matter of practical appeal to managers pursuing shareholder wealth or economic value maximisation goals, that citizenship activities enhance corporate reputation and hence long-term financial performance, which in turn enables citizenship activities.[1] At the least it is held that a bad reputation will damage long-term financial performance. A multinational enterprise operating in an integrating world economy should practise global corporate citizenship: it should be a good citizen (and neighbour) in every host country in which it operates. This chapter examines the evolution of the corporate citizenship notion and offers some cautions concerning how best to interpret the notion.

Taken at face value and as an ideal, and briefly leaving aside the question of true motive, the notion must seem superficially unassailable: no one wants unvirtuous citizens who operate expressly as bad or oblivious neighbours. Civic virtue is a desirable, perhaps necessary, feature of democratic polities (contrast Putnam

---

1   The Conference Board (of New York City) recently listed on offer some 20 reports under a corporate citizenship rubric. Their listing included reports on the following topics: public–private partnerships, corporate contributions, corporate ethics practices, corporate community economic development, corporate volunteerism, corporate community involvement and corporate brand, image and reputation management.

1993 with Banfield 1958 concerning Italy)—an idea traceable to Machiavelli, who explicitly contrasted types of 'virtue' defined differently in princely and republican states (see de Alvarez 1980: xix-xxii). Some traditional complaints against business responsibility can be cast aside quickly. There have always been doubts whether, strictly speaking, corporations should practise philanthropy with what is after all the owners' assets (or perhaps a socially approved private tax shifted ultimately to consumers). But limited corporate philanthropy[2] meets the business judgement rule (ALI 1994: 58). The American Law Institute (ALI 1994: 65) argues the case for allowing 'corporate resources to be devoted to public welfare, humanitarian, educational, and philanthropic purposes even without a showing of expected profits or ethical norms' owing to consideration of a firm's social impact, its stakeholder concerns and 'the co-operation of corporations' with public policy, including desirable diversity of philanthropic participation. The ALI goes on to say, however, that 'corporate activity that is justified solely by social considerations should be subject to a limit of reasonableness' (1994: 65). Even Milton Friedman's (1970) famous (or notorious) critique of discretionary corporate social responsibility by management explicitly conceded a plausible role for prudential altruism, as distinct from discretionary altruism, where the former is defined as strategic concessions for the protection (or promotion) of long-term profits.

Although a prudent appearance of altruism does not make strategic investment a moral activity, and Orts (1992: 71-72, note 381) warns against short-term concessions intended to gain long-term benefits (on the grounds that, in each succeeding round of owner–stakeholder interactions, stakeholder demands for more concessions may simply rise), the notion of prudent conduct at least suggests a broader, stakeholder-responsive (if not, strictly speaking, a moral responsibility) conception of business strategy. Business has, at least in appearance and rhetoric, shifted from the 19th-century Social Darwinism contempt for the public interest that prevailed prior to the Progressive Era, tempered in some degree by the post-exploitation philanthropy pioneered by Carnegie, Rockefeller and Vanderbilt, to a recognition, however expedient, of Davis's (1973) proposed 'Iron Law of Responsibility' holding that businesses misusing social power will lose social legitimacy, particularly in the face of rising societal expectations.

Davis defined social responsibility as beginning where legal compliance ends: it must exceed minimum legal obligations. Corporate citizenship is more a matter

---

2   The *Statistical Abstract of the United States* reports general information on philanthropy. In 1997, of US$143.5 billion donated, some US$8.2 billion (5.7%) came from corporations, and US$13.4 billion from foundations (which can be business-related); the rest came from living individuals (the vast bulk) and charitable bequests (USDC 1999: Table 646, p. 405; based on AAFRC Trust for Philanthropy, New York City, *Giving USA* annual). In 1987 (the last year reported in the following form), the percentage of pre-tax net income donated in a sample of 1,200 corporations giving at least US$100,000 was 1.31 on average (up from 0.93 in 1984), 1.73 in manufacturing (up from 0.90)—ranging between 0.62 in textiles and 3.05 in electrical machinery and equipment—and 0.66 in non-manufacturing (down from 1.01 in 1984) (USDC 1989: Table 891, p. 538; based on M.N. Duffy, *Annual Survey of Corporate Contributions*, New York: The Conference Board).

of strategic policy including legal compliance than any application of moral principle (Wilson [1989] draws a tripartite policy–law–ethics distinction). At a minimum, corporate citizenship—understood explicitly as strategic investment in the firm's social and natural environments for sustainable corporate growth and profitability—arguably aligns corporate and social interests to mutual benefits in win–win outcomes for all stakeholders of the firm. The essential idea thus arguably both broadens and enriches the older notion of corporate social responsibility. If so, even gross imperfection of motives should not be treated as the implacable enemy of at least some good outcomes (to paraphrase and modify what has been said in another context).

There are, nevertheless, certain difficulties with corporate citizenship as a concept and practitioner movement. These difficulties suggest lessons and caveats to be reflected on. Elsewhere in this volume, A.B. Carroll (Chapter 8) cautions that true corporate citizenship requires moral leaders; such ideal leaders may prove relatively scarce. If so, true motives are important, at least to a degree. A strategic calculation is not *per se* a moral principle. Imperfection is, then, possibly a signal of deeper issues embedded in the corporate citizenship notion. Corporate citizenship is, moreover, a diffuse notion (see footnote 1, page 39)[3] and literally a fiction in two senses. First, the domestic enterprise is tacitly portrayed as equivalent to the ordinary individual citizen. Citizenship conveys the sense of 'one person, one vote' and equality of constitutional, legal and political standing in a democratic polity. The corporate citizenship notion conflates citizen (which a firm cannot be) and person (which a firm can be but only as a legal fiction). The portrayal is fictional in that, although for many purposes a corporation is treated in law as if a person with rights of private contracting, public expression and political activities, the corporation cannot vote or hold office, not even through agents— the key hallmarks of citizenship defined as a share in sovereign power in a democratic polity.[4] Any presumption that the corporation is an association of citizens who thus in some sense vote collectively ignores the agency problems resulting from separation of ownership and control. The corporation is viewed as a non-voting citizen precisely because of its power to affect others greatly, and corporate citizenship should serve to blunt or channel that power. Fictional personhood is not a sound basis for artificial citizenship.

Second, the multinational enterprise is typically portrayed as a citizen of the world, a notion that constitutionally and legally does not exist (there are as yet no UN-chartered businesses). Rather, the meaning of the terminology must plainly

3 Davenport (2000: 213) designed two questionnaires around the Delphi expert panel method for dealing with 'lack of agreement or an incomplete state of knowledge' about a problem. 'The majority of study participants agreed on three' indicators of 'good corporate citizenship': (1) rigorous ethical behaviour; (2) stakeholder commitment (including community, consumer, employee, investor and supplier commitments); and (3) environmental and sustainable development commitment (2000: 216). Some 20 specific principles, criteria or measures (Davenport uses all three of these terms; 2000: 17) were identified.

4 Citizenship is 'the manner in which a person responds to . . . duties as a member of a community' (*WRDEL* 1982: 183).

be that the enterprise is a non-voting (if influential) force in each nation-state in which it operates (i.e. it has direct effects) or which it otherwise affects (i.e. via indirect effects). Although some countries recognise dual citizenship, the notion has never extended to embrace multiple citizenships of the sort suggested by global corporate citizenship. Moreover, the notion of a home country—that is, a nation-state whose interests are superior to those of other countries in which the enterprise operates—evaporates, and this evaporation may not prove consistently popular with national governments. Corporate citizenship may be an eminently practical rhetoric, but analogies, fictions and metaphors alike should be carefully scrutinised before accepting their practical implications.

The remainder of this chapter develops as follows. The next section briefly characterises (rather than details) the evolution of the corporate citizenship notion and movement. The third section characterises and evaluates the conventional interpretation of the notion. The fourth section proposes an alternative progressive responsibility approach. There is a brief summary and conclusions section.

◢ A brief developmental history of corporate citizenship

The exact origins and evolution of the corporate citizenship notion and movement are not traced in systematic detail here: some careful historical research is definitely wanted. What can be provided presently is a general sense of the likely developmental history aimed at isolating key elements. Corporate citizenship is, strictly speaking, not new language at all.[5] The US Supreme Court explicitly rejected an early argument for treating corporations as if they were citizens (1839) and then much later accepted the corporate artificial person fiction (1886).[6] The 1919 decision of the Michigan Supreme Court in *Dodge v. Ford Motor Co.* (204 Mich. 459, 170 N.W. 668) supported the primary importance of profit maximisa-

5 The term 'corporate citizenship' features prominently in the subtitle of a book resulting from a 1980 conference on 'Corporate Governance in the '80s' held at Rice University's then Jesse H. Jones Graduate School of Administration (now Management) and co-sponsored by the then Coopers & Lybrand (Greanias and Windsor 1982). Letts (1982: 118-19) argued two themes transparently recurrent in the recent corporate citizenship literature: 'The job is not to render management more accountable for its decisions, but to get managers and directors alike to abandon too narrow a definition of their duty. We must get our managers to say, "My shareholders are the public, and they want what the public wants" . . . Bad corporate citizenship and good corporate citizenship are reflected in stock prices. As a result, it is becoming clear that there is a positive economic benefit to shareholders in having the corporation be perceived as socially responsible.'

6 Chief Justice Taney declined to call a corporation a citizen (*Bank of Augusta v. Earle*, 13 Peters 519 [1839]). Chief Justice Waite agreed to treat the corporation as a person with constitutional rights (see *YLJ* 1982) within the meaning of the Fourteenth Amendment (*Santa Clara County v. Southern Pacific Railroad Co.*, 118 US 394 [1886]) (Miller 1968: 54).

tion on behalf of owners and the business judgement rule granting reasonable discretion to managers.[7]

Davenport (2000: 211) states that 'corporate citizenship became a commonly used term by practitioners' in the 1990s and is a more accurate descriptor of corporate behaviour than is 'corporate social performance', which 'is a theoretical construct from the academic community'. Since the corporate social performance approach (as reformulated by Wood 1991) is composed of (in incomplete form and content) multi-dimensional responsibility, responsiveness and outcomes notions, the greater accuracy argument must turn on some clearer specification of corporate citizenship in terms of concrete activities. Davenport's analysis strongly suggests a practitioner movement among corporate and philanthropic managers. Kinsley (1987), editor of *New Republic*, characterised corporate citizenship as viewing 'the corporation as a political institution that should be dealt with as such'. Kinsley reiterated in effect Friedman's argument against discretionary corporate social responsibility practised by managers. Kinsley stated, citing the hypothetical case of a corporation producing peanut butter:

> The proper social role of the corporation is to produce the best peanut butter at the lowest price . . . corporations should keep to their own sphere and not attempt to become all-embracing social-service agencies . . . I am not impressed by corporate charity and cultural benefaction, which amounts to executives playing Medici with other people's money . . . a good image is good for profits . . . But if it's actually a hard-nosed business decision, why give the corporation credit for generosity? (1987: 29).

Kinsley associated the corporate citizenship movement with the Council on Economic Priorities report on 'Rating America's Corporate Conscience' (Lydenberg *et al.* 1986).

The corporate citizenship movement appears to reflect four key developments or elements. The first, historically, was the academic debate over the conceptual ambiguity and substantive merit of corporate social responsibility. Mitchell (1989) 'traced the emergence of corporate social responsibility in the 1920s as an ideological movement intended to legitimise the power of large corporations' (Oberman 2000: 239). Friedman (1970) viewed discretionary corporate social responsibility practised by managers as 'theft' from a firm's customers, employees and owners (i.e. the other key stakeholders). Friedman stipulated profit maximisation within customary legal and moral rules of the game, governmental regulation to promote competition (however minimalist) and, as explained earlier, prudential altruism (i.e. strategic concessions for the protection of the firm's profits). Davis (1973) conceded the ambiguity of corporate social responsibility. But such ambiguity arguably continues to affect social performance and corporate citizenship conceptions as well.

---

7 As reported by Nunan (1988), Henry Ford had wanted to discontinue a special dividend in order to reduce prices to consumers and increase wages to employees, so as to share the benefits of industrial civilisation rather than as an explicit strategic action aimed at increasing market share.

The second development historically, spreading worldwide from Canada, the USA and the UK, was the attempted cutback in growth of governmental domestic activities during the Reagan and Thatcher era of the 1980s. Ideologically, conservative governments preferred deregulation, privatisation, tax reduction and volunteerism (i.e. civic virtue). A decline in public-sector responsibility, coupled with government and philanthropic calls for voluntary action by individuals and businesses, led on to the corporate citizenship movement filling but arguably not resolving an intellectual void left by the debate over social responsibility.

Corporate citizenship was readily interpreted as action in response to and/or on behalf of various stakeholder groups. The Canadian Centre for Philanthropy (CCP 2000) commented: 'As government cuts back, the public wants Canadian businesses to be more actively involved in supporting the community and social services that make Canada's quality of life among the best in the world'. A US Secretary of Labour, Reich (1996), advanced the same argument with respect to employees, their families and local communities: 'If the government is to do less, then the private sector will have to do more' in terms of 'responsibility for Americans' economic wellbeing'.

The third development historically was recognition of the evolution of a more integrated and competitive world economy (see TCB 1999; Tichy *et al.* 1997). Reich (1996) asserted there was an 'implicit social compact between corporations, their employees and communities' for benefit sharing during the 1950s through the 1970s that has subsequently disappeared owing to increased competition (resulting from information technologies, deregulation, global competition and the decline of entry barriers). Reich states that an 'electronic capitalism' has replaced the gentlemanly investment system that had given 'industrial statesmen' the discretion to balance the interests of shareholders against those of employees and communities'.

So characterised, such discretion must have rested on both management semi-independence and corporate market power relative to customers. A Hitachi Foundation publication (Logan *et al.* 1997) explicitly argues that the 'home' of the multinational enterprise is 'now much more global and multicultural'. It expands the scope of the term 'corporate citizenship' to include 'corporate responsibility, corporate community involvement, corporate community investment, and corporate community responsibility' (cited in Preston and Mihalko 1999: 46; see also footnote 1, page 39). Global corporate citizenship may arguably serve to integrate corporate social responsibility and stakeholder management within a corporate social performance framework.

The Hitachi Foundation publication defines good corporate citizenship as a firm 'meeting, within reason, the expectations of all its societal stakeholders to maximise the company's positive impact and minimise the negative impact on its social and physical environment, while providing a competitive return to its financial stakeholders' (cited in Preston and Mihalko 1999: 46). Preston and Mihalko (1999: 47) note that the Hitachi Foundation publication explains global corporate citizenship in terms of the business need to increase the consumption capacity of developing countries as the essential basis for maintaining 'profitability and growth rates' in circumstances in which the 'industrialised world has become saturated with producers'.

The fourth development historically gave a very specific shape to corporate citizenship activities. Companies such as General Electric, Coca-Cola and AT&T pioneered various forms of shareholder wealth maximisation or economic value maximisation strategies (see *Economist* 1999f; Tully 1993). The essence of this development is to require that all functions and activities of the firm show value creation. The development shaped corporate citizenship activities toward purely strategic investment policies and programmes. Corporate philanthropy has been subjected to the requirement that it add bottom-line value. This requirement implies objective setting and outcome measurement (see CoF 1996). The Council on Foundations's national survey of a sample of US heads of household, supported by 16 corporate sponsors and conducted by Walker Information of Indianapolis, found that 14% of respondents claimed to seek out corporate citizenship in purchases, and 40% regarded corporate citizenship as a tie-breaking consideration (CoF 1996).

◢ Evaluating the conventional approach to corporate citizenship

A consensus among business managers, philanthropic managers and scholars that is favourable to the corporate citizenship notion viewed as a win–win proposition is understandable. And, in a steadily rising and extending economy, all interests can presumably gain; but such a consensus simply takes advantage of improving circumstances to assert its case rather than developing a moral principle. Yet, as Himmelfarb opined in related circumstances (concerning civil society), 'There is something suspect about a concept that appeals to so many people of such different persuasions' (1999: 31). Conventionally, corporate citizenship simply suggests what would be ideal: a positive relationship between corporate good conduct and corporate financial performance (Vidal 1999), a suggestion for which empirical confirmation is as yet weak.

One may find a corporate citizenship report from Philip Morris International: 'We have had a prominent international corporate citizenship programme for more than 30 years in the many communities where we do business.' A previous web address[8] in effect placed tobacco and corporate responsibility together. The three main areas of business of the corporation are food, beer and tobacco. Another example is provided by the journalist Hicks, who criticised Caterpillar for flunking the corporate citizenship test in York County, PA (1996). Hicks listed historical evidence of the firm's previous good citizenship: provision of jobs,

8 philipmorris.com/tobacco_bus/pmi/corp_resp/citizen.html (accessed 28 May 2000; see www.pmintl.com/corp-resp/citizen.html, accessed 4 April 2001).

training and high compensation, and community participation (especially phil-anthropy). According to Hicks, Caterpillar allegedly 'ceased being a good corpo-rate citizen in York County' when it placed profits ahead of employee safety.[9]

Carroll (1991) delineated corporate social responsibility into four dimensions: economic (including, but broader than, financial performance), legal, ethical and discretionary (i.e. philanthropic)—depicted visually as a pyramid in that order from base (economic) to peak (philanthropic). He treated economic and legal responsibilities as socially mandatory, ethical responsibility as socially expected and philanthropy as socially desirable. He interpreted modern corporate citizen-ship as having these 'four faces'—that is, these responsibilities in different shape (Carroll 1998).

Recognising first the effective power (i.e. the influence and impacts) of impor-tant businesses, one can say then that corporate citizenship amounts to the following. Good citizens comply with the legal and moral rules of the 'game'. Technically, obedience to law and ethics is socially mandatory, but the vital issue is voluntary compliance, even though such compliance may rest largely on, for example, US sentencing guidelines that reduce corporate penalties where 'strong' ethics programmes exist. A business cannot properly act against the public interest: it is a licensed supplier of goods and services to customers. But enforce-ment costs are low where compliance is largely automatic. Good neighbours are also benevolent, but corporate altruism, like corporate compliance, is strictly prudential (and limited): it must return value (or at least exhibit a break-even relationship). It should be noted that the ALI document explicitly criticises legal compliance based on a purely cost–benefit calculus (1994: 60), because such compliance is a duty and not a calculation.

The difficult aspect of evaluating corporate citizenship involves the trade-offs that occur within economic performance dimensions among various stake-holders, especially consumers, employees and owners, in addition to the victims of uncompensated externalities. (Such trade-off issues concerning employees and communities are the heart of Reich's [1996] complaint, cited in the previous section.) That corporate altruism is ultimately funded by consumers who might rationally object to such private taxation—precisely as they may object to, for example, US government restrictions on imports of sugar with subsidies for excess US sugar production[10]—or that Bill Gates's philanthropy may arguably rest, in this author's opinion, on what a federal district judge has ruled to be antitrust violations are neglected issues.

9 Caterpillar initially refused entry to investigators from the National Institute of Occupational Safety and Health (NIOSH) who wished to examine whether cadmium exposure levels exceeded OSHA standards.
10 Sugar price support programmes both raise sugar prices above market levels and redistribute income to a few thousand farmers (*Houston Chronicle* 2000). The US General Accounting Office recently reported that in 1998 these programmes cost cus-tomers about US$1.9 billion. The price floor is maintained at 18 cents a pound for cane sugar and 22.9 cents a pound for beet sugar, relative to 8.5 cents a pound on the world market (note, however, that sugar production may be subsidised in other countries for competitive advantage).

Social responsibility of necessity involves legal and moral compliance; corporate altruism is a strategic investment for many companies. Corporate social responsibility, performance and citizenship are equally diffuse notions. Corporate citizenship makes a virtue of necessity and then turns that virtue to strategic advantage. Reich (1996) notes the same strategic calculus applies to value redistribution as distinct from value creation: 'In too many instances, top executives are not creating value; they are merely redistributing income from employees and their communities to shareholders'.

As commented earlier, critical observations—even if valid—are perhaps beside the point as long as business and society progress together. But two potentially significant social costs are inherent in the corporate citizenship construct itself: (1) minimisation of potential corporate social responsibilities compared with those of the ordinary individual citizen; and (2) release of the global corporation from traditional national sovereignty constraints.

Citizenship involves privileges and immunities as well as obligations (see *YLJ* 1982). The current corporate citizenship approach suggests equivalence of the corporation with ordinary individual citizens—an equivalence potentially of advantage in criminal and civil cases against corporations. The ALI (1994) corporate recommendations on corporate governance propose, in effect, that a corporate citizen be subject to the same, but not have any greater, duties relative to the individual citizen. Citizenship thus sounds more positive than corporate social responsibility and yet can be a more minimalist, voluntarist notion, with natural liberty and freedom of contract overtones, that conceptually limits externally imposed responsibilities. The duties are mandatory; the key matter is whether the duties ought to be greater for businesses than for ordinary individuals.

Corporate citizenship suggests a strategic balancing of considerations. Reich (1996) notes:

> In a 1951 address that was typical of the era, Frank Abrams, chairman of Standard Oil of New Jersey, proclaimed, 'The job of management is to maintain an equitable and working balance among the claims of the variously directly interested groups . . . stockholders, employees, customers and the public at large'.

The entire notion of the balancing of partially conflicting interests requires more careful scrutiny than has occurred to date. The World Bank and the International Monetary Fund (IMF) were recently expected to fund 'a controversial energy project' in the West African countries of Chad and Cameroon (Ivanovich 2000). Oil fields in landlocked Chad with a pipeline to the Atlantic coast through neighbouring Cameroon would transform the two countries. An oil company spokesperson stated: 'We believe that the citizens of Chad deserve the right to benefit from responsible development of their resources.' The opposition comes chiefly from environmentalists and human rights advocates concerned with 'possible disruption of the lifestyle of local Pygmies' and 'long-term survival of the black rhinoceros'. Cameroon ranked worst on the 1999 Corruption Perceptions Index published by Transparency International (of Berlin), and Chad has been through a civil war. Both countries were characterised by Ivanovich as corrupt and abusive of human rights. (There have also been criticisms that the two countries are receiving an inadequate share of the projected oil revenues.) A balancing perspective would aggregate the distributions of various benefits and losses with some implicit weighting scheme. Values cannot be balanced but rather must be ranked hierarchically (cf. Dworkin 1978: 26-27; Lewis 1955: 53-55).

A second matter generated by the notion of global corporate citizenship is the release of corporations from traditional national sovereignty. Globally 'footloose' firms might be less responsive to local stakeholders' interests, precisely because the firm can more readily move activities to less 'costly' locations involving lower standards of conduct. Unocal was sued in a US federal district court over allegations that its joint venture (to bring Andaman Sea oil by pipeline across southern Burma [Myanmar] to Thailand) with the repressive military regime of Burma (Unocal is not the only firm involved) results in various harms to the local population (*John Doe I, et al., v. Unocal Corp., et al.*, 963 F. Supp. 880 [1997]). If such harms have been imposed in fact, they cannot simply be balanced (at least by a firm facing potential conflicts of interest) against benefits arguably generated by Unocal. There are significant policy conflicts for global corporations operating in various countries. On more than one occasion, a US corporation (or industry) has wanted to do business opposed by the US government on national security grounds. Recently, US firms have lobbied the US government with respect to business opportunities in China and Libya. Obviously, another government may order a local subsidiary of a US firm to do something opposed by the US government.

◢ A proposed theory of progressive corporate responsibilities

Machiavelli, in *The Prince* (1980 edn), stresses that the ruler of a principality (as distinguished from a republic) 'ought to take great care that nothing goes out of his mouth which is not full of the five qualities' (pity, faith, integrity, humanity and religion) such that 'he appears to be, when one sees and hears him, all pity, all faith, all integrity, all humanity, and all religion' (ch. 18, 'On the Faith of Princes', p. 109). He explains in the same passage that princes (especially when new to office) must often work against those same five qualities in reality in order to maintain the state (a principality being equated by Machiavelli with the prince's will), and Machiavelli explicitly apprehends there the strategic role of reputation.

The translator, de Alvarez (1980: xv-xvi), comments on what one must appreciate as, in effect, laws of deception studied in Machiavelli (i.e., as de Alvarez states, explaining Machiavelli's approach, 'appearances are deceiving'):

to go beyond appearances demands a method; that is, we must have a way of protecting ourselves against the deceptions of sight. We must first begin to understand in what ways one can be misled, and in what ways one can touch and therefore have certain knowledge.

If corporate social responsibility in fact evolved in the 1920s as a managerial ideology (as argued by Mitchell 1989), then what vouchsafes today's corporate citizenship movement unless modern managers are truly different in motive (see Jackall 1988, who characterises corporate life in terms of moral mazes)? The reader should bear in mind here Adam Smith's observation in *The Wealth of Nations* (1776: Book 4, Ch. VII, Part 3) concerning his complaints about the British East India Company: the complaints were not directed at particular individuals, as most persons would have behaved similarly in the place of the company's officials.

If one is to take corporate citizenship seriously, then, contrary to the current approach, unequal distributions of wealth and power in society imply a fundamentally different theory of progressive responsibilities for corporations. The more powerful and wealthy the firm, the greater that firm's responsibilities to neighbours and the community must be. The argument is strongest for legal and moral compliance. It is useless to construct a case for increasing corporate altruism (which must come out of monies belonging to owners or consumers), which must always arise from strategic calculation, although public policy may induce or compel philanthropy as a direct substitute for government taxation. And one cannot trade some good for some bad in this argument. The argument begins with the individual citizen, who although equal before the law with respect to basic (i.e. constitutional) rights is not equal with respect to social responsibilities either in terms of ethics or in terms of public policy. To paraphrase what has been said by others, freedom is simply the opportunity to do that which is right with respect to others. This view is embedded in Rawls's (1971) proposed principle that policy changes from what is in effect a random lottery of individual outcomes in life should always benefit the disadvantaged the most. (Milton Friedman [1962: 191-95] advocated a negative income tax on wealthier citizens for alleviation of poverty rather than waiting for market forces to handle the matter over time.) The US has embraced in this century progressive income and wealth taxation.[11] Progressive citizenship responsibility is, for individuals, built into the notion of graduated income-tax liabilities. Progressive taxation rests arguably on an uneasy case (Blum and Kalven 1970), but the case for ability-to-pay taxation was made by Adam Smith in *The Wealth of Nations* (1776: Book 5, Ch. I, Conclusion).

One may visualise a very simple chart (not depicted here) with responsibility on the vertical axis and gradations of wealth and power (in some combination) on the horizontal axis. A line measuring responsibility will begin at some positive point

11 A proportional tax rate applied after an initial exemption yields some degree, however mild, of progressivity. A true flat tax (i.e. a single proportional rate) cannot, strictly speaking, have such an initial exemption; so-called 'flat tax' proposals typically reduce tax rates to two or three levels.

on the vertical axis above the zero origin point for an individual ordinary citizen: there are basic responsibilities for every member of the community. But the line should thereafter rise with wealth and power, and large corporations should be classified with the wealthy and the powerful and not with the ordinary individual citizen. This analysis is analogous (bearing in mind the above caution concerning the uneasy case for progressivism) to progressive taxation. Davis's (1973) 'Iron Law of Responsibility' for business is not set at the basic responsibility point for citizens but higher. (The rising curve will become vertical, reflecting infinite responsibility, at the point of criminal responsibility for misconduct. Such businesses are in effect taxed to death.)

A progressive responsibility case that applies to individual citizens must apply most particularly to large and hence influential corporations. More is expected of Bill Gates, not the same or less, with respect to his conduct of Microsoft's business precisely because of its success. Where an individual and a large corporation's employee pour a single can of oil on the ground (neither should do so, of course), the responsibility is greater for the corporation, not simply equal to that of the individual. (The corporation is licensed by society and in theory professionally managed. The employee is an agent, and, where one can is poured, another will probably follow. Many citizens must pour oil to match the volume of misbehaviour by a single corporation.) The current notion of corporate citizen promotes a minimisation of socially imposed responsibilities equivalent to those expected of an individual ordinary citizen.

The current limited view of corporate citizenship is ultimately grounded in a narrow perspective concerning legal standing in criminal and civil actions. The bar of justice should be blind with respect to various distinctions among citizens. Any defendant in a criminal trial is presumed innocent until proven guilty, and the burden of proof (to be demonstrated to some independent tribunal) falls on the government; a defendant in a civil suit is subject to a standard of preponderance of evidence and equitable remedies, and the burden of proof (to be demonstrated to some independent tribunal) falls on the plaintiff. In principle, no other considerations are relevant. (That wealth is important in obtaining best legal representation or that firms are subjected to deep-pocket milching are not theoretically the central issues. No judicial process will be perfect. But the presumption must be one of equality at law.) The argument made here is not that the corporation should be presumed guilty or accountable, or that civil juries should feel free to milch (most particularly out-of-jurisdiction) firms. But criminal and civil law (statutory and common) are narrowly circumscribed, and should be distinguished (as does Wilson 1989) from either ethics (i.e. moral responsibility) or public policy (i.e. what representative institutions decide to do within constitutional rules of choice). Different standards of conduct—that is, of social expectation of conduct—can be enacted into public policy where appropriate.

The policy-making process may well find the implementation of progressive corporate responsibility difficult. It is much easier to craft universal responsibility policies with the appearance of equalisation among 'citizens'. In part this reality may trace to the Lindblom (1977) thesis that in the USA business is a relatively powerful sector. This thesis has recently been broadened in global application by Mitchell (1997). This power is not so much exercised as it is pervasive, in the sense that government depends on the economic performance of the business sector in many ways. Despite his criticism, Reich (1996) did not foresee a return to what he termed 'industrial statesmanship': 'That era, too, is over.' Moreover, with respect to stakeholder interest balancing, 'it is far from clear that society should vest such power in private citizens'. However, Reich's explicit proposal was to adjust corporate income taxes as incentives for particular corporate actions (see Quinn and Shapiro 1991)—that is, to affect the strategic calculus of businesses by rewards. The proposal ties corporate social responsibility explicitly to the tax system. In weighing such tax incentives, it might be wise to bear in mind that corporate responsibilities are arguably progressive and not minimal. And those responsibilities can and should increase with rising social expectations over time, in accordance with Davis's (1973) 'Iron Law of Responsibility'.

◢ Summary and conclusions

Corporate citizenship is a managerial and philanthropic ideology: a strategic doctrine and movement evolved by practitioners. (An ideology is here simply a world-view, and the term is thus *per se* neutral.) Corporate citizenship is consistent with voluntarism advocated by conservative government, and both strict compliance and limited benevolence accomplish some social good. Although corporate citizenship embeds older traditions of corporate social responsibility and responsiveness, fundamentally it crafts an instrumental, self-serving view of the relationship between business and society. Hence corporate citizenship is still a two-edged sword to be handled carefully. One edge admits both the ultimate power of society to impose corporate responsibilities and the strategic advantages of business alignment with societal expectations, but the duties are also restricted to be no more than the duties of ordinary individual citizens. This posture refurbishes the 19th-century legal doctrine of corporate personhood developed in the US Supreme Court as economic substantive due process and serves to blunt any possible development of progressive corporate responsibility.[12] The other edge advances a novel theory (rejected by the US Supreme Court in the 19th century) that the corporation should be treated as if a citizen in terms of legitimating the political influence and activities of business executives.

Corporate citizenship is a marriage of two circumstances: (1) rising societal expectations of corporate benefits in an age of governmental cutbacks; and (2) strategic management aimed at value creation in all functions and activities of a firm. It is a strategy for arguing that direct benefits (i.e. actual gains or reductions

---

12 It may be unfair to argue that the posture was intended to do so, but the implicit opportunity for abuse must be evident, at least in the narrow sense of retarding more radical legal developments in criminal and civil cases and in promoting tort reform.

in losses) are generated for all stakeholders of a firm through value creation orientation. If negative impacts of corporate activities were in fact reduced and minimised, and all affected parties received either such reduction or some gain, then corporate citizenship would correspond to an increase in corporate social performance. But the circumstances would then be a standard and a test for serious corporate citizenship.

CORPORATE CITIZENSHIP
Rethinking business beyond corporate social responsibility*

David Birch
**Corporate Citizenship Research Unit,
Deakin University, Australia**

◢ Holistic corporate citizenship

Lester Thurow wrote, nearly 40 years ago, in *The Future of Capitalism*, that, 'Paradoxically, at precisely the time when capitalism finds itself with no social competitors—its former competitors, socialism or communism, having died—it will have to undergo a profound metamorphosis' (1966: 326). That metamorphosis of capitalism lies at the very heart of the discussions about corporate social responsibility and, more recently, corporate citizenship that have ebbed and flowed throughout most of the 20th century. As more and more pressure is put on capitalism to perform as basically the only major economic system the world now has left, the focus on the social and environmental impact of that system will inevitably increase.

We are seeing that focus now, as more and more people, individuals and groups call on all organisations, including business, to be economically, environmentally and socially sustainable; to be accountable and transparent; to be inclusive; to be ethical and more equitable. These are some of the key issues within the corporate social responsibility discussions as they have developed since the 1940s and within the corporate citizenship debates as they have built up in the 1990s. This chapter explores some of these issues, and their relevance for contemporary business, and concludes with a conceptual framework of corporate citizenship

* My thanks to Mark Glazebrook, Greg Bourne, Ian Fliedner and the participants of the BP seminars.

worked out in consultation with BP in Australia as a systemic, holistic approach that goes well beyond the externalities of corporate social responsibility.

Sustainable capitalism, to use John Elkington's (1997: 258) term, as a building ideology for rethinking business beyond corporate social responsibility activities towards holistic corporate citizenship requires systemic cultural change. That cultural change involves investing in the long term, and in building a sustainable society as part of it, not just a sustainable business in economic terms. This is at the core of holistic corporate citizenship and is what distinguishes it from the very important, but much narrower, generally programme-based, discussions on corporate social responsibility of the past 40 years or so. Holistic corporate citizenship is best viewed, I would argue, not as a programme of activities but as a holistic system of organisational behaviour affecting every level and aspect of an organisation's policies and practices.

◢ The social 'must'

Kenichi Ohmae argued in *The Borderless World: Power and Strategy in the Interlinked Economy* that

> A corporation is a social institution whose responsibilities extend far beyond the wellbeing of its equity owners to giving security and a good life to its employees, dealers, customers, vendors and subcontractors. Their whole life hinges on the wellbeing of the corporation (1991: 214).

If that is the case, and I believe it is, then holistic corporate citizenship is not simply about philanthropy, corporate generosity, business community partnerships, executive leasing to community organisations, cause-related marketing, good causes and so on (though these may well be some of the concrete [externalised] realisations of corporate social responsibility)—it is about a changing business ethos. If the organisation is to survive, if it is to be sustainable, if it is to create wealth it absolutely requires what Thurow described over 30 years ago as a 'social must' (1966: 303).

The social and environmental have to be incorporated, then, not as add-ons to a company's economic activities but as essential, integral, redefinitions of that company in order to better reflect the rapidly changing post-industrial economy (see Bell 1974, cited in Beesley and Evans 1978: 16). This is easier said than done, of course, which is mostly why much of the very developed literature in this area in the 1970s, saying these sorts of things, was never really taken on board beyond a number of environmental imperatives.

Peter Drucker, in his now classic *The Concept of the Corporation*, said over 50 years ago that what is needed in a redefining of a corporation as a social institution 'is an integration of the worker as a partner in the industrial system and as a citizen in society' (1946: 137), arguing strongly that 'the relationship between the self-interest of the citizen and the interests of society is the most fundamental question of a free society' (1946: 214). That argument has since been applied well beyond the individual to the corporate world and is where corporate citizenship, as a significant way of rethinking business, most significantly functions today (see also Birch 1999a; Marsden and Andriof 1998; Moon 1995).

Courtney C. Brown, in *Beyond the Bottom Line*, recognised in 1979 that systemic change was, and still is over 20 years later, a very large order to achieve. It needs considerable authority from business leaders to drive the changes but, he argued, they would have little choice because 'the public insistence on moving quality of life considerations to centre stage is proving hard to resist' (1979: 4). 'The corporate quest' only for 'improved efficiency, competitive success, and maximised profits', Brown argued, is no longer sufficient (1979: 4). 'New tasks have been assigned by public pressures', he wrote, 'tasks for which executive management in many cases is not prepared' (1979: 5). This is still the case, for the most part, because in the past 20 years or so it has been 'easier' to concentrate on corporate social responsibility as something effectively external to an organisation's internal workings, with little of the activities involved seriously changing internal corporate behaviour or ethos, except where a major crisis has initiated that change.

Holistic corporate citizenship is very much more demanding than that, and requires, I would suggest, if it is to be effective at all, that internal behaviour changes so that every decision that is made at every level of an organisation is measured against deeply rooted principles of corporate citizenship. Concentrating the debate on corporate social responsibility, as is happening in many areas today, distances the organisation from the really hard, internal, decisions that have to be made if any serious claim to corporate citizenship is to be made. Courtney Brown went on to argue that

> The real values of the business corporation—and they are social and political as well as material—will be restored to credibility in the present climate of opinion only when business spokesmen [*sic*] are able to articulate a set of guiding principles that relate the conduct of business to a wide range of human aspirations, not just to material abundance alone (1979: 18).

This is as true today as it was in 1979. For the most part, the difference between corporate citizenship and corporate social responsibility is that those guiding principles have been articulated more as externalities than as holistic criteria in comprehensively redefining an organisation internally.

Holistic corporate citizenship, I would argue, requires the external face of the organisation to be guided by its internal structures, and too often those structures and behaviours are rarely, if ever, examined as deeply as they might be. Being socially responsible is still very much a matter of external affairs in most companies. But being a good corporate citizen is more than external affairs—it needs to be intrinsic to every facet of a company's profile. That is not easy and few companies around the world have risen to that challenge, even though many have excellent reputations for their environmental and social responsibility. BP in Australia is one that has accepted the challenge, and this chapter concludes by looking at recent (and ongoing) approaches within that company towards a more holistic, systemic, understanding of corporate citizenship that is designed specifically to go beyond the externalities of corporate social responsibility.

◢ Business as a public culture

The sort of holistic, systemic, understanding of corporate citizenship currently being developed within BP in Australia clearly requires greater conceptual awareness of some foundational principles and processes of corporate citizenship. Peter Schwartz and Blair Gibb, in *When Good Companies Do Bad Things: Responsibility and Risk in an Age of Globalisation*, for example, argue that a company's goal has to be 'in the end, not discovery of a model of social responsibility, but development of a process that will create its own living understanding of its place in the wider world' (1999: 82). But, as Neil Chamberlain pointed out in 1982, 'to pretend that social purpose can simply be grafted onto the existing corporate organisation is an illusion and an evasion' (1982: 12); it requires systemic, holistic, cultural change.

The cultural change required, therefore, goes well beyond externalities, requiring business to increasingly understand itself as a public culture (see Birch and Glazebrook 2000a). As Malcolm McIntosh, Deborah Leipziger, Keith Jones and Gill Coleman, in their 1998 book *Corporate Citizenship: Successful Strategies for Responsible Companies*, make clear, corporate citizenship can really no longer be seen as discretionary (1998: xxiv,). If this is the case, however, this requires a level of disclosure of information, transparency, inclusiveness and accountability from business which is likely to far exceed traditional practices and is likely to mean disclosure on highly organic social goals such as economic justice, stability and freedom (Johnson 1979: 9)—goals not generally associated with the core activities of business. The conclusion is inescapable. Business receives its licence to operate from society and ultimately it is accountable to the society for what it does and how it does it (see Anshen 1980: 6; see also Gladwin *et al.* 1995; Handy 1997; Piore 1995; Reder 1995; Sheikh 1996; Turner and Crawford 1998). In other words, if a business does not radically transform itself to meet its social, environmental as well as its financial obligations it will *de facto* lose its licence to operate in that society, and to carry out that transformation it needs to rethink itself beyond the externalities of corporate social responsibility. As David C. Korten, in *When Corporations Rule the World*, challenges so uncompromisingly:

> If our concern is for a sustainable human wellbeing for all people, then we must penetrate the economic myths embedded in our culture by the prophets of illusion, free ourselves of our obsession with growth, and dramatically restructure economic relationships to focus on two priorities:
>
> • Balance human uses of the environment with the regenerative capacities of the ecosystem, and

- Allocate available natural capital in ways that ensure that all people have the opportunity to fulfil their physical needs adequately and to pursue their full social, cultural, intellectual and spiritual development (1995: 50).

Trust, commitment and co-operation, as Will Hutton suggests, are key elements in this debate but are often missing in the equation for successful and sustainable businesses to create successful and sustainable societies. Hutton talks of the moral economy, arguing that what is needed to redress some of the imbalances is 'a recognition that firms are formed by human beings with human as well as contractual claims on each other and behind this social world lies the moral domain' (1995: 23). These are variables, uncomfortable to many in business, that lie at the heart of rethinking business beyond corporate social responsibility towards corporate citizenship, which has, at its core, a deep-rooted commitment to sustainable development. Rethinking business strategy, therefore, along these lines requires a change in the culture of an organisation but it also opens up 'new opportunities to reassess other aspects of business' (Welford 1995: 77). The challenge is to establish a corporate culture 'consistent with the concept of sustainable development' (Welford 1995: 114). Richard Welford suggests the following ways of rethinking corporate behaviour:

- Shift from objects to relationships
- Shift from parts to the whole
- Shift from domination to partnership
- Shift from structures to processes
- Shift from individualism to integration
- Shift from growth to sustainability (1995: 117).

What is needed, Welford and others argue, in order to achieve objectives such as this is to work much 'smarter' (Halal 1986) and to think more systemically than perhaps we have done before. Peter Senge has made similar points, arguing that business is disabling itself if it continues to:

- Think in terms of individual jobs rather than in terms of the whole organisation
- Blame problems on people or things that are outside the organisation
- Believe that organisations can always solve their problems by taking aggressive action against whatever external force they believe is causing problems
- Become fixated on specific sudden events
- Be unable to perceive threats that result from slow gradual processes
- Operate under the myth that management teams interact cross functionally to solve problems when in reality these teams often spend tremendous energy defending the self-interests of individual members (1990: 142).

Tilman Peter Oehl, in his 1993 paper 'Thoughts about the Changeability of Corporate Cultures' recognises that 'A corporation that regards itself as a corporate citizen is necessarily more political. It cannot remain neutral if something goes wrong in a society its success is based on' (1993: 211). To that end, Will Hutton, in *The Stakeholding Society*, argues persuasively that an imperative for sustainability, and, therefore, effective, holistic, corporate citizenship, 'must be to build a free moral, socially cohesive society based on universal membership, social inclusion and organised around the market economy' (1999: 88). Society, therefore (at least Western developed society), can no longer be considered in unitary terms—it needs to be understood as pluralistic (Drucker 1993: 51), not only in its make-up, now, but also in its expectations.

Peter Drucker talks about the need to redefine society in terms of social ecologies (1993: 52). Linking business inextricably to society, he argues that 'every organisation of today has to build into its very structure, the management of change' (1993: 59), or else business 'will lose performance capacity and with it the ability to attract and to hold the knowledge specialists on whom it depends' (1993: 60). Loyalty, Drucker argues, cannot be obtained by the pay cheque: 'it will have to be earned by proving to knowledge employees that the organisation which presently employs them can offer them exceptional opportunities to be effective' (Drucker 1993: 66). He continues, 'Partnership with the responsible worker is the only way to improve productivity. Nothing else works at all' (1993: 92). This is a systemic change in the distribution of power and lies at the very core of effective corporate citizenship and sustainable development.

As Charles J. Fombrun suggests, moral principles alone constitute a relatively fragile defence for encouraging corporate social responsibility, and he proposes that 'the argument for corporate citizenship is significantly strengthened when buttressed by two additional structural pillars, social integration and the long term sustainability of the business enterprise' (1997: 35). Social integration and long-term sustainability, in Fombrun's terms, cannot happen without serious redefinitions of some of the key defining imperatives of contemporary Western society. And, if that sounds too big a task for business to be involved in (and many in business would probably suggest it was), then, in effect, we will have reached an impasse, and we will remain 'trapped' in a corporate social responsibility paradigm and never be able to get beyond this to a more holistic, systemic, corporate citizenship.

Some companies are, however, attempting to move beyond this paradigm, with BP in Australia one of them. The rest of this chapter is a short account of some of the principles BP in Australia is now working with in order to move the agenda beyond corporate social responsibility towards a more holistic systemic corporate citizenship. Established as part of a draft paper for discussion, entitled 'Charter of Corporate Citizenship', in consultation with the Corporate Citizenship Research Unit, Deakin University, the following generic principles of corporate citizenship were established, through discussions and through an evening seminar series with senior management, as the basis for drafting a proposed charter.

◢ A conceptual framework of corporate citizenship

Discussions with BP in Australia began with an account of the corporate social responsibility debates of the past 60 years or so, concluding that, if there are lessons to be drawn from the discussions so far on these issues, it is that the tensions between capitalism and democracy as currently defined are irreconcilable without serious change. We agreed that we would not achieve long-term sustainability without change. Business needs, therefore, significant policy directions to enable this change to occur, not just within business practices but also within society overall. These are not small responsibilities; they are responsibilities generally associated with government, but they are responsibilities business—as a social institution, as a social enterprise, as a public culture—has to take on board. Business, and in this case BP in Australia, we agreed, will effectively take these on board by considering as central to its core business activities, operations, values and policies the following 12 generic principles of corporate citizenship.

Making a difference

Corporate citizenship is about making a difference in society. It is more than philanthropy. It is about more people having more say, through dialogue and partnership, about the ways in which sustainable success is to be achieved both in the corporate world and in society at large.

Employee and stakeholder empowerment

Corporate citizenship seeks to ensure that every person associated with an organisation is empowered to be able to contribute creatively. Recognition that people want to become involved and the creation of strategies that will ensure this happens are at the heart of corporate citizenship.

Transparency

Corporate citizenship is about transparency. This does not mean being uncompetitive. Studies have shown that the more transparent an organisation, the more benefits flow back in the long term.

Accountability

Corporate citizenship is about improved accountability and shared programmes, which bring benefit to all. To do that requires recognising the value of community partnerships with business. Auditing (and verification) of the organisation's environmental, social and economic bottom lines will enable the business and its stakeholders to make a difference to the continuous improvement of the organisation.

Sharing responsibility

Corporate citizenship is about business sharing responsibility without losing profitability.

Inclusivity

Corporate citizenship is about employee and stakeholder-inclusivity. Stakeholder inclusion requires a long-term, and continuous, relationship to be developed with all stakeholders both inside and outside the organisation.

Sustainable capitalism

Corporate citizenship recognises that at the heart of successful business, government and community relations there needs to be prosperity, and that this prosperity needs to be sustainable.

A triple bottom line

Corporate citizenship is a recognition that a business, corporation or business-like organisation has social, cultural and environmental responsibilities to the community in which it seeks a licence to operate, as well as economic and financial responsibilities to its shareholders or immediate stakeholders. Corporate citizenship is about business redefining the way in which a company focuses on a 'single' bottom line, with companies seeing themselves as responsible only to their shareholders, towards a more socially, ethically and environmentally aware focus on what it means to do business in the public eye (see Tichy *et al.* 1997).

Long-termism

Corporate citizenship recognises the need for moving from a philosophy of short-term transactions to one of long-term dialogue, exchange and partnership.

Communication

Corporate citizenship is about communication between all stakeholders in society in order to build social capital in order to build sustainable societies. To do this involves business, government and community recognising that business is a significant social enterprise shaping community values, attitudes and cultures.

Engagement

Corporate citizenship is about engaging with changing cultures—corporate, government, community and individual—in order to achieve sustainable social, environmental and economic success.

Dialogue

Corporate citizenship involves an organisation coming to terms with the need for often radical internal and external changes in order to better meet its responsibilities to all of its stakeholders (direct or indirect) in order to establish, and maintain, sustainable success for the organisation and, as a result of that success, to achieve long-term sustainable success for the community at large rather than just short-term gains. This involves substantial dialogue with the three main domains of business: the internal organisation of the business, the core business activities and the relations of the business with community.

◢ A suggested charter of corporate citizenship for BP in Australia

The above 12 generic principles were applied to BP in Australia, in particular using BP's own existing business policies outlined in its statement *What We Stand For*. They were then synthesised from a generic conceptual framework of corporate citizenship, applicable to all business, into a specific 'Charter of Corporate Citizenship' specifically designed for BP in Australia and addressed to BP's stakeholders. The charter, given in full in Box 3.1, is a draft charter only and formed the basis for discussion within BP in Australia and should not be seen, in any way, as current BP policy.

Whether this charter in this, or some other, form will become policy in BP in Australia is yet to be determined, but as the basis for discussion internally within BP in Australia and elsewhere the process of drafting this charter has been one that has dramatically increased awareness within the company of the difference between establishing a corporate social responsibility programme in the company and the company becoming a corporate citizen by holistic and systemic cultural change. At its core is an understanding that corporate citizenship is as much (if not more) about the internal organisation within business as it is about business doing business, and business 'doing' things in the community. Recognising employees as primary stakeholders is crucial in this, as is making it clear in all policies and practices within the business that corporate citizenship will not be sustainable unless internal organisation, core business and community links are brought together in inclusive ways.

◢ The way forward

The overall target of a company such as BP in Australia, then, in tandem with its core business activities, internal organisation and community relations, is the

Making a difference

BP aspires to be a good corporate citizen by committing the company to be an ethical, inclusive, mutually advantageous, safe, profitable and social enterprise, where the creation of wealth and sustainable jobs is considered to be a social responsibility for the mutual benefit and empowerment of all employees and stakeholders.

Accountability

As a good corporate citizen BP is committed to conducting business, in an accountable, trusting, open and transparent environment, with a high regard and respect for human dignity, individual rights, the environment and the law.

Sharing responsibility

BP recognises that good corporate citizenship is more than corporate philanthropy, sponsorship or business/community involvement, but that it requires employee and stakeholder inclusivity on a daily basis, expressing how everyone in the Company ensures that our core values, as expressed in *What We Stand For*, are at the heart of everything we do.

Sustainable capitalism

BP is committed to being a socially, environmentally and economically responsible business. This means maximising profit in order to create wealth and sustainable jobs, always intending to have a positive social and environmental impact. Our aim is to optimise long-run rewards, including profit, in order to build long-term value for all our stakeholders. To do this, BP is committed to developing a triple bottom line to include social, environmental and financial measurement of our sustainable success.

Long-termism

Good corporate citizenship is our licence to do business in the community. We are obligated to a social, environmental and financial contract with the community and the public at large where we do business, making sure that we run the business sustainably, ethically, efficiently, openly and profitably. We recognise that as good corporate citizens our investments—financial, social and environmental—will bring sustainable success to all our stakeholders, if we recognise that our first investment priority is with people. Effective communication is vital to that investment.

Engagement

BP recognises that good corporate citizenship requires dialogue with all employees and stakeholders, and that our social, environmental and financial, responsibilities require us to open avenues for that dialogue to take place in order to both recognise achievements, and also to bring about change, where necessary. BP's corporate citizenship defines our behaviour as a company doing business in the public eye. That behaviour is a sum of all the parts at BP. Everyone in BP is responsible for engaging in corporate citizenship.

Box 3.1 **A suggested charter of corporate citizenship for BP in Australia** establishment of sustainable, holistic corporate citizenship, through systemic cultural change. Any business will need to determine the principles that will enable this to happen within the context of its own core values. How this is to be achieved will differ from business to business, depending on differing priorities and constituencies. However, sustainable success for the business and, as a consequence, sustainable success for society are more likely to be reached by asking the following questions of every policy and operation of the company or organisation—on a daily and recurring basis.

- Will this make a positive or negative difference—socially, environmentally and financially?

- Is this fully transparent and accountable in terms of the triple bottom line?

- Is this fully inclusive, involving employee and stakeholder dialogue and feedback?

- Is this ethical, sustainable and profitable?

- Does this add value to the long-term triple bottom line?

- Will this enable all of us to be proud of our current behaviour and the legacy we leave for others?

These questions need to be asked of:

- The internal organisation

- The core business

- The community at large

These are core questions at the very heart of a holistic approach to corporate citizenship and might be achieved in a number of strategic ways, some of which might be to:

- Establish the central role of people and employee involvement in the organisation, recognising that employees are primary stakeholders

- Recognise that corporate citizenship is more than corporate social responsibility and is not simply project-based: it is about three domains
  - The organisation itself
  - The core business
  - The community in which the organisation operates

- Establish a realisable stakeholder consultation process within (and outside of) the company to ensure extensive stakeholder participation in decision-making

- Ensure that the principles of corporate citizenship inform every decision that is made by every member of the company

- Instigate implementation and evaluation processes
- Continuously assess the principles, strategy, policy and values of corporate citizenship against the core competences and constituencies of the business
- Continuously distribute examples of good practice
- Develop site-specific training
- Establish rewards systems
- Set clear goals in an open communication environment
- Calculate the social and environmental impact of all decisions
- Price social and environmental costs
- Review corporate governance
- Establish effective and regular social and environmental auditing
- Monitor changing social values and social attitudes
- Establish effective forecasting of social and environmental futures
- Be willing to change
- Become involved in public policy debates
- Understand what is happening worldwide
- Contribute to research in the area
- Decide whether to go beyond minimum compliance with legal requirements for business and professional practice by evaluating where going beyond compliance will benefit both business and community
- Place more emphasis on non-economic values and quality-of-life issues both within and outside of the business
- Be prepared to enter into big-picture debates
- Recognise that business can successfully create two kinds of value—commercial and social
- Be prepared for innovation
- Decide on the amount of time and resources to spend on developing corporate citizenship within the organisation itself and within the community, and determine the ways in which community involvement will be realised: long-term partnerships, short-term sponsorship, one-off donations, training schemes for community groups, employee volunteer schemes and business education partnerships and so on

◢ Conclusions

It is clear, then, that we have to change the narrow emphasis on economic growth at all costs if we are to be sustainable in the future. Charles Handy argues that

> a three percent growth rate continued for one hundred years would mean that we would be consuming sixteen times as much stuff as we do today. We cannot, can we, buy sixteen times as many cars or television sets, travel all of us, sixteen times as far or as often, eat sixteen times as much food or consume that amount of extra oil and gas? (1997: 45).

His solution is to 'perhaps create more activity outside the purely economic sphere where the motivation will be unconnected with efficiency and more to do with intrinsic satisfaction and worth' (1997: 48), an argument at the core of corporate citizenship discussions.

This stands in strong opposition to a very common, and generally uncontested, view that, in Handy's words, seems 'to be saying that life is essentially about economics, that money is the measure of most things and that the market is its sorting mechanism' (1997: 73). But most of us, increasingly, do not accept this view. As Handy suggests, trapped though we may be in the rhetoric of modernist economics, 'there is a hunger for something else which might be more enduring and more worthwhile' (1997: 73). I believe that the example of BP in Australia presented here demonstrates a positive, and sustainable, reaction to that hunger, and that we do not need to reinvent the issues and principles but to pick up on what has been said so well by so many before us in the past 60 years or so and to now turn that into action by rethinking business beyond the externalities of corporate social responsibility to sustainable, systemic, holistic, corporate citizenship.

GLOBAL CORPORATE CITIZENSHIP IN A DOT.COM WORLD

The role of organisational identity

James E. Post and Shawn L. Berman
Boston University, USA

On 26 July 2000, executives from 50 multinational corporations met with the Secretary-General of the United Nations to commit their companies to a set of principles in the areas of environment, labour and human rights. The leaders of a dozen labour unions and civil society organisations were also present for the historic meeting. The signing of the UN Global Compact is one in a series of recent events underscoring the rising importance of corporate citizenship. The UN Global Compact began to take shape at the 1999 World Economic Forum in Davos, Switzerland, when UN Secretary-General Kofi Annan challenged business and political leaders in these terms:

> I want to challenge you to join me in taking our relationship to a still higher level. I propose that you, the business leaders gathered in Davos, and we, the United Nations, initiate a global compact of shared values and principles, which will give a human face to the global market.
>
> Globalisation is a fact of life. But I believe we have underestimated its fragility. The problem is this. The spread of markets outpaces the ability of societies and their political systems to adjust to them, let alone to guide the course they take. History teaches us that such an imbalance between the economic, social, and political realms can never be sustained for very long (Annan 1999: 1-5).

The UN Global Compact is another recent milestone in the development of global corporate responsibility. For example, John Browne, chief executive of BP Amoco, broke ranks with the petroleum industry and publicly acknowledged the problems of global climate change and the need for corporate action. And Goran Lindahl, chairman of ABB (Asea Brown Boveri), a manufacturer of power transmission equipment, with major investments in China, South Africa and the war-torn Balkans, issued a public call for global corporations to take the lead in meeting civic duties and to become 'co-guarantors of human rights'. He wrote,

> As a businessman with almost 30 years of international experience, I see globalisation as basically a good thing. But I also know that transparency and a free flow of trade, capital, skills, technology, and information, even mixed with the human aspiration for a share of the better life, will not automatically lead to a better life for all . . . The pursuit of profit alone cannot hold societies together . . . Globalisation has thrust on the international business community another even more challenging dimension to our new civic role. An already worrying gap is widening between the international norms and declarations on human rights, such as the UN Charter, and current societal and business realities. Big companies need to step into the breach to ensure that globalisation delivers more than a litany of dashed hopes. We must now act as co-guarantors of human rights (Lindahl 2000: 3).

The 'compact' to which executives of 50 companies, including Bayer, Daimler-Chrysler, DuPont, Ericsson, Heatheon/WebMD, Nike, Royal Dutch Shell and Unilever committed involves pledges to support human rights, eliminate child labour, allow free trade unions and refrain from polluting the environment wherever they do business. The UN Secretary-General stressed the importance of encouraging companies that operate across borders to spread Western-style human and environmental values or risk seeing the erosion of the consensus that favours open trade and investment (Kahn 2000).

Most corporations remain far from their potential for aligning civic roles with their business models. Yet, the promise is surely there. The drivers of change—intense competition, new technologies, globalisation, a concern for ethics and values, ecological issues and the changing role of government—will continue to prod companies and managers to reinvent their businesses and their vision of citizenship. As they do so, relationships with stakeholders will become more vital. Reputation, image and corporate identity are of growing importance as price and product quality become less differentiating in a world where customers have many choices. Can any company assume that customers will not select the firm with the better reputation? Increasingly, the 'supplier of choice' will have to be the 'neighbour of choice' (Burke 1999).

◢ Corporate citizenship

The modern corporation is one of the great institutional developments of the past century. Despite its economic success, the corporation's social and political power have drawn extensive criticism and generated a continuing debate about the role of business in society. The dialogue has led many business leaders and corporations to engage in philanthropic, public relations and community activities. Enlightened self-interest has prompted efforts to meet public expectations and temper pressures for political and regulatory action. In many companies, civic engagement is part of the culture.

As the first decade of the21st century unfolds, the role of the corporation is under a new kind of debate. Global commerce raises questions of global accountability and responsibility. Critics ask whether corporations should profit by imposing risks and harm on unsuspecting individuals and countries. Sharp disagreements exist over the proper way to share economic benefits with the communities or countries that bear the risks of wealth creation. Against a backdrop of global economic expansion, these important questions are forming the foundation for an era focused on global corporate responsibility and citizenship. These issues are the contextual underpinning of the UN Global Compact initiative. The salient questions include the following:

- What does it mean to be a global corporate citizen?

- What does global corporate citizenship mean for business strategy?

- What practices can society reasonably expect from its corporate citizens?

These questions are part of a high-stakes dialogue in the global business and political community. Prosperity has been unevenly shared across the global economy; serious social and political problems exist alongside economic opportunity. At the macro level, world leaders wrestle with a global financial system that remains unstable, and we live in a global trade regime rife with inequities that generate deep political and social tensions. At the micro level, social and environmental issues challenge governments, corporations, labour unions and civil society organisations to develop effective responses.

Corporate citizenship remains a concept in search of a definition. Based on a recent study of global corporate citizenship activities by firms in many industries, we offer the following definition:

> Global corporate citizenship is the process of identifying, analysing, and responding to the company's social, political, and economic responsibilities as defined through law and public policy, stakeholder expectations, and voluntary acts flowing from corporate values and business strategies. Corporate citizenship involves actual results (what corporations DO) and the processes through which they are achieved (HOW they do it)' (Post 2000a: 8; emphasis in original).

Because technology and globalisation are redefining the nature of communities that companies interact with, every company's citizenship model must be realigned with its business model to accommodate new realities. New industries and new forms of commerce raise complex competitive, social and ethical issues. The modern corporation is at the centre of these changes, and leaders recognise that there is no place for the corporation and its managers—or society and its citizens—to hide.

External pressures are not the only drivers of corporate citizenship. In many companies, managers and employees understand that a company's core values shape citizenship activities as well as strategic goals and business plans. Firms with significant community presence (e.g. banks, electric utilities) illustrate how citizenship becomes an intrinsic part of the firm's business model. Companies also link citizenship principles to business activities when operating on a global scale. At Motorola, for example, the company's core values ('respect for the individual' and 'uncompromising integrity') require active management responses to ethical issues that arise around the world. The company has created a global ethics process that engages senior corporate managers with those who are at the front lines of day-to-day business conduct in locations around the world. Coupled with training programmes that forthrightly address the dilemmas that occur, the objective is to encourage each employee to apply the company's core values— respect for the individual and uncompromising integrity—to their everyday business activities. The result is a combination of 'push' and 'pull' factors leading all employees to think about the relationship between their business objectives and the company's citizenship responsibilities and opportunities (Post *et al.* 2002a).

◢ Corporate identity

Corporate identity is a fundamental dimension of corporate citizenship. Every organisation develops an identity that enables its members to answer the fundamental question, 'Who are we?' (Albert and Whetten 1985; Benning 1999). An organisation's collective 'sense of self' reflects its history, shared values and the standards of behaviour expected of its members. In a world where stakeholder relationships are complicated and important to a firm's success, corporate identity provides value to employees, customers, business partners, investors and other stakeholders. Stakeholders want answers to such questions as 'What does this company stand for?' 'How does it behave?' 'What performance can be expected?' The frequency and importance of these questions has moved stakeholder management to the foreground of senior management competences. The management of identity is a key aspect of that competence.

Corporate response to stakeholder issues is shaped by a company's identity. After all, corporations *are* what they do (Post *et al.* 2002a). Rhetoric is not performance, and words are not deeds. But rhetoric creates and shapes stakeholder expectations. Business exposure, top management philosophy, external affairs organisation and design, and political strategy all influence the way organisations respond to external issues (Miles 1986). Amid an often lengthy and diverse agenda of issues, corporate values help managers prioritise what matters most.

Identity has strategic relevance to the firm. Albert *et al.* (2000) argue, for example, that identity has both generative and integrative qualities that enable an organisation's members to comprehend where they are and where they are going. Identity can be a strategic asset, providing members with a 'North Star' to which they can turn when faced with confusing facts, circumstances and uncertainties. Leaders also use an organisation's identity to help stakeholders understand and articulate the impact of change and the need to adapt to it.

Identity is an integrative concept, providing a unifying explanation for diverse activities. However, Pratt and Foreman (2000) have shown that an organisation may have multiple identities—that is, it may present itself in different ways to various interests. Benning (1999) found that a faith-based social service agency manifested multiple identities, each designed to connect with different groups of stakeholders. The organisation's religious service identity appealed to church members who provided donations to support the agency. The agency was a 'responsible manager' to those government agencies with which it entered into service provider contracts. To the social workers and other professionals who work with, and for, the organisation it possessed a professional service identity. These are not simply different images of the organisation. The organisation actually was a religious service entity, professionally managed and committed to high standards of professional practice. As Benning shows, various groups of internal and external stakeholders selected among the three identities when responding to the question, 'Who are we?' The art of leadership in such a setting is to communicate with various audiences in the context of the organisation's identity.

The history of a company's interaction with government, community groups, non-governmental organisations (NGOs), media and other stakeholders shapes its identity and its distinctive corporate citizenship profile. The way a company has dealt with past public issues, stakeholders and community concerns affects employee perceptions of what matters. Motorola, a leading manufacturer of telecommunications equipment, was surprised to learn that it was being criticised for being involved in the production of landmines. Semiconductor chips manufactured by Motorola had been sold to a European dealer who, in turn, sold them to a third-party assembler of landmine components. Once disclosed, Motorola withdrew from that business relationship and instituted new controls to monitor its market channels. Today, Motorola has more comprehensive mechanisms for analysing global corporate responsibility issues on a worldwide basis, including a revised code of business conduct and a top-management task force for reviewing global corporate responsibility policy (cf. Post *et al.* 2002a).

◢ Identity and corporate citizenship

A small number of companies develop corporate citizenship identities that are so strong as to actually define their business identity. Levi Strauss, for example, has long valued its citizenship commitments to the extent that it has sacrificed business success in order to pursue community commitments. Ben & Jerry's, Dayton-Hudson (now Target Stores), The Body Shop and Newman's Own are firms for which the pursuit of a social mission is at the core of their very existence.

Most firms develop a citizenship identity that is compatible with their business identity. International Paper wishes to be known as a company committed to sustainable forestry; Rio Tinto for responsible mining practice; and Monsanto to environmental safety and protection. America Online (AOL) is establishing its identity as a leader in community services (e.g. philanthropy) via the Internet. These identities complement the business identity in meaningful ways that appeal to important stakeholders.

Finally, there are firms whose citizenship identity (positive or negative) exists apart from any concept of the business. These firms may engage in various community good works, but it is not part of the definition of what they are. Still, as the competitive marketplace puts growing value on the importance of trust, reputation, brand identity and an organisation's ability to effectively manage a multitude of stakeholder relations, the importance of identity becomes more important as an expression of shared values.

Given these variations, we believe that some organisations consciously create and project an integrated identity whereas others create and project multiple identities. This proposition, if confirmed, has important implications for the study and practice of corporate citizenship. As illustrated in Figure 4.1, organisational identity is linked to reputation, corporate image and brand identity. It is an intangible asset and a valuable component of the firm's 'brand equity'. What is unknown is whether an integrated identity, in which citizenship attributes are integrated with business attributes into an overall identity, or multiple identities, in which citizenship attributes are viewed as separate—and perhaps distinctive—from business attributes, is preferable. Indeed, it is unclear whether companies actually succeed in projecting integrated or multiple identities to their stakeholders.

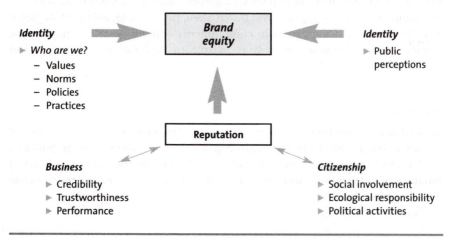

Figure 4.1 **The strategic role of corporate identity**

Identity in a dot.com world

Citizenship is often an element of a firm's published identity. Core values, codes of conduct, policy statements and publications (on the World Wide Web or in print) typically refer to the firm's commitment to its customers, employees, suppliers, investors and local communities. Companies in the forest products, mining, petroleum, banking and insurance industries typically address stakeholder expectations, public issues and corporate performance through these means, and the firm's civic role is often an extension of the dominant business model in these industries.

In the Internet era, companies in both the 'new economy' and the 'old economy' use websites to describe their organisation, its products and services and its key features (values, policies, practices, activities). Web pages are designed to highlight information that the organisation wishes to share with inquirers and to provide information that responds to frequently asked questions (FAQs) about the company. This combination of 'push' and 'pull' forces effectively leads the organisation to clarify its identity in ways that will 'speak' to the audience.

Preliminary research suggests that firms with low exposure to public issues are not likely to provide information about their citizenship activities on corporate websites. Rather, they tend to emphasise the firm's products, services and workplace. Firms with high exposure to public issues (e.g. those in the tobacco industry), however, include information on their websites that describes their position and describes action taken on key issues. In 1999, Philip Morris redesigned its global website to emphasise the 'People of Philip Morris' as a community citizenship theme and to draw distinctions between the tobacco business and the company's food and beverage businesses.[1] Many firms in the gaming industry now stress 'responsible entertainment' themes; businesses with a high ecological impact (chemicals, forest products, mining, petroleum) frequently include information about their environmental management programmes. And companies that have been sharply criticised for wrongdoing employ websites in their efforts to rehabilitate public images. Royal Dutch Shell, for example, designed its global website to emphasise citizenship commitments—environment, human rights, community involvement—as well as petroleum exploration, production and distribution activities.[2]

The study

To further examine how companies from both the 'new economy' and the 'old economy' communicate their citizenship model in relation to their business model, we examined 100 corporate websites. The sample contained nearly equal numbers of old-economy and new-economy firms and was constructed to examine two propositions:

1 www.philipmorris.com
2 www.shell.com

- That organisations will communicate one or more identities to their stakeholders in response to the question, 'Who are we?'

- That new-economy firms will more likely communicate a single identity on their websites than will old-economy firms

A group of 100 respondents observed the websites of a sample of companies. Each respondent was asked to examine six corporate websites: three old-economy firms and three new-economy firms. The companies were identified by name but not by industry. No reference was made to old economy or new economy. Several respondents observed each company's site, creating a total of 599 'observations' of the company websites. Respondents were given a maximum of two minutes to examine each website. (Our pilot study showed that one minute was too little time to grasp the 'message' of the site; a three-minute option was deemed to be 'too much time' by the pilot sample.) Each respondent was asked to answer four basic questions:

- Does the company communicate one clear answer to the question 'Who are we?' (yes/no)?

- If yes, please describe the answer in your own words.

- If no, does the company communicate several answers to the question 'Who are we?' (yes/no)?

- If so, please describe the answers in your own words.

Net identity

As illustrated in Figure 4.2, we hypothesised that corporate websites would reflect either a single identity or multiple identities. Our primary question was whether new-economy firms are more likely, or less likely, to include information about

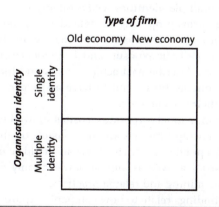

Figure 4.2 **Relations between firm type and identity**

their citizenship activities on websites than are old-economy firms. Further, are firms engaged in e-commerce more likely, or less likely, to project an integrated identity than are old-economy firms?

Based on a total of 599 observations (see Table 4.1), we found that:

- 50.75% of websites were categorised as describing companies with a 'single identity'.

- 36.06% of websites were categorised as describing companies with 'multiple identities'.

- 8.35% of websites were categorised as describing 'both', suggesting some confusion about the message or purpose of the website.

- 4.84% of responses were categorised as describing 'neither' a single identity nor multiple identities, suggesting confusion about the message or purpose of the website.

Breakdown of observations	Old-economy firms	New-economy firms	Percentage*
Single identity	137	167	50.75
Multiple identity	122	94	36.06
Both	30	20	8.35
Neither	13	16	4.84
Total	**302**	**297**	

* The total number of observations (old-economy firms plus new-economy firms) as a percentage of the total number of observations (599; 302 + 297)

Table 4.1 **Identity patterns in old-economy and new-economy firms**

The strongest finding is that new-economy firms tend to project a single identity rather than multiple identities. Old-economy firms are almost equally divided, with 22 of 45 firms projecting a single identity, and 23 of 45 projecting multiple identities through their websites. This may be attributable to a number of factors, including public issue exposure and the tendency of old-economy firms to use their websites to describe past achievements and future directions (e.g. e-commerce). New-economy firms tend to have a sharper, more coherent and unified message for their stakeholders.

An examination of individual corporate websites showed some support for the proposition that citizenship activities are more visible on the websites of firms that face controversial public issues. This was true of old-economy businesses in high-exposure industries as well as among new-economy firms involved with issues of privacy, data mining and related practices.

How might these findings relate to how companies approach the challenge of corporate citizenship in the 21st century? First, old-economy firms appear to use their websites for business activities and corporate citizenship purposes. At least some of these firms seem determined to highlight both their corporate citizenship model and their business model. New-economy firms are less likely to blur their messages but are also less likely to recognise that a corporate citizenship model accompanies their business model. Very few of the new-economy firms provided significant corporate citizenship information on their websites (notable exceptions include Ericsson and AOL Time Warner).

Citizenship patterns

Distinctive patterns of corporate citizenship exist across industries. Companies in the natural resources industries (e.g. petroleum, mining, paper and pulp) have a strong geographic approach to citizenship issues. Emphasis is placed on resource stewardship and cultivating positive relationships with local communities. Industrial manufacturers, with large facilities and concentrated impacts on local communities, place a high priority on local government and community relations. Traditional retailers have a strong geographic focus, although adverse impacts are quite different in scale and scope than with heavy manufacturing firms. Banks, insurers, electric companies, telecommunications, and cable television firms display profiles that are influenced by geographical and non-geographical factors (Post 2000a).

Many companies understand the relationship between successful business strategy and corporate citizenship and implement effective programmes in their home country. According to recent studies by the Foundation for Public Affairs, for example, support for the community relations function is quite strong among senior executives (FPA 2000; Post and Griffin 1997). More than 70% of all (*Fortune* 1000) companies studied in recent years engaged in organised community relations functions that are linked to corporate philanthropy, volunteerism and community involvement. In some industries, the percentages are even higher. A similar pattern of support exists in Australia, according to a recent survey of community involvement best practice (CCPA 2000).

In the international arena, however, a more complex picture emerges. According to a recent study by the Boston College Centre for Corporate Community Relations (1999), 62% of 111 respondent companies reported operating in multiple countries; only 42% of these companies, however, have an established community relations programme in any of the their international locations. When asked what programmes or services are offered for communities at their international locations, 83% mentioned financial contributions, 64% mentioned in-kind services, 67% mentioned volunteerism and 62% mentioned partnerships. These responses paint a portrait of companies that are mostly trying to export successful domestic programmes to new locations.

The 'glocal' corporation

To achieve global competitiveness, many firms strive to integrate global business strategies and local civic activities. International business research has shown that the introduction of a global brand in a developing country with a promising consumer market is not likely to succeed against domestic competitors unless the global company establishes its credibility as a local company. This may require working with a local partner or building a visible local presence through activities in the community.

This integration of global strategy and local delivery is the essence of a 'glocal' approach. The success of McDonald's and Coca-Cola in integrating global brand identity with local market presence underscores the power of the 'glocal' concept. These companies have integrated knowledge from marketing, operations, public affairs and community relations into an active global citizenship philosophy that joins their business and citizenship models (Post 2000a).

Models

Traditional patterns of corporate citizenship changed considerably in the 1990s. Philanthropy and community relations became less altruistic and more systematically tied to strategic business goals. Decision processes were streamlined in many companies; overhead expenses and staff positions were reduced in virtually all firms. Corporate community relations was transformed as a result of corporate restructuring, technology and other drivers of change (Altman 1997; Altman and Vidaver-Cohen 2000). The new models have been shaped by two factors: current scope of the business and traditional industry pattern of activity. A summary of the models and representative company examples are shown in Table 4.2 and discussed below.

Scope of the business

The scope of a multinational corporation's business involves the number of countries in which it does business, the geographical proximity and cultural distance of those countries and the degree of co-ordination occurring in the supply chain and market channels. These factors affect whether managers think about citizenship issues on a country-by-country, regional or global basis.

Most industries have developed models of corporate citizenship through trial and error. In these industries global corporate citizenship has evolved as the scope of business has evolved, from domestic to global settings. The domestic model refers to the company's home country or dominant market. The multi-domestic and global models refer to the number of countries involved and the interconnectedness of these countries with one another. In practice, there is overlap among these models and individual corporations display a mix of features. Still, the models described below illustrate essential factors that define distinct ways of thinking about corporate citizenship.

	Geographic scope of the business[†]		
*Industry citizenship orientation**	*Domestic*	*Multi-domestic*	*Global*
Natural resource	Western Mining	Rio Tinto BHP	BP Amoco Exxon Mobil Royal Dutch Shell
Industrial		General Motors Asea Brown Boveri (ABB)	Dow Chemical IBM[‡] Intel
Service			IBM[‡] FedEx BT[‡]
Retail		Wal-Mart	Coca-Cola[‡] McDonald's
Internet (e-commerce)		Dell Computer America Online (AOL)	BT[‡] Microsoft IBM[‡] AOL Time Warner

* The citizenship orientation increases as the table is descended.
† The geographical scope increases from left to right.
‡ This company's operations properly place it in more than one category.

Note: All of the companies cited are continuously re-evaluating their business strategies. For example, AOL has expanded from its dominant home market (USA) to a number of foreign venues and is becoming a multi-domestic corporation. The company's merger with Time Warner will move the new company from a multi-domestic scope of business to a global scope of business.

Table 4.2 **Citizenship models and geographic business focus, including representative company examples**

The domestic business model

The history of many corporations begins with success in a home-country market from which they evolve an international market strategy. Global industries such as petroleum, motor vehicles and telecommunications equipment are populated by firms that were successful in their domestic market before initiating international expansion. In terms of citizenship, these firms tend to have a strong national approach to how citizenship activity should be conducted.

The multi-domestic business model

In some global corporations the overarching strategic vision is to position the company as a 'domestic firm' in every country where it conducts business. At ABB (Asea Brown Boveri), the Swiss–Swedish industrial giant that operates in more than 120 countries, it is important to be seen as a 'local company' wherever it bids for public-sector contracts or builds industrial equipment (Belanger *et al.* 1999). To this end, ABB supports country-level citizenship strategies that emphasise locally appropriate community involvement activities. The company's projects in

China, Indonesia and other countries are typically accompanied by a carefully designed community and government relations presence.

Multi-domestic businesses cultivate local citizenship wherever they operate. Executives usually serve on community boards, the companies are involved in industry associations and employee volunteers participate in a range of local causes. The multi-domestic citizenship model, like its business model counterpart, emphasises local identity and presence rather than the company's 'global name'.

The global enterprise model

One feature of the truly global enterprise is its effort to simultaneously be seen as both global and local. Companies that cultivate this model of business and citizenship develop distinctive identities as global corporate citizens. They recognise and respond to the unique challenges posed by international supply chains and market channels, cross-border environmental issues, international labour markets and global communication and transportation systems. They are 'glocal' businesses and 'glocal' citizens.

The truly global enterprise develops citizenship strategies that harmonise, or integrate, local action with global themes and commitments. For example, IBM has developed a global commitment to education that translates into country-specific initiatives where the company has local facilities and markets (cf. Post 2000a). Enterprise-wide initiatives send a single message—for example, IBM and education go together—and can build local understanding of the company's citizenship objectives.

Traditional industry pattern

Firms in the same industry tend to display similar citizenship features. This is not surprising, since imitation of successful behaviour is to be found throughout business policy and practice.

The natural resources model

Businesses involved in the extraction, development or use of natural resources inevitably impact local communities. Companies involved in petroleum exploration, mining, forestry and land development recognise the importance of earning a company's 'social licence to operate'. Community involvement requires mitigation of negative effects, consultation processes, support of community activities and provision of services for employees and residents. The natural resources industry model is visible in the 'company towns' of Australia, Brazil, Papua New Guinea and other countries where exploration occurs in remote areas and where local economic activity depends on employees who are flown in and out of the area. Exploration companies also encounter 'communities' of indigenous people, residents, employees and activist organisations (including international NGOs).

The industrial or manufacturing model

Industrial and manufacturing companies face community issues similar to those of natural resource firms. Residents, businesses and neighbourhoods who are put at risk may resist the establishment of such firms in their region until satisfactory commitments are made to protect the community. In such cases, the company's 'social licence to operate' is contingent on the community's approval and on confidence in relationships with management. Stewardship programmes, risk management and community consultation are the core elements of a successful community relations programme for industrial firms.

The service model

The service firm—bank, insurance company, business service company—is rarely challenged in terms of its social licence to operate. It is challenged, however, to meet community standards and to address the community's expectations of corporate involvement. Corporate image and identity are important assets in service industries. Reputation matters greatly as the company strives to meet the challenges of innovation, distribution and marketing. Companies whose community presence and involvement earns respect often reap the benefits of sales patronage, customer loyalty and institutional customers. Reputation can also make a difference in a company's ability to attract employees with scarce talents. The distinctive benefits of community involvement are evident in the linkages between citizenship, employee support and cause marketing. Service firms depend heavily on impressions—the perceptions that others have of the firm as a good employer, supplier and citizen.

The retail model

Retailers develop citizenship profiles that emphasise active involvement with consumers and local communities. Entertainment and consumer products are often associated with public events, ranging from rallies and civic actions to promote awareness of community needs, to company-sponsored events, such as concerts, festivals or celebration of holidays. The citizenship profile of global retailers—who also manage vast supply chains—can be organised around marketing themes, social causes or links to charity organisations (AIDS Action, Special Olympics). As companies emphasise their 'brand' names (e.g. Reebok, Levi Strauss, Timberland), positive corporate image and identity as citizens becomes more important. Of course, visible names can assume negative connotations, as shown by the anti-Nike campaign or the strong reactions from communities in which a Wal-Mart store is about to be located (cf. Post *et al.* 2002b).

The Internet or e-commerce model

Information technology and the explosive growth of electronic commerce (e-commerce) are giving rise to another model of corporate citizenship. This model, still in its infancy, bears some resemblance to others but with such unique features as to merit separate consideration. Many new technology companies seem hopelessly self-absorbed as they struggle to survive in extremely competitive environments. For these firms, competition is fierce, technology changes at a dizzying rate and external affairs are characterised by media hype and posturing for investor favour in anticipation of initial public offerings (IPOs). There seems to be little space for corporate citizenship in the culture of these entrepreneurial companies.

There is reason to expect that, as Internet companies mature and become more global in their business activities, corporate citizenship will become more relevant to their business models. Companies such as AOL, Cisco Systems, EMC, Lucent and a host of Internet service providers (ISPs) already grapple with complex issues of corporate responsibility involving employees, customer privacy and content restrictions on products and services. Many are displaying distinctive and emergent citizenship profiles. Dell, for example, is becoming more of a global citizen as it becomes more of a global competitor (Post 2000a). Citizenship is now integral to its business model. In a profile of high-technology companies operating in China, *Fortune* contrasted Intel's close relationship with the leading Chinese personal computer firm (Legend) with Dell's focus on Chinese consumers. Dell's critics argue that the direct sales model will not work in a country where customers like to see and touch a product before they buy. But Dell's Asia-Pacific boss Phil Kelly argued that the critics missed the key point: 'The most important thing in China is *guanxi*, or relationships. That's what Dell is all about. It's taking the middle person out so that a customer can deal with the father rather than the son' (Chowdhury 1999).

◢ Toward dot.com citizenship

The Internet creates opportunities for companies in all sectors to redefine the way they do business. Firms are building relationships with customers, suppliers and business partners in new ways. Three converging forces are shaping this strategic logic:

- Digitisation of business platforms
- Knowledge and intellectual resources
- Interdependent business relationships

Whereas products and services were once the *sine qua non* of commercial success, business relationships—the ability to link with the best suppliers of every part of the entire value chain—are now the most prized element of the commercial equation. The digitisation of modern commerce puts information technology at the very centre of business models and corporate strategy, and evidence is mounting that no industry or competitor is immune from this revolution. As Venkatraman (1998: 18) states,

> Far from being just another staff function, information technology (IT) has moved to the core of business platform design. No longer tangential, information—and the technological capability to get it and use it—is central to all business strategy.

The relationships between service provider, content provider and customer are faster, more frequent and infinitely more varied than they are in service industries. Cause marketing, philanthropy, public-service information and volunteer programmes are already a part of the Internet model. The first 'NetAid' global concert and fundraising event took place in 1999; more Internet mega-events are certain to follow. Communities of interest and practice intersect and overlap in a staggering number of ways. Each component of the traditional citizenship equation is already being developed in new electronic forms. But experts suggest that other, more unique, citizenship elements are also evolving. Cyber communities engaged in human rights, environmental sustainability, social equity and corporate responsibility issues make it likely that new forms of external pressures will also shape the Internet citizenship model.

Whatever a company's traditional posture toward its stakeholders and civic role, the reality of competing in a 'dot.com' world will galvanise new thinking and action. The modern corporation is increasingly understood as a portfolio of capabilities existing in a web of stakeholder relationships. These relationships are visible to end-consumers and play a central role in delivering value to them. It is the company's relationships with its stakeholders (suppliers, vendors, alliance partners) that are critical to delivering value to a company's end-consumers. Citizenship activities can be leveraged to strengthen, create or enhance key relationships in this new environment. Communities of people with specialised knowledge, interests or risks can become a critical business relationship as a source of customers, employees or expertise.

Impact on corporate citizenship

The digital revolution will affect corporate citizenship in two distinct ways. First, the amount and quality of information will increase, enabling individuals, activists and communities to learn about the firm and its activities much faster than they were able to in the past. Organisational boundaries will become more permeable to community influence, with information flowing at cyber speed from corporation to community. Second, digital technology will enable the corporation to respond faster and better to issues of concern to stakeholders. Information about risks, business operations, community programmes and other activities can be shared faster, and more effectively, than it was in the past. Some firms use online community forums and chat rooms to communicate with stakeholders; others are doing extensive electronic polling to assess community support or resistance for activities such as plant expansion (Altman and Vidaver-Cohen 2000).

Corporate citizenship 'products' are also affected. Web pages are used to post information about the company's citizenship activities and initiatives. Assistance to schools and other organisations often takes the form of new or upgraded technology. New configurations of donor–donee relations have emerged. Greatergood.com, for example, is an organisation that extends affinity and social cause marketing to e-commerce. By clicking on the Greatergood.com site, prospective customers are linked to the websites of more than 300 non-profit organisations that sell goods and services. Customers learn that the non-profit organisation of their choice will receive 5% of profits from their sales purchase.

◢ Conclusions

Citizenship is a challenge that companies cannot ignore and that managers cannot avoid. New 'communities' are part of every company's reality, generating new problems and creating new opportunities. The Internet enables businesses of any size to 'go global' in their search for customers, suppliers and allies. For companies that were founded in a pre-Internet world ('old-economy' firms), the digitisation of commerce affects products and processes first, then the basic business model, then the citizenship model. For companies that were founded as e-commerce start-ups in the 'new economy', the business model always begins with a definition of the Internet 'communities' that will be drawn to the product or service.

The growing importance of communities, both geographic and virtual, is setting the stage for a new era of corporate citizenship. In the 21st century, corporate citizenship may become the standard expectation for global business enterprises. The reason is clear: the benefits and costs of business activities are so extensive that no society can develop without seriously thinking about the role of the global corporation. UN Secretary-General Kofi Annan's comments, quoted in the opening of this chapter, underscore the challenge of achieving a balance between economic and social wellbeing and place the problem in sharp relief: businesses will not reap the economic benefits of open global markets without responding to their social and political responsibilities. They must be global corporate citizens. Citizenship must become part of their corporate identity, for it truly is who they are.

THEORISING
BUSINESS CITIZENSHIP*

Donna J. Wood
**University of
Pittsburgh, USA**

Jeanne M. Logsdon
**University of
New Mexico, USA**

The concept of corporate social responsibility is being replaced by the term 'corporate citizenship'. It may not be a bad idea to make this shift in terminology. But we are concerned that the core content of social responsibility may be lost in favour of a more narrow and voluntaristic concept of corporate community service. We argue in this chapter that the broad ethics-based norms of social responsibility must be intentionally integrated into corporate citizenship. We suggest that the alternative term 'business citizenship' may better incorporate the broader perspective on business rights and duties, stakeholder relationships, opportunities and challenges that accompany the global socioeconomy of the 21st century.

In order to develop a working theory of business citizenship, we first extract several key ideas about citizenship of individual persons and apply them to business organisations. This step requires an analysis of two perspectives on the individual, the organisation and the state: the minimalist or the libertarian view, and the communitarian view. Next, we transpose the concept of business citizenship from a single community perspective to a global perspective. We do this by contrasting the communitarian view of citizenship with the universal rights view. This approach allows a view of business citizenship that accommodates strong moral guidance, structural and institutional realities and the flexibility necessary

* An earlier version of this work was presented by invitation at the Ruffin Lectures in Business Ethics, University of Virginia, October 1999. An extensive version of the Ruffin paper will be published in *Business Ethics Quarterly*.

The authors wish to thank the Sloan Foundation for financial support, and the Olssen Centre for Business Ethics, University of Virginia, for an opportunity to present an early version of this work.

to respond to the changing circumstances of particular company–stakeholder relationships.

◢ Corporate social responsibility and corporate citizenship

Although the concept had existed for decades (see Dodd 1932), the term 'corporate social responsibility' was initially proposed in the 1950s and 1960s (Bowen 1953) as a kind of business self-regulation device, a way of ensuring the social control of business without depending on the uncertainties of individual ethics or the potentially coercive authoritarianism of government. The scholarly articulation of corporate social responsibility was part bully-pulpit, part an appeal to self-interest and part justice-oriented. William C. Frederick (1986: 4), for example, expressed corporate social responsibility as follows: 'The fundamental idea of "corporate social responsibility" is that business corporations have an obligation to work for social betterment.'

Business executives have focused much attention on corporate social responsibility at least since the 1950s. In the 1960s in the USA many business leaders were genuinely concerned about social unrest, urban decay and the natural environment. Corporate social responsibility gave businesses a role to play in dealing with serious social problems. The problems, however, were much bigger than the ability of business to solve them. In addition, the mid-1960s to mid-1970s brought a spate of 'social' regulation of business practices in pollution control, equal employment opportunity, workplace safety and health, banking practices, advertising, product safety and much more. By the end of the 1970s, businesses began to chafe under an increasing regulatory burden. For some, corporate social responsibility was viewed as a potentially powerful way to avoid burdensome government intervention by instead implementing self-regulation. For others, corporate social responsibility was a 'Commie plot'[1] to subvert capitalism by reducing individual opportunities and macroeconomic growth.

Over the decades, however, the early strong flavour of corporate social responsibility—the idea that business could and should contribute to a more just and healthier society—was criticised in a world of high inflation, over-regulation and threats of international competitiveness. In addition, the popularity of free-market conservative rhetoric beginning in the mid-1970s, the 'Reagan–Thatcher Revolution' of the 1980s and even the transformations of the former Soviet Union and Eastern Europe in the late 1980s and early 1990s seemed to make corporate social responsibility an old-fashioned and unnecessary concept. Many large corporations learned the new language of corporate growth and success—re-engineering, downsizing, rightsizing, outsourcing and so on—and the former mean-

---

1 'Communist plot'.

ings and applications of corporate social responsibility were not easily adapted. IBM, for example, was praised in the 1970s for its lifetime employment policies and its low-risk growth, but in the 1980s, with the rising dominance of the finance view of the firm, these same policies were damned as irresponsible.

In the 1990s, scholarly attention shifted from the concept of corporate social responsibility to the concept of 'corporate citizenship'. Funding initiatives, conferences and research by major institutions such as the Hitachi Foundation (Logan *et al.* 1997) and The Conference Board (Alperson 1995) pointed to intense interest in corporate citizenship as a vehicle for social change and/or corporate transformation. New academic centres for corporate citizenship as well as new awards programmes sprang up. Little new research appeared on corporate social responsibility, but numerous new books, journals and conference presentations were published on corporate citizenship (e.g. Altman and Vidaver-Cohen 2000; Davenport *et al.* 1999; McIntosh *et al.* 1998; Tichy *et al.* 1997).

The precise connection between corporate social responsibility and corporate citizenship was not always clear in these works. In some cases it appeared that corporate social responsibility and corporate citizenship were simply synonyms. In other works, it appeared that corporate citizenship was focused almost exclusively on corporate–community relations. Table 5.1 illustrates this lack of clarity by comparing a broad view of corporate social responsibility with a narrow view of corporate citizenship. For example, corporate social responsibility has always been difficult to operationalise; it has not been possible to arrive at any consistent, logical means of evaluating corporate social performance. The narrow view of corporate citizenship, on the other hand, concerns a much smaller group of stakeholders and issues, making it easier to measure the concept and to evaluate company performance.

Corporate social responsibility	Corporate citizenship
Hard to operationalise, measure and evaluate	Limited and specific; easier to measure
Obligatory and voluntary (through tax payment and law abidance as well as discretionary problem-solving activities)	Largely voluntary, often with a corporate strategic focus (i.e. use corporate resources to help the community and the company as well)
Broad concern for many issues and stakeholders, and for society at large	Narrow focus on local community and charity
Self-interest benefits are possible and acceptable but not assumed and are not primary in any case; ethical and legal concerns take precedence.	Self-interest benefits are desirable and perhaps essential to serve as incentives for behaviour that benefits local communities.
It is threatening to popular neoclassical economic theories of capitalism.	It is reassuring: speaks to 'constrained liberalism' and 'compassionate conservatism'.
Moral grounding is assumed and ambiguous; it has a 'Sixties-liberal' orientation, and a US focus.	'Give-back' and 'tit-for-tat' grounding does not require any philosophy or deep thinking.

Table 5.1 **Comparison of corporate social responsibility with corporate citizenship**

In addition, the obligatory aspects of corporate social responsibility are replaced by a weak legalistic obligation (pay taxes, obey the law) and a voluntaristic approach to community problems and opportunities. Corporate social responsibility's emphasis on big sociopolitical issues (poverty, racism, sexism, etc.) gives way, in corporate citizenship, to a narrow focus on 'sticking to the knitting' of business and getting involved in community affairs if the company wants to, primarily through charity and employee voluntarism.

Another important difference involves the concepts' fit with the neoclassical economic model. Corporate social responsibility considers the moral and legal obligations of business to have precedence over self-interest. Corporate social responsibility appeared to be threatening to neoclassical economic theories because of its relegation of self-interest to a lesser status. For advocates of corporate social responsibility, corporate self-interest may or may not be met through socially responsible actions—and it is irrelevant anyway, because companies should bear the full costs of their production, and a company that cannot operate responsibly should not be in business. By contrast, corporate citizenship as narrowly conceived is compatible with standard economic analysis. It supports both 'compassionate conservatism' and 'constrained liberalism' in that voluntaristic charity is possible and supportable but not essential or obligatory. The corporate citizenship view tends to hold that self-interest serves as an incentive to businesses to engage in behaviour that benefits communities. Corporate citizenship tends not to consider cases where self-interest and collective interest conflict.

The moral grounding of corporate social responsibility, which was assumed but not clearly explicated, resonated with earlier Progressive ideas about the need for corporations to conform to social expectations. The ideological grounding of corporate social responsibility, also assumed, was based on a 1960s US liberal–democratic public policy view of human welfare. Corporate citizenship, by contrast, has a 'give-something-back-if-you-can' moral grounding that sounds good and feels right. Indeed, there were good reasons for corporations to become increasingly concerned about their relationships with local communities. As Burke (1999) has argued so persuasively, local communities were becoming more powerful in determining whether and how business activities could take place, and so businesses needed to learn how to become 'neighbours of choice' in order to survive. However, as corporate citizenship began to replace corporate social responsibility as the 'concept of choice' in scholarly and business literature, more than a shift in terminology occurred.

◢ Getting to business citizenship in two steps

We propose that, if corporate social responsibility is replaced as a conceptual centrepiece of business and society–business ethics thinking, then corporate citizenship, because of its close association with corporate–community relations, may be too narrow to express the depth and variety of business–society relations. Instead, we suggest the term 'business citizenship'.[2] The key variables needed to make this transition are shown in Table 5.2.

	LEVEL OF ANALYSIS	
	Local, community or national scope	**Global or universal scope**
The individual person as citizen	**Cell 1: the individual citizen** Relationship of the person to the state; rights and duties of citizens; national and cultural identity	**Cell 3: the universal citizen** Common humanity; interdependence; universalism; less grounded in fixed rules or laws; asserted based on philosophical ideas
The business organisation as citizen	**Cell 2: the corporate citizen** Business as a responsible player in its local environments; emphasis on voluntarism and charity, as well as on the organisation's rights and duties in and for the community	**Cell 4: the business citizen** Business as a responsible local actor and a consistent global actor; emphasis on the organisation's rights and societies within and across national and/or cultural borders; there is a need for analysis of hypernorms

Table 5.2 **Four states of citizenship**

The first challenge is to move from cell 1 to cell 2 (Table 5.2), that is, to establish the manner in which business organisations can and cannot be considered citizens. The question here is, 'Is a corporate citizen the same as an individual citizen, and, if not, what are the differences and similarities?' The second challenge is to move from cell 2 to cell 4, that is, to establish the nature of business citizenship that is not tied to a particular polity. The question here is, 'What are global businesses citizens of, and what does this mean?'

As we see it, the situation illustrated in cell 4 offers business organisations more freedom at a price of more accountability. Pragmatically, cell 4 is the most compatible with the desire of business for a stable and more predictable environment. It is also compatible with greater adaptability of business to changing social, political, technological and economic conditions.

---

2   The term 'organisational citizenship' would make sense, except that it has already been used to focus only on internal activities of employees with regard to the welfare of the organisation (Organ 1988).

The left-side vertical label reads: UNIT OF ANALYSIS

◢ The nature of citizenship

Defining, defending and evaluating the construct of individual citizenship is a task that has occupied philosophers, political theorists, rulers, legislatures and many others for thousands of years. For the individual, 'citizen' is ordinarily used to denote a political status with regard to the state, a set of rights and duties to maintain that status and/or an essential aspect of one's social identity. It has roots in political theory, philosophy, law, sociology and psychology.

Citizenship thinking in much of the post-World War II period focused primarily on possession of individual rights. T.H. Marshall's (1965) definitive essay 'Citizenship and Social Class' established the conventional post-war view that citizenship rights can be categorised into the civil, the political and the social, and that a natural evolution occurs in political systems from the most basic civil rights toward a gradual expansion of the pool of rights and of those eligible to claim them. Marshall observed that in Britain these rights were provided over approximately three successive centuries and to an expanding range of groups. Civil rights, such as free speech and the right to own property, were granted to property-owning British males in the 18th century. The championing institution was the judicial system, which was sparring with parliament at the time over the degree of individual liberty that would be tolerated. Political rights, including rights to vote and to hold office, were granted in Britain in the 19th century and were gradually expanded to include first non-property-owning males, then to women in 1918. Social rights, by which Marshall means rights to education, healthcare and other aspects of human welfare, came to be provided in the 20th century. Citizenship, to Marshall, was the status that ensured that everyone would be treated as an equal member of society.

In the 1990s, after several decades of post-Marshallian quiescence, citizenship has re-emerged as a central concept for intellectual discourse (Kymlicka and Norman 1995). One important debate distinguishes the concept of citizenship-as-legal-status from the concept of citizenship-as-desirable-activity. The minimum requirements to be called a citizen are very different from the requirements to be called a 'good citizen'. This has become ever more important in societies characterised by voter apathy, social pathology and radical individualism. In particular, controversies about immigration and citizenship status of non-whites have taken place in many industrialised Western nations in recent years, making it ever more important to define who can be a citizen, how citizenship is conferred and what citizenship offers and requires.

Debate has also emerged in political theory about the need for correlative responsibilities—as well as rights—to be embedded in theories of citizenship in order for societies to thrive. For example, the New Right has championed workfare in place of traditional welfare programmes so that the indigent have the 'opportunity' of working in return for basic subsistence income. More diverse and complex views have been articulated about the need for civic virtue to accompany the citizenship rights that Marshall identified. Variants of these arguments call for greater democratic participation in civil society, more involvement in voluntary associations and more explicit education in the civic virtues (Kymlicka and Norman 1995).

Debates such as these are easier to understand and more amenable to business applications when we consider the different intellectual pathways to citizenship that have garnered widespread support. Parry (1991) identifies three such contemporary approaches: the minimalist theory of civic association, the communitarian model and the universal human rights model, which are compared in Table 5.3.

The minimalist theory of citizenship begins with the notion that citizens are merely residents of a common jurisdiction who recognise certain rules that regulate their conduct (Parry 1991). These free agents are striving to achieve their individual goals, and compliance with certain laws is seen as contributing to their achievement of these goals. Civil association is not to be confused with community, which has the special meaning of a shared enterprise. The fundamental and moral relationship among citizens in a civil association requires the right to justice and equal treatment under law. These rights could be operationalised as basic legal rights such as the right to bring charges, the right to legal representation and so on. Rights evolve and are extended to more groups as the association discovers problems that are not dealt with effectively under the more constricted system of rights. This essentially libertarian view of citizenship requires equal treatment in the sense of negative rights—that is, the right of citizens to pursue their interests without interference—but it does not necessarily require citizen participation in rule-making. The minimalist theory shows the legacy of Roman views about citizenship, particularly in its relatively unambiguous separation of private and public spheres of activity, although the Romans were neither libertarian nor democratic (Pocock 1995).

Communitarian reasoning, according to Parry, embeds the citizen in a particular social context, rather than viewing persons as autonomous and detached moral agents as the other two models do. One's personal identity is bound up with the nature and history of one's community. Boundaries and rules of membership become highly significant, and the obligation to consider one's community as more important than other communities becomes justifiable and perhaps even required. From the Greeks, citizens of the community have the duty to participate in making rules about membership and in carrying them out in order to preserve the distinctive culture of the community. Rights, in the communitarian view, have been overemphasised to the detriment of collective wellbeing, where the individual's duties to the group are just as important, if not more so, than personal rights. In addition, communitarians recognise that guaranteeing rights is a costly and time-consuming process, and thus the more stringent requirements for membership and the resulting in-group/out-group social structure make sense in political–economic terms.

A third view of citizenship is based on the moral assumption of universal human rights as necessary for the achievement of human agency—the freedom to pursue one's interests, or autonomy of action. The primary role of government is to secure and protect these conditions of human agency. Not only must the state

MINIMALIST VIEW	COMMUNITARIAN VIEW	UNIVERSAL RIGHTS VIEW
Nature of citizenship		
The good society maximises individual liberty.	The good society supports and provides human identity based on community membership.	The good society guarantees fundamental rights for all humans.
Civic association exists so that individuals can pursue their personal goals without interference from others.	There is no ideal of the free agent or autonomous person: people exist and are defined by their own histories *and* by their membership in a community Private and public life are not distinct.	Government exists to protect human rights, and can do so forcefully if necessary.
Citizens voluntarily choose to follow the rules and laws of the jurisdiction where they happen to be.	Citizens create rules to provide for the wellbeing of their particular community group.	Citizens create government and can act against it if human rights are not being supported.
Nature of bonds to the state		
Self-interest-based	Identity- and loyalty-based; focused on a specific group	Social contract-based
Rights and duties		
Emphasis on negative rights: right to be left alone	Little emphasis on rights; strong emphasis on duties	Emphasis on negative *and* positive rights
Only the right to individual liberty is absolute.	There are no absolute rights; rights are contingent on the particular community and its definition of the good.	Civil, political, and social rights are absolute—the problems are just practical ones of working out the details.
Civil rights		
Accepts rights to liberty, property ownership, speech and assembly, due process	Accepts rights to liberty, property ownership, speech and assembly, due process	Accepts rights to liberty, property ownership, speech and assembly, due process
Political rights		
Granted in order to secure civil rights, if necessary; citizens must be vigilant to make sure that the state acts *only* to maintain human autonomy and agency.	May or may not be granted, depending on the particular community's definition of the good.	Are as fundamental as civil rights, and government needs to act positively to secure political rights (to participation) for all.

Table 5.3 **Three views of citizenship for individuals** *(continued opposite)*

MINIMALIST VIEW	COMMUNITARIAN VIEW	UNIVERSAL RIGHTS VIEW
Social rights		
Neither inherent nor likely in this system of thought	Not inherent in the system, but are likely to be provided in some measure because they help to preserve the community	Derive from the human right to wellbeing; government needs to provide the conditions for wellbeing in a democratic fashion.
To whom do rights apply?		
Rights apply to all who happen to be within a jurisdiction and who agree to abide by its rules.	Rights *and* duties apply only to members, those who share the common bonds and identity of the community; because rights and duties are costly to provide and enforce, good reasons arise for excluding outsiders (or making entry difficult) to preserve the community.	Rights apply to all humans.
Duties		
Subscribe to law Don't interfere with others	Subscribe to law Participate in government Guard the community's integrity of identity	Subscribe to law, unless law does not support human rights Don't interfere with others unless interference is necessary to secure human rights Act so that all people have the conditions of human autonomy and agency
Boundaries		
Are behavioural; all who follow the jurisdiction's rules are within bounds as citizens.	Are well defined and closely guarded; there is a clear demarcation of an in-group—based on shared beliefs, location, nationality, ethnicity, religion, etc. —which defines who is entitled to citizen rights and is obligated for citizen duties.	Are merely an administrative practicality that allows rights to be provided.

Table 5.3 (continued)

protect negative rights of non-interference—those guarantees of human liberty such as protection of the right to free speech and assembly and the right to vote— but also it must identify and protect positive rights that must be provided in order to achieve human potential, such as the right to education and the right to health-care. Here resides a philosophical position to support Marshall's assessment of civil, political and social rights. This perspective is critical when dealing with people and situations outside of 'our community', and especially outside 'our borders'. The question is whether a set of common norms can be extracted (or designed) and supported across cultural and political boundaries.

From individual citizenship to corporate citizenship

Our next step will be to change the unit of analysis, to see whether the concept of corporate citizenship makes sense when grounded in common understandings of individual citizenship (moving from cell 1 to cell 2 in Table 5.2). Key points are noted in Table 5.4.

As it turns out, the minimalist position on individual citizenship is quite compatible with the neoclassical 'nexus of contracts' view of the firm, so that the challenge in moving to corporate citizenship is one of articulating the value for businesses of belonging to a community and abiding by its norms and values. Therefore, we will focus in this section on comparing the minimalist and com-munitarian views of citizenship, holding the universal rights perspective for the next step in the analysis.

The minimalist orthodoxy

An influential interpretation of the theory of the firm focuses on the corporation as a 'nexus of contracts' among suppliers of various inputs, whose rights are negotiated as part of their contracts with the firm. In this view, shareholders are providers of the input of capital and acquire property ownership. Management's role is to co-ordinate the negotiating process among the various input providers, acting as agents for the shareholder-principals. Shareholders are vulnerable because their delegation of power to agent-managers leaves them with high monitoring and control costs and a subsequent higher risk that managers will succumb to moral hazard (or opportunism) and act in their own interest instead of those of shareholders. However, in this theory, market forces are generally structured to link managers' incentives to shareholders' interests, thus providing an institutional control mechanism in favour of shareholders' interests. Corpo-rate law, in this view, exists in part to protect the shareholders from managerial opportunism, but only as a supplement to market forces, that is, as a correction to the rare market failure.

Just as the minimalist view sees individual citizenship as a status of conve-nience, detached from culture and oriented to individual liberty, a business citi-

MINIMALIST VIEW	COMMUNITARIAN VIEW
Nature of citizenship for persons	
The good society maximises individual liberty. Civic association exists so that individuals can pursue their personal goals without interference from others. Citizens voluntarily choose to follow the rules/laws of the jurisdiction where they happen to be.	The good society supports and provides human identity based on community membership. There is no ideal of the free human agent; people exist and are defined by their own histories and by membership in a community; private and public life are not distinct. Citizens create rules to provide for the wellbeing of their community group.
Chief characteristics	
Self-interest-based Maximum: individual liberty and discretion Minimum: social control	Identity- and loyalty-based Focus on community wellbeing; personal liberty less important
Nature of the business organisation	
The firm is a nexus of freely chosen individual contracts.	The firm is a member of the local community.
Can a business organisation be viewed as a citizen?	
No, a company cannot be a citizen.	Yes, a company can be viewed as a *corporate* citizen.
Why?	
Organisations are merely a legal fiction within which individual contracts are negotiated. Managers are agents of shareholders, who want to maximise their own self-interests and are not concerned (in the context of business) with collective interests.	An organisation is a combination of the community's resources and takes on an existence and identity separate from individuals, but which reflects community values. Business wants to remain in good standing and is thus likely to conform to local norms. Business cares about the community, wants it to thrive, and will contribute.

Table 5.4 **Moving from individual to corporate citizens**

zen or manager–citizen in the minimalist view would claim those rights essential to the pursuit of self-interest and would fulfil only those obligations mandated by the convenience of having a collective entity to guarantee those rights. Simply put, in a minimalist world, an organisation is merely a shell within which individuals make contracts with one another. If and only if those individuals perceive it to be in their self-interest, they may direct the organisation to act in citizen-like ways. The organisation itself, however, cannot 'be' a citizen in this perspective.

The communitarian revolution

The communitarian view, in contrast to the minimalist view, does not see the business organisation as an empty shell but as a functioning member of a community, separable from the individuals who participate in it. In this view, businesses have both rights and duties because of their important role in society. In many ways this view is compatible with early definitions of corporate social responsibility—businesses should be responsible for how the harms and benefits of their actions are allocated, regardless of intentionality and regardless of cost to the firm.

It is clear that business organisations have important roles to play in society and are more than shells within which individual contracts are negotiated. But would we say that a corporate citizen has the same status and identity as a human citizen? The general view on this question is that corporate citizens and human citizens are not identical. For example, Bovens (1998) warns of the dangers of continuing to endow business organisations with citizenship rights and duties by emphasising the role of citizenship in preserving the autonomy of individuals, who are entitled to such rights because of their humanity. That is, humans and organisations are not the same kind of entity. Moreover, he argues that granting the same type of citizenship to individuals and to corporations would disrupt the social balance of power by making it more difficult for governments to intervene on behalf of human rights. Finally, he observes that the power inequalities between individuals and complex organisations are so severe that granting equal rights to both types of entity would destroy the capacity of individuals to protect themselves from organisations. For Bovens, and we concur, organisations can be no more than secondary citizens, subject to the primacy of human citizenship. For example, in the USA, corporate citizens are granted certain legal rights but not others—for example, they have the right to engage in certain political actions but not the right to vote in elections.

Practically speaking, moving away from the minimalist position has meant focusing more attention on the interactions of businesses with their local communities. This has the effect of making 'social responsibility' or 'good citizenship' very concrete and observable. When a paper mill dumps effluents into the river, the negative consequences for neighbours are apparent; when a factory sponsors an employee drive to fund a new community centre, the benefits to neighbours are equally apparent. Business organisations as citizens are legitimate community actors, imbued with community values. However, because they are secondary citizens and primarily members of the economic institution, their rights are limited and so are their duties. This idea is seen clearly in the notion of corporate citizenship, where a business organisation is expected and required to pay taxes and obey the law but is not required (though may be expected) to contribute to solving local problems—thus the emphasis on voluntaristic projects in the literature on corporate citizenship. Voluntary contributions to the community are likely to be praised and rewarded, even though not required. Similarly, an individual citizen may not be expected or required to do more than pay taxes and obey the law, but is likely to be perceived as a 'good citizen' if she or he does more.

◢ From corporate citizenship to business citizenship

Scholars who want to make the jump from individual citizenship to business organisation citizenship must concentrate on moving the minimalists closer to a communitarian view. This is a critical first step in redefining business–society relationships in the modern environment, as we saw in the previous section. There is another step to be taken, however. Now that we understand how citizenship can make sense at the organisational level, we need to change the scope of analysis by examining the condition in which the business citizen is not exclusively bound by the rules of a local polity but is also responsive to the collective norms of a global community (moving from cell 2 to cell 4 in Table 5.2). In order to do this, we will compare attributes of citizenship for individuals and for business organisations according to the communitarian and universal rights perspectives (Table 5.5).

The communitarian orthodoxy and the universalist revolution

In international business, there are two common approaches to the question of how a business organisation should conduct itself within the societies in which it operates: the multi-domestic view and the global integrated view (Daniels and Radebaugh 1995). In the multi-domestic approach, the corporation is encouraged to 'conform to local practice', a directive that is quite consistent with the communitarian view of citizenship. In the absence of a global government or a single known set of rules, one defers to the local community's (or nation-state's) norms, whether as an individual or as a business organisation. It is not difficult to see that this approach to international business and this view of business citizenship would support current conceptions of 'corporate citizenship' as voluntaristic, locally oriented activities that vary from one site to another and from one corporation to another.

The global integrated view, by contrast, encourages the corporation to maintain policies, processes and structures that are consistent with the company's expressed mission and values across all relevant cultures. This view is quite compatible with

COMMUNITARIAN VIEW	UNIVERSAL RIGHTS VIEW
Nature of citizenship for persons	
The good society supports and provides human identity based on community membership. There is no ideal of the free human agent. People exist and are defined by their own histories and by membership in a community. Private and public life are not distinct. Citizens create rules to provide for the wellbeing of their community group.	The good society guarantees certain fundamental rights for all humans. Government exists to protect human rights, and can do so forcefully if necessary. Citizens create government and can act against it if human rights are not being supported.
Chief characteristics	
Identity- and loyalty-based Focus is on community wellbeing; personal liberty less important	Based on a value for balancing freedom with social welfare
Nature of the business organisation	
The firm is a member of the local community.	The firm is a participant in a network of stakeholder relationships.
Can a business organisation be viewed as a citizen?	
Yes, a company can be viewed as a *corporate* citizen.	Yes, a company can be viewed as a *business* citizen.
Why?	
An organisation is a combination of the community's resources and takes on an existence and identity separate from individuals, but reflecting community values. Business wants to remain in good standing and is thus likely to conform to local norms. Business cares about the community, wants it to thrive and will contribute.	Organisations are vehicles for manifesting human creativity. They permit creation of surplus value, allowing people and societies to do more with resources. Companies are members of stakeholder networks whose interests and actions span multiple locales and cannot be completely captured in contracts.

Table 5.5 **Moving business citizenship from local to global**

the universal rights perspective on citizenship. In this perspective, business citizens are encouraged to recognise that there are hypernorms and consistent norms that take precedence over local values in the case of conflict, although there is plenty of room for 'moral free space' in which local norms can guide appropriate organisational behaviours (Donaldson and Dunfee 1999). This idea of universal rights and the citizenship behaviour that would accompany its execution is the ongoing agenda for firms operating across borders today.

Business citizenship from three perspectives

In Table 5.6, the three perspectives on business citizenship are compared on a number of criteria. These include the perspective's dominant approach to guiding values, representative ethical decision rules, behavioural and organisational manifestations and some of the challenges that remain to be worked out under each perspective.

◢ Business citizenship in support of human rights

The realities of the global economy demand that businesses and societies move toward a new and widespread set of expectations regarding global business citizenship. Above all, these expectations are concerned with supporting the conditions necessary for the universal exercise of human rights. No matter which intellectual tradition one follows, individual citizenship exists to provide a template for governing power relations among people and between people and the state. In most traditions, individual rights are protected from state intervention. It matters not whether the state is seen as a necessity for maintaining human happiness, or as the ultimate arbiter of conflicts among individuals, or as the setting in which individuals become fully human, or as the ever-possible juggernaut that can crush human agency and must be guarded against. Ultimately, individual citizenship is always, at a minimum, a construct in support of human liberty.

Similarly, corporate social responsibility is, at a minimum, a concept in the service of a fundamental value for social justice. Regardless of the specific issue-content one emphasises, corporate social responsibility exists to provide a conceptual grasp of the idea that business organisations exist because of people and to serve people's interests, and that business and society relationships are governed by duties to the collective as well as by the pursuit of managerial autonomy and organisational self-interest. Those duties typically include guarantees of process justice in the firm (e.g. fair administration of workplace rules) as well as some striving toward distributive justice through the firm's many types of interaction with its stakeholders (e.g. political action, issues management, community relations, stakeholder management, environmental protection, voluntary philanthropy and so on).

MINIMALIST VIEW	COMMUNITARIAN VIEW	UNIVERSAL RIGHTS VIEW
What is a firm?		
A nexus of contracts among individual and organisational actors	An embodiment of community values	A vehicle for fulfilling certain needs and wants of of stakeholders
Can a firm be a citizen?		
No, the firm is not a real entity.	Yes, a *corporate* citizen	Yes, a *business* citizen
Approach to guiding values?		
Opportunistic view: emphasis on hard-nosed tit-for-tat exchanges, guided by the individual local values and values of involved business actors	Multi-domestic view: emphasis on relativistic conformance to local values and practices	Global integrated view: emphasis on hypernorms and consistent norms in business practice while respecting local norms via moral free space
Ethical decision rules		
If it's ethics, it's not business; if it's business, it's not ethics (the separation thesis).		Hypernorms and consistent norms underlie all business decisions.
Cause no harm that will cost the company money.	Cause no harm that violates important local community values.	Local norms and values can guide business decisions if they are not inconsistent with hypernorms.
'Do good' only if you can make money doing it.	'Do good' if the local culture values the action and the firm can justify it as a good business decision.	In value conflicts, hypernorms take precedence.
Community orientation		
Resistance to participation in collaborative relations with community ventures unless self-advantage is clear	Corporate community relations with long-term as well as short-term pay-offs in view	Corporate citizen behaviours such as community relations and local philanthropy, plus contributions to non-local efforts to secure conditions supportive of hypernorms
Other behavioural and organisational manifestations		
Cause-related marketing and strategic philanthropy, in some instances	Local philanthropy to address local problems and issues	Integrated public affairs and issues management
.	Volunteer projects, local memberships	Participation in peak organisations to define and enforce global norms and to adjudicate conflicts
	Participation in collaborative ventures to improve the community	

Table 5.6 **Business citizenship from three perspectives** *(continued opposite)*

MINIMALIST VIEW	COMMUNITARIAN VIEW	UNIVERSAL RIGHTS VIEW
Other behavioural and organisational manifestations (continued)		
When opportunism yields harms to others, the minimalist firm will search for additional opportunistic choices, e.g. blame someone else, stonewall, shift financial responsibility, etc.	Willingness to take (or at least share) responsibility for the business's own harms to local communities and for community problems that affect the business but are not caused by it	Focus on a triple bottom line: social, economic and environmental impacts Transparency and accountability via social auditing (to evaluate the firm's performance) and continuous dialogue (to inform and hear stakeholders)
Challenges		
Avoiding or controlling opportunism (chances to violate contracts) because agents have an incentive to cheat Maintaining legitimacy: can be too difficult to justify negative consequences (externalities) as a necessary result of guaranteeing individuals' free choice	Avoiding or controlling ethnocentrism (disrespect for other cultures and values) because identity is so tightly tied to the local community (colonialism, fascism) Avoiding excessive inward focus and isolation from world events Avoiding in-breeding that ultimately may be destructive to the culture	Creating a coherent identity not based on locale Sustaining an adequate ethical base without adherence to a particular culture Balancing an excess of demands: being confronted by bounded rationality, must make choices and justify them (the essence of ethics)
The bottom line on citizenship		
No such thing as citizenship for business	**Corporate citizenship**	**Business citizenship**

Table 5.6 (continued)

Note that individual citizenship and corporate social responsibility each contain mandatory and voluntary components. For corporate social responsibility, the breakdown is straightforward. In Carroll's (1979, 1998) hierarchy of corporate social responsibility duties, the mandatory components for the firm are these: meeting the firm's economic needs, obeying the law and abiding by ethical rules. The voluntary component, for Carroll, includes discretionary stakeholder relations and philanthropy, which he equates with 'corporate citizenship'.

For individual citizenship, the particular voluntary and mandatory components depend a great deal on which intellectual stream one chooses to apply and which polity is in question. Minimalists, for example, say that humans are in a voluntary contract with the state, and so with each other, simply when they choose to abide by the rules of a jurisdiction. Communitarians offer a stricter set of mandatory and reciprocal duties on behalf of both the state and its citizens, and the voluntary component of this intellectual stream appears to exist primarily in an individual's choice to stay with the community or leave it. Rights theorists propose that the state's guarantee of human rights is mandatory, but that citizens' participation in governance is voluntary—a right that can be exercised, but not a duty that must be fulfilled.

Business citizenship can incorporate all the best of corporate social responsibility and individual citizenship while also offering assistance to businesses in dealing with the new challenges of the global environment. In short, we propose that business citizenship involve the following components:

- In support of human liberty: business citizenship involves the rights and duties of every business, in every location, to support the conditions necessary for the exercise of human agency

- In support of social justice: business citizenship involves the rights and duties of every business, in every location, to experiment with ways to enhance the quality of life, to insist on due process under law and to work to distribute fairly the harms and benefits it creates

- In recognition of business's vital functions for human beings and their societies: business citizenship involves limited rights and duties for business organisations in order to facilitate a business's accomplishment of human purpose

An ongoing issue in discussions of corporate social responsibility and corporate citizenship is that of specifying the duties or social obligations of businesses. One answer to this question derives from revisiting Aristotle's three primary duties of the citizen (Pocock 1995) and extrapolating to organisational duties. Aristotle's extensive discussions of citizenship, in the 'civic republican' tradition, illuminate three fundamental civic duties: participation in the political process (to rule and be ruled in turn), payment of taxes and militia service. Strictly speaking, of these three, corporations are liable only to pay taxes. However, if we recognise that the free-born male citizens of ancient Greek city-states do not fully represent citizenship in the modern world, we can redefine Aristotle's duties to show the similarities and differences in citizenship status for modern individuals and for business organisations (Table 5.7).

A question that necessarily arises from the last cell of this table (firm duties regarding militia service) is this: 'What are the common enemies of the business institution?' Our answer is straightforward: conditions that threaten, distort or prevent human moral agency are enemies of the business institution. Capitalism depends on strong legal and moral conceptions of private property and free moral agency (i.e. individual liberty). So, though one can hardly imagine business organisations marching off to war, one can indeed imagine them demanding and working for the conditions of human moral agency that make it possible for capitalism to thrive.

Aristotle's category	Contemporary implications	Individual duties	Firm duties
Participation in civic governance, personal involvement in community decisions	Participate in political processes	Elect government representatives Participate in political discourse Vote on issues Avoid undue or unfair influences (bribery, coercion, nepotism, etc.)	No voting rights, but lobbying and other legal political action is expected. Also, investor and consumer markets vote with dollars. Avoid undue or unfair influences (bribery, coercion, unjust process, etc.)
Payment of taxes	Provide financial support for the collective good and common projects	Pay taxes Voluntarily support welfare and social justice activities	Pay taxes Voluntarily support welfare and social justice activities
Militia service	Participate in defence against common threats and enemies	Engage in military service if called	Support national defence, including military service of employees Defend against enemies of the business institution whether in or across political borders

Table 5.7 **The Aristotelian view of individual and business duties**

Democratic political theory generally suggests, and Max Weber (1958) laid out a similar strong argument more than a hundred years ago, that human liberty is an essential ingredient for the success of free-market capitalism. Without liberty, there is no right to private property. Without liberty, there is no ground for contracting. Thus, because capitalism requires human liberty as much as human beings do, business organisations are readily obligated to seek out and support those business settings where human liberty exists or has the possibility of arising. Nielsen supports this view, offering the idea that a prime duty of organisations is to protect the civil liberties of individuals. Nielsen writes (1984: 199):

> A large part of managers' civic responsibility is for the manager as a citizen of an institution to develop the habit of thinking and judging independently as a basis for discussing and acting with others to build and preserve the good characteristics and behaviours of institutions while resisting the immoral 'ideal type' behaviours and characteristics.

What real-world business duties might be implied by these theoretical components? Supporting the conditions necessary for the exercise of human agency might involve corporate behaviour such as:

- Giving up the use of secret workplace monitoring devices in order to protect people's right to privacy

- Establishing corporate ethics programmes supported by a culture that encourages and rewards individual ethical reasoning and decision-making

- Working within local cultures to help provide the civil and political rights that are deemed fundamental to the exercise of human liberty; corporate political action skills could readily be turned to interventions on behalf of basic human rights

- Refusing to do business with corrupt, coercive or totalitarian governments or in regions controlled by such governments

In the international context, the problem arises about what to do with states that do not support such rights. Such states are often the sources of exploitable cheap labour and present opportunities for businesses to achieve a short-term competitive cost advantage. From the universalistic perspective, however, such a state lacks legitimacy and needs to be 'fixed'. Over time, extreme variations in national human rights policy and rampant violations of human rights create a destabilised, unpredictable business environment and thus a nightmare for strategic planning and top management team implementation.

The duty of business citizens to support experimentation toward social justice is a more interesting idea. It is clear to most business and society/business ethics scholars, philosophers and social scientists that ideas of social justice vary even more than do conceptions of individual citizenship, and legitimately so. It is generally agreed (as in Rawls's [1971] veil-of-ignorance thought experiment) that rules of process justice can be readily achieved, but that rules of distributive justice are more difficult to attain. Should the distribution of collective benefits and burdens be based on need, on contribution, on merit, on agreed-on attributes such as gender or race, on geographic location (southern versus northern hemispheres) or on national boundaries? There are a number of defensible ideas about what the 'good society' would look like in terms of who reaps which benefits and who pays which costs.

When searching for a good definition of distributive justice in a world where power and resource inequalities are common, and where legitimate disagreements exist on what constitutes just distribution, it is essential that jurisdictions, corporations and individuals alike focus on small experiments in broadening access to a higher standard of living and in correcting the imbalances of wealth, class, gender, race, culture, religion and all the other factors that prevent fairness in societies and cultures. Indeed, many examples of social justice-related duties of business citizenship are the voluntaristic and community-oriented programmes of 'corporate citizenship'. Business citizenship takes these programmes one step further and institutionalises a process of experimentation with the aim of arriving at a just distribution of benefits and burdens.

Our idea here is that corporations can operate within the 'moral free space' of local possibility laid out by Donaldson and Dunfee (1999) with pragmatic, locally oriented attempts to achieve workable and fair distributions of wealth, health, longevity, autonomy, education and all the other 'goods' of human social existence. 'Moral free space' allows variations in company policies that reflect the cultural and individual differences of localities, cultures and workplaces. These differences are allowable and necessary, as long as hypernorms—the basic rights and obligations of human moral agents—are maintained. We suggest that, for business citizenship, the most important 'hypernorms' are those that represent the fundamental conditions necessary for human liberty. It is in the cultural 'moral free space' of Donaldson and Dunfee that companies can initiate thoughtful experiments toward social justice.

◢ Conclusions

The argument has been made (Wood *et al.* 1997, 1998) that corporate social responsibility and business citizenship have a legitimate place in a business curriculum because of the educational institution's core function of helping individuals learn how to balance the demands of liberty (via self-interest and concerns for individual survival and success) with the demands of justice (via collective interest and concerns for the social welfare). Here we suggest that balancing the demands of liberty and justice is a task for all institutions—business, labour, government, education, family and religion.

'Business citizenship', thus defined and explained, provides an overarching rationale for corporate social performance, for the study of ethics in business, for stakeholder theory and issues management, for business–government relations and for concerns over major social, political and human issues such as labour rights and environmental protection. Business citizenship can be one of the conceptual balance beams of the long-standing paradox of self-interest and other-interest, of individual versus collective outcomes.

So, if business citizenship is thought of as only a 'voluntary' concept with a limited content of local charity or self-interested strategic advantage, it has little chance to correct power imbalances or to guard against them. We believe that global businesses will move toward liberty and justice for all—toward fulfilling their duties as business citizens—because these are the conditions necessary not only for nurturing human autonomy and quality of life but also for the survival of capitalism itself. We offer this concept of 'business citizenship' as another step along the way.

BUSINESS CITIZENSHIP OUTSIDE AND INSIDE ORGANISATIONS
An emergent synthesis of corporate responsibility and employee citizenship

Diane Swanson and Brian P. Niehoff
Kansas State University, USA

In this chapter we examine two distinctly separate perspectives on citizenship. The first is external and deals with the expectation that corporations should carry out a host of responsibilities that benefit society as a whole. The second is internal and focuses on employee behaviour that specifically benefits the organisation and its members. Neither of these approaches, referred to respectively as 'corporate citizenship' and 'organisational citizenship', gives a holistic statement on what citizenship means for business. The development of such a statement awaits a better understanding of how citizenship behaviours inside the organisation relate to external expectations of corporate responsibility and vice versa. In other words, we argue for an integration of research on citizenship instead of a separation. This exploration of synthesis is part of a mounting interest in defining citizenship inclusively, as evidenced by the variety of topics listed in the table of contents of this very book.

To address the problem of separation, we explore business citizenship as an emerging synthesis of corporate social responsibility and employee citizenship. Our research strategy is straightforwardly threefold. First, we conceptualise some tenets or acknowledged principles, both of corporate responsibility and of employee citizenship. Second, we compare their differences and similarities. Third, based on the comparative analysis, we propose an integrative framework that unites the conventional wisdom of both approaches with that of exemplary organisational leadership. To preview, we propose that the pivotal 'linchpin' for business citizenship is the executive steward who can direct employees to respond constructively to issues that impact the organisation as well as its external constituents or stakeholders.

The proposed framework capitalises on affinities between 'citizenship-as-cor-porate-conduct' and 'citizenship-as-employee-behaviour', but it also accommo-dates differences. Because the framework points to the possibility of integration, it has an emergent quality. We conclude with a discussion of some implications for research and practice.

◢ Conceptualising two views of citizenship

Before we review the two approaches to citizenship, some caveats are in order. To reiterate, this chapter represents an initial attempt to blend two long-standing and separate fields of inquiry. To our knowledge, very little (if any) research has been done in this area of integration. Given the preliminary status of this research, we do not delve into the many intricacies of corporate responsibility and employee citizenship. Instead, we explore a synthesis of their main tendencies as princi-ples or tenets. Additionally, it is important to note that the framework for synthe-sis, proposed later, does not constitute theory. Rather, it codifies the conventional wisdom of two outlooks on citizenship. In a manner of speaking, the model constitutes a roadmap for exploring the possibility of integration. This roadmap is not comprehensive, and our hope is that it will be expanded as scholars explore citizenship across interdisciplinary boundaries. With this goal in mind, we turn to the first part of our research strategy, which is a conceptualisation of citizen-ship as some acknowledged principles of corporate social responsibility.

Corporate citizenship as social responsibility

Research on corporate social responsibility provides much of the foundation for conceptualisations of corporate citizenship (Altman 1998b; Waddock 2001). For at least five decades, scholars of corporate responsibility have attempted to find and develop a constructive relationship between business and society. This search has taken many forms, including philosophical inquiry into the moral status of the social contract between business and society (Donaldson 1989; Werhane 1985) and formulations of business and society as inter-penetrating systems (Preston and Post 1975) or mutually sustaining relationships between business organisa-tions and their constituents or stakeholders (Freeman 1984). According to the social contract, corporations have responsibilities to stakeholders beyond the sole pursuit of profit. For, if corporations fail in their responsibility to enhance community life in general, then the institution of business risks both economic survival and social legitimacy. Typically, business and society scholars have explored the nature of corporate responsibility by analysing cases of actual corporate conduct (see e.g. Carroll and Buchholz 2000; Post *et al.* 2002b).

Although no grand theory of business and society has yet been developed, some main tenets of responsibility have been captured in corporate social performance models or classifications of research on corporate conduct.[1] Our adaptation of an earlier model (Swanson 1995) underscores how principles of responsibility can be used to define corporate citizenship across four levels of analysis, conceptualised as (1) a macro principle, (2) a leadership principle, (3) a corporate culture imperative and (4) corporate citizenship as performance.

The most general statement of responsibility given in Figure 6.1 is an institutional or macro principle that business organisations have economic and ecological responsibilities that are required, expected and desired by society. This statement blends Frederick's (1995) value-based research with Carroll's (1979) components of responsibilities. According to Frederick, business organisations economise by efficiently converting inputs to outputs through co-operative efforts among employees and competitive behaviour among firms in industries. On the other hand, business organisations ecologise when they exhibit symbiotic linkages with their external environments that function adaptively and collaboratively to sustain life. Since both economising and ecologising support community life, they constitute the legitimate responsibilities of business, according to the social contract.

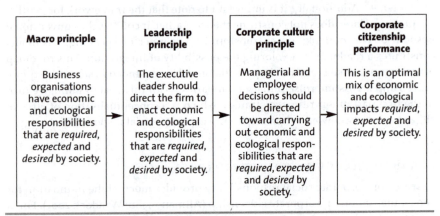

Figure 6.1 **Corporate citizenship as responsibility**

Source: adapted from Swanson 1995

Sometimes economising and ecologising are mutually reinforcing, as when the business sector collaborates with the scientific community to develop new technologies that lower costs of production and improve standards of living. Yet economising and ecologising can also be subject to tension and intractable trade-

---

1 The models of corporate social performance include work by Sethi (1975), Carroll (1979), Wartick and Cochran (1985), Wood (1991) and by one of the current authors (Swanson 1995, 1999). Each model is a classification of research topics that extends and revises previous frameworks. The point of corporate social performance models is to show interrelationships among diverse topics and provide unifying themes for future research (Jones 1983).

offs. Dumping industrial waste into rivers can be economical for business organisations but threaten the health of ecosystems and communities downstream. A meaningful theory of business and society necessarily will come to terms with the trade-offs between economising and ecologising and point corporate activity toward an optimal blend of their impacts (Swanson 1995).

Figure 6.1 depicts economising and ecologising in terms of social norms or what society **requires, expects** and **desires** of corporations. This portrayal is consistent with Carroll's (1979) original identification of responsibilities as economic, legal, ethical and discretionary. Economic and legal responsibilities are required by society whereas ethical and discretionary responsibilities are expected and desired, respectively. Economic responsibilities include efficient production, the payment of wages and dividends and the generation of profit and retained earnings. Legal responsibilities, also required, are meant to protect both economic and ecological goals. For example, business is subject to antitrust laws aimed at preventing monopolies that decrease competition, yet the legal system also protects ecological values, as evidenced by laws that place greater value on the safety of consumers than on profit maximisation.

Whereas economic and legal responsibilities are required, ethical responsibilities are optional in that they have not yet been codified as law. Consumers may expect refunds for defective products, regardless of legal mandates. A more compelling example of ethical expectations is suggested by the practice of selling infant formula internationally. It may be perfectly legal for companies to market and sell infant formula to consumers in developing nations. Yet corporate managers who carry out such policies risk public opinion that conditions in developing nations (such as unsanitary water and illiteracy) render the formula lethal to thousands of infants (Sethi 1994). Such adverse public opinion can pressure corporations to forgo economic gains in favour of preserving community life-networks. When this occurs, expectations of ecological responsibilities are at the forefront of social consciousness.

The remaining component of responsibility in Figure 6.1 is the discretionary component. Groups in society often desire corporations to voluntarily make charitable or philanthropic contributions to communities. Although such contributions can strategically serve economic goals, as when corporate philanthropy generates consumer goodwill and increased revenue, philanthropy can also facilitate ecologising. Indeed, earlier statements of corporate citizenship were cast narrowly as philanthropic, consistent with Carroll's original arrangement of responsibilities hierarchically from most to least important (as economic, legal, ethical and discretionary). In contrast, Carroll (1998) has recently envisioned the four aspects of responsibilities on a continuum showing that corporate decision-makers can carry out a mix of economic, legal, ethical and discretionary responsibilities simultaneously. Our adapted model elaborates on this continuum by depicting economic and ecological responsibilities as taking legal, ethical and discretionary forms.

It is important to note that the responsibilities of corporate citizenship are relative. What is required, expected and desired of business will depend on the issue at hand and whether economic and ecological responsibilities are seen as mutually reinforcing or conflicting. For instance, a policy of maximum production could fit with a firm's economic responsibility yet lead to unsafe work conditions and pollution. That managers are sometimes counted on to protect consumer and environmental safety beyond legal requirements is a function of social norms (Carroll 1998). To complicate matters, norms of responsibilities are neither monolithic nor static. Groups in society often disagree on what constitutes required, expected and desired corporate conduct. Standards are in flux. Another complication is that it is difficult to differentiate conduct based on a true sense of responsibility from that driven by the intention to manage stakeholder perceptions strategically. Of course, it is beyond the scope of this chapter to resolve such matters definitively. The task at hand is simply to describe how tenets of responsibility pertain to corporate citizenship.

The macro principle of responsibility in Figure 6.1 points to a principle for leadership: executives should direct the firm to enact the economic and ecological responsibilities required, expected and desired by society. It follows that executives should forego self-centred power seeking and empire building in favour of directing organisational behaviour toward socially beneficial impacts. This code of leadership implies a 'corporate culture imperative': managerial and employee decision-making should be aimed at enacting the economic and ecological impacts required, expected and desired by society. Said differently, corporate culture can be an important means for trying to achieve goals of responsibility. The last component of the model depicts corporate citizenship as some optimal mix of economic and ecological impacts.

In the final analysis, corporate citizenship can be viewed as an effort to accommodate economic and ecological norms of society. In contrast to this broad institutional perspective, organisational citizenship focuses narrowly on employee behaviour within organisations, discussed next.

Organisational citizenship as employee behaviour

Within an organisation, citizenship refers to the discretionary actions of employees. Sometimes referred to as the 'willingness to co-operate' (Barnard 1938), 'performance beyond role requirements' (Katz and Kahn 1966) or 'extra-role behaviours' (Graham 1991; Van Dyne et al. 1995), employee citizenship consists of classes of behaviour that fall outside specific job descriptions. This behaviour, encapsulated as 'organisational citizenship', is not formally rewarded (Organ 1988), yet an organisation probably cannot survive without such behaviour (Barnard 1938; Katz and Kahn 1966).

The model in Figure 6.2 illustrates the main tenets of employee citizenship as three groupings of empirical research. The first, shown in the uppermost box, defines the dimensions of employee citizenship to be interpersonal helping, compliance with or obedience to organisational rules or norms, demonstrated loyalty to the organisation and active participation in organisational governance. (Multidimensional models of employee citizenship have been developed by a number

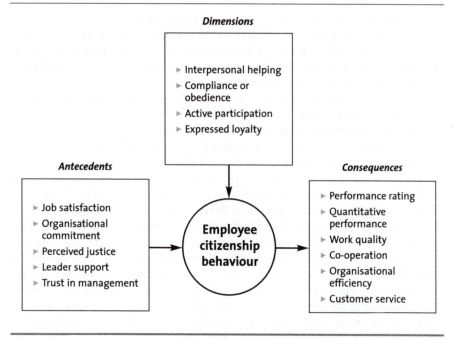

Figure 6.2 **Employee citizenship as constructs of behaviour**

of researchers, including Moorman and Blakely 1995; Organ 1988; Smith *et al.* 1983; Van Dyne *et al.* 1994.) From management's point of view, these forms of employee conduct are desirable but difficult to legislate openly.

The second collection of research focuses on antecedents to employee citizenship, found in the lower left-hand side of Figure 6.2. The most prominent of these—job satisfaction, organisational commitment and perceptions of justice— are understood to be employee cognitive responses to characteristics of the work environment rather than expressions of individual personalities (Organ and Konovsky 1989). Taken as a whole, the antecedents convey a main principle of employee citizenship: that employees respond affirmatively to leadership that facilitates trust and a sense of justice (Fahr *et al.* 1990; Moorman 1991).

The third group of research pertains to desirable consequences of employee citizenship (lower right-hand side of Fig. 6.2). Indeed, a main tenet of employee citizenship is that constructive behaviour among employees is positively correlated with measures of organisational efficiency and effectiveness, including work quality, customer service and group-based performance ratings (Podsakoff and MacKenzie 1997). Citizenship is generally viewed as an aggregated phenomenon. The behaviour of a single employee may have little impact, but positive consequences can emerge, as constructive behaviour becomes more widespread (Organ 1988; Walz and Niehoff 2000).

Although the empirically driven tenets of employee citizenship are generally accepted, their focus on altruistic motives has been challenged. Citizenship and impression management can be highly correlated (Bolino 1999; Eastman 1994), meaning that employees who exhibit helpfulness and co-operation may not have the good of the organisation in mind. Instead, more self-aggrandising motives may drive behaviour. Additionally, obedience and compliance may simply preserve an undesirable status quo. That co-operative behaviour can passively endorse bad management is at odds with the very goals of employee citizenship. These contradictions strain theory development.

Yet there are theoretic frameworks that shed light on the apparent contradictions. A potentially fruitful area of inquiry has been found in political theory on civic citizenship (Graham 1991). Seen through this lens, employees exhibit citizenship because they have developed covenants with organisations based on mutual trust and shared values. More specifically, in environments marked by trust and shared values, employees may be more likely to demonstrate obedience and loyalty toward management and participate in organisational governance. In other words, employees are likely to behave as 'good citizens' in 'good organisations'.

Theories of social exchange and psychological contracts complement the political explanation for employee citizenship. According to social exchange, employees exhibit constructive behaviour to reciprocate for supportive organisational leadership (Moorman 1991; Organ 1988). In terms of psychological contracts, employees are more likely to participate in governance if they perceive that the organisation is fulfilling its part of an implicit agreement (Robinson and Morrison 1995).

Although research seems to bear out the political and social–psychological explanations, there is no overarching theory that satisfactorily integrates all tenets of employee citizenship. Notably, this state of affairs parallels the lack of general theory in the area of corporate social responsibility. With this in mind, we compare the two forms of citizenship and explore their integration.

◢ Comparing citizenship inside and outside organisations

Obvious differences

To repeat, corporate responsibility and employee citizenship developed as independent streams of research. Not surprisingly, they exhibit differences. We focus on three. The first is that corporate responsibility tends to be outward-looking and concerned with the impacts of corporate conduct on society at large. In contrast, organisational citizenship is more micro-oriented and narrowly interested in the good of the organisation. In short, each approach to citizenship emphasises a different goal and domain of analysis.

The second difference pivots on conceptual theory versus empirical research. Principles of responsibility developed more as theoretic statements than as empirical findings (even though, as mentioned earlier, case studies support theoretical views). On the other hand, research on employee citizenship has been shaped more by empirical investigation than on theoretical development.

Finally, the two approaches grant contrary weights to 'the normative' and 'the descriptive'. Although responsibility involves description (*vis-à-vis* case studies), it is ultimately normative or focused on what corporate conduct should be. In contrast, research on employee citizenship emphasises description of what is. As a result, scholars stop short of formulating ethical prescriptions. For instance, there is no accepted prescription that all employees must exhibit citizenship; only a 'critical mass' is necessary. This raises a normative issue of equity that has not been adequately addressed.

To summarise, citizenship-as-responsibility and citizenship-as-employee-behaviour exhibit some diametrically opposed inclinations toward societal and organisational outcomes, theoretical and empirical research and normative and descriptive inquiry.

Similarities or shared interests

Although the perspectives differ, they exhibit at least four interrelated and rather striking similarities. First, both rely on reciprocal covenants or social contracts. Corporate responsibility is based on the ideal of a constructive partnership between business and society whereas employee citizenship invokes the idea of reciprocating behaviour among employees. Second, both contract orientations deal with economic and ecological goals, albeit in different domains. Corporate responsibility, on the one hand, emphasises the civic-mindedness of economic and ecological goals for society at large. Employee citizenship, on the other hand, deals with the internal dynamics of organisations and the teamwork or mutualistic behaviour that supports economic performance. A third similarity follows. Both approaches call for the extra role or discretionary behaviour of helpfulness. Employee citizenship elaborates on the importance of such behaviour within organisations whereas corporate responsibility calls for the civic participation of organisations in society at large. Finally, there is a shared interest in how leadership can facilitate the covenants of citizenship.

An emergent synthesis

The two approaches bear enough resemblance to suggest the possibility of integration. Yet, paradoxically, the most compelling reasons for integration may lie in differences. Notably, research on corporate responsibility addresses the broad social context that organisational behaviour lacks. In contrast, research on employee citizenship involves some fine-grained measures of organisational behaviour that could potentially illuminate the nature of responsible corporate conduct. More pointedly, constructive employee behaviour can be understood as means for carrying out the goals of responsibility. Indeed, the grand paradigms that have eluded both approaches might unfold as a combination of their normative and descriptive inclinations across individual, organisational and societal domains. Figure 6.3 depicts the potential power of this synthesis as the executive stewardship of employee and corporate citizenship.

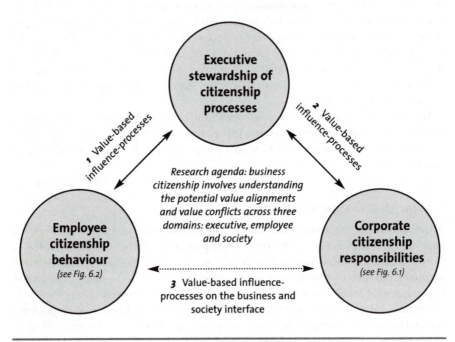

Figure 6.3 **Toward a synthesised model of business citizenship**

According to the model, business citizenship can be understood as three interrelated platforms:

- Employee behaviour can be a practical means for enacting corporate responsibilities.
- Economic and ecological responsibilities are important goals for employee behaviour.
- The executive leader has the dual boundary-spanning role of aligning employee conduct with organisational goals and social norms.

This linchpin role of executive stewardship involves searching for optimal solutions when organisational and societal goals appear to conflict. Although the idea of stewardship is not new to management research (see Davis *et al.* 1997), its centrality to citizenship has yet to be developed.

◢ Implications for theory and practice

Charting a research agenda

Our research agenda, outlined here, is an exploration of value-based influence-processes, shown as two-way arrows across domains of citizenship (Fig. 6.3).

Executive stewardship and employee citizenship

In Figure 6.3, arrow 1 denotes the influence executive stewardship might have on employee citizenship and the reciprocating effects of employee citizenship. Research indicates that employees tend to exhibit values that executives effectively communicate and demonstrate (Schein 1992; Simon 1947). Moreover, leadership that establishes and maintains trust is thought to promote co-operative behaviours among employees and to increase their commitment to the organisation (Podsakoff *et al.* 1997). Less recognised, however, are the effects of employee values on the executive's vision of corporate responsibility. It is important to study such value-based influences. Since values represent beliefs that people prize as deeply meaningful, understanding them in terms of organisational dynamics could help differentiate between citizenship that is meaningful, on the one hand, and civic behaviour that is superficially impressionistic, on the other.

Executive stewardship and corporate citizenship

Value interactions mark the relationship between executives and external stakeholders, as indicated by arrow 2 in Figure 6.3. Indeed, empirical studies suggest that the values held by top executives drive a firm's management of public affairs (Miles 1986). Similarly, the personally held values of stakeholders help determine what economic and ecological impacts are required, expected and desired of corporations (Frederick and Weber 1987). Hence, values are paramount to distinguishing corporate citizenship that is superficially impressionistic from that prompted by an executive's genuine commitment to stakeholders.

Employee citizenship and corporate citizenship

Arrow 3 (Fig. 6.3) represents value interactions between employees and external stakeholders as a major 'interface' between business and society. Indeed, our whole platform of business citizenship is based on the assumption that employee citizenship and corporate social responsibilities are related and that the former can be a means to achieving the latter. Since relatively little is known about the linkages between employee citizenship and corporate social responsibility, the connecting arrow in Figure 6.3 is broken, suggesting that many questions need to be asked in this area. For instance, to what extent is citizenship among employees a necessary condition for carrying out responsibilities that are required, expected and discretionary? Does an organisation's demonstrated commitment to community influence the extent to which employees exhibit citizenship? Further, does a community's demonstrated commitment to an organisation influence employee citizenship? What employee-held values serve economic and ecological goals? Finally, to what extent do violations of covenants in one domain affect citizenship in another?

Executive stewardship of citizenship domains

Given the conventions described so far, the interactions across citizenship domains can be viewed as potential 'conduits of shared trust' for reconciling organisational and societal goals. But how can shared trust be established and maintained? One avenue of inquiry is to explore the values leaders espouse and demonstrate and to study the effect of breached contracts. For instance, what happens when the executive espouses a commitment to product safety but fails to implement commensurate standards of production? The apparent breach of citizenship (failure to adhere to an expected ecological responsibility) could enhance economic performance yet pose a dilemma for employees. Should they respond based on direct knowledge of the breach of contract and 'blow the whistle'? Alternatively, should employees and other stakeholders trust the executive to redress the apparent violation, even though a breach of trust gave rise to the very dilemma at hand? We raise these questions merely to indicate that a synthesis of citizenship will not necessarily be easy.

Formulating guidelines for practical management

Although no integration of citizenship exists, the combined tenets of corporate responsibility and employee citizenship imply certain guidelines for practical management. Conversely, citizenship in practice can inform citizenship in theory. Consider, for example, Johnson & Johnson's massive recall of Tylenol (see Frederick *et al.* 1992). Briefly, eight people died in Chicago in 1982 and in New York in 1986 as a result of cyanide put in Extra-Strength Tylenol capsules by an unknown poisoner. In both cases of product tampering, the response of James Burke, chief executive officer of Johnson & Johnson, was hailed as an exemplar of what we have called 'executive stewardship'. In terms of arrow 1 in Figure 6.3, James Burke helped mobilise employee co-operative behaviour to serve community (ecological) wellbeing. Employees willingly accepted extra responsibilities, helping each other and the organisation, working all hours day and night to recall massive amounts of Tylenol through established distribution channels. Indeed, Johnson & Johnson's recall went far beyond what was required and expected by the US Food and Drug Administration and other stakeholders.

During the crises, James Burke and the employees invoked the firm's mission statement as a credo that expressed their willingness to forgo economic goals in favour of consumer safety and community wellbeing. Indeed, most analysts agree that Johnson & Johnson set a new standard for responsible corporate conduct.

This shows that executives can influence what society requires, expects and desires of corporate conduct. Put differently, executives as stewards can take the lead in defining the practical possibilities of citizenship, instead of narrowly adhering to laws or waiting to react to adverse social pressure.

The citizenship of Johnson & Johnson can be understood in terms of our model of synthesis. Executive stewardship involves protecting organisational interests while discerning what society requires, expects and desires of organisational performance. The case of Tylenol suggests that, when stakeholders (in this case customers) face extreme risk of harm, citizenship means providing the greatest protection possible through appropriate organisational conduct. A basic guide-line is that executives should strive to understand the views of all impacted stakeholders, especially those of employees who will be called on to implement policy. Executives should also communicate citizenship goals to employees and other stakeholders, including customers, the media and public policy-makers. Put differently, executive stewardship involves a communicative ethic or process whereby all viewpoints and concerns are heard, respected and considered. Such dialogue could potentially facilitate citizenship as channels of shared trust among organisational participants and external stakeholders (see Calton and Kurland 1996; Calton and Lad 1995).

Since a crisis necessarily limits the opportunity for dialogue, the ideal scenario is that a communicative ethic is integrated into the strategic management process in the first place. As the case of Johnson & Johnson demonstrates, a mission statement or credo can serve as a touchstone for citizenship. It follows that an information system could be used to reinforce a firm's stated mission and facili-tate channels of communication and trust across citizenship domains. For this purpose, flatter organisations with less vertical division of labour function better than organisational structures with elaborate layers of administration (see Halal 1994). Hence, citizenship points to redesigning organisations, including some integration of functional areas, such as human resource management, informa-tion systems and marketing (Marsden and Andriof 1998; Waddock 2001). The relevance of cross-functional integration goes along with the extra-role behaviour and teamwork of employee citizenship. Since research on the implementation of corporate responsibility is scarce, theory probably lags behind practice in matters of organisational design.

Maintaining realistic expectations for theory and practice

Dealing with the spectre of relativism

Earlier we pointed out that the norms of corporate citizenship are relative, depending on the culture and issue at hand. Consistent with a tradition in busi-ness and society research, case studies can be used to shed light on relativism. Again, the case of infant formula comes to mind. The charge of corporate mis-conduct is loudest when infant formula is marketed to consumers in developing nations (Sethi 1994). Marketing the formula in advanced industrial nations does not appear to violate social norms. Cases that factually demonstrate the relativity of citizenship suggest that the nature of covenants between organisations and societies vary. We submit that Figure 6.3 can be used as a template for realistically coming to terms with business citizenship on a case-by-case basis.

Finding the limits to citizenship

It is important to acknowledge the practical limits to business citizenship. One quandary is that a zealous pursuit of economising can adversely affect community, as when cutting costs means relocating a plant and laying off workers. When this occurs, employees and other stakeholders will most probably feel a breach of trust. Yet executives cannot be expected to forgo all plans that run counter to community expectations. Rather, it is the role of government to ameliorate disruptions in the social contract. Public policy should be aimed at harmonising organisational and community goals, as when local government offers special tax incentives aimed at retaining businesses. In other words, business citizenship needs a complementary theory of public policy. Along these lines, we propose that executives who understand citizenship inclusively will deal more effectively with public policy than those who do not.

◢ Conclusions

In this chapter we have explored business citizenship as an emerging synthesis. We have compared corporate responsibility with employee citizenship and have proposed a framework for uniting them around exemplary executive leadership. Because the framework links two fields of inquiry across individual, organisational and societal domains, it points to fruitful research and guidelines for practice beyond what either approach to citizenship offers as presently formulated. Ultimately, we hope the model will stimulate interdisciplinary research that yields a realistic conception of citizenship for the business sector.

Part 2
GOVERNANCE AND
LEADERSHIP OF
CORPORATE CITIZENS

CORPORATE CITIZENSHIP AS AN ETHIC OF CARE
Corporate values, codes of ethics and global governance

Michel Dion
Université de Sherbrooke, Canada

The term 'corporate citizenship' has often had various meanings and scope. Most of the time, the problem is not one of terminology but concerns the kind of ethical conflicts that business ethics deal with (managerial dimension) and the ethical values that are actually involved in each case (the value-centred dimension). This chapter will try to establish a clearer distinction between those ethical questions and values that characterise the corporate level (corporate ethics), those that appear on the institutional level (the business milieu as a social institution), those that are typical to a given society or culture (social ethics) and those that are properly ethical issues involved in international business transactions. Such a distinction is crucial to determine the scope of corporate citizenship.

In the next section, I will present the 'top ten corporate values' determining the import of the concept of corporate citizenship. I will go on to show how such values are defined in a more or less legalistic context, through a content analysis of the corporate codes of ethics of 15 Canadian multinational corporations (MNCs) in various industries. Finally, I will explain how the concept of corporate citizenship must be developed in the broader context of global governance, presenting a threefold concept of corporate citizenship: working together (struggling for co-operation), hoping together (searching for understanding) and living together (respecting basic human rights).

◢ Corporate ethics

A business enterprise is a moral agent that has its own moral and social responsibilities, following from the implicit social contract between the society and
business milieu (Buchholz 1989; Dion 1994; Macdonald 1995). But, because of the
cultural and religious pluralism of our societies, corporate ethics must deal with
values and norms of ethical behaviour in a pluralistic organisational context, and
then with the value conflicts that may follow from such a context (Dion 1996;
1995; McCoy 1985; Sims and Gioia 1986).

Corporate ethics implies a critical assessment of discourses and practices in
organisations. It starts from a moral sociology, from the existential, organisational
life as it is perceived within the organisation, from the ethical paths used by
organisational members. Corporate ethics thus cannot avoid an analysis of the
moral consensus in order to be able to present realistic solutions to the moral
dilemmas with which the organisational members are confronted. The corporate
language that is used to express organisational culture is determined by corporate values and their relative compatibility with those of competitors, of other
industries in the given society and of the global culture of countries in which the
company operates.

◢ The top ten corporate values

I would now like to present, very briefly, the 'top ten corporate values' that one
may generally observe expressed in most corporate codes of ethics. Such values
should be considered as the 'heart' of corporate citizenship. In any corporate code
of ethics, one may observe that the concept of corporate citizenship is closely
linked in terms of social and environmental issues and in terms of ten values that
constitute the basis of such social and environmental concerns. These ten core
values will be defined as integral parts of integrity values (C values: integrity,
honesty, justice, equality, objectivity) and relational values (D values: loyalty,
devotion, respect, prudence, tolerance).[1]

Integrity

Integrity is the quality that prompts a person to try to safeguard what he or she
perceives to be his or her own being, protecting it against every pressure towards
inauthentic distortions; an organisational member tends to be an anonymous
subject (Heidegger 1962), destroying him or her in the long term. Integrity is

---

1 Values may be subdivided as follows: A values, profitability values; B values, socially
  induced values; C values, integrity values; D values, relational values.

closely related to authenticity and involves avoiding self-contradictions, trying to keep one's own essence, resisting those distortions that may be imposed by social, economic, political, cultural and sometimes religious structures. Integrity means resisting 'structures of non-being' that tend to cause the self-decay of the human being, with terrible psychological, physical and moral consequences.

Honesty

Honesty presupposes one to conform to the spirit of law and to customs, but above all to conform to one's own moral duties, to do 'what one should do'. Honesty is linked, on the one hand, to the exercise of practical reason (reflecting the usual moral norms of a given society) and can be safeguarded through positive law. On the other hand, honesty is linked to the human being acting either by moral duty or by regard to virtue. Honesty is a key value that gives to an individual various reference patterns for his or her own actions: conformity to his or her reason, the practice of some virtues or the actualisation of moral duties. Honesty is generally one of the main principles of corporate ethics.

Justice

Justice is often discussed in the midst of organisational discourses and practices, whether it reflects an attitude of fairness, the respect of basic human rights, a 'meritocracy' or a key value for positive law and thus a natural characteristic of human beings, giving rise to laws and regulations. Justice implies the redress of harms, the aim of equal rights for and obligations to each other, respect for the individual as well as collective rights. Justice is closely linked to the vague concept of common good or public interest. Only limitations or constraints to individual or collective rights can ensure an authentic meaning for justice. One should avoid becoming exclusively concerned with abstract structures and rules and thus disregarding the adequacy of such legal forms to the human reality that they have to shape. One should also avoid overlooking the need for legal forms and structures. In corporate codes of ethics, justice is presented as key to organisational change towards 'what should be'. Justice is, then, another pillar of corporate ethics.

Justice is often seen as a universal value, as part of human nature. If we were searching for justice, then transparency and accountability, generosity and sharing, fairness, integrity and honesty would be the natural by-products of that quest. The more we have, the more we should give. Globalisation has made clearer the deep disparities between rich and poor individuals as well as between developed and developing countries. The internationalisation of business through protectionist attitudes and social dumping mechanisms has led to the widening of the extent of poverty, so that one could say that globalisation is globalising poverty. We have to find out ways to make globalisation more attentive to natural justice. Otherwise, we are creating a self-destroying world. We must set up mechanisms to ensure interdependence between social justice (collective needs and interests) and personal health and growth (individual needs and interests). According to Robert Putnam (1996), civil society organisations seem to be the main generators of social capital.

Equality

Equality implies a will for forces to be in equilibrium, for a harmonisation of human needs and interests, for public recognition of an individual by others, whatever his or her social characteristics. Equality is linked to a flexible organisational climate in which every person is respected for what he or she is and wishes to be. Equality presupposes a prior comparison of various beings, out of their innate nature, of their acquired characteristics or of their intrinsic value as living beings. Equality seeks to prevent the occurrence of those abuses that are based on such natural differences.

Objectivity (or impartiality)

Objectivity is presented as being safeguarded through the rule of law applied without any prejudice. However, we should be aware that the absence of prejudices is nothing but a utopia. Moreover, prejudices can be and actually are useful: they form an integral part of the way we know beings, things and events (Gadamer 1976). There is no knowledge without prior prejudices. Pure objectivity is nothing but an illusion. Objectivity presupposes an exclusion of affections, of sensitivity in the decision-making process. At present, affections and sensitivity, which constitute a set of emotions (such as anger and fear) and feelings (such as love), are absent from the economic framework, so that traditional enterprises (centred on an absolute respect for hierarchy, decorum and obedience and thus on the collective life within the organisation) reflect only the social trend towards the enhancement of economic and technical rationality rather than any humanist and existential values, which are centred on individual lives.

Loyalty

The concept of loyalty is found in the midst of discourses of chief executive officers (CEOs). In most cases, the loyalty described is a one-sided loyalty—that of employees towards their organisation. Only rarely will an enterprise commit itself to loyal relations with its employees (two-sided loyalty). Originally, loyalty had a strong meaning of conformity to an implicit contract with the monarch and thus was a political value. It is quite strange to see such a value enhanced in the workplace, where 'common' workers see only continuous power struggles. The absence of loyalty is identified with manipulation, that is, the use of others as objects for one's own prestige or social status. However, the absence of loyalty is also identified with instinctive behaviour, with the absence of practical reason.

Devotion

In a business context, devotion implies self-sacrifice, that is, the neglect of one's own needs and interests to the profit of organisational needs and interests. However, such a devotion to an organisation can give one the status of an 'organisational hero'. Devotion means showing goodness and generosity, a sense of harmony, a disinterested attitude, a deep 'feeling' for the organisation. We should always beware of the psychological trap: through devotion we can develop an idolatric vision of the organisation concerned. Devotion can become a 'class egoism', to the profit of status quo within the organisation, reinforcing the position of those who hold organisational power, leaving those 'below' them powerless and poorer. Organisational members may then become merely physical extensions of the organisation and may develop their own personal identity to be strictly compatible with corporate culture. The trap of devotion in business corporations lies in the inner tendency to annihilate one's own personal identity and to integrate the organisational culture within oneself, even though it may be in contradiction with one's personality (leading to the creation of, for example, 'organisation-man').

Respect

Respect for others is a looking towards others, an enhancement of what one finds in others. We are unable to respect someone we cannot consider as 'magnificent', that is, expressing some desirable human characteristics with an unusual intensity. It is therefore necessary for the characteristics to be present with an unusual intensity. Respect for others implies public recognition of the Other as human being, that is, a being participating in the world humanisation process (from which nobody can be excluded). It also implies the actualisation of the best potentialities within humanity. Respect for others presupposes that actions I undertake towards others will be led by the feeling that I cannot be myself if I am unable accept the facilitation of the self-actualisation of others. I am 'I' only in the face of the Other.

Respect is a key value in social and organisational life. In fact, there is no room for a pluralistic world without mutual respect for other nations and peoples. Respect for each other goes beyond tolerance and emphasises our common human nature. Within monotheistic religions, respect has opened the door to sacred reality. In Islam, respect has a deep religious dimension and is a necessary condition for communicating with Allah (Dion and Ibrahim 1995).

Respect for others implies a focus on human dignity. Human dignity is the foundation of all ethical values and basic human rights, such as equality, tolerance and freedom. It implies that all human beings are equal and should be equally respected as individuals. Human dignity presupposes that each person must, as Kant (1983) said, always be treated as an end and never only as a means.

The search for human dignity requires the abandonment of individualism (championed by Adam Smith [Smith 1937] and Thomas Hobbes [Hobbes 1996]) as the cornerstone of society. It also implies the abandonment of John Stuart Mill's (Mill 1956) concept of allowing 'maximal liberty' as long as nobody inflicts avoidable harm on others. In addition, human dignity implies a basic freedom of will, so that we may live in conditions allowing us to become what we want to be.

Human rights and civil liberties are universal standards by which everyone can live in dignity, so that the violation of such standards implies the treatment of another as a 'non-person', as an object, as a means for our self-interest. Global governance implies the obligation to respect the dignity of each other, as a universal hypernorm.

Prudence

Although some definitions of 'prudence' may include consideration for one's own interests (*Collins English Dictionary*, 1998 edn), here 'prudence' is defined as a kind of wisdom following from intuition and reason. In an organisational context, it is a systematic reflection by an organisational member on the effects or consequences of his or her actions and decisions on beings and things in his or her environment and on the local communities. Prudence is above all a concern for others, a deep concern for their wellbeing, so that a consideration of others is present in the midst of our own decisions and actions. Through prudence, we are concerned with the actual effects of our actions and decisions on others, so that we cannot be authentic without being concerned with the wellbeing of others. There is no authentic being without a concern for others.

Tolerance

Tolerance is concern for difference, otherness. Given tolerance, radical difference can become a source of paradigmatic change in one's attitude towards the meaning of life. Tolerance implies an attitude of gentleness, of sweetness, which can contribute to the transformation of differences into possibilities for enrichment for us. Tolerance is limited by what we define as being an integral part of human nature and that must be universally respected. Tolerance considers moral and cultural pluralism as a path for individual growth and international peace. Tolerance implies compassion for others. Compassion and loving kindness follow from caring for each other and remain basic values in many world religions and spiritualities, such as Buddhism and Christianity. As said the Dalai Lama (Dalai Lama and Cutler 1998), compassion requires an altruistic attitude, that is, overcoming one's self-interest to become centred on the urgent needs of others and displaying peaceful behaviour following from one's altruism. Compassion cannot rise without peace. Compassion and loving kindness express an altruistic intent and concern as well as altruistic behaviour. They are centred on social achievement and self-discipline (Kanungo and Conger 1993).

◢ Institutional ethics and corporate codes of ethics

Business ethics is a critical reflection on moral practices, discourses and values, transmitted in the business milieu as a social institution. Business ethics thus takes a globalising approach to ethical issues in the business milieu and shows the various interests and values held by different stakeholders (Freeman 1984). As a system of production, an enterprise puts products and/or services on the market for its clients. As a system of power, the enterprise presupposes functions of authority that are necessary to any kind of leadership. An enterprise is a system that is in interaction with other systems, each having its own characteristics and basic orientations, so that corporate citizenship cannot be the exclusive responsibility of a single enterprise. Other stakeholders play their own part in corporate citizenship (Freeman 1984). Corporate citizenship deals with the social and cultural conditioning of business practices and looks at their ethical justification. Corporate citizenship must reveal linkages between organisational culture and social culture, between corporate ethics and social morality, and thus can draw from such an analysis various value orientations that will characterise a given business milieu.

Content analyses of corporate codes of ethics in Canada

Small and medium-sized enterprises and multinational corporations

In a survey of 224 provincial manufacturing companies in Canada, each with more than 100 employees, Lescarbeau and I found that 66% of the sample did not have a corporate code of ethics; 40% of these were, however, concerned with the necessity to provide a code of ethics in the near future (Dion and Lescarbeau 1994). The survey was realised through two sets of questionnaires: (1) one for those companies that already had a code of ethics; (2) one for other companies in which there was neither a code of ethics nor a projected code. We asked the companies to send us all relevant ethics documents. We usually received only codes of ethics, although corporate policies should also have been sent (for instance, environmental policy, health and safety policy, conflicts of interest policy) when such policies exist in co-ordination with a given corporate code of ethics. However, respondents either understood that provisions of such corporate policies were repeated or summarised in the codes of ethics, or their interpretation was that ethics simply relates to the code itself. Our questionnaires were also useful in discovering to what extent managers know the contents of their code (first questionnaire), or to what extent they would like to have a corporate code of ethics in the future (second questionnaire).

The codes were usually written by middle managers (92%) and applied to all employees (67%). Honesty and integrity were the most common values in such codes of ethics (94%). In terms of ethical conflicts in business, the most commonly cited were as follows: conflicts of interest (92%), disclosure of confidential information (87%) and unfair competition (63%). Conflicts of interest often accounted for a substantial proportion (up to 25%) of the text. There are numerous prohibitions included in sections dealing with unfair competition, but there are many more in codes dealing with conflicts of interest.

Other ethical conflicts are discussed in such codes: environmental responsibility (58%), product safety (55%), political contributions (54%), insider trading (36%) and misleading advertising (34%). In general, such sections involve few prohibitions (Dion and Lescarbeau 1995; Dion and Marquis 2001). Some ethical conflicts such as equal opportunity programmes, protection of the environment, product safety and political contributions are clearly not at the top of corporate concerns, although such issues are covered by the concept of corporate citizenship. Codes dealing with insider trading and misleading advertising are relatively rare and give rise to few prohibitions.

Most such codes of ethics have been set up since 1982, and the Canadian experience of corporate codes of ethics should be identified as a side-effect of the US 'ethical wave' in the mid-1970s. Corporate codes of ethics and their implementation and monitoring processes make 'corporate social performance' an integral part of business life.

Analysis
Through a content analysis of corporate codes of ethics, one can observe that such codes are very often more 'legalistic' than truly 'ethical'. The more that corporate codes of ethics are legalistic, the less they reflect a wide concept of corporate citizenship. Legalistic codes are more a kind of commentary on laws and regulations than a text about 'How can we raise ethical behaviour beyond legal requirements?' The legalistic character of a code can be identified through three main factors. A legalistic code will:

- Contain many references (approximately 11 or more) to laws or to respecting laws and regulations
- Describe many prohibitions (approximately 11 or more)
- Make few mentions (approximately 4 or less) of values of integrity and relational values (defined in the section above on the top ten corporate values as C and D values), yet make frequent mention of profitability values (A values)

Indeed, there are few corporate codes of ethics that are truly ethical. Codes that exhibit the first two factors listed above yet not the third may be called 'hybrid codes'. Although they show great potential to be a true ethical discourse, such potential is counterbalanced by the high recurrence of prohibitions and references to respect of laws and regulations.

Multinational corporations

The following content analysis deals with the corporate codes of ethics of 15 of the most important Canadian MNCs (being among the top 50 of the 500 largest

Canadian companies in terms of their annual revenues) (*Le Journal Les Affaires* 1999). The following industries were represented in the sample: manufacturing (2 MNCs), telecommunications (2), oil and gas (3), foods and tobacco (3), banking (3) and insurance (2). The five MNCs in banking and insurance were in the top seven Canadian banks and life insurers. The codes had been generally been set up or reviewed since 1993.

Hypothesis
I take as a hypothesis that those companies that put a greater emphasis on integrity values and relational values (C and D values) than on profitability values (A values) show a higher level of ethical discourse within their codes of ethics. I assume that socially induced values (B values) are basically the result of social progress and the influence of interest groups, so that their role in determining the legalistic or ethical character of corporate codes of ethics should be considered as 'neutral'.

As to the concept of corporate citizenship, although, as already discussed, it reflects the influence of the 'top ten corporate values' mentioned above, one could say that, more globally, corporate citizenship is a concept made of socially induced values (B values), integrity values (C values) and relational values (D values). I will use the following typology (including 40 corporate values) to reflect various ethical frameworks in corporate codes of ethics (Dion 2000). The 'top ten corporate values' discussed above are integral parts of integrity values (C) and relational values (D):

- Profitability (A) values (10 values): these can be divided into two sub-groups:
  - Values associated with products and services, such as productivity, product quality, efficiency, innovation, competence and corporate success
  - Values associated with stakeholders (mainly the public and competitors), such as corporate image, accurateness, clarity and competition

- Socially induced (B) values (6 values): these can be divided into two sub-groups
  - Values closely linked to community, such as the protection of the environment, life quality of consumers and social responsibility
  - Values closely linked to employees, such as health and safety in the workplace, wellbeing of employees and human rights

- Integrity (C) values (9 values): these can be brought together into three sub-groups:
  - Fairness values, such as equality, justice and fairness
  - Impartiality values, such as objectivity and impartiality
  - Honesty values, such as probity, integrity, truth and honesty

■ Relational (D) values (15 values): these can belong to two sub-groups:

- Intra-organisational values, such as respect, trust, loyalty, faithful-ness, collaboration, discernment, understand, devotion and freedom
- Inter-organisational values, such as openness, modesty, courtesy, hospitality, politeness and prudence

Results

Given that the emphasis of the codes of ethics should necessarily be on ethical values, some 26.7% of codes studied showed a negative outcome, that is, they placed greater emphasis on A values than on C and D values. In 53.3% of the cases, there is a neutral outcome, that is, the emphasis is equally on A values and on C and D values, or there may be only one of each of A, C or D values. Some 20% of the companies' codes exhibited a positive outcome, that is, a greater emphasis on C and D values than on A values. As to the list of corporate values enhanced within corporate codes of ethics, a significant number of MNCs have more than ten 'core values' (out of the 40 values defined), but most of them have fewer than six values.

If one looks at the various industries in Canada under study, one may observe that some corporate values receive more emphasis in some industries than in others. For instance, the issue of competition is present in the code of ethics of every industry, but much more so in the telecommunications industry, and much less so in the tobacco industry. The issue of integrity is also present in all codes, but much more so in the telecommunications industry and much less so in the banking industry. Honesty is emphasised more in the codes of ethics of the telecommunications industry than it is in those of the insurance and banking industries. Accurateness, justice and trust are present mostly in the codes of the telecommunications industries, but much less so in those of the insurance and oil industries. Respect is emphasised only in the codes of the telecommunications industry. Protection of the environment is emphasised in the manufacturing and telecommunications industry codes but is not given such great emphasis in the codes of other industries.

Most of the corporate codes of ethics studied included 15–26 references to respect for laws. (In this study, for a code to be considered 'legalistic', there must therefore be a minimum of 15 references to laws [see the 'Analysis' section below].) Very few had less than 11 such references, so that they could not be con-sidered as 'ethical' codes as opposed to 'legalistic' codes. Only the food and tobacco industry codes contained fewer than 15 references to laws. Few codes had more than 30 references to respect for laws that would place them firmly in the 'legalistic' category. Oil and gas company codes had between 15 and 17 references to laws and so this industry represents one of the least legalistic Canadian indus-tries as far as codes of conduct are concerned. The telecommunications industry, having between 26 and 30 references to respect for laws, is the most legalistic Canadian industry in this respect.

Most corporate codes of ethics included 25–29 prohibitions, so for the purposes of this study it was decided that for a code to be considered prescriptive it must contain at least 25 prohibitions. In no case did a code actually meet the condition of having ten or fewer prohibitions and so could not be regarded as purely 'ethical' in that sense. The banking and telecommunications industries are those that show the highest rate of making prohibitions (30–68), whereas the food and tobacco industry had the lowest rate of making prohibitions (6–25).

There are two main types of prohibition: strong and weak. Strong prohibitions are those that are unambiguous and are in no way equivocal. Strong and weak prohibitions may be complemented with exceptions and/or the requirement of prior authorisation. When one considers the various ethical conflicts covered by corporate codes of ethics, one observes that weak prohibitions are more present in sections dealing with competition, relations with clients, disclosure of confidential information, gifts and conflicts of interest. Strong prohibitions are more present in sections discussing financial records and accounts, insider trading, relations with suppliers, use of corporate assets for personal ends and conflicts of interest (including gifts and advantages). Strong prohibitions complemented with the requirement of a prior authorisation are much more in evidence in sections on conflicts of interest, use of corporate assets for personal ends and disclosure of confidential information. Finally, strong prohibitions accompanied by exceptions are more typical of sections dealing with insider trading and conflicts of interest. There are usually no weak or strong prohibitions within sections dealing with protection of the environment.

In the same manner, there are some types of behaviour that are tolerated by companies. This tolerance can be classified as following: a simple tolerance, a tolerance accompanied by a few exceptions and/or the requirement of prior authorisation and a tolerance with few conditions attached. Simple tolerances are more frequent within sections dealing with gifts and privileges. Tolerated behaviour with the requirement of prior authorisation is more in evidence in sections dealing with conflicts of interest, whereas tolerances with few conditions attached generally appear within sections dealing with relations with the community.

Analysis
In order to realise an ethical assessment of corporate codes of ethics, one must to set up an 'ethical ladder' as to the three main criteria:

- Recurrence of certain corporate values (A values compared with C and D values)
- References to respect for laws and regulations
- The number of prohibitions

Codes may be regarded as 'ethical' if they:

- Place a greater emphasis on C and D values than on A values
- Contain fewer than 11 references to respect for laws
- Contain fewer than 11 prohibitions

If the company code meets two of these three criteria, it will fall in the 'ethical –' (ethical minus) sub-group.

For a code to be regarded as a 'hybrid' it must meet one or both of the following requirements. It must be close to having:

- The lower limit of references to respect for laws and regulations (15 citations)

- The lower limit of prohibitions (25 citations)

The 'hybrid' label can be divided into three sub-groups: 'hybrid –' (hybrid minus, being quite similar to the 'ethical –' label), 'hybrid' and 'hybrid +' (hybrid plus, being quite close to a 'legalistic –' label, defined below).

Corporate codes of ethics that have a good record as to the corporate values criterion but that contain more prohibitions or references to laws than the average, or codes having fewer prohibitions or references to laws than the average but a bad record as to the corporate values criterion will fall into the category 'hybrid –'. The 'hybrid +' label presupposes that codes have either more prohibitions or more references to laws than the average.

The 'legalistic' label is divided into three sub-groups: 'legalistic –' (quite close to 'hybrid +'), 'legalistic' and 'legalistic +'. Corporate codes of ethics that have not clearly met the corporate values criterion and have many more prohibitions and references to laws than the average will be identified as 'legalistic +'.

In the study sample, only one company code actually falls into the 'hybrid +' sub-group (6.7%). A high number of company codes (5 [33.3%]) fall into the 'legalistic +' sub-group. Similarly, a high number of company codes (6 [40%]) could be identified as belonging to the 'hybrid –' sub-group.

If the sample is broken down by industry one finds that the telecommunications industry and manufacturing industry codes fall into the 'legalistic +' sub-group; insurance industry codes are typically 'hybrid –'; food and tobacco industry codes falls into the sub-group 'ethical –'.

Discussion

In the sample studied, it was found that most Canadian MNCs have 'legalistic' codes of ethics and thus these codes are far from illustrating any concept of corporate citizenship. The fact that there is a significant group of MNC codes of ethics that fall into the 'hybrid' sub-group actually shows how there is a deep confusion between ethics and law, how MNCs cannot distinguish ethical from legal issues. One of the most important aims of such codes would be to clarify ethical behaviour and legal requirements, since ethics begins to act and speak when laws and regulations have finished imposing their basic moral norms. Such results also point out how the CEOs of Canadian MNCs need to be more aware of the ethics–law confusion, so that they will be able to lead people to higher ethical standards in their organisational behaviour. Otherwise, company codes will simply repeat existing laws, reinforcing their punitive function through prohibitions, yet will neglect corporate values, providing no corporate discourse that could actually lead people towards ethical considerations rather than towards respect for existing laws.

◢ Social ethics

Social ethics is particularly concerned with socially induced values, such as the protection of the environment, and is thus quite close to the concept of corporate citizenship, however defined. One has here a social expectation and a corporate response. In both cases, with regard to the environment, it is not necessarily the same representation of 'Nature' that is at stake. Generally speaking, business corporations adopt an anthropocentric viewpoint, since the environment must be safeguarded for the needs, desires and interests of human beings. This is especially clear in corporate environmental policies (Dion 1998a, 1993). An enterprise has very few alternatives for action: it must ensure its own survival and growth in the long run and give an acceptable answer to questions regarding social expectations. There is no truly biocentric company, since one cannot do business by being centred on the needs, desires and interests of every living being, given that all living beings are equal! The ideal course of action would be to safeguard wilderness, but reality consists of competition and of survival in the short run as well as in the long run.

Sometimes, an enterprise may be confronted by environmentalist share-holders, particularly institutional shareholders. Such situations have in the USA given rise to some 'proxy resolutions'.[2] However, shareholder activism is not limited to environmental issues. One also sees the emergence of 'ethical mutual funds', with protection of the environment as one of many ethical criteria (Dion 1998b).

It is evident, therefore, that protection of the environment remains a strong social expectation, despite the fact that the scope of involvement required from an enterprise with respect to environmentalism is not entirely clear. It is clear, however, that protection of the environment must be included in any concept of corporate citizenship. The current awareness of the global effects of human actions may explain the firmness of this social expectation.

The expectation of health and safety in the workplace is strong in Western societies. The public in general expects that part of corporate profits will be used to improve working conditions, since working conditions affect physical well-being.[3] But, insofar as the perceptions of the effect of such conditions is highly subjective, health and safety in the workplace remains a weak social expectation in comparison with that of protection of the environment. However, the way

2 A 'proxy resolution' is an attempt (during the Annual Shareholders' Meetings) by activist shareholders to prevent given corporate decisions or to require from top managers that they undertake given actions.
3 'Wellbeing' here refers to a state of physical, mental and spiritual health.

health and safety laws are enacted depends on existing cultural values and social rules. Depending on the culture in question, social expectations of standards could be higher regarding health and safety in the workplace than for protection of the environment. Nevertheless, it is an integral part of any concept of corporate citizenship.

The wellbeing of employees is located in the midst of business ethics and is actually a response to social expectations. In a small number of cases, members of organisations appear to derive meaning in their lives purely through their participation in organisational life, so that it seems the organisation is the only source of meaning in their lives. Such a phenomenon I have identified as 'corporacentrism'; it gives rise to what I call organisational messiahs or saviours (Dion 2001a), the organisation playing a redeeming role in those people's lives. An organisational messiah saves the organisation and provides a 'meaning of life' for all organisational members. The idea of wellbeing of employees implies in a more general sense the satisfying of their basic physical, psychological and spiritual needs. However, the notion of basic needs is not entirely clear, in terms of, for example, the scope of involvement required from the enterprise to satisfy such needs. For this reason the wellbeing of employees will remain a weak social expectation, although it is part of corporate citizenship.

The ethics of international business, global governance and a threefold concept of corporate citizenship

In this section on the ethics of international business I aim to make a critical assessment of business practices on the international scene in order to reveal ethical questions that are inherently linked to such practices and to propose reference patterns to resolve ethical conflicts in daily international business transactions.

Some codes of ethics for international business come from non-governmental organisations (NGOs) and international organisations. Five of the main texts of such international organisations are:

- The Principles for Global Corporate Responsibility
- The Interfaith Declaration
- The Rules of Conduct to Combat Extortion and Bribery
- The Tripartite Declaration of Principles Concerning Multinationals and Social Policies
- The Convention on Combating Bribery of Foreign Public Officials in International Business Transactions

The Principles for Global Corporate Responsibility

These principles were adopted by three religious organisations from England, Canada and the USA, on 19 September 1995—the Ecumenical Committee for Corporate Responsibility of the United Kingdom, the Task Force on the Churches and Corporate Responsibility of Canada, and the Global Corporate Accountability Issue Group from the Interfaith Center on Corporate Responsibility (USA) (Interfaith Center 1995). The principles include respect for human dignity and for collective as well as individual rights. Corporate citizenship here is defined with reference to:

- Ecosystems (protection of biodiversity)
- National communities (respect for basic human rights and promotion of high standards of health and safety in the workplace)
- Local communities (respect for basic human rights in foreign countries)
- Shareholders (actualising their interests in co-ordination with those of employees and other stakeholders)
- Employees (in terms of equal opportunities)
- Consumers and suppliers (showing transparency in decisions and actions as a 'good corporate citizen')

The Interfaith Declaration

This Declaration is a code of ethics on international business for Christians, Muslims and Jews, written by various researchers and business people from these three monotheistic religions (*Interfaith Declaration* 1993). The Declaration acknowledges that the three monotheistic religions have the following common concepts:

- Justice
- Mutual respect
- The stewardship of Divine creation
- Honesty

Justice is seen in terms of fairness and exercising authority in maintaining the state of law. Mutual respect is regarded as an attitude of love towards others, of caring, of being-with-others. As Heidegger (1971) said, it is respect for others, for what they are, so that a human being becomes a being-in-the-world-with-others. Mutual respect means to be caring. Caring is to involve oneself with others as a being-in-the-world. According to Locke (1966), it is compassion as a moral duty, participating in the pain of one's neighbour, trying to prevent or eliminate such pain. Compassion, then, is the foundation of morality, of self-transcendence. A moral agent, said Schopenhauer (1978, 1966), is a person who is able to act with compassion, so that compassion is the ultimate source of goodness, justice and love. Stewardship of Divine creation is defined as the task of safeguarding the Universe (or that part of the Universe which we can control), which ultimately is the property of God only. Honesty is defined as truth and reliability in thought, words and action.

The Declaration also outlines a few principles applicable to the political economy, emphasising the need for free competition and avoidance of monopolies, advocating the setting up of a collective wealth for the profit of all social groups and pointing up the moral duty of the state to provide a legal framework requiring business corporations to do business with fairness and honesty, to aim at the common good and not only its own private interests

The Declaration also states that corporate policies should be grounded in honesty, fairness and trust. Adherence to the principles of the Declaration requires ensuring that working conditions meet high standards in terms of health and safety, fair wages and respect for every organisational member, whatever his or her beliefs, family responsibilities or self-realisation needs. Relations with suppliers should be based on mutual trust. As to local communities and governments, business corporations should take into account the effects of their activities and operations everywhere they operate. Finally, the Declaration prohibits some types of behaviour, such as bribery, power abuse and disclosure of confidential information for personal ends.

The Rules of Conduct to Combat Extortion and Bribery

The Rules of Conduct to Combat Extortion and Bribery were formulated by the International Chamber of Commerce (ICC) in 1996 (ICC 1996). The ICC encourages its members to adopt corporate codes of ethics, including a whistle-blowing mechanism in cases of bribery or attempted bribery. MNCs should invest part of their profits in the countries in which they operate. They should co-operate with these countries in terms of hiring local people in their foreign subsidiaries. Finally, the Rules suggest that MNCs should not require any payment for technology transfer when such technologies hold no real value for them.

The Tripartite Declaration of Principles Concerning Multinationals and Social Policies

The Tripartite Declaration of Principles Concerning Multinationals and Social Policies was made by the International Labour Organisation (ILO) in 1977. The Declaration contains a number of principles, such as the prohibition of making threats to employees to transfer a given plant, in order to influence the collective bargaining process. As in the Rules of the ICC, MNCs should promote the hiring of local employees in the countries in which they have operations. The ILO adds that MNCs should give stability to their employees, provide adequate training, set a minimum wage corresponding to employees' family needs and meet high standards of health and safety in the workplace (including communication with employees as to the hazards of the products being made). Finally, the ILO suggests that MNCs should co-operate with local governments in order to give fair compensation to those workers they may lay off.

The Convention on Combating Bribery of Foreign Public Officials in International Business Transactions

The Convention on Combating Bribery of Foreign Public Officials in International Business Transactions was published by the Organisation for Economic Co-operation and Development (OECD) on 17 December 1997 (OECD 1997b). This Convention affirms that bribery has become widespread in international business transactions and that it undermines economic development and distorts competition. The Convention acknowledges the responsibility of states to prevent solicitation of bribes from individuals or enterprises, and that real progress presupposes co-operation between states and business through a periodic audit of business practices. Each signatory state must establish that it is a criminal offence for anyone to offer, promise or give undue economic or other advantages, directly or indirectly, to a foreign public officer in order to ensure that that officer will accomplish or will omit to accomplish his or her own public functions. To combat bribery of foreign public officers, each signatory state must take the necessary measures to ensure that corporate records, accounts and annual reports are audited and to prohibit 'off-the-book' accounts, the presence of non-existent expenses or the use and/or creation of false documents.

Summary

The ethics of international business is concerned with an implicit social contract between MNCs and society. It may be unrealistic to require MNC headquarters to have ethical standards extra-territorial to their countries. However, reliance on the various ethical standards prevailing in countries where the MNC has operations may lead to an attitude of indifference in that MNC. We need to draw some ethical parameters by which MNCs will be able to present their corporate ethics as good, or to modify those ethics according to the cultures and religions of their business partners, depending on what is at stake (protection of the environment, health and safety in the workplace, equal opportunity programmes, conflicts of interest; see De George 1993).

◢ Corporate citizenship as an ethic of care

Corporate citizenship is nothing but an opportunity to become more deeply aware of our perceptions of ourselves, of our world and sometimes of our God. We are continuously creating our meaning of life, our paradigmatic beliefs about reality, so that out of such beliefs we become involved in the world (Gandz and Hayes 1988; Piper 1993). Corporate citizenship has to deal with moral pluralism so that individuals can confront, on a daily basis, their fear of others. Fear of others is not simply a fear of the social, political, economic and cultural threats that others may represent to us, or the need to protect the self against such threats as perceived by our moral imagination. It is an anxiety that we will lose our meaning of life through the invasion of our consciousness by the otherness. Our intolerance of ambiguity, our anxiety when reviewing our own value system as a result of some striking discussion or our anxiety that we will lose our absolute certainty that we hold the truth—all such attitudes should be reviewed through corporate citizenship, because corporate citizenship opens the door to the 'absolute certainty of a relative uncertainty', even in our ethical behaviour. Day by day we deal with ethical or unethical behaviour, first through our values and then by reference to our meaning of life (Tillich 1952).

Corporate citizenship starts from 'being-in-the-world-with-others' (Heidegger 1962). It should aim at internalising an 'ethic of care' (Welch 1990). An ethic of care should imply:

- A moral courage, that is, one should act in accordance with some basic ethical values, such as honesty, respect for others, fairness and trust
- Empathy with and compassion towards others
- A proactive attitude, a visionary perspective that may create solidarity and a more meaningful life for all

Corporate citizenship should, then, adopt a cross-cultural and inter-religious approach to ethical issues in the international scene as well as on the national level (where cultural and religious pluralism has been present for many years in Western and Eastern countries), insofar as many ethical conflicts are perceived through the prism of cultural and religious values and norms of behaviour, whether the religion be Islam (there are even some substantial cultural differences between Islamic countries of South-East Asia and those of North Africa), Buddhism, or Christianity (for instance, in the Philippines, where most of the people are Christian, in contrast to, for example, Canada). A whole cross-cultural and inter-religious dialogue is becoming more and more necessary as a result of the internationalisation of business. We can no longer do business in the long run without having a deeper understanding of the cultural and religious background of our business partners, whether it is in Muslim, Hindu, Buddhist and Confucian countries. Such a dialogue, which is a growing condition for international corporate citizenship, implies three basic values:

- Struggling for co-operation, implying an openness to the viewpoint of others, so that we could accept the modification of some of our own cultural and religious practices and beliefs
- Searching for understanding other people's cultural and religious roots, realising that the other may know something better than us and having the ability to question the validity of our prejudices (Gadamer 1976)

■ Respecting basic human rights, implying a respect for people having different cultural and religious roots from ourselves

There is no sense in having the concept of corporate citizenship unless business leaders have a deep feeling and conviction that collaboration is strongly required. Corporate citizenship implies a culture of 'togetherness', which is grounded in caring for others. It is expressed through various means of working together (struggling for co-operation), hoping together (searching for understanding) and living together (respecting basic human rights).

Working together: struggling for co-operation

Co-operation implies empowerment of the powerless, so that people can control and shape their collective destiny and exert a major influence on global processes. The act of working together involves co-operating to create a more harmonious, peaceful world and thus continuously trying to overcome the 'reef barriers of mutual understanding', that is, conflicting interests. To create a better world, there seems to be no other alternative than to work together.

Working together is a requirement for the emergence of a real global civil society, as public interest groups have various viewpoints and interests to defend: women's rights, labour rights, farmers' interests, etc. Indeed, sharing in decision-making that affects our livelihood is a basic human right. Global governance not only implies popular participation but also, mainly, a strong record of co-operation showing how much political, social and business leaders are ready to accept cultural and religious pluralism and to improve democratic participation mechanisms. Working together means that we are able, as political, business or social leaders, to face various needs, interests and values, and to change our management style and decision-making process, if necessary, in order to improve the conditions required for collaboration. Corporate citizenship, which has economic, political, administrative and systemic aspects, implies working together to create a democratic, open and co-operative world. We are creating a context in which people can participate in the life and activities of the community. In other words, we are developing habits of democratic participation, openness and co-operation through action. Corporate citizenship implies global citizenship and global decision-making that are more participatory and more democratic. It implies the promotion of universal 'hypernorms', or globally based norms, such as personal freedom, physical security and wellbeing, informed consent, political participation and, more generally, the core human rights (Fritzsche 1997). Corporate citizenship implies the mastery of dialogue, the capacity to question our own assumptions (Sérieyx 1993). It avoids the 'mobilisation of bias', that is, the fact that we can operate, unconsciously or overtly, to preclude some courses of action from entering into our considerations.

Civil society implies many different groups of citizens pursuing various interests, such as labour organisations, professional associations, advocacy groups, charitable organisations and so forth. Within civil society organisations, citizens are generally concerned with public policy issues. Civil society serves as a 'guardian of democracy' and will criticise democratic institutions in their functioning when important issues are at stake, such as protecting the environment, safeguarding basic human rights and ensuring international peace.

Hoping together: searching for understanding

Business needs political courage and political vision; both are required for good government. Visionary business leaders show a high level of courage in their decisions, that is, the courage to make hard choices, in considering all affected groups. Such leaders are also aware that having a specific vision for a given country also requires them to look at the effects of that vision on other nations. So, because of globalisation, business leaders must show a global vision that contains the 'power of hope'.

Hoping together is sharing the hope that the world can be better managed and harmonised and is to hold such a hope for our respective countries. There is a strong social need for hoping together, because growing disenchantment with politicians and the political process is widespread. Higher standards of integrity in public life, as 'confidence-building measures', should help to reinforce people's trust in governments. We should invent means and mechanisms to insure a '3R corporate citizenship' concept, one that is responsible, responsive and representative. Corporate citizenship thus means democratic participation as well as a responsible and a responsive exercise of power on matters of public interest. It consists of exercising power in a way that one is always aware of the main social expectations as to what constitutes the common good, in a way that one actually meets such social expectations.

We should implement an effective global decision-making process, given that corporate citizenship is a multi-dimensional phenomenon, presupposing democratic participation, flexibility and openness between partners. Only in a peaceful society, a society that always refers to the rule of law and tries to develop mutual respect and love between its citizens, can we hope for a better world. And that implies a shared vision developed, at least, by business leaders actualising a high level of corporate citizenship (Drath and Palus 1994).

Living together: respecting basic human rights

The great challenge for corporate citizenship is to find out and deepen the meaning of common values and to develop a sense of common responsibility, within the reality of global diversity (implying at least a cultural and religious pluralism). Common or shared responsibility not only means respecting the basic rights of each other but, above all, that we all have shared duties for the sustainability of our world. We cannot erase our responsibility. We have common responsibility for preserving our world, because it is a collective heritage. Corporate citizenship is, then, the process through which various social institutions exercise their rights and duties in accordance with universal values and hypernorms.

Corporate citizenship implies an ethical leadership, which is both visionary and globalising (Dion 2001b). Ethical leadership is a kind of leadership that allows us to meet the challenge of assuming responsibility for the predicament of the others. It is a kind of leadership by which we can create the social, political, economic, cultural and religious conditions required for living together. It is a type of leadership concerned with solidarity.

Organisational self-renewal occurs when a CEO provides effective and ethical leadership and when organisational members have the ability to easily adapt themselves to organisational change. There seems to be a set of homeostatic conditions by which, consciously or unconsciously, organisational equilibrium is safeguarded through a combination of the ethical leadership of the CEO and the ability of people to adapt themselves to organisational change. An organisation's capacity for self-renewal can be developed in a way that we more and more are able to live together.

Living together means being-with-others (Heidegger 1962), so that our survival and self-actualisation are closely linked to the survival and self-actualisation of others. Living together implies avoiding a concept of otherness that destroys human community. In international business, basic ethical disagreements may often occur, as when people from different cultures see the same facts yet disagree on the moral issue. For this reason we need cross-cultural dialogue and a decision-making process that involves all business partners and organisational members. There are two major pitfalls we must avoid: ethnocentrism (trying to impose our culture and ethics on others) and cultural relativism (being no longer concerned with ethical dilemmas).

At present, the market is a mechanism that ignores justice; we must thus humanise it. Globalised markets, with the impulse of protectionism, have globalised poverty. Globalisation, as led by *laissez-faire* ideology, is aimed directly at deregulation and profit maximisation, with very little consideration of corporate social responsibilities. The current process of anarchic globalisation must be reoriented through the use of international mechanisms, such as a mechanism to reduce the adverse effects of massive capital outflows. We have all seen the results of this phenomenon, combined with intervention by Western countries, on international organisations during the recent financial crisis in South-East Asia. We cannot really be human without being-with-others, without having a deep concern for their wellbeing, regardless of cultural and religious pluralism. Corporate citizenship engenders better means for living together, and that implies having the political courage to change the world by modifying the way each business corporation pursues its own interests and needs and, more basically, by changing the way businesses perceive each other on the international scene.

THE MORAL LEADER
Essential for successful corporate citizenship

Archie B. Carroll
University of Georgia, USA

How can business and other organisations be good corporate citizens? The key is understanding the essential elements of corporate citizenship and providing the moral leadership for this understanding to be implemented in practice.

It is essential before we proceed to have a robust comprehension of what corporate citizenship really means. In this chapter, I will argue that corporate citizenship has four 'faces' that the moral leader must understand for effective leadership. These four faces are: the economic, legal, ethical and philanthropic (Carroll 1979, 1998). First, successful corporate citizens need to understand that they must be profitable to continue to exist (the economic face). That is, they must be successful enough to carry their own weight financially. In the early 1900s, US President Theodore Roosevelt said that 'the first requisite of a good citizen is that he [or she] be able and willing to pull his [or her] own weight'. With respect to business organisations, this translates into the economic responsibility to be profitable. Profit-making is not antithetical to good corporate citizenship. Rather, it is a baseline obligation—a *sine qua non* to successful corporate citizenship. The organisation that cannot support itself financially cannot fulfil its other roles in society.

Second, good corporate citizens must obey the law; that is, they must fulfil their legal responsibilities to the society and community in which they reside. Laws represent a form of codified ethics since they embrace notions of appropriate behaviour, activities and practices, and many of them are designed to protect important stakeholders such as employees, consumers, owners and the community (for example, environmental laws). Though laws are necessary in the functioning of society, there are at least three reasons why they are inadequate on their own:

- Laws cannot cover every conceivable situation a manager may face; there are gaps that must be addressed by some other way of thinking.

- Laws tend to lag behind ethics; once passed, it is often years until a law is modified or brought up to date. Research may later reveal that the legal standards were not adequate in the first place. In addition, new technologies for measurement may render previous standards obsolete. Therefore, laws are inadequate in and of themselves.

- Laws are made by legislators who are not always looking after the various stakeholders' best interests, but rather are looking after their own interests. Laws are often the result of political compromise and therefore may not always reflect the degree of concern that is needed to protect human life and the environment.

Someone once said there were two things he did not want to see made—sausage and laws. There is some truth in this old adage.

Third, good corporate citizenship must go beyond the law—that is, business people must engage in ethical practices. Many managers today suffer from what philosopher Christina Hoff Summers calls conceptual moral chaos. By contract, effective corporate citizens must be leaders in the ethical sphere. In the next section, in which I begin a discussion on moral leadership, I will develop this idea of the responsibility to be ethical.

Last, good corporate citizens are expected to 'give back' to the community and society. This final, discretionary 'face' of corporate citizenship relates to business giving, or philanthropy. Philanthropy is commonly believed to be a desire to help humankind through acts of charity, whether done by private citizens, foundations or corporations. Though this face has an ethical underpinning to it, it is important to distinguish it from the 'ethical face', which is concerned with treating stakeholders fairly and avoiding harm. Today, the citizenry of most countries expects corporations and other organisations to fulfil their philanthropic roles by voluntarily adding to the quality of life in communities around the world.

Building on a solid foundation of what corporate citizenship really means, organisations require a 'moral leader' to implement this conception. In the next section, an introductory discussion of the relationship between ethics and leadership will set the stage for further considerations.

◢ Ethics and leadership

It has become fashionable in recent years to call for ethical leadership on the part of managers at all levels. To some, this call is genuine; that is, it reflects an authentic belief that moral leadership is needed because it is the right thing to do. To others, it is less genuine. To them, it just sounds pleasing to the ear, or faddish.

To yet others, it is believed to be related to desirable organisational outcomes. That is, it is instrumental. Whatever the motivation, ethical leadership is a vital topic as we embark on a new millennium of organisational management, both in the for-profit sector and in the not-for-profit sector.

There is an extensive literature on the two separate topics of ethics and leadership. To be sure, much of the literature on ethics presumes its importance not only because of the belief that it is the right thing to do but also because of the belief that managers, leaders and organisations need it or other stakeholders desire it. There seems to be an often unstated presupposition on the part of those writing in business ethics that the topic is important, needed or vital. To others, ethics is seen as something managers and leaders now need to consider because the public demands it, stakeholders expect it, it is instrumental in leading to a more profitable enterprise and it helps the organisation to stay out of trouble. For most writers and researchers on business ethics, it could be safely surmised that they see intrinsic value in business ethics.

On the leadership side, however, it is not clear that ethics has always been, or is, a presumed part of leadership style or method. Leadership theory and research has been more centred on accomplishing organisational objectives through people, with the emphasis more on instrumental means and ends than on the morality, ethicalness or righteousness of the means and ends. For example, if one examines the lead articles in the 1998 special issue on 'Leadership' of the *Harvard Business Review*, a special collection of the most influential articles on leadership published in that flagship magazine for executives, most pay scant or no attention to the ethical dimension or facet of leadership. The concerns are more with such topics as 'The Manager's Job: Folklore or Fact' (Mintzberg 1998), 'What Leaders Really Do' (Kotter 1998), 'Managers and Leaders: Are They Different?' (Zaleznik 1998) and 'The Work of Leadership' (Heifetz and Laurie 1998).

To be fair, a couple articles are included that address ethics-related topics: 'The Discipline of Building Character' (Badaracco 1998) and 'The Human Side of Management' (Teal 1998), but these influential articles were published only in the past five years. When one examines the body of leadership research, a similar pattern is generally found.

In more recent years, the topics and literatures of ethics and leadership have started to be bundled together. A prime example of this would be the volume, *Ethics: The Heart of Leadership*, edited by Joanne B. Ciulla (1998). In this book of essays, direct efforts are made to link the two fields. It is worth observing, moreover, that Ciulla comes at this topic from the ethics field, not the leadership field. Much to her credit, however, she does include in the volume several pieces written primarily by leadership theorists (e.g. Bass 1998; Hollander 1998).

It is clear that, over the next decade, more and more initiatives to unite the fields of ethics and leadership will be made. It is a natural linkage, and it is unfortunate that it has taken so long for it to be explicitly addressed. For some time now, ethics and management have been a much-discussed relationship. It is only a small step to start finding applications in the ethics literature to the challenges, topics and problems of leadership and to associate them with effective corporate citizenship.

To advance this discussion, it is important to further link some literature from ethics and management and to demonstrate its relationship with leadership. Though some commentators make subtle distinctions between managers and leaders, such as Zaleznik's (1998) article cited above, it is safe to say that many writers, including myself, have presumed that there is significant overlap between these two roles. Leaders who are not managers, or managers who are not leaders, will not last very long in today's organisations. The two roles are complementary and probably were never intended to be separate. It was only through the observation that some managers became imbalanced and thus emphasised one aspect to the detriment of the other that the distinction between management and leadership became an issue in the first place. It is useful to think about this movement from moral management to moral leadership.

Management and leadership models

In the next section I want to develop the idea that the model of the moral manager (see Carroll 1987, 1991), when more fully developed, becomes a model of the moral or ethical leader. The characteristics of the moral manager need to be more completely set forth to be sure that leadership aspects are amply embraced. Further, it will be argued that the moral manager model is an excellent prototype for ethical leadership.

One way of understanding the moral manager model is to compare it with two other types of management—immoral management and amoral management. Taken together, these three models of management morality depict a range of categories in which management behaviour has been noted, described and illustrated (Carroll 1987, 1991, 1995). In a sense, they depict a set of categories that capture much of the observed behaviour, patterns or types of ethical management that may be found in organisations today. The descriptions of immoral and amoral types will be brief, but they help us to understand the category of moral management, or leadership, which is the primary topic of interest in this chapter.

Immoral management and leadership

The immoral management model is a fairly straightforward concept.[1] Immoral management, or leadership, is a posture or approach that is devoid of ethical principles and precepts and is actively opposed to what is moral. Management decisions, behaviour, actions or leadership style are discordant with ethics or morality, even loosely defined. The immoral management model holds that management's motives are selfish and that it cares only, or principally, about the individual's or the organisation's gains.

---

1 The words 'unethical' and 'immoral' are used interchangeably in the following discussion.

If management is actively opposed to what is regarded as ethical, the clear implication is that management to some degree knows right from wrong and chooses to do wrong. Immoral management may be motivated by greed. Its goals are profitability and organisational (or personal) success at almost any price. Immoral managers do not care about others' claims or expectations to be treated fairly or justly. Immoral management regards the law as a barrier to be overcome in accomplishing what it wants. Immoral managers have no problem with circumventing the law if it achieves their ends. The basic strategy of immoral management is to exploit opportunities and people for personal or organisational gain and to cut corners when it appears to be useful (Carroll 1987, 1991, 1995). In the vernacular, immoral managers are the 'bad guys'—they are not good corporate citizens.

Amoral management and leadership

The amoral management model of leadership is a posture or approach that is devoid of ethics, that is, it is a model that does not factor the ethical dimension into decision-making and practice. It is not actively immoral as the above-described model. Rather, it is conceptualised as a posture without ethics. Amoral managers or leaders may be categorised into two different types—intentionally amoral and unintentionally amoral. Intentionally amoral leaders do not factor ethical considerations into their actions because they believe business activity resides outside the sphere in which moral judgements apply. These leaders are neither moral nor immoral; they simply think that different rules apply in business compared with other realms of life. These individuals do not make good corporate citizens.

Unintentionally amoral leaders, by contrast, are amoral for an alternative reason. These leaders are morally casual, careless, unaware or inattentive to the fact that their decisions and actions may have detrimental or deleterious impacts on other stakeholders. These leaders lack ethical perception, sensitivity or aware-ness. They blithely go through their organisational lives not thinking that what they are doing has an ethical facet or dimension to it. They may be well inten-tioned but they are insensitive to or unaware of the fact that their actions and decisions may be hurting or adversely affecting others. Either intentionally or unintentionally, the amoral leader's 'ethical gears are in neutral'. Amoral leaders use the letter of the law as their guide rather than the spirit of the law (Carroll 1987, 1991, 1995). Therefore, as long as they maintain their amoral perspective they cannot be good corporate citizens.

◢ From moral management to moral leadership

For decades, writers and researchers have been attempting to distinguish between managers and leaders, or between management and leadership. This is not an easy task as the two concepts are closely related. Generally speaking, management is more concerned with the overseeing of processes leading to the achievement of organisational objectives. Management involves planning, organising, controlling, motivating and communicating. In many respects, management is more task-focused than people-focused. A manager could come up with an excellent organisational strategy or operational plan but not have the skills or leadership ability to put it into practice or to motivate organisational members to move in the desired direction. Leadership, by contrast, is frequently thought to embrace a greater sense of vision, mission, change, creativity, challenge and engagement with people as humans.

Chapman and O'Neil (2000) distinguish between managers and leaders through a series of comparative statements. They assert that, whereas managers protect their operations, accept responsibility and minimise risk, leaders advance their operations, seek responsibility and take calculated risks. Whereas managers pacify problem employees, strive for a comfortable working environment and delegate cautiously, leaders challenge problem employees, strive for an exciting working environment and delegate enthusiastically.

Capowski (1994) has distinguished between managers and leaders in a similar fashion, by comparing the two. She argues that the manager is driven by his or her 'mind' and is characterised as rational, consulting, persistent, problem-solving, analytical, structured and uses position power. The leader, on the other hand, is driven by his or her 'soul' and is represented or perceived as visionary, passionate, creative, flexible, inspiring, innovative, courageous, imaginative and uses personal power. Clearly, many of these same attributes are needed among those who serve as manager and leaders, and although the ethics or morals of these two types may not be at odds with one another it is useful to see what characteristics might distinguish the two groups.

In earlier works, I set out the general characteristics of moral managers (or moral leaders) as follows (Carroll 1987, 1991; Carroll and Buchholtz 2000). Moral managers and leaders conform to high standards of ethical behaviour or professional standards in terms of their conduct, motives, goals, orientation toward the law and general operating strategy. Moral leaders aspire to succeed, but only within the confines of sound ethical precepts—fairness, justice and due process. Ethical leadership is commonplace in this model. Obedience toward the letter and spirit of the law is evident. The law is seen as a minimal level of ethical behaviour and the moral leader prefers to operate at standards that are higher than the law mandates. The strategy of moral leaders is to assume a leadership position when ethical dilemmas arise.

Moral management or leadership, as described, is very similar to and compatible with what Lynn Sharp Paine (1994) refers to as an 'integrity strategy'. The integrity strategy is characterised by a conception of ethics as the driving force of an organisation. Ethical values in this strategy provide a common frame of reference and serve to unify different functions, lines of business and employee groups (Paine 1994).

In the next section, a fuller development of the attributes of moral leadership will be set forth. For effective corporate citizenship to take place, moral leadership is essential. Quite often, moral leadership is a function of habits embraced by leaders.

◢ The seven habits of highly moral leaders

With respect to moral leadership, how might one further articulate the essential attributes of moral leaders or moral leadership? What qualities do leaders need to possess and display to be thought of as moral leaders? In this section, I identify seven important attributes or habitual qualities of moral leaders:

- They have a passion to do right.
- They are morally proactive.
- They consider all stakeholders.
- They have a strong ethical character.
- They have an obsession with fairness.
- They undertake principled decision-making.
- They integrate ethics wisdom with management wisdom.

Borrowing from the language used by Stephen Covey in his best-selling book *The Seven Habits of Highly Effective People* (1989), I could easily term these 'the seven habits of highly moral leaders'. Like Covey, I would argue that these qualities need to be so prevalent and present in the leader's approach that they become habitual as a leadership approach.

A passion to 'do right'

Moral leaders have a passion to do the right thing. This passion, motivation or inspiration is the glue that holds everything together. It builds on what James Wilson (1993) termed the 'moral sense'. It is consistent with what Louis Pojman (2000a, 2000b) might think of as 'the moral life'. Powers and Vogel (1980) might refer to this as a 'sense of moral obligation'. Like many personality or dispositional attributes, it is not always clear where the motivation to do right comes from. Some may be born with this sense; others develop it over time through spiritual, rational or experiential sources. Regardless, it is difficult to see someone functioning as a moral leader without it, and it becomes the essential quality that leads to the other attributes or habits.

Leaders who possess the moral sense, or motivation to do what is right, have doubtless internalised the basic purposes of or justifications for morality. Whether morality is seen as idealistic or instrumental, these leaders see at least the following purposes for morality: to keep society from falling apart; to ameliorate human suffering; to promote human flourishing; to resolve conflicts or interest in just and orderly ways; and to assign praise and blame, reward the good and punish the guilty (Pojman 2000b: 39). To all of this could be added, of course, 'because it (being moral) is the right thing to do'.

Morally proactive

The moral leader must be morally proactive. The moral leader is sensitive, astute and aware and is prepared to seek out ethical issues and exert ethical leadership. The moral leader uses 'moral imagination'. He or she attempts to imagine or foresee situations in which people might get hurt and takes action ahead of time. The moral leader does not wait for ethical problems to arise or for decisions to be made that do not factor in the moral dimension. Moral leaders are always anticipating and proacting. They are at the cutting edge of identifying ethical issues and dimensions.

One way in which moral leaders are able to behave proactively is through background–foreground shifting. Whereas the amoral leader perceives business to be in the foreground and ethics in the background, the moral leader shifts this arrangement and sees moral issues in the foreground and business issues in the background. What this means is that the moral leader perceives business issues and problems through the lens of ethics and therefore is better able to quickly discern potential ethical problems and to act proactively.

It is difficult to find examples of moral proactiveness in its purist form. In most instances, leaders who anticipate ethical issues by sensitively interpreting stimuli in the environment would be regarded as morally proactive. Even in this situation, it is difficult to accurately perceive motives. For example, some might impute moral proactiveness to the decisions and actions of Steven Sliwa, president of Colt, one of the oldest gun-makers in the USA. Others might see in his decisions a pragmatic fear of government regulation. Sliwa's plan is to develop a 'smart' pistol—one that can be fired only by its owner. Hired for his high-technology brilliance, Sliwa has applied for his own patent on a smart gun for self-defence and expects to have a consumer or police version on the market in two years. Sliwa believes that Colt is about to introduce the 21st-century gun. The notion of moral proactiveness would assume that this decision be made because the president anticipated the growing problem with guns and weapons and decided to do something about it for moral reasons (Bai 1999).

Stakeholder-inclusiveness

Moral leaders go out of their way to consider all stakeholders in their decision-making, to consider the implications of their decisions for all stakeholders. Whereas some managers or leaders think only in terms of transactions with economic-oriented stakeholders (suppliers, employees, owners, consumers, financiers), moral leaders employ a broad definition of stakeholders in their thinking and decision-making. Such a broader concept might bring into play special interest groups such as environmentalists, community groups and other social activist groups.

Wheeler and Sillanpää argued strongly for the notion of stakeholder inclusion in their book *The Stakeholder Corporation: A Blueprint for Maximising Stakeholder Value* (1997). They argued that, during most of the 20th century, in the United Kingdom and the USA, where their data was gathered, stakeholder-inclusive enterprises fared better than 'shareholder-first' companies. They express no doubt that stakeholder inclusion leads to better long-term business performance.

If one builds on this notion, moral leaders would subscribe to the 'principles of stakeholder management', also termed the Clarkson Principles (CCBE 1999). These principles evolved after years of discussion, by numerous scholars around the world, about the stakeholder concept. The first principle pointedly addresses our concerns here:

- Managers should acknowledge and actively monitor the concerns of all legitimate stakeholders, and should take their interests appropriately into account in decision-making and operations.

The other principles exhort managers to (CCBE 1999: 4):

- Listen to and communicate with stakeholders

- Adopt processes sensitive to stakeholder constituencies

- Recognise the interdependence among stakeholders

- Work co-operatively with stakeholders

- Avoid activities that would jeopardise the human rights of stakeholders

- Acknowledge the potential conflicts between their own role as corporate stakeholders and their legal and moral responsibilities for the interests of other stakeholders

An example of stakeholder-inclusiveness is found in the case of the Wainwright Bank and Trust Company, a US$300 million Boston commercial bank, founded in 1987 by Robert Glassman and John Plukas. If you go to the bank's website, you find that it is infused with a sense of mission in that it speaks openly of the bank's commitment 'to all its stakeholders' with a 'sense of inclusion and diversity that extends from the boardroom to the mailroom' (Kaltenheuser 1998: 11). Wainwright is a national leader in financing shelters for the homeless, and community development loans constitute one-fifth of its portfolio. Environmentalists note that the bank is a signatory to the demanding CERES (Coalition for Environmentally Responsible Economies) Principles; feminists point with pride to the fact that the bank is a signatory to the Women-friendly Workplace Pledge created by the National Organisation of Women. Socially responsible investors note that Wainwright made a major investment in Franklin Research and Development Corporation, the largest independent firm specialising in socially responsible investing.

An innovation of the bank is its 'Community Certificate of Deposit', Federal Deposit Insurance Corporation (FDIC)-insured certificates of deposit that earn competitive rates and are utilised to do good works. The funds are channelled into loans to socially responsible organisations and projects such as health service centres, breast cancer research, inner-city business development, the production of affordable housing, homeless shelters and special-needs housing, and immigration services. Founder Glassman sums up his philosophy as follows: 'I believe it is important to use the platform the Bank affords me to inform, educate, and introduce different constituencies [stakeholders] to issues of social justice' (cited in Kaltenheuser 1998: 11). This example also illustrates a passion to do right, an obsession with fairness and a strong ethical character.

Strong ethical character

The moral leader will possess a strong ethical character and will typically be courageous. This point is somewhat related to the others; however, it was felt that it ought also to be mentioned separately. Philosopher Robert Solomon (1984) has pointed out that the word 'ethics' derives from the Greek word *ethos*, meaning 'character' or 'custom'. He goes on to say that the etymology of the word 'ethics' suggests its basic concerns with

- The individual's character, including the issue of what it means to be a good person
- The social rules that govern our conduct, known by many as morality

Thus, the notion of character is inseparable from discussions of leadership ethics.

Norman Schwarzkopf, former commander of the US Central Command, and Commander of operations Desert Shield and Desert Storm during the Gulf War, has argued that 'the main ingredient of good leadership is good character' (1998: 5). He goes on to say that this is because leadership involves conduct, and conduct is determined by values. He said that 'without good character, we live in a frightening amoral world' (1998: 5).

A recent example of character on the part of a leader was seen in the case of the Omni hotel chain's decision to phase out adult movies from its hotels. Omni chairman Bob Rowling thinks that the hotel chain should not make revenue on pornography, and he had the courage, along with the company's president, to eliminate adult movies—typically a money-maker at its hotels and motels nationwide. As his justification, Rowling said that he was the father of two boys and did not think this was the kind of thing his company ought to be doing at its hotels. The move was seen by many as gutsy because pay-per-view adult movies are a profit-maker for most hotels (Yancey 2000). This example could also be thought of as principled decision-making and a passion to do right.

An obsession with fairness

Moral leaders are obsessed with being fair. They strive in everything they do to be fair. Moral leaders understand that fairness means many different things to different people and that fairness can be calculated in a variety of different ways. Moral managers strive to employ ethical due process. They want to make sure that decision-making processes as well as the outcomes of those processes are fair.

Principled decision-making

Moral leaders strive to be principled decision-makers. They think deeply about the great ethical principles of moral philosophy and work hard to employ these principles in their actions. They 'think ethically' because moral principles guide their outlook on organisational life. Many companies do not use, at least by name, the same principles that might be used by philosophers or business ethics educators; however, they may be principled nonetheless.

An example of such a company is Medtronic, a winner of *Business Ethics* magazine's important annual business ethics awards. Medtronic Inc. is a Minneapolis-based firm that makes medical devices and technologies, from pain-blocking neurostimulators and implantable drug-delivery systems to the world's most prescribed cardiac pacemakers. Medtronic has steered clear of the temptations that have befallen a number of other companies in the healthcare industry. This is a testament to the company's leadership and to a mission of committing the company to being 'the unsurpassed standard of comparison and to be recognised as a company of dedication, honesty, integrity, and service'. Medtronic's founder, Earl Bakken, wrote the above mission statement in 1960, and the company's entire culture revolves around upholding these principles.

One story that illustrates this commitment is the story of the president of Medtronic Europe who once had to deal with an ethical quandary. This president approved 'promotional funds' that found their way into the Swiss bank account of an important customer. The president pleaded with his CEO to 'let us do business the way others do'. Instead, he was fired.

In an interview, Bill George, CEO of Medtronic Inc., was asked whether his idealism compelled him to lead his industry on a more ethical path. He responded, 'The Biblical or spiritual answer is to let your light shine—be an example for others and let them see what you are doing.' It is easy to see how Medtronic and its CEO are principled decision-makers.

Another way in which companies demonstrate their principles is through value statements that are frequently posted on websites and made available to employees on a regular basis. An excellent illustration of this is the value statement of Boeing, the aircraft firm, posted on its website.[2] Its value statement articulates that in all its relationships it will demonstrate 'a steadfast commitment to', for example, leadership, integrity, quality and customer satisfaction. The statement

2 www.boeing.com

on integrity reads as follows. 'Integrity: we will always take the high road by practising the highest ethical standards, and by honouring our commitments. We will take personal responsibility for our actions, and treat everyone fairly and with trust and respect.' This statement illustrates another way in which companies exert moral leadership through the articulation of principles by which company members live.

The integration of ethics wisdom with management wisdom

Moral leaders do not see issues as 'ethics' issues or 'management' issues. They see both aspects in situations and strive to effectively integrate both considerations into their deliberations. Powers and Vogel (1980) speak of an ability to integrate managerial and moral competence. Moral issues in management do not arise in isolation from traditional business decision-making but 'right smack in the middle of it'. The scandals that major corporations have faced did not occur independently of the companies' economic activities but were embedded in a series of decisions that were made at various points in time and culminated from those earlier decisions. Excellent examples of this point include companies that have produced and sold what have turned out to be dangerous products. The tobacco industry comes to mind.

Immoral or amoral leaders see ethical decisions as isolated and independent of managerial decisions and managerial competence. Moral leaders see every evolving decision as one in which a moral perspective must be integrated into a managerial perspective.

Leaders who seek to integrate ethics wisdom with management wisdom will find ways to address social problems while fulfilling the mandate to be profitable. Such a strategy is presented as 'a new model for corporate citizenship' by the World Resources Institute (WRI) and by the Initiative for Social Innovation through Business (an initiative of the Aspen Institute). While maintaining corporate profitability, this new business strategy

> involves engaging in collaborative problem-solving, developing products that meet societal standards for labour and for environmental and human safety, building employee relationships, maximising the potential of human capital, partnering in communities and with non-profit organisations, communicating company values and standards, and reporting progress on corporate environmental and societal commitments (WRI 1999: 2).

◢ Conclusions

Moral leadership is critical for successful corporate citizenship. Of the four faces of corporate citizenship, the ethical or moral face can be the most challenging to fulfil. The transition from moral management to moral leadership is similar to the transition from management to leadership—generally. One cannot be a moral leader without first being a leader. Moral leaders possess a number of important qualities. Perhaps these qualities could be referred to as 'habits', which distinguish them from immoral or amoral leaders. Among these qualities are the following. Moral leaders have a passion to do the right thing. They are appropriately motivated. They are morally proactive—they take the initiative and are on the cutting edge of doing the right thing. They are stakeholder-inclusive. They adopt and use the stakeholder model of the organisation. They strive to be sure that all relevant stakeholders are taken into consideration. They have a strong ethical character and an obsession for fairness. Moral leaders are principled decision-makers and they know how to integrate ethical wisdom with management wisdom in all that they do.

Although recognising that very few leaders fully achieve these seven habits, it should nevertheless be stated that moral leaders achieve most of them or are a long way 'down the road' to achieving them. At a minimum, they stand as baseline standards against which leaders might be compared. In the final analysis, moreover, strong corporate citizenship is unattainable without moral leadership.

HOW AUSTRALIA'S TOP 500 COMPANIES ARE BECOMING CORPORATE CITIZENS

Mark Glazebrook
Corporate Citizenship Research Unit, Deakin University, Australia

◢ Public policy

Since 1998, Australia's Prime Minister, Mr Howard, has clearly opened up the public policy debate on corporate citizenship by outlining his vision for a more socially responsible corporate Australia by calling on business to become more closely involved with supporting the community sector through what he has described as a new social coalition. This culminated, in January 1999, into a major part of his Federal address entitled the 'Australian Way' where he described the importance of 'creating a strong, social coalition':

> Few Australians would deny the proposition that Governments alone cannot solve immense social problems. They need the help and under-standing of great community organisations, dedicated individuals and the corporate sector . . . I resolve to build a stronger social coalition, renewing my call to business both large and small to play their part. To give back to the community from which they profit, to follow the example of many genuine Australian philanthropists, to advise, to donate in cash or kind, to mentor (1999).

Within the media, this issue attracted considerable attention at the time, partic-ularly within the print media, with the headlines 'PM ups the ante on goodwill' (Grattan 1998: 4) and 'Corporates must "give for profit" ' (Evans 1998: 4) highlight-ing the Prime Minister's particular emphasis on creating 'a greater philanthropic tradition'. However, the media had also been active on this issue well before the Prime Minister's decision to make it part of his government's public policy plat-form. Major articles earlier in 1998 and back as far as 1997 stressed how corporate funding levels of charities and foundations were shrinking. In December 1997, prominent philanthropic leader Baillieu Myer headed a contingent of Australian businesspeople to the Philippines, to highlight the need for the business community to become more active in corporate philanthropy (Eccleston 1998: 10; Hartcher 1997: 1-10; Painter 1998: 1).

Although it could be argued the Prime Minister reacted in part to an already-emerging groundswell, he has maintained a consistent stance on this issue ever since, raising it again and again on 62 separate occasions across the country, choosing carefully the setting in which the message is repeated. Events where this issue has profiled heavily include those focusing on unemployment, breast cancer, drugs, families, health, indigenous and rural issues (Howard 1998, 1999).

Although this emphasis by the Prime Minister has been significant, his vision for developing a new agenda for business responsibility, through increasing acts of philanthropy and the giving of money, has been extremely limited in scope. In addition, it has been disconnected from the massive cultural and organisational changes already emerging across corporate Australia and from the vigorous debate opening up within the courts, parliament, the media and university circles about the social expectations of business. Within parliamentary circles, this debate has become fragmented and disjointed, with the Prime Minister's social coalition agenda unfolding quite separately from a range of related debates occurring elsewhere in the parliament concerning the negative impacts of business operations.

Supporting the Prime Minister's new agenda, Alan Cadman MP, when debating an amendment bill to the taxation laws aimed at increasing gift and charitable donations, said that he would like to see

> an extension of this process so that we see a rising and improving attitude towards philanthropy in Australia, so that large corporations and businesses are encouraged and given incentives from the government to take under their wings organisations that need aid and help (2000: 15,090).

Set against this perspective, parliament generally has chosen to debate corporate responsibility along much more contentious lines, which although often picked up by the media has yet to adequately challenge the shortcomings of the Prime Minister's social coalition agenda. In relation to rural issues, for example, Mr Horne MP, a member of the Labour opposition, took the government to task in relation to the massive job cuts that the government majority-owned telecommunications company Telstra had announced at the same time as recording massive profits. He went on to say that 'shedding jobs like this does very little other than make management look neater . . . and it certainly does nothing for the corporate citizenship of Telstra' (2000: 14,157). Similarly, the government came in for harsh criticism during question time over the closure of the BHP (Broken Hill Proprietary Company Ltd) steelworks in Newcastle, NSW. Assurances by workplace relations minister, Tony Abbott MP, that BHP had acted as a truly model corporate citizen during the closure served only to enrage several members of the Labour opposition, who challenged the government, saying it had not done enough to address the large number of job losses (Abbott 1999: 10,905-10).

Likewise, the recent waterfront dispute between the shipping company, Patricks Stevedores, and the union representing waterside workers, the Maritime Union of Australia, clearly raised further questions about the capacity of Mr Howard's social coalition agenda to apply to the more contentious issues of corporate responsibility, especially where these challenge his broader reform agenda: for example, industrial relations. When questioned at a press conference during the dispute about the behaviour of Patricks, Mr Howard stressed, 'I'm a Prime Minister. I don't give a running commentary on every corporate citizen of Australia' (Howard 1998).

Why, then, did his own minister, Tony Abbott, comment on BHP's corporate citizenship? Examples such as these suggest corporate citizenship and social coalition actually mean different things to the government at different times, depending on the specific message it wishes to convey. Sometimes the government considers this agenda to mean a company 'giving something back' to the community in the form of charity and philanthropy and at other times it means the need for responsible business operations, but seldom are both aspects linked together in the same debate. Government policy in this area, then, continues to contradict itself, with the Prime Minister calling on businesses to do more to support the Australian community (e.g. in the area of unemployment) while at other times accepting that job losses emerging from BHP, Telstra and the waterfront are simply part of business adjustment and represent examples of good corporate citizenship if handled well.

In recent months, however, the government has begun to lose its traditional hold on determining public policy on this issue, especially within the media. Australian businesses are no longer passive players reacting to the debate as laid out by the Prime Minister, but are choosing instead to enter the public debate with a whole new agenda of their own, challenging their own ranks, government and the rest of the community to work together in forming more inclusive public policies.

President of the Business Council of Australia (BCA), Campbell Anderson, recently outlined this new agenda in the press, indicating that business should not just get the agenda right but should help shape public policy and have an open mind to engage with all levels of the community. He believes that there is a 'great opportunity for business to assume the high moral ground by embracing and demonstrating best practice in environment, corporate citizenship and other issues' (Fox 2000a: 70). He also called on business leaders such as the chief executives of large and small companies to become more proactive in engaging with people and their concerns, changing where necessary and better communicating the thinking behind business decisions, not just ignoring the issues or 'keeping its head down' to avoid community antagonism. 'Instead of ignoring these pressures,' he said, 'business needs to join in debates and even discuss what its role in society should be' (Fox 2000a: 70).

Greg Bourne, President of BP Australia, is one prominent business leader who has taken up this challenge of moving into the public debate. In June 1999 he entered the debate by challenging the Prime Minister's social coalition agenda as concentrating too much on philanthropy (Bourne 1999). Since that time, he has continued to challenge the Prime Minister's view in the press, suggesting recently that

> when the Prime Minister first started talking about business involve-ment and philanthropy it sounded a bit like he was saying 'OK guys chuck some money over the fence, pay for your right to exist and then your obligation is over' . . . In our view [referring to BP], giving has to be done with true involvement, it would be marginalising if we were asked to contribute cash without being involved in the community in which we operate (Taylor 1999: 18).

Similarly, Professor David Birch, Director of the Corporate Citizenship Research Unit, also an author in this book, has challenged current notions of corporate citizenship as extremely limited, urging the Prime Minister

> to consider extending the debate on social coalition beyond this dis-course of helping the needy; beyond business giving back to the com-munity in which it seeks a license to operate; beyond a concentration on the individual, to recognising the huge and enormous potential that business has, and is willing to make, in establishing more significant partnerships by investing in social capital in ways that can include, but also go way beyond philanthropy or helping out the disadvantaged, to building a real social coalition—a socially cohesive Australia (1999: 15).

Barry Cusack, Managing Director of Rio Tinto, also shares this position, describ-ing its partnerships with environmental and human rights organisations as being about a desire to engage with the community and not altruism or philanthropy: 'we want to be involved in a way that gives the community and ourselves various benefits . . . we cannot lose sight that we must be adding value to our share-holders in the long term' (Taylor 1999: 19).

Addressing corporate citizenship on a more operational level, Graeme Thomp-son, the Deputy Governor of the Reserve Bank of Australia, on approving a rural bank closure, warned that alternative electronic services needed to be provided, otherwise 'banks risked being seen by disgruntled customers as bad corporate citizens' (Cornell 1998: 62).

Such is the power of this backlash that one of Australia's largest banks, the ANZ, was recently forced to reverse its decision to impose charges on child and student banking after a public outcry by political leaders and youth advocates who saw the move as a new low in corporate citizenship (Brocklehurst and Mangnall 1999).

Examples such as these clearly demonstrate a significant dimension to the corporate citizenship debate that the Prime Minister is yet to address.

Rather than waiting to be caught out by these types of issue again and again, Australian businesses have recently started to undertake serious research in the area and, importantly, to take notice of the findings. Recently, in a major national survey titled 'What Ordinary Australians Think of Big Business and What Needs to Change', respondents not only indicated an interest in the financial viability of business but also expressed a strong desire for companies to be regarded as good corporate citizens not by simply being charitable but also by balancing profits with ethics when addressing stakeholder interests (Clemenger Report 1998: 10-11).

Opinion within the business community is still divided, however, with Paul Anderson, chief executive officer (CEO) of BHP, Australia's largest mining and resources company, signalling that his company's capacity to be a generous community benefactor had probably ended. In reviewing the closure of its Newcastle plant, he questioned whether the company would continue elsewhere to fund the social impacts of its business as extensively as it had in Newcastle (Wood 1999: 1).

The first signs of business entering the public debate and changing how it relates to society has attracted some criticism, especially from within the non-government sector. Elsa Aitken, of the New South Wales branch of the National Trust, has questioned the impact this shift will have on the funding of community organisations that find it hard to align themselves to a particular corporation. She describes the Australian business culture as now based on partnerships. 'They don't see beyond their noses', she said, recalling how one company where she acted as a consultant, Westpac Bank, now talks in terms of synergy, something it feels it does not have with the National Trust. Importantly, as corporate Australia enters this new phase of defining corporate citizenship beyond philanthropy, some thought will need to be given to Elsa Aitken's warning that groups concerned with heritage or other issues viewed as limiters to business growth will find it difficult to meet this new prerequisite for synergy with business, when many company interests are currently at loggerheads with these issues (Fox 2000b: 62).

◢ Governance

In a recent study, I found evidence to suggest that corporate citizenship within Australia's top 500 companies is evolving as part of business planning and reporting, with 37 of Australia's top 500 companies (7%) now viewing corporate citizenship as central to the strategic direction of their businesses, demonstrating this commitment through vision statements, business objectives and overall performance measures for company directors (Glazebrook 1999: 122). Findings from this study also indicate 15 of these companies only took such steps in the past 12 months.

The study, examining annual reports, CEO statements and company publications over the four-year period 1995–99, identified those companies describing themselves as corporate citizens as well as how they go about putting this into practice. Australia's top 500 companies are beginning to interpret corporate citizenship as central to the way they do business and in much broader terms than does the Prime Minister Mr Howard's current focus on philanthropy. Significantly, the study also reveals that philanthropy was completely absent in the profiles of companies describing themselves as corporate citizens (see Table 9.1).

Ranking	Interpretation: issue involved	Percentage of firms
1	Governance	40
2	Ethics	30
3	Sponsorship	14
4	Stakeholders	7
5	Partnerships	5
6	Product stewardship	32
7	Environmental responsibility	1
8	Social responsibility	1
Unreported	Cause-related marketing, philanthropy, triple bottom line, sustainability	0

Note: The firms represented here are those firms in the top 500 Australian companies who regarded themselves as corporate citizens.

Table 9.1 **How Australian companies interpret corporate citizenship**

Source: author's survey

Although individual companies differ in how they go about achieving corporate citizenship, trends indicate an emergence of seven key priority areas that companies are adopting to put corporate citizenship into practice: governance, ethics, sponsorship, stakeholders, partnerships, product stewardship, environmental responsibility and social responsibility. Rather than corporate citizenship being viewed as something extra to what a business does, these findings indicate that companies are interpreting corporate citizenship as being much more central to how they do business. Changes in governance practices—making company directors and CEOs more accountable for achieving corporate citizenship, the introduction of ethical procedures and expectations and a new emphasis on valuing the importance of stakeholders (e.g. responding to the needs of employees, customers and suppliers as well as investors)—are all clear signs that corporate citizenship is increasingly being viewed as a core business activity.

For the companies moving in this direction, governance and ethics are clearly the most significant definers of what companies are doing in terms of corporate citizenship. Indeed, several major companies, including Coles Myer, MMI Insurance and BHP, now have corporate citizenship as a performance measure for the company and/or its directors. My study also revealed that companies choosing to adopt a corporate citizenship position are not just the ones with bad reputations. Companies committing to developing corporate citizenship are emerging from a cross-section of industries (Fig. 9.1), with less than half of these being brand-name companies.

During the 1990s, Australian business clearly showed an increasing interest in developing corporate citizenship within business operations. Importantly, this

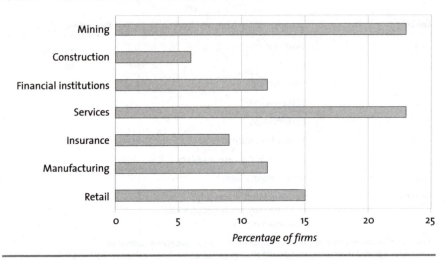

Figure 9.1 **Corporate citizenship, by industry: Australia's top 500 companies**

Source: author's survey

trend is most apparent when one examines how corporate citizenship evolved as a priority within each company from year to year. Companies such as Coles Myer, the leading retail company in Australia, evolved corporate citizenship from a minor commitment in 1995—as part of its community programme section of its annual report—to a major commitment in 1999, locating it as part of its overall vision statement and performance expectations of its board, as well as of senior management. So strongly is corporate citizenship now viewed within Coles Myer that at Coles Myer's 1999 annual general meeting, its chairman, Stan Wallis, went into considerable detail to outline to its shareholders the scope of the agenda, which ranged from charitable contributions through to how the company is meeting its operational and supplier responsibilities (Wallis 1999: 15,002).

However, current interpretations of corporate governance are expanding significantly, no longer constricted by the artificial borders of nation-states or accurate in a world that now trades and communicates globally. Governance has been used haphazardly and narrowly to describe various functions of government.

Governance as we know it is fundamentally changing in ways that the world has not witnessed before. A number of factors—including the expansion of world trade fostered by the General Agreement on Tariffs and Trade (GATT) and the World Trade Organisation (WTO), the associated private capital flows in the past 50 years and the steady shift of publicly owned business enterprises and services (bound by geographic borders) into the private sector (operating globally)—have blurred the rigid boundaries that once separated business, government and the community. For John Elkington, the issue is clear: 'we've successfully globalised capitalism but not governance' (2000). Much of what was considered to be public enterprise is now private, people are no longer described as citizens but rather as customers, and employees no longer just work hard but compete globally. Just as government is offloading public assets and modelling its operations on business, business is developing a social and environmental conscience in response to changing needs in the marketplace, taking itself more and more into the realm of ballot box government. Thus the difference between the two is being erased.

The president of the World Bank, Jim Wolfensohn, recently brought attention to this blurring of boundaries and how this is impacting on democracy. He suggested that 'a vital element in a modern democracy is modern corporate governance . . . just as with governments, firms must be run transparently; management must be accountable' (Wolfensohn 1998: 38). His view and that of the Global Corporate Governance Forum being developed in conjunction with the World Bank are moving current notions of corporate governance well beyond assurance and regulatory compliance measures. His comments suggest an elevation of corporate governance into the realm of overall governance of society. These changes extend the very basis for corporate governance significantly from what authors such as Monks and Minow (1995: 20) view simply as a relationship between government and business based purely on laws that govern the behaviour of the corporation with its stakeholders.

Legislation appears to be unable to restrict the cultural direction in which business is leading us. And laws can only ever be a 'snapshot' of society's values at any given point in time. Laws, especially corporate laws, are usually about compliance and about setting general standards, which are largely irrelevant for the more progressive companies and an 'obstacle course' for poor performers to navigate around.

Applied to the Australian context, Coles Myer, in its 1999 annual report,[1] demonstrated a clear intention to move corporate governance beyond being about legal compliance by extending its transparency provisions to include an 'objective of honest and open disclosure in dealing with stakeholders', stating that 'such disclosure may exceed statutory requirement'. Clearly, the last statement, 'may exceed statutory requirement', is quite unambiguous in its intent and is a strong indication of how this company is prepared to act beyond its legal obligations to demonstrate its corporate citizenship.

Within the banking industry, the chairman and managing director of the National Australia Bank, Don Argus, had a similar message that 'the challenge for industry leaders such as the National is to ensure that the nature and impact of the changes it is implementing, and the reasons for them, are both understood and valued by its key stakeholders'.[2]

◢ The law

It is at this point that the debate about corporate citizenship within Australia begins rather than ends. Although corporate citizenship profiles heavily in public

1 See www.colesmyer.com.au.
2 National Bank 1999 annual report, at www.national.com.au.

policy debates and especially in the media, it also has become a significant issue in a far less well-known area of activity: namely, the law. Here, corporate citizenship has less to do with broader issues of business, government and community responsibility and more to do with how corporate citizenship applies to the individual citizen or, at times, individual companies. Within Australia, the courts have examined 55 cases since 1990 that have been argued at least in part on the merits of corporate citizenship. In contrast to the rhetoric flowing through the media and parliament—rhetoric that claims to represent public opinion—the courts serve as a much more accurate social barometer, providing a unique insight into the actual public experience of the corporation in action.[3]

Issues related to corporate citizenship brought before the courts include defamation, work injury, industrial relations, administrative appeals, environmental protection, privacy, superannuation and consumer matters. So widespread are these cases that they have been heard in all court jurisdictions, in each state and territory as well as in the Commonwealth courts.

Despite this level of activity, corporate citizenship has not been afforded any specific legal recognition.[4] Courts appear to accept corporate citizenship implicitly as meaning a company of good standing, and therefore the concept is most often used in support of a company facing charges against them in relation to their practices.

As part of a personal injury case, counsel representing BHP argued

> for a sizeable reduction in the penalty otherwise applicable . . . I have in mind the considerably improved safety performance of the defendant over the period from 1995 to 1999, particularly in the rail operations area of the steelworks, and its undoubted good-standing as an industrial and corporate citizen. The defendant's commitment to occupational health and safety issues, as evidenced by its stated policy and safety performance, I think, also are in its favour in terms of mitigation. The defendant entered an early plea of guilty, it was acknowledged by the prosecutor to have 'fully and frankly co-operated in the investigatory process' and it has implemented remedial action to prevent a recurrence . . . I am of the view that those factors operate to significantly reduce what the penalty might otherwise be (*Workcover Authority v. BHP* [2000]).

Likewise, in a case regarding trade practices, counsel representing a major retailer charged with supplying faulty goods to a customer argued as one of 11 mitigating factors that the company represented a good corporate citizen and a responsible employer of a large number of employees, had a good reputation as a retailer but faced financial difficulties at that time. Despite this defence, the company was fined Aus$7,000 (*Pretorius v. Venture Stores* 1991).

In a landmark case that attempted to link the concept of corporate and individual citizenship, Caltex, an oil company, attempted to claim privilege from having to produce documents that may have incriminated the organisation. The High Court in its determination ruled that an incorporated company is not entitled to privilege (as enjoyed by individual citizens) commonly known as privilege against self-incrimination. For the court,

3 Australasian Legal Information Institute 2000, at www.austill.edu.au
4 Wheelwright 3 May 2000, personal communication.

the current widespread use of the expression 'corporate citizen' seems to owe more to the objects of the public relations industry than to the analysis of the legal concept of citizenship. But, even if an artificial entity can be regarded as a citizen [referring to a corporation], the argument based on privacy is not, in my opinion, a strong one for holding that a corporation should be able to claim the privilege (*EPA v. Caltex* [1993]).

Cases such as these suggest that corporate citizenship occupies an emerging role in the legal process, albeit one that fluctuates in interpretation by the courts. If, as the public debate suggests, more and more corporations will continue to move their business practices beyond compliance levels, one wonders if the courts are likely to take this development into account in future judgements and, if not, whether this will act as a disincentive in changing corporate behaviour.

◢ Incentives

Research into how corporate Australia is portrayed in the media, annual reports and the courts indicates that the main drivers in developing corporate citizenship credentials can be grouped into three types of incentive: accolades, imperatives and opportunities (Glazebrook 2000).

Accolades

Media research has shown that large sections of Australian business are still using acts of philanthropy and sponsorship as examples of good corporate citizenship to attract attention within the media and thus benefit from free publicity. In a study of the print media specifically, sponsorship and philanthropic programmes were by far the most reported forms of corporate citizenship. Articles of this type usually profiled an event serving as an accolade, a launch, an important day marking some particular issue or cause, or a new relationship between a corporation and a community organisation. So strong is this particular message that the press could be accused of placing greater emphasis on these types of event, as examples of corporate citizenship, particularly as they usually provide good photo opportunities and visuals, at the cost of other emerging practices (Glazebrook 1999).

Similarly, the emergence of new awards for excellence in business and community partnerships developed by the Prime Minister, John Howard, as a tangible extension of his social coalition agenda, and the trend in accolades coming from within business itself, such as the 'Perth Rotary/American Chamber of Commerce Corporate Citizen of the Year' award, indicate some companies see considerable merit in having their community activities acknowledged publicly through an award process (Mason 1999: 65).

Imperatives

In contrast, some companies are embarking on a very different form of corporate citizenship, one more attuned to responding to actual imperatives that are beginning to impact directly on their financial bottom line. Australia insurance companies, for example, are feeling the strain of huge pay-outs due to two massive storms that killed six people in the Sydney–Hobart yacht race and caused damage to 20,000 houses (Elias 1999: 1).

As David Elias suggested recently:

> The insurance industry is now asking itself the question, what if, as a consequence of global warming, storms like these become more com-monplace? But, as the frequency and speed of the big winds increase and the cost of claims reaches US$15 billion [Aus$22.8 billion] a year, they say they don't have the time to wait for answers. The insurance industry has found itself in the eye of an environmental storm and it is preparing to assume its new role as the world's ecological police (1999: 1).

So concerned is the industry that 90 large underwriters in 27 countries have offered to use their financial clout to push the industry towards the use of renewable energy sources, as part of the United Nations Environment Programme (UNEP) in Geneva that will seek to sign up insurance companies in Australia. Raymond Jones, general manager of the QBE Insurance group, Australia's sole UNEP insurance signatory (UNEP 1995), hopes that, after 'Geneva', his company will no longer be the only voice in the wilderness, particularly in Australia: 'We got involved four years ago because we wanted to be a good corporate citizen and we wanted to understand the environment as part of a good risk assessment process' (Elias 1999: 1).

With so many issues emerging for the corporate world, it is becoming crucially important to predict which industry is about to be the next 'caught out'. A visiting researcher from the USA warned the gaming industry in Australia to take notice of the experiences of another, the tobacco industry. Durand Jacobs, of the Loma Linda University Medical School, suggested on a recent trip to Australia that the industry faced class actions from gambling addicts on the same level as tobacco companies (Heggen 1999: 15).

Exploring how business can better meet these emerging imperatives has been my aim throughout my three-year doctoral study. Findings from this research indicate that lying at the core of all corporate citizenship activity is an intention by companies to compensate in some way for the social and environmental ineffi-ciencies (waste, deforestation, unemployment, etc.) of its own business opera-tions or, at times, for what other businesses and even government have created. Economists describe these costs as externalities; marketers call them uncompen-sated costs of exchange; sociologists refer to them as social costs; environ-mentalists prefer to call them environmental costs (Blau 1964: 88; Mundt and Houston 1996: 73; Perkins 1994: 239). Companies can choose from a 'smorgas-bord' of possible corporate citizenship responses. At one end of the spectrum, they may give these anomalies only superficial attention in the form of 'giving something back' through sponsorship and philanthropy; at the other end of the spectrum, they may carry out targeted triple-bottom-line ('doing it along the way') reporting. The important message in this analysis is that the true or actual cost of a company's operations may not be reflected in the price charged for its products. Consider whether $10 for a packet of cigarettes really represents the full cost of smoking. The multi-billion-dollar US pay-out by tobacco companies to compensate for the negative health and social costs associated with smoking suggests it does not. Years of ploughing millions into motor racing and other brand recognition strategies have not excluded these companies from their responsibilities as citizens. The only question is, 'Which industry is next?'

Opportunities

Although there are clear imperatives for business to respond to this agenda, there are also substantial opportunities. For example, although the concept of externalities has merit if one wishes to understand the impact of business on society, much of the literature tends to concentrate on negative or harmful components of production, neglecting the potential benefits or positive externalities arising out of relevant products. A company that successfully addresses its negative externalities combined with developing new positive or restorative externalities could join in with government in addressing relevant social and environment issues as part of their normal business operations rather than as something extra they do.

This has already been conceptualised, particularly in the environmental area, by Amory Lovins and the Wuppertal Institute under their Factor 4 (a 75% reduction in energy) and Factor 10 (a 90% reduction in energy) approaches. However, these are yet to be seriously adopted, along with social equivalents, within industry (Hawken *et al.* 1999: 11; von Weizsäcker *et al.* 1997). One company, however, that is attempting to meet this challenge is BP Australia (BPA).[5]

BPA's first phase is seeking to deliver on the 'triple bottom line' (see the left-hand side of Fig. 9.2), integrating social and environmental objectives into its overall performance (Elkington 1997). BPA's second phase takes the company radically beyond current thinking in the field of corporate citizenship and indeed business practice generally, developing a position on how it can 'shape a better tomorrow' (see the right-hand side of Fig. 9.2).[6]

The significance of BPA's approach is a desire to develop an entirely new form of corporate accountability, one that is less 'dollar-denominated' and more reflective of sustainable success. Like other companies, BPA is seeking to reduce the direct impact of its operations through triple-bottom-line performance but, unlike other companies, it intends to develop new ways it can help shape a better future through technology and forwarding thinking, reversing the effect of past impacts

---

5 Data was gathered as part of my field research within BPA, from 1999 to 2000.
6 Bourne, 3 May 2000, personal communication; Elkington 1997; Logan *et al.* 1997; McIntosh *et al.* 1998; Tichy *et al.* 1997.

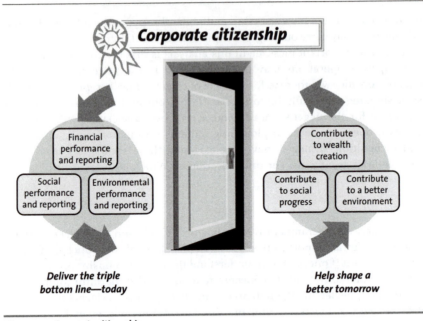

Figure 9.2 **Corporate citizenship**

and harm caused through human activity. This step clearly has risks, taking its operations into uncharted territory, but the potential benefits of developing a business model for turning an overall negative impact into a positive impact are too great to ignore.

Within this implementation, BPA, as part of the global BP Group, is adopting a radical new strategy called 'Global Social Investment'. Listed below are the criteria that drive the application of the strategy, which clearly departs from other forms of corporate citizenship strategy existing within other companies, representing greater synergy with the notion of 'venture capital' for sustainability than the usual 'arm's-length' or cause-related marketing emphasis of a community affairs approach. The strategy:

- Must have a business outcome
- Must make a meaningful contribution to society
- Should, ideally, engage employees
- Should have a positive effect on the reputation of BP

To operationalise this, BPA might choose in the future to establish new facilities in a locality left contaminated by previous industrial activity, restoring it, through use of the appropriate technology, as close as is possible to its original state.

◢ Conclusions

Corporate citizenship within Australia is clearly undergoing a period of rapid change and debate. What has not been fully appreciated, however, is just how extensively this activity permeates through every institution and aspect of Australian life. Unlike in the past, the business sector is now taking a lead role in carving out this new agenda and, significantly, is assuming the political high ground.

Although Australian business still remains diverse in how it approaches corporate citizenship, there are strong signs that some businesses are not prepared to wait for the next crisis, choosing instead to steer their organisations towards a risky but potentially more sustainable future. Even more significantly, this shift is also seeing business lobbying in areas that traditionally were counter to its own interests. Australian business has now joined the debate, joining unlikely allies such as the non-government sector in challenging the government to shape public policy to reflect issues of sustainability and governance generally. Far from being a just business imperative, corporate citizenship is now opening up a whole new debate; namely, it is asking: 'Who should contribute to democracy and the future of society?'

WHEN MULTINATIONAL CORPORATIONS ACT AS GOVERNMENTS
The Mobil corporation experience

Alejo José G. Sison
Institute for Enterprise and Humanism,
University of Navarre, Spain

◢ Multinational corporations and corporate social responsibility

Strangely, there is no agreed definition for a 'multinational corporation' (MNC). In 1976 the Organisation for Economic Development and Co-operation (OECD) published the document *Declaration and Decisions on International Investment and Multinational Enterprises* (reprinted in OECD 1997a). In this document it also employed the term 'foreign-controlled enterprises' for entities operating in one country yet owned or controlled directly or indirectly by nationals of another country. In the 1997 reprint, *OECD Guidelines for Multinational Enterprises*, the OECD states that 'a precise legal definition of multinational enterprises is not required', explaining, nevertheless, that

> these usually comprise companies or other entities whose ownership is private, state or mixed, established in different countries and so linked that one or more of them may be able to exercise a significant influence over the activities of others and, in particular, to share the resources with the others (1997a: 9).

Ironically, a major thrust was to promote 'national treatment', whereby member countries commit themselves to deal with 'foreign-controlled enterprises' no less favourably than they deal with their own enterprises. This 'non-discrimination' principle sought to mitigate differences between domestic and multinational or foreign-controlled enterprises. The OECD *Guidelines* were the first international framework for co-operation between governments and multinational enterprises.

There is a preference for 'multinational enterprise' over 'multinational corporation' in official texts. The former seems more inclusive, applicable to any kind of organisation, whereas the latter is limited to profit-seeking businesses. However, the issues considered (competition, employment and industrial relations, environmental protection) generally arise in relation to firms, not to non-governmental organisations (NGOs) (Enderle and Peters 1998). Furthermore, 'corporations' have the advantage of possessing a legal charter and state recognition, unlike 'enterprises' in general. Therefore, although 'multinational corporation', 'multinational enterprise', 'foreign-controlled enterprise' and 'transnational corporation' may be taken as synonymous, it is 'multinational corporation' (MNC) which best expresses their overall meaning.

By MNC we are to understand a company that has production and sales operations in more than one country. Why organise economic activities around an MNC? MNCs make more efficient use of capital, technology and human resources, thus contributing to the economic growth and social development of home and host countries. Usually, less developed host countries are less developed for lack of financial capital. Funds can be sourced through foreign aid or through private bank loans, but often the first is insufficient and the second too expensive. The remaining option is to welcome MNCs as bearers of foreign direct investment (FDI). MNCs are usually based in developed countries. The FDI that MNCs bring consists of money, know-how and management expertise; they build factories and offices; they provide jobs and training. Through MNCs the 'comparative advantages' of different countries are best exploited.

MNCs have evolved together in terms of their technological, economic and political environments (Dunning 1993a, 1993b; Elfstrom 1991; Vernon 1998). Three distinct phases may be identified in recent history: the first begins after World War II and extends to the early 1970s; the second continues from the end of the first period until the fall of the Berlin Wall; the third period coincides with the contemporary period of globalisation.

The first phase was characterised by the dominance of US MNCs, as a result of the US victory and the fact that, practically, its production facilities alone were intact. US MNCs did their manufacturing at home and set up subsidiaries abroad to source raw materials and to take care of exports. In due course, European and Japanese MNCs began to follow the US strategy and consolidate 'national champions'. Excluded were the Communist countries and others that, under Communist influence, pursued policies of self-reliance and import substitution, that were nationalist and isolationist and hostile to foreign capital. In the early 1970s there was a wave of 'nationalisations' of foreign-owned assets in developing host or third world countries.

The second phase began with cautious (re)negotiations among MNCs' home and host countries regarding the ownership and control of production assets. The oil crisis, the proliferation of petro-dollars and the financial debacle triggered by third world debt helped little in this regard. Nonetheless, the emerging economies of East Asia became most agreeable to the lifting of controls on trade and investment, and benefited accordingly. Trade liberalisation on regional and global levels was spearheaded by multilateral agencies in the form of the General Agreement on Tariffs and Trade (GATT).

The third phase of MNCs will be discussed in detail later. With it came the 'transnational' variant of MNCs. Unlike the traditional MNC, the operations of which run independently and are loosely co-ordinated from headquarters, the transnational corporation (TNC) carries out inextricably linked operations. In its clearest form, a TNC consists of vertically integrated units, turning out goods and services at different stages of production, in at least two countries. A conventional MNC, on the other hand, is composed of free-standing units replicated in different countries. Despite organisational differences, the sociopolitical and economic impacts of conventional MNCs and TNCs are essentially the same. They are alternative ways of pursuing resource efficiency and comparative advantages.

With the second phase of MNCs came a growing awareness of 'corporate social responsibility' (De George 1993; Hoffman *et al.* 1986; Wartick and Wood 1998). Public debate was stoked by scandals involving corruption, harmful products or hazardous wastes, and 'insider trading'. Between 1972 and 1973, for example, Lockheed, the US aviation firm, paid a US$12 million bribe to the Japanese government for the purchase of 21 Tristar jets. Certainly, Lockheed derived a profit and kept hundreds of jobs, fulfilling a 'strictly business' purpose. Furthermore, it had broken no law. But, in the end, Prime Minister Tanaka had to resign from office, his Liberal Democratic Party disgraced and US Congress impelled to pass the Foreign Corrupt Practices Act (Kotchian 1977).

By and large, business ethics arises from the realisation that the 'profit motive' and compliance with purely legal obligations are no longer sufficient justifications for a firm. There are other hidden 'costs'—environmental, human or social— that have to be met. These demands are not satisfied by mere donations; adherence to good business ethics is not so much corporate philanthropy as a thoroughly ethical way of doing business. Neither is it just the concern of individual employees or managers, but of the company as a whole, as a corporate moral agent and citizen. Good business ethics are reflected in corporate culture rather than in isolated actors or practices.

To assume a broader 'corporate social responsibility' necessarily means accepting that a firm exists not for shareholders alone but for other 'stakeholders' as well (Goodpaster 1991). Major stakeholder groups include equity owners, employees (management and staff), clients or customers, suppliers, competitors, local communities, government and even the environment and future generations. These are granted the right to participate, to the degree they are affected, in corporate decisions. Stakeholder theory underscores the fact that the firm, far from being an 'atomised' economic production unit, is actually a mini-community embedded with families, other intermediate associations and the state in civil society. Apart from the exclusive 'profit motive' of capitalist owners, there are other 'social interests' that firms should consider. The good done by the US Federal Corporate

Sentencing Guidelines of 1991 (Nagel and Swenson 1993) consists in creating legal and economic incentives for furthering 'social interests', thus effectively aligning them with the 'profit motive'.

A high point in the exercise of 'corporate social responsibility' and recognition of 'social interests' came with the agreement among MNCs to abide by the Sullivan Principles (De George 1993: 56), thereby contributing to the defeat of the South African apartheid regime in the early 1980s.

◢ From nation-state to welfare state

A world without government is a myth. If such a world ever existed it could not have gone very far. This does not mean, however, that governments and states have always come as we now know them (Held *et al.* 1999: 32-86). 'Nation-states' are a modern invention and their legal foundations were not set until the 17th-century Treaty of Westphalia (Krasner 1999: 20-25).

The main ingredients for a nation-state are land and people. Land refers to a territory enclosed by borders. For a nation-state to be viable, the land should provide sufficient resources for the populace. The people are those born in that land, or their children. Aside from birthplace and 'blood', the people of a nation-state share the same language, culture and religion. Also, they are bound by the same laws and subject to the same authorities. Thus it is hoped that, within the nation-state, people will be able to achieve their common purpose of a flourishing, inherently social, life.

The Treaty of Westphalia transformed European nation-states into self-contained units, governed by a sovereign. In theory, each nation-state was vested with autonomy in its internal affairs, promised non-interference in the internal affairs of others and was guaranteed equal treatment in the nebulous matters of international society (Krasner 1999). Inside the nation-state was a consolidation of political, economic and social structures and a concentration of power and authority, often culminating in 18th-century absolutist regimes: the sovereign embodied the state. The strict division between internal and external spheres, often justified as necessary for the defence of the state, was in truth an indispensable condition for the (self-)perpetuation of the sovereign.

The rise of liberalism in 19th-century Europe sounded the death-knell of absolutist monarchies. Tradition was no longer a source of authority in religion, nor was a divinely appointed birthright in politics. The sovereign's monopoly of power had been broken and no longer was anyone considered above the law. Power and authority was vested in the 'people', however limitedly construed. Concretely, property-owning enlightened gentlemen came to be understood as possessors of inalienable rights that the state was obliged to respect.

No matter how imperfectly, liberalism paved the way for democracy in the 20th century. The rights to decide on who should govern and how, as well as the 'political freedoms' or protection from state abuse, were extended to an ever-widening circle of citizens. The growth of cities, industrialisation and capitalism jointly influenced these developments. In due time, 'citizens' included women and workers of inferior socioeconomic status.

In its present form, the welfare state arose in response to the negative side-effects of liberal capitalism. Certainly, the untrammelled exercise of economic freedom produced enormous wealth, but this was concentrated among the few owners of capital. Workers were condemned to make do with subsistence wages or risk falling out of the economic system altogether. Such inequality caused serious upheavals by the disenfranchised classes, unable to meet their basic needs, to the point of endangering the stability of the state itself.

As a result of the Great Depression of the 1930s in the US and World War II in Europe, a new 'social contract' was brokered. The great masses of workers and poor renounced violence, as long as the state committed itself to a more equitable distribution of the social product, even at the expense of curtailing economic freedoms. The state assumed the role of providing poverty relief and converted socioeconomic equality into a primary goal. This could be achieved only through an exponential growth in bureaucracy and public expenditure. The state ended up smothering and displacing private initiative while transforming itself into the sole dispenser and guarantor of public welfare. Citizens became the state's dependants. Politicians took advantage of this patron–client relationship for their own ambitions. 'Civil rights', formerly understood as the freedoms citizens enjoy with respect to each other before the state (non-discrimination on the basis of sex, race or religion), now meant entitlements the state is obliged to provide (pensions, disability and unemployment benefits, education, healthcare, housing), the denial of which must pass strict constitutional safeguards.

Presently, the universal ideal and dominant form of state is a liberal and democratic one that assumes welfare functions in varying degrees (Rawls 1971, 1993, 1999). In theory, this entails the separation and balance of power, the rule of law, the guarantee of political and civil rights of citizens and the acknowledgement of fundamental human rights for all. The original nation-state model is breaking down as a result of demographic changes, migration and multiculturalism, among other things.

◢ Contemporary globalisation and its impacts

By 'contemporary globalisation' we understand the present trend towards the integration of national economies. Economists and historians trace its roots to half a century before World War I, when the interdependence of capital, goods and labour markets (FDI as a proportion of gross domestic product) was especially high for major European powers. Yet, considering the influence of politics and ideology on who does business with whom, one could say that globalisation did not 'take off' until after the fall of the Berlin Wall and the thawing of the Cold War in 1989. Additional enabling conditions came with advances in 'net' technologies (transport, telecommunications and computers; pre-eminently, the Internet), the liberalisation of commerce (e.g. through GATT, the World Trade Organisation [WTO], the European Union [EU], the North American Free Trade Agreement [NAFTA], the Association of South-East Asian Nations [ASEAN] and Mercosur) and the growth of MNCs.

There is hardly any trouble in identifying the characteristics, conditions, causes and chronology of contemporary globalisation. Disagreements emerge in ascertaining its end, meaning, future or purpose. There are three main schools of thought (Held *et al.* 1999: 3-10). The first is composed of the 'hyperglobalists', for whom globalisation results in the definitive triumph of the market over the state, as the ultimate framework and reference of human action (Guéhenno 1985; Ohmae 1995; Wriston 1997). In the new, cosmopolitan, market-driven civilisation, no tears are shed for the nation-state, for the market has more than competently taken over its functions of producing and distributing wellbeing.

The second school consists of 'sceptics', for whom globalisation is a myth, a mask behind which three regional blocks, the American, the European and the Asian, backed by powerful nation-states, continue to determine the course of world events (Hirst and Thompson 1996). If anything, what we have is a heightened form of 'internationalisation', where national governments have initiated— and still very much regulate and control—global exchange. The 'clash of cultures or civilisations' perspective is a variant of this view (Huntington 1996).

The third is the 'transformationalist' school, for which the only thing certain about globalisation is change: not absolute change, however, but transformation (Castells 1996; Giddens 1990; Scholte 1993). The debate is on what is transformed, into what other things, and on which things remain the same. Thence one hears talk of 'reinventing' the state and the market (extensible to MNCs), of 'restructuring' world politics and the world economy in a global civil society. The motto could very well be, to quote Lampedusa, 'something has to change, for everything to remain the same' (Lampedusa 1991).

In the next section, to advance our understanding of globalisation, and the changes it has wrought on governments and MNCs as well as on the notions of sovereignty and wealth creation, respectively, that these exemplify, I will present a study of the case of Mobil Corporation. Particularly, I will present an analysis of its trajectory, as gleaned from its external communication efforts, from the time Lucio Noto assumed the top post in 1994 until the completion of the merger with Exxon Corporation in 1999. One may be tempted to dismiss the 30-year series of opinion columns as a mere advertising gimmick, but if one is to make a fair judgement one should not reject off-hand the possibility that they express deep-seated corporate principles and management beliefs.

◢ Mobil Corporation (1994–99) and corporate global citizenship

On 1 March 1994, Lucio Noto, president and chief operating officer of Mobil Corporation, replaced Allen Murray as chairman and chief executive (Salpukas 1994). The rise of this Brooklyn-born (1938) son of Italian immigrants (his father served as secretary general of a garment workers union) is quite atypical, for he 'earned his stripes' in planning and marketing overseas rather than in explorations or in a job at US headquarters. He joined the company in 1962, was first assigned to Japan in 1968, then to Italy in 1973, and afterwards to Saudi Arabia in 1979. Throughout these postings, he built a reputation for financial 'savvy', detailed knowledge of operations, cultural sensitivity and social skills, winning himself friends among foreign government officials and industry executives. These are extremely valuable assets, since nearly two-thirds of Mobil's production comes from outside the USA, and prospection is held in such politically perilous places as Vietnam, Russia and Kazakhstan. He returned to the USA in 1985, on appointment as vice president for planning and economics.

Mobil traces its roots to John D. Rockefeller's Standard Oil Trust, organised in 1882. In 1911, the US Supreme Court found Standard Oil Trust in violation of the Sherman Act and split it into 34 companies,[1] Standard Oil Co. of New York (Socony) and Standard Oil Co. of New Jersey (Jersey Standard) among them. These two were the predecessors of Mobil and Exxon, respectively. For two decades after the break-up, Socony developed every segment of its businesses, from production and pipelines to refining and research. It also embarked on expansion projects in the USA and abroad. It acquired 45% of Magnolia Petroleum, and, in 1931, it merged with Vacuum Oil. In 1933, Socony-Vacuum entered a 50:50 joint venture with Jersey Standard, forming 'Standard-Vacuum Oil Co.' (Stanvac). Stanvac had operations in 50 countries, from East Africa to New Zealand, before being dissolved in 1962.

After World War II, Socony-Vacuum took advantage of growth opportunities in the transformation of refinery by-products into basic petrochemicals and derivatives. In 1955 it changed its name to Socony Mobil Oil, and in 1966 to simply Mobil Oil. The Arab oil embargo and the Iran revolution in the 1970s disrupted supplies and produced extreme price hikes. In consequence, other countries implemented conservation measures and explored alternative energy sources. Mobil Corporation, which had absorbed Mobil Oil as a wholly owned subsidiary in 1976, escalated prospections outside of the Middle East, into the North Sea, the Gulf of Mexico and parts of Africa and Asia. By the early 1980s oil prices had already fallen.

For the remainder of the 20th century the petroleum and petrochemical sector could be described as 'low-price' and 'low-margin': in 1998, crude oil registered prices similar to the pre-embargo levels of the 1970s. US and European markets

1 www.exxonmobil.com/emhistory

have matured, and competition in technology, productivity and efficiency have reached cut-throat levels. Regulations against monopolistic practices and environmental harm have become more stringent. In response, in the 1990s companies resorted to staff and operations cutbacks (between 1989 and 1994, Mobil laid off 15,000 workers and shed Montgomery Ward and the Container Corporation) as well as entering into partnerships (in 1996 Mobil combined its European refining and marketing operations with British Petroleum). When these proved insufficient, companies turned to mergers. In August 1998, British Petroleum (BP) bought Amoco for US$48 billion, and by late November of that year, Exxon and Mobil announced their US$77 merger. Shortly afterwards, France's Total said it was buying Belgium's Petrofina for US$13 billion. In a follow-up move, BP Amoco declared another merger with Atlantic Richfield (Arco) in April 1999. But, before analysing from an integrative business ethics viewpoint the issues behind the Exxon–Mobil merger, let us return to Mobil's corporate social responsibility record during the Noto years.

Mobil's former Internet homepage contained a corporate overview and an index of Op(posite)-Editorial advertisements. On the upper, right-hand corner of the index page was a link that permitted the visitor to send her or his views to members of the US Congress. These articles, expressing corporate stands on issues critical to business, the community and the world at large, began in 1970 as a 'dialogue with the American people' (for a list of advertorials, see the Appendix on page 181). Given Mobil's and the USA's prominence, their relevance cannot be ignored. The articles were published in the *New York Times* and other US and international journals.

The OECD, in its 1997 *Guidelines for Multinational Enterprises*, lists seven crucial areas in the relationship with states:

- Disclosure of information
- Taxation
- Employment and industrial relations
- Environmental protection
- Financing of the arts
- Science and technology
- Competition

All these areas, and more (e.g. politics), have been covered by the Mobil 'advertorials'. What is surprising is not that Mobil speaks out with one corporate voice—obviously, important corporate interests are at stake in environmental policies. What requires explanation is why Mobil makes a statement on such public issues as civil justice reform, regulatory improvement, trade sanctions and corruption. The position it assumes and its reasoning are secondary to the fact that, seemingly, Mobil has 'got out of bounds', behaving as a state-like political actor.

Disclosure of information

The OECD disclosure requirement concerns information on the structure, activities and policies of an MNC. Minimum financial data may be legally required, although this is often insufficient for the host country's planning purposes. Neither does it favour an MNC's long-term commitment or any positive involvement with the community.

Through the advertorials, Mobil informs about its products, itself and its industry (Mobil 1995: 14–16; 1996: 11, 12; 1997: 14, 28; 1999: 48–50).[2] These talk about gasoline prices getting lower (adjusted for inflation) as a result of improved manufacturing, distribution and marketing systems and about taxes getting higher. The story is similar for petrochemical derivatives such as asphalt, paint solvents and additives and for ingredients for food, medicine and clothing (Mobil 1996: 44; 1997: 12).

Articles refer to Mobil's 'ripple effect' in wealth creation (1994: 16), its international partnerships and 'global citizenship' (1995: 32; 1996: 34, 50; 1998: 56). Sometimes, these take a defensive stance regarding, for instance, the failed Santa Barbara onshore drilling project (1996: 7). They may take a position against moves to disqualify major oil producers from US Congress financial relief (1994: 40; 1999: 9, 29). Alternatively, they may clarify the misconception that companies control the world's oil and gas reserves (1996: 39).

Finally, columns explain Mobil's understanding of 'corporate philanthropy' (1998: 17), its contribution to disaster relief (1998: 50; 1999: 4, 13) and its collaboration with not-for-profit NGOs (1997: 29, 52; 1998: 1, 51, 54; 1999: 35, 41, 46, 47).

Taxation

The 1997 OECD *Guidelines* urge MNCs to provide information for a correct tax assessment and to refrain from transfer pricing not in conformity with the 'arm's-length' standard. Previously, we have referred to taxes being a high, fixed cost of gasoline pump prices (1998: 10, 53). Mobil has lobbied for the repeal of the 'alternative minimum tax' (1995: 37) and against the immediate taxation of foreign profits (1997: 15; 1999: 28). The articles call for streamlined tax procedures (1995: 27) and a balanced budget (1995: 41). They argued against the subsidies electric cars receive and against state mandates for 'zero-emission vehicles' for heavily distorting the market (1994: 37, 38).

In 1998, however, Mobil settled a lawsuit alleging that it had underpaid the US Treasury by about US$40 million on royalties for drilling on federal land (Lewis 1999). The suit was brought to court by Project on Government Oversight, which received nearly US$1.2 million under the Federal False Claims Act. Apparently, an official from the Interior Department and another from the Department of Energy

---

2 Lists of the Mobil advertorials for the period 1994–99 are provided in the Appendix on page 181 and are identified by year and number.

partook of the rewards at $350,000 each. A year later, the Justice Department began investigations on whether the payments constituted a bribe, an illegal gratuity or improper outside income.

Employment and industrial relations

Concerning employment and industrial relations, the 1997 OECD *Guidelines* admonish MNCs to respect the right of employees to associate and be represented by unions, to upgrade the skills of local labour, to be fair in hiring, discharge, pay and promotion policies and to observe standards no less favourable than those of comparable employers in the host country.

Mobil editorials promote equal opportunity and diversity in the workplace through support of labour organisations (1994: 6, 14; 1996: 51). They also voice concern over social security issues such as retirement pensions and healthcare, given an ageing population (1994: 22–25; 1996: 9; 1999: 3). Although universal access to healthcare is a priority, this does not imply government provision nor price controls; private enterprise and market mechanisms should take the lead, with the state making up for the remainder. The articles distinguish between those who are uninsured by choice and those who simply cannot afford health plans (despite paying, indirectly, through taxes, for others). People who cannot afford health plans are the target beneficiaries of state subsidies.

Editorials rallied behind the Health Insurance Reform Act of 1995, which increases the portability of employer-sponsored health insurance (1996: 9). On occupational safety and tort law, although self-congratulatory about its record (1994: 41; 1997: 25), Mobil strongly advocates the limitation (or elimination) of joint liability, punitive damages and 'non-use value' damages (1995: 7, 12).

Nevertheless, there could be some incongruity between this apparent 'people (employee)-first' attitude and the US$2.8–4.0 billion expected merger savings to be financed by the 9,000 lay-offs from the 80,000 and 40,000 employees of Exxon and Mobil, respectively (Myerson 1998; Myerson and Salpukas 1998a).

Environmental protection

In the 1997 OECD *Guidelines* MNCs receive a mandate to assess the environmental impact and health-related consequences of their activities. They are also encouraged to minimise through education and training the risk of accidents and to co-operate with local authorities when untoward incidents occur.

Mobil has dedicated the greatest number of columns to environmental protection: the 'Clearing the Air' series (1994: 33–39; 1995: 1–4; 1996: 29–31), the 'Kyoto Protocol' series (1997: 10, 27, 32, 34, 43–47, 49–51; 1998: 6, 16, 21, 40, 47) and the 'Climate: Technology and Carbon Dioxide Emissions' series (1999: 17, 19, 30–34). These endeavoured to separate fact from fiction about air and water quality (1995: 39, 40), to objectively consider the economic impact of the greenhouse gases emission control strategies (1999: 15) and to inform about Mobil's and the sector's efforts, from the reduction of emissions (1994: 4), the development of lubricants for improved engine efficiency (1994: 27), the funding of hydrocarbon fuel research (1998: 31), to reforestation (1996: 26; 1999: 25).

Since 1995, Mobil has published yearly an 'Environmental, Health and Safety Performance Report'. It has also been a major actor in the formulation of US energy and environmental policy (1994: 17; 1996: 16, 18–21), with mixed feelings about the Department of Energy's 'Domestic Natural Gas and Oil Initiative' (1994: 5), complaining about its disproportionate contribution to the 'Superfund' for toxic waste clean-up (1996: 10) and being, on the whole, critical of the Environmental Protection Agency's policies in favour of the ethanol-fuelled car (1994: 3, 9, 13, 15, 17, 21, 28, 31, 43; 1996: 38; 1997: 2, 5, 6, 9, 20) and the electric car (1994: 2, 11, 42; 1995: 17–23; 1996: 3, 15, 48) policies.

The sea has also been an object of attention (1994: 26, 32), through efforts to make offshore platforms friendly to coral reefs (1994: 1; 1997: 19) and the building of double-hull carriers (1994: 10; 1996: 32; 1997: 7).

Financing the arts

Since the 1970s, Mobil has sponsored the Masterpiece Theatre programme (1996: 37; 1997: 3, 37; 1998: 32, 49). It has also funded the Pegasus Literary Prize since 1977 (1994: 44; 1995: 42; 1999: 42) and has supported various museums, monuments and exhibits (1994: 20; 1997: 21, 40, 53; 1998: 3, 29; 1999: 21).

Not everyone, however, is comfortable with this generous flow of corporate 'soft money' even for non-partisan, altruistic uses as education. Mobil's sponsorship of shows at the National Gallery in Washington, where Capitol Hill officials are invited to black-tie dinner openings, has been criticised as unfair business practice (Apple 1997).

Science and technology

Regarding science and technology, the 1997 OECD *Guidelines* ask MNCs to contribute, to the extent allowed by industrial and intellectual property rights, to the know-how of host and home nations.

Advertorials have expressed the need for improved economics (1994: 45), reading (1998: 30) and maths and science (1997: 1; 1998: 9) education and have fought against gender, minority and other biases (1994: 18, 30; 1998: 2, 55; 1999: 5, 36). They have applauded the 'Goals 2000' Bill of 1994, which aims to promote national educational standards in the USA (1994: 46; 1995: 31). A three-pronged approach concerning teachers (1997: 48; 1998: 13), parents (1997: 4; 1998: 15) and schools (1996: 14, 47; 1998: 12; 1999: 8) has been advocated. Columns have backed the 'Ed-Flex' Bill, the Elementary and Secondary Education Act of 1999 and the principle that money should be spent in instruction instead of administration (1999: 11).

The articles have served to keep abreast of computer-aided prospecting (1996: 45), flexible drilling (1997: 13) and of compositional modelling and biomimetic refining (1996: 46; 1997: 23, 1998: 37, 41). They have also rallied support for fuel–vehicle research (1998: 11, 42; 1999: 20, 23, 24) against government-imposed, tax-subsidised electric cars (1995: 45; 1996: 13). They have spoken of the benefits of the use of vehicles fuelled by liquefied natural gas (1997: 8; 1998: 44).

The articles have endorsed the use of VTS 2000 port traffic management systems (1996: 28). Last, they have afforded insights on the significance of the Internet (1995: 48), NASA's Mars Pathfinder (1997: 30) and the anticipated Y2K (Year 2000) computer problem (1999: 38).

Competition

Mobil articles have strongly supported free trade (1995: 24–29; 1996: 23–25, 36, 40; 1998: 18–20, 22, 24), NAFTA (1994: 8; 1997: 41), GATT and the WTO (1994: 12, 19, 29; 1997: 11; 1998: 52, 1999: 43), co-operation with the EU (1995: 49), the IMF (1998: 8), participation in the Davos World Economic Forum (1998: 7) and in local and international business councils (1996: 35; 1999: 16, 45).

Through the 'Sanctions Debate' (1994: 47; 1996: 42; 1997: 18, 22, 24, 26, 31, 38, 39; 1998: 5, 34; 1999: 10). Mobil has rejected unilateral trade sanctions and secondary boycotts on environmental, labour, human rights and political grounds, against countries such as Indonesia, Saudi Arabia, Nigeria, China, Iran, Libya, Iraq and Vietnam (1996: 17, 41; 1998: 28, 36, 43, 46, 48; 1999: 6, 14, 18, 22, 26, 40, 44, 51). Mobil finds these measures detrimental to its own global competitiveness, aside from believing such measures to be most harmful to the very people they are intended to help. It favours 'constructive engagement' instead. Throughout the years, Mobil has run an 'International Partners' series in the United Kingdom, Singapore, Norway, Kazakhstan, Venezuela, Equatorial Guinea, Canada and Qatar, among others (1995: 32–35, 38, 43, 44, 46; 1996: 1, 2, 5, 22; 1997: 16, 42, 1998: 4, 14, 25, 26, 33, 35; 1999: 12, 37, 39).

Politics

With reference to the involvement of MNCs in domestic and foreign politics, the 1976 OECD *Declaration* establishes three safeguards. The first, the 'national treatment' principle, has already been discussed. The second, the 'International Investment Incentives and Disincentives' instrument, purports to improve co-operation on measures affecting international direct investment. The third is the 'Conflicting Requirements' instrument. While bilateral state meetings may at times prove more effective, the OECD nevertheless provides a multilateral alternative through its International Investment and Multinational Enterprise Committee. This Committee acts as an intermediary by notifying parties, examining issues (exceptions to 'national treatment') making proposals and adopting decisions, with the assistance of the Business and Industry Committee and the Trade Union Advisory Committee. Such decisions are open to accession by the EU.

Some advertorials have gone as far as setting legislative agendas for the US Congress. The 'Sensible Solutions' series (1995: 5–13, 30, 36, 47; 1996: 8; 1997: 33, 35; 1998: 38, 39, 56) suggested: a tax policy overhaul, the reduction of government size, regulatory reform (cost–benefit analysis), civil justice reform, presidential line-item veto for trade laws and a balanced budget. In 1996 Mobil pushed for a review of entitlement programmes and education policies (1996: 49; 1996: 27); while in 1999, among the 'national priorities', it cited fixing the international financial system (1999: 1, 2, 27). Articles also encouraged participation in elections (1996: 33, 43; 1998: 45).

Nigeria

In 1996, Mobil prided itself in reinvesting US$5 million annually in Nigerian communities, about one-third of the total contribution from the US Agency for International Development (USAID). By 1998, the figure was up to US$8 million, mostly going to the Eket region or 'Mobiland', an area of 100 square miles, where Mobil has effectively become the local government, providing water, electricity, roads, hospitals, schools and jobs. Its investments amounted to US$2.5 billion, and the Ubit offshore platform, pumping 250,000 barrels a day, was its largest single production unit.

On 12 January 1998 a 24-inch offshore pipeline snapped, releasing 40,000 barrels of oil into the Niger Delta. Thanks to the fiercely secretive regime of General Sani Abacha, which received 70% of oil revenues, the news was silenced. The hanging of Ken Saro-Wiwa in 1995, into which Royal Dutch Shell reluctantly got dragged, received full coverage, however (Moldoveanu *et al.* 1999a, 1999b). A combination of factors—such as the high quality of Nigerian crude (unusually sulphur-free and light), favourable wind and sea conditions—helped alleviate the crisis (Cohen 1998). After having received initial claims of US$4.5 billion, the spill cost Mobil only around US$40 million: US$10 million for the clean-up, and US$30 million in settlements (Cohen 1998).

Discussion

Such was the state of affairs in Mobil, from the global corporate citizenship viewpoint, until its merger with Exxon. Earlier, I alluded to some reasons behind this strategic move—the low price of oil and the high cost of exploration drove companies to refuge in scale. However, the determining factor was the dismal performance of oil shares compared with new technology and industrial stocks (Gilpin 1998; *Economist* 1998). Between 1989 and 1999, oil firms have consistently destroyed shareholder value, with returns on capital lower than cost, to the point that it became cheaper to buy reserves at Wall Street than to drill for oil oneself. It was thought that the best way to improve on returns was to expand from the mature markets of Europe and North America into far riskier and expensive places such as the Caspian Sea, West Africa and China (*Economist* 1999a, 1999b, 1999c).

With close to US$80 billion in stock and US$204 billion in sales in December 1998, Exxon Mobil became the world's largest corporation (Myerson and Salpukas 1998b). The merger was done through a 'pooling of interests', where Exxon shareholders would own 70% and Mobil shareholders 30% of the combined corporation.

General, chemical and 'upstream' (exploration and production) headquarters would be in Texas, whereas 'downstream' (refinery and marketing) headquarters would be in Virginia. Lee Raymond, with a reputation for being an unrelenting cost-cutter and efficient technician, became the chairman, chief executive officer and president of Exxon Mobil; Lucio Noto, the born salesman, able diplomat and power politician, became the vice chairman (Salpukas 1998). On 27 May 1999 the merger received shareholder approval, on 29 September the European Commission gave the go-ahead and on 30 November of the same year the final nod from the US Federal Trade Commission was given (Labaton 1999).

◢ Cues for global governance from the Mobil experience

I have based this study on Mobil as an example of a contemporary global US MNC. It has gone beyond legal obligations and profit-seeking goals to champion social responsibilities assigned by different stakeholders. By holding the content of advertorials against the OECD checklist, it has been found that Mobil has pursued its objectives in a manner reminiscent of governments and states—not only because of its resources and organisation (US$43 billion assets and 41,500 employees in 1998) but also because of the breadth and depth of its concerns and influence (operations in 140 countries).

Without being a government, a state, an international body of states or a worldwide NGO, but precisely by being a global MNC, Mobil has exercised global governance. Unlike Westphalian nation-states, Mobil has never claimed independence from, nor has it ever given up involvement in, the state where it has operated. It owes its existence to the laws of states, and its history has been marked by state intervention: from the US Supreme Court mandated break-up of Standard Oil Trust in 1911, through the Saudi Arabian Aramco nationalisation of the 1970s, to the Exxon merger in 1999 (with divestitures imposed by the EU and the US government). Mobil may own land, but only as a state franchise, and its employees remain subject to state laws. It has never appropriated security or defence functions, leaving the state's monopoly on legitimate violence intact. Neither has it ever collected taxes, nor issued its own money. But it has definitely played a role, sometimes a leading one, in diplomacy and in national policies of home and host countries.

Not being a state for lack of sovereignty, Mobil has, however, fulfilled state functions, such as the providing 'public goods'. It has done this in four ways. First, it has fulfilled state functions through its involvement in relief, welfare and educational (including research and development [R&D]) programmes. Second, it has offered environmentally friendly products and services (the price of which may be considered as 'user fees') that contribute to human wellbeing. Third, it has provided jobs, salaries and employee benefits (healthcare, pensions). Last, it has created shareholder wealth. Therefore, albeit conditioned by its hierarchical corporate structure, Mobil has behaved like a welfare state.

How far does Mobil go in terms of the liberal-democratic values of welfare states? Literature has championed diversity, open communication, trust and fair treatment; for US stakeholders, legal safeguards for political and civil rights are in place. However, guarantees do not apply to non-US stakeholders without access to US courts. It appears as if, in their cases, for the time being, economic benefits override political, civil and human rights. The resurrection of the 1789 Alien Tort Law, by which US firms may be sued at home for offences overseas, would be helpful (*Economist* 1999d). Otherwise, one will be mixing business with politics, or imposing one's values. Whether economic engagement is strategically more effective than embargoes in democratising oppressive regimes is still an open question. Equality is also somewhat challenged by managerial hierarchy and capitalist ownership; but we could probably assume their legitimation through the post-World War II 'social contract'.

Perhaps the biggest problem of MNC global governance is how to assure legitimacy—that is, how to achieve the free and informed consent of everyone reasonably affected ('stakeholder democracy'). It is not just a matter of determining different conflicting stakeholder interests but is one of brokering a workable agreement based on trade-offs: 'corporate governance' (Charkham 1995). This is accomplished at the highest level by the board, whose members represent various corporate constituencies. Certainly, the rights of states, owners, workers, communities and so on should be upheld and their preferences be taken into account. But once this is done, measures for maximum shareholder participation and stakeholder access in decision-making should be adopted. Good corporate governance is aided by a code of ethics that delves into the mission, function, composition and structure of the board. Best practice suggests a group of no more than 20 people—including non-executive directors and people independent of the corporation—with varied professional backgrounds, divided into operating committees and led by someone other than the chief executive officer. The group is then tasked with the oversight of a 'triple bottom line' (people, planet and profits). Advanced information and telecommunication facilities should serve not the concentration and abuse of power but the promotion, through transparency of the above-described 'democratic' purpose.

Earlier, I spoke of the transformational effect of globalisation. On the plus side of the 'globalisation ledger' (ATK/GBPC 2000) are improvements in political freedom and civil rights and growth in social spending (health and education). On the negative side are worsening corruption and pollution. For the new breed of global MNCs, this could be their most valuable contribution: like a state, it may increase a people's overall welfare, but without recourse to coercion or force; like a firm, it will engage in the efficient production of goods and services, but with democratic accountability. Good corporate governance and adherence to multilateral regimes as the OECD, WTO or Kyoto Protocol (albeit through governments) could certainly help in attaining such goals.

◢ Appendix: Mobil advertorials

The following advertorials (or articles) cited in text were to be found on the Mobil website, at (Exxon) Mobil Corporation, www.exxonmobil.com. Citations in text are by year and number.

1994

1	'Full fathom five'
2	'California dreaming (still)'
3	'They're baaack . . .'
4	'Some of the brightest lights in American business . . .'
5	'Let's get back to basics'
6	'The new faces of American business'
7	'Reasoned regulation'
8	'The economic Olympics'
9	'Adding voices'
10	'The Eagle has launched'
11	'Coming soon: the alternative fuel of the future'
12	'Going to bat for GATT'
13	'An improving environment'
14	'The job corps: working for 30 years'
15	'Adding (more voices)'
16	'When ripples make waves'
17	'33/50: an experiment that works'
18	'Mixed messages are bad business'
19	'Let's not forget GATT'
20	'A tour at sea'
21	'A matter of opinion'
22–25	'The health care debate'
26	'The coast (should be) clear'
27	'The death of a legend'
28	'When is a deal, a deal?'
29	'Motherhood, apple pie and GATT'
30	'It's a chance to change the world'
31	'When is a fact, a fact?'
32	'Ready, willing and able. If needed'
33–39	'Clearing the air'
40	'Excuse us?'
41	'Reinventing the wheel'
42	'Alternative fuels: the jury's still out'
43	'Future (sticker) shock'
44	'A rare find . . . in Turkish'
45	'A, B, C, D, Economics'
46	'The gift'
47	'Rules of the game'

1995

1–4	'Clearing the air'
5–13	'Sensible solutions'
14–16	'An interesting industry'
17–23	'The hidden price tags'
24–29	'The global economy'
30	'A lost opportunity'
31	'The challenge for tomorrow's employees'
32–35	'International partners'
36	'Unfinished business'
37	'Reforming the alternative minimum tax'
38	'Oh, Canada!'
39, 40	'The environment . . . better than you think'
41	'A balanced budget: where there's a will, there's a way'
42	'Latin America's newest voice'
43	'Kazakstan: a good investment climate'
44	'Qatar: pearl of the Arabian Gulf'
45	'The evidence keeps mounting'
46	'The summer of '85'
47	'Edmund Burke'
48	'Caught up in the Web'
49	'A trans-Atlantic agenda'

1996

1	'Norway: beyond the fjords'
2	'Equatorial Guinea: a bright spot on the African continent'
3	'Car crazy: a hard habit to break'
4	'Vietnam: building lasting bridges'
5	'Venezuela revisited'
6	'Sanctions: the last resort'
7	'A clear view of uncertainty'
8	'Opportunity lost, opportunity (re)gained'
9	'Healthcare reform: let's not kill a good thing'
10	'America: it's time to clean up our act'

THE WORLD'S BUSINESS
The United Nations and the globalisation of corporate citizenship

Jonathan Cohen
United Nations Association of the USA

The end of the Cold War and the acceleration of globalisation have brought the tremendous growth of markets and led to a dramatic increase in the number and power of transnational corporations (TNCs), which have far outstripped the jurisdiction and ability of national governments to exert effective authority over them. Whereas 7,000 TNCs existed in 1970, their number grew to more than 53,000 by 1998 (French 2000: 33). The United Nations (UN) stands as the only truly global inter-governmental organisation with a comprehensive mandate that can take the lead on corporate citizenship and harness the power of TNCs and globalisation on issues such as human rights, labour standards and the environment. Business and the UN, however, have traditionally engaged in an adversarial relationship.

The UN has transformed itself from an institution previously known for being caught up in Cold War-wary attitudes toward business. Gone are the days when pitched battles were regularly fought in the UN General Assembly over a 'new international economic order' (NIEO), which called for developing nations to be able to nationalise and expropriate foreign-owned property, and when the UN had a Centre for Transnational Corporations that was less than business-friendly (Bennett 1984: 244). One of the few current sources of contention between the UN and business is the blistering attacks on the tobacco industry by the World Health Organisation (WHO), which has been developing a framework convention on tobacco control. A distinction is made here between UN agencies and UN member states, which have been known to rail against corporations from time to time.

Today, the UN constellation of 30 agencies and over 50,000 employees is engaged in an all-out courting of the private sector that in less than a decade has resulted in dramatic increases in partnerships between the two. The globalisation and embrace of corporate citizenship is spreading through the work of the UN. The UN now serves as a central international forum capable of formalising relationships between governments, business and non-governmental organisations (NGOs) as well as bringing together leading experts to further the field as a whole. The concept of corporate citizenship—defined as the practice of a corporation's direct responsibilities to employees, shareholders, customers, suppliers and to the communities in which it conducts business and serves markets—is inherently universal and consequently requires a universal institution as its champion (Regelbrugge 1999: 10). The UN, however, will need to form partnerships with business carefully in order not to jeopardise its credibility and reputation.

The UN can be characterised as having undergone three phases of development with regard to its relationship with business. Its development may be described in terms akin to those used in Jörg Andriof and Chris Marsden's (2000) framework for the development of corporate citizenship as a whole:

- Awakening
- Engaging
- Networking

The awakening in phase 1 involved a sea change in the internal culture of the UN with respect to its attitude toward business. Following the new UN approach being accepted by the 'first movers' in leadership positions the floodgates of engagement are currently open in phase 2. The next step in phase 3 will be to manage the process of engagement with business internally and externally to fulfil the UN's mandate more effectively, with clear systems in place to choose partners, train staff, define objectives and measure progress.

Business has been involved with the UN since its inception. In fact, business and NGOs joined the 51 nations that gathered in San Francisco, CA, in 1945 to sign the United Nations Charter, and expected to be part of a tripartite relationship on behalf of peace and development. Despite the Cold War, the UN and business worked together, but primarily in sectors where common international standards were needed. Anyone who has eaten food harvested or processed abroad or used prescription drugs manufactured by transnational pharmaceutical companies has benefited from standards set by the UN Food and Agriculture Organisation and the WHO, respectively. The world body now seeks a new partnership with business to actively fulfil the mandate of the world body by 'reducing poverty, promoting environmentally sustainable growth and extending the benefits of globalisation to the poorest countries' (UNJIU 2000, citing UNOPS 2000b).

◢ The United Nations and corporate citizenship

The strengths of the UN with regard to its work on corporate citizenship are its global reach, its constellation of agencies, which cover a vast array of issues related to a progressive mission, its inter-governmental nature, numerous communication vehicles in the world's major languages as well as institutional credibility, particularly with the developing world.

Some 189 member states currently make up the UN, covering every geographical area on the planet. Although this world body's global nature makes it ideal to work with TNCs, its network of country offices also has the potential to reach large numbers of small and medium-sized enterprises (SMEs). The UN Development Programme (UNDP), for example, has 132 country offices and serves more than 170 countries and territories around the world (UNDP 2000). UNICEF (UN Children's Fund), carries out programmes in 138 countries (UNDPI 1995: 24). Also, NGOs that are accredited with the UN work closely with UN agencies and offer opportunities for multi-sector partnerships.

One model for UN–business interaction is the International Labour Organisation (ILO). The ILO, which was founded in 1919 and predates the UN, is unique among UN agencies in that its decision-making structure is tripartite, with representatives of workers, employers and governments participating and voting (UNDPI 1995: 74).

Some of the many issues in which the UN boasts expertise, which makes it ideal to foster multi-sector partnerships, include agriculture, cities, crime, drugs, education, health, human rights, intellectual property rights, international law, labour, landmines, NGOs, outer space, sustainable development and women. Also, the UN has the ability to forward issues across the world's major languages—English, Spanish, French, Russian, Arabic and Chinese—through extensive translation services, print, radio, television and the Internet.

As an inter-governmental organisation, the UN has the ability to forward corporate citizenship by working not only with business but also with government, by, for example, calling for stronger regulatory frameworks and use of incentives to encourage socially responsible behaviour.

The popular perception about the UN is that it primarily works on peacekeeping. In fact, less than 30% of UN activity is devoted to peacekeeping. The majority of its work focuses on development and humanitarian assistance. In doing so the UN works on an impartial basis by not favouring any national or commercial interest. Developing countries have a leadership role and stake in the process of the UN's non-peacekeeping work. As a result of these factors, the UN is able to earn respect from its constituents, particularly in the developing world (UNDPI 1998: 15-16). As domestic markets in the developed world tend to be competitive, making sales growth difficult, the developing world offers new markets, which the UN can help access as it seeks to foster corporate citizenship principles in those markets (Kell and Ruggie 1999). The UN's credibility allows it to play the pivotal role of broker.

The UN is the only organisation that boasts such an extensive global reach, system of agencies, broad technical expertise, language capability and credibility, making it an ideal central hub for corporate citizenship.

◢ Phase 1: the awakening

The UN Secretary-General, Kofi Annan, is responsible for redefining the UN's relationship with business. Shortly after taking office in 1997, he declared the importance of this relationship as well as plans for engaging with business (Annan 1997). The Secretary-General subsequently announced in a speech at the World Economic Forum (WEF) in Davos, Switzerland, a few months later, that a 'fundamental shift' had occurred at the UN that signalled that the world body understood that peace and prosperity required partnerships between government, business and the non-governmental sector (UNJIU 2000: 5). This declaration was intended as much for UN personnel as the business world, because Annan had staked the future of the organisation on transforming its culture in order to work with business to forward the UN's mission.

One year later, also at the WEF, the Secretary-General called for a global compact between business and the UN on the issues of human rights, labour standards and environmental practices. These three issues were chosen because they are

> the areas in which universal values have already been defined by international agreements, including the Universal Declaration of Human Rights, the International Labour Organisation's Declaration on Fundamental Principles and Rights at Work, and the Rio Declaration of the United Nations Conference on Environment and Development (Annan 2000a).

Subsequently, a new UN Global Compact website (www.unglobalcompact.org) was launched in January 2000 at WEF. The website stands as a voluminous and growing resource for information concerning corporate citizenship, with sections detailing corporate citizenship principles, translating from principles to practice, profiles of partners and initiatives, information profiles of more than 180 countries as well as a review of literature on globalisation and news updates.

Business has responded favourably to the Secretary-General's overtures. A meeting was held in February 1998 between the International Chamber of Commerce (ICC) and the UN at which two main areas of co-operation were agreed upon. The first was establishing an effective regulatory framework for globalisation, including investment, capital markets, competition, intellectual property rights and trade facilitation. The second was raising the productive potential of the least developed countries by building up the private sector and encouraging foreign investment (ICC/UN 2000). Despite the fact that the ICC has held consultative status with the UN through the Economic and Social Council (ECOSOC) since 1946, relations between the two institutions have been marked by a past of mutual suspicion and periodic antagonism until after the end of the Cold War (ICC/UN 2000).

The motivations for the UN and business, respectively, to enter into these new partnerships are identical to those of NGOs and business. SustainAbility, a British strategy consultant, cites the following motivating factors for NGOs, which also applies to the UN (Elkington and Fennell 1998: 50):

- Growing interest in markets as vehicles to fulfill the organisation's mission
- Disenchantment with government as provider of solution
- Need for more resources, such as funding, as well as technical and management expertise
- Credibility of business with government
- Cross-fertilisation of thinking
- Access to supply chains, and
- Greater leverage

Motivations for business include:

- Markets
- NGO [read 'UN'] credibility with the public on issues and priorities
- Cross-fertilisation of thinking
- Desire to head off negative public confrontations
- Desire to engage stakeholders

With an American-educated Secretary-General leading the way, the UN transformed its internal culture in the latter half of the 1990s, through a series of policy changes and communications events, into an entity that aims to work with rather than against business to fulfil its mandate. The three issues of environmental practices, labour standards and human rights stand as the pillars of this new relationship, rooted in clearly defined international agreements. The international business community, for its part, has responded to the UN's overtures and has engaged in increasing numbers of activities with the world body that represent positive corporate citizenship practices.

◢ Phase 2: engaging

The Engaging Phase of the UN–business relationship could also be characterised as opening the floodgates. Box 11.1 provides a brief sketch of the steady drum-beat of UN–business activity that has taken place in 2000 alone. The following are more specific cases of UN–business activity and illustrate the potential it has for fostering corporate citizenship.

- On 19 June 2000 Ericsson, a telecommunications company, announced the launch of a pilot project to enhance the level of disaster preparedness and response in countries such as Turkey, Vietnam, Thailand, Iran, Guatemala and Costa Rica, which are prone to disasters. Ericsson will work with local experts from the UNDP and the International Federation of Red Cross and Red Crescent Societies to determine the current preparedness level of these countries, what resources exist and what they

▶ **4 January:** the UN Environment Programme (UNEP) Insurance Industry Initiative called on governments to ratify the UN Kyoto treaty on climate change.

▶ **1 February:** the World Bank and the World Business Council for Sustainable Development (WBCSD) launched a joint programme on Business Ethics and Corporate Responsibility

▶ **1 February:** the UN's Division of Sustainable Development co-hosted an international workshop on sustainable energy issues with several private corporations.

▶ **2 February:** the World Bank, private insurance companies, universities, NGOs and governments established the ProVention Consortium, a partnership that seeks to equip developing countries with the means to better cope with natural disasters.

▶ **12 February:** the World Bank's International Finance Corporation and Softbank announced a partnership to 'Invest in Internet Enterprises for the Developing World'.

▶ **10 April:** the UN Food and Agriculture Organisation, and Parmalat, Italy's largest producer of dairy products, agreed to join forces to fight world hunger and raise awareness.

▶ **5 May:** the International Chamber of Commerce and UNEP presented their first business awards for environmental achievement to a dozen companies.

▶ **11 May:** the UN Programme on HIV–AIDS (human immunodeficiency virus/acquired immune deficiency syndrome) opened a new dialogue with pharmaceutical companies to improve access to HIV–AIDS-related treatment in developing countries.

▶ **23 May:** the International Fertiliser Industry Association formally endorsed the UNEP International Declaration on Cleaner Production.

▶ **31 May–1 June:** the UN Office for Project Services (UNOPS) organised 'The UN and Business: A Partnership for the New Millennium', which was the first conference on public–private partnerships between the world body and the business community to ever be held in the USA.

▶ **3 July:** UNEP launched the World Conservation Monitoring Centre to develop a biodiversity information and monitoring system that will support the work of decision-makers in governments, the private sector and NGOs.

▶ **26 July:** the UN Secretary-General's Office launched the Global Compact with nearly 50 transnational companies, prominent NGOs, labour unions and UN agency heads at headquarters in New York.

▶ **9 September:** UNDP, the Corporate Council on Africa, which consists of US business executives, and the Southern African Development Community, which has 14 member countries, launched a corporate campaign to fight HIV–AIDS. The campaign aimed to raise $40 million for action against HIV–AIDS in workplaces and communities across the region.

▶ **12 September:** the World Health Organisation (WHO) launched the Global Alliance for TB Drug Development with public- and private-sector organisations to combat tuberculosis by discovering, developing and distributing anti-TB drugs at affordable prices, particularly in countries hit hardest by the disease.

▶ **9–10 October:** the presidents and chief executive officers of 19 national employers' organisations from the Asia–Pacific region met in Singapore and endorsed the UN Global Compact

Box 11.1 **UN business activity in 2000** *(continued opposite)*

Source: Cohen 2000

▶ **2 November:** UNEP and the WILD Foundation honoured four companies and their advertising firms for responsible use of wild nature in advertising to enhance corporate consciousness, promote responsible use of wildlife and wilderness in advertising and encourage corporate philanthropy that supports the conservation and sustainability of the wild world.

▶ **4 December:** a high-level meeting of more than 20 Indian business leaders was held in Bombay where support was pledged for the UN Global Compact. A Steering Group was created and decided to focus on HIV–AIDS, sustainable cities and basic education.

▶ **7 December:** the UN Secretary-General announced the launch of the International Partnership against AIDS in Africa, which brought together the continent's governments, donors, NGOs, the private sector and the United Nations.

▶ **11–12 December:** the UN Financing for Development Conference preparatory committee held hearings with the private sector concerning themes such as corporate citizenship in emerging markets at UN headquarters in New York.

Box 11.1 *(continued)*

would need in order to begin to build common preparedness plans and communication response plans in the event of a disaster (Ericsson 2000).

▧ The UNEP Financial Institutions Initiative on the Environment was founded in 1992 to engage a broad range of financial institutions—from commercial banks, through investment banks, venture capitalists, asset managers, to multilateral development banks and agencies—in a constructive dialogue about the nexus between economic development, environmental protection and sustainable development. The initiative promotes the integration of environmental considerations into all aspects of the financial sector's operations and services as well as fostering private-sector investment in environmentally sound technologies and services. Another goal is to foster endorsement of the UNEP Statement by Financial Institutions on the Environment and Sustainable Development, which commits signatories to incorporating environmentally sound practices into their operations. As of 15 March 2000 a total of 171 companies from 45 countries have become signatories (UNEP 2000).

▧ In October 1999 the WHO signed up the Partnership for Quality Medical Donations (PQMD), an umbrella organisation of US-based pharmaceutical companies and NGOs, concerning its Interagency Guidelines for Drug Donations. This represents a significant step forward to ensure that only those drugs that are needed by recipients, accompanied by clear packing lists, and that are not close to or past their expiration date are donated. WHO will track the quality of drug donations and provide feedback to those organisations that do not adhere to the Guidelines. Hundreds of tons of unusable drugs were donated following recent crises in Turkey, Kosovo and elsewhere; these drugs now constitute an environmental hazard (WHO 1999).

● UNDP and Cisco Systems, a provider of networking for the Internet, launched a programme in August 1999 to bring Internet education to students in developing countries in the Asia–Pacific region. UNDP and Cisco Systems jointly funded and set up ten Cisco Networking Academies in nine developing countries in the region to provide students with advanced information technology curricula to leverage the opportunities created by the Internet while creating a qualified talent pool for building and maintaining networks (Freeman 1999).

● The UN Industrial Development Organisation (UNIDO) partnered with Acerlan, a Mexican foundry, as a result of pressure to apply environmental controls placed on the company by the government. Acerlan participated in a demonstration project of UNIDO/UNEP's Mexican Cleaner Production Centre to improve energy management, labour standards and production processes. Benefits derived from the project included: savings of approximately US$120,000 per month by improving the control of steel oxidation and a 10% reduction in use of oxygen; 14% fuel savings from the installation of air and fuel programming controls; and electricity savings of 5%; reductions in emissions of smoke and flames as a result of the improved maintenance of seals on electric arc ovens (UNDESA 1999: 33).

A litany of briefings, panels and workshops has paralleled this partnership activity, as well as research produced by agencies such as the UN Research Institute for Social Development and training by the UN Institute for Training and Research.

The most prominent UN–business–NGO gathering took place at the UN headquarters in New York on 26 July 2000 with the formal launch of the Global Compact. Nearly 50 TNCs from such diverse sectors as media, mining, automotive, services, telecommunications, banking, petroleum, pharmaceuticals, software and footwear joined with the heads of the ILO, UNEP, and the UN High Commissioner for Human Rights, labour unions and prominent NGOs, such as Amnesty International, Conservation International and Transparency International. The companies pledged to translate the principles of the Global Compact into practice through advocacy and publicity, posting examples of such activity on the Global Compact website annually and joining the UN in partnership at the policy or operational level. The goal of adding to the Global Compact coalition 100 large TNCs and 1,000 companies overall from across the world's regions within a period of three years was announced (UN 2000b).

◢ Phase 3: networking in the future

The next step for the UN, in phase 3, will be to more effectively plan and manage its networking in the future with business concerning corporate citizenship measures. Central policies and guidelines on what constitutes an ideal corporate partner, uniform UN-wide training of staff that will be involved with such partnerships and clear evaluation tools are needed.

This is slowly starting to happen. The UN Staff College is working with the Prince of Wales Business Leaders Forum and groups such as the New Academy of Business to train UN staff on how to understand the ramifications of the new relationship with business, as well as build, manage and evaluate partnerships (UN/PWBLF 2000).

The UN needs to co-ordinate its overtures to business and avoid duplication, whether from within or across agencies. While a business may see only one UN, UNDP may make a clear distinction between itself and UNEP or WHO, for example. These agencies may be in competition to work with particular companies as well, especially if members of staff are evaluated in the future based on these agencies' partnerships with the private sector.

By espousing ideals for business to achieve, the UN opens itself up to greater scrutiny by those same businesses as well as by NGOs. An example of this is the ground-breaking UN Office for Project Services (UNOPS) announcement in June 2000 that it would be the first UN entity to sign on to a certification agency, the Council on Economic Priorities' SA 8000. SA 8000 provides a standardised, global system for companies interested in evaluating and providing incentives to improve the social accountability (SA) of their suppliers and vendors as well as their own facilities (CEP 2000). UNOPS has broadened its impact on companies and suppliers that may not otherwise have been likely to become involved with SA 8000, thereby fostering a faster spread of international social norms (UNOPS 2000a). UNOPS has established a benchmark that eventually all other UN offices will have to meet. In 1998, UNOPS purchased US$331 million-worth of goods and services (UNOPS 2000b); the UN as a whole purchases approximately US$3 billion of goods and services annually, which results in the ability to make quite an impact on business and supply-chain certification (UNJIU 2000: 3).

Currently, few staff are devoted to issues relating to corporate citizenship in the Secretary-General's office. A lead agency for corporate citizenship will be necessary if the UN is to become the global leader of corporate citizenship, as it has professed it intends to be. Fortunately, the Secretary-General announced at the Global Compact on 26 July 2000 that such a move will take place in the future (Annan 2000b).

◢ United Nations and corporate citizenship challenges

Partnerships between the UN and business have the potential to positively alter the face of globalisation. However, this new relationship is not without its pitfalls. The UN risks its reputation if it is not careful in forging effective internal guidelines for engaging with business partners and acting transparently; in addition, it has to do this while managing an unwieldy and sizeable system of agencies. Also, the motivations behind the UN's work with business will impact on the effectiveness of that work, as will the structural limitations of the UN.

The UN has a weak normative framework in relation to business. Although a body of rules governing relations with NGOs has been developed over the past few decades, starting with Article 71 of the UN Charter, a similar body of rules concerning the private sector is lacking (UN 2000a). NGOs apply for formal consultative status with UN bodies. Over 1,500 NGOs have such status with ECOSOC, and more than 1,600 with the Department of Public Information, for example (UN 2000a).

Collaboration with business could open the UN to criticism of helping to bluewash poor corporate reputations if partnership activity is not conducted transparently and results are not communicated—whether successful or not, for example. As yet, the UN system does not have a uniform code of conduct governing its agencies' relations with business. Some agencies, such as UNICEF and the UNDP, have codes, but many others do not. Even the existence of such codes does not necessarily guarantee accountability if members of staff are unclear as to the purpose of the partnership. The absence of a system-wide code and training reflects the decentralised structure of the UN system. Many UN agencies are autonomous organisations, each with its own charter, budget and staff, largely outside the purview of the Secretary-General.

An internal report released in January 2000 from the UN's Joint Inspection Unit addressed concerns about UN–business partnerships and recommended more effective communication within the world body about why they are undertaken, as well as greater attention to engaging business in the developing world as well as small and medium-sized enterprises (SMEs) worldwide. Also, the report took pains to point out that fundraising 'is not the primary objective' of partnerships with business; rather it is to encourage the private sector to 'espouse the values of the United Nations' (UNJIU 2000: 5-6). Another concern among some member states and NGOs has to do with the belief that the UN 'only relates to wealthy multinational corporations and business circles in developed countries' (UNJIU 2000: 7).

The UN is particularly vulnerable to a business working in co-operation with the world body in one area and in bad faith in another. An example of this is a multi-stakeholder review of voluntary initiatives by business that began in 1998 at the UN Commission on Sustainable Development (UNCSD) which involved the ICC, the UN and NGOs. The idea behind the review was to identify the key elements of successful and unsuccessful voluntary initiatives. Often, they are declared with great fanfare, but not monitored. The ICC pulled out at the start of the 2000 UNCSD, without notifying the NGO partners. Even worse, the justification for withdrawing from the review of voluntary initiatives cited to the UN was that their work with the Global Compact was preferable to continuing with the review (NGOTOBI 2000).

NGO opposition to the UN fostering socially responsible corporate citizenship practices through partnerships with business offers a separate challenge. On 28

January 2000, exactly one year after the launch of the Global Compact, NGOs challenged the UN and business leaders at the WEF to endorse a Citizens' Compact on the relationship of the private sector to the UN. The Citizens' Compact calls on the UN to (Corporate Watch 2000a):

- Enact policies to monitor TNCs

- Avoid endorsing or promoting any products or brand names of any private corporation

- Avoid any public association or financial relationship with companies with destructive practices or that make products that are harmful to human health or the environment

- Establish open and transparent processes of dialogue with NGOs prior to entering any relationship with a corporation

- Ensure that any corporate donations go to programmes that have no connection with commercial projects for that company

The Citizens' Compact has been endorsed by over 70 NGOs. Pressure from groups supportive of the Citizens' Compact contributed to UNDP's proposed Global Sustainable Development Facility (GSDF) being scratched in mid-2000. Information leaks by UNDP employees who did not agree with the GSDF also contributed to the programme's demise. The GSDF sought to involve corporations in unspecified development projects in exchange for US$50,000 each (Corporate Watch 2000b).

NGOs are not of one mind on this approach. Georg Kell and John Ruggie, of the UN Secretary-General's office, characterise smaller NGOs as viewing UN–business relations as a 'Faustian bargain at best' (Kell and Ruggie 1999). However, they characterise the larger and more transnational NGOs as viewing the strategy of 'constructive engagement' (in contrast to confrontation) positively. Such NGOs are working with the UN. Interestingly, however, Kell and Ruggie (1999) acknowledge that 'without the threat of confrontation, engagement would be less likely to succeed'.

Words of caution have even come from a UN agency head. Carol Bellamy, the Executive Director of UNICEF, warned the UN community not to view partnerships with business as a panacea. She gave a now-famous speech at Harvard University on 16 April 1999 that took issue with 'one widely talked-about rationale for the UN working in partnership with the business community'—money, 'based on the assumption that the resources of government are not plentiful enough' (Bellamy 2000). Bellamy refused to let governments off the hook. Nor should the UN 'be uncritical' in its dealings with the private sector, she said. She went on to say that 'it is dangerous to assume that the goals of the private sector are somehow synonymous with those of the United Nations, because they most emphatically are not'. Bellamy called for care to be taken in choosing business partners, as UNICEF, the UN agency with the longest history of business involvement, has done. UNICEF does not work with any business involved with activities such as landmine production, exploitative child labour, tobacco or manufacturers of infant formula (Bellamy 2000).

SustainAbility cites the following brakes on business partnerships for NGOs, which also apply to the UN (Elkington and Fennell 1998: 51):

- Belief that company is only seeking public relations benefits, rather than real improvement
- Perceptions of inconsistency in company behaviour (inability to deal with schizophrenic [*sic*] tendencies of companies)
- Conflicts with membership and fundraising base
- Decisions to devote energies to protecting the regulatory structure

Brakes on partnerships for business include:

- Concerns over confidentiality of information shared with NGOs [read 'UN']
- Difficulties of addressing broadening agenda of sustainability-focused groups
- Inability to deal with schizophrenic [*sic*] tendencies of the NGO [read 'UN']
- Short-term financial concerns

The UN can take steps to protect itself from the downside of working with business, by:

- Establishing and following a stronger normative framework
- Concentrating on the management and technical expertise, as well as distribution systems, of the private sector, rather than on money
- Including SMEs, and not only TNCs, in corporate citizenship activity
- Ensuring that business cannot work 'both sides of the street', which will enhance the support of some NGOs
- Acting transparently

The fundamental weakness of the UN's role as a global leader in corporate citizenship is that it does not possess any enforcement capability. At best, it has only moral authority. Indeed, a theme of the NGO participants at the launch of the Global Compact was the need for independent monitoring of application of the Global Compact principles, public reporting and measures to be taken against those members of the Global Compact that continually violate it. In the end, NGOs will have to play the role of monitor and critic.

◢ Conclusions

The post-Cold War era has opened the door for the only global inter-governmental organisation to work with business and seek the mantle of corporate citizenship leader. A universal concept requires a universal champion. The UN is undergoing a three-phase development in its odyssey with business to fulfil a mandate of reducing poverty and promoting sustainable development, human rights and labour standards.

The awakening of phase 1 altered a long-standing culture within the UN toward the potential of working with rather than against business. Business, despite a history of animosity with the UN, embraced the overture on the basis of pragmatism and self-interest in obtaining benefits such as new markets and a share of the world body's credibility. The present engagement of phase 2 resembles more of an opening of the floodgates, with new UN–business initiatives launched regularly across the 30 agencies and 50,000 employees of the UN system. The networking of phase 3 will require greater management of an unwieldy and decentralised relationship with business, internally and externally.

The trend of third-party certification of procurement by the UN started by UNOPS should in time spread throughout the system. The formulation of uniform policies concerning choice of business partners, staff training, evaluation tools and transparency, as well as a lead agency, are all essential for a global leader of corporate citizenship.

UN strengths in promoting corporate citizenship include a global constituency and network of agencies, an all-encompassing progressive mission, vast communications vehicles in the world's major languages and credibility. Challenges facing the UN in promoting corporate citizenship include establishing policies that all of its agencies embrace, including reaching out to SMEs, approaching partnerships with business as more than opportunities to supplement funding by governments and the need to implement screening criteria. Even one wrong move and the resulting damage to one UN agency will damage the entire UN system of agencies. The UN needs to reserve the right to be a constructive critic of business, in general, and of partners, specifically, when warranted. The future of the world body may well depend on the judgement it exercises in managing its relationship with business.

The UN has elevated corporate citizenship higher than before on the global agenda with the introduction of the Global Compact. The careful engagement of business in partnerships with the agencies of the UN system to improve environmental, human rights and labour standards has great potential. There is the possibility of sharing best practices and bringing increased expertise, resources and delivery systems to the table, and to the developing world in particular, in previously unknown proportions. Institutionalisation of partnerships with socially responsible business through the UN offers the best way to humanise globalisation.

The Secretary-General believes that a contradiction does not exist between profit and the goals of the UN. Critics, however, fear that business will take on an ever-greater say in the affairs of the UN to the detriment of its mission. With extensive safeguards, the UN has the potential to institutionalise stakeholder partnerships on a global scale that is without precedent.

Part 3
STAKEHOLDER
ENGAGEMENT
AND SOCIAL
ACCOUNTABILITY

PARTNERSHIP ALCHEMY
Engagement, innovation and governance*

Simon Zadek

Institute of Social and
Ethical AccountAbility, UK

◢ New challenges to old problems

Businesses, communities and individuals are learning to live with the realities of the 'new economy', characterised in terms of economic globalisation, technological transformation, demographic change and political transition (Zadek *et al.* 2001). The forces of privatisation, market liberalisation and electronic communication have meant a massive transfer of assets and attention to the private sector and a radical reorientation of the role of the state. These new realities are creating unprecedented opportunities for many citizens but are causing increased insecurity and inequality for others. In almost every country, it is possible to find cosmopolitan pockets of growing affluence, high technology, world-class social services and increased economic competitiveness existing side by side with areas of rising unemployment, inadequate skills, low incomes, poor housing, family breakdown, crime, ethnic conflict and environmental deterioration.

The widening gap between those who are beneficiaries of change and those who are excluded from its benefits poses a fundamental threat to the project of economic and political modernisation that countries at all levels of development are pursuing. Bridging this gap has therefore become a central goal for policy-

* This chapter draws on the publication *Partnership Alchemy: New Social Partnerships in Europe*, which I co-authored with Jane Nelson and which was supported and published by The Copenhagen Centre. Fig. 12.5 was prepared by Lisa Curtis, Renaissance Worldwide, as part of her presentation at the annual AccountAbility conference.

makers, whether in government or whether leaders in business, trade unions and the community.

◢ Partnership times

Traditional roles are under threat. Governments often seem impotent in the face of the economic and social forces that their predecessors have helped to create. The labour movement appears stunned by the collapse of its power base of organised labour and disturbed by the emerging influence of other civil society actors. These other actors—an eclectic blend of non-governmental organisations (NGOs)—are unprepared for power and remain unable to effectively handle the politics of engagement rather than marginalised resistance. And then there is the business community. As the era's most powerful constituency, this community—particularly its largest, transnational members—has been thrust into the limelight of public policy debate and practice.

There is growing recognition of this shifting balance of power between the state, the market and civil society. Familiar configurations of power are being replaced by more complex and fluid patterns of interactions, transitory alliances and long-term relationships between the key institutional actors and individual citizens. We have entered 'the age of the partnership'.

There are many kinds of partnership. Companies come together to drill for oil or to share airline codes. They also join forces to lobby for or against legislation and often work continuously with trade unions to ensure a productive and profitable business environment. NGOs join forces to campaign for new legislation to secure environmental improvements and to influence corporate governance. Equally, they work closely with business and government in mobilising resources to battle disease and poverty. Governments join with each other to fight wars, provide humanitarian aid and to make laws. Equally, governments join with business in bringing private finance to public projects and to inject public finance into private business.

There are the many forms of 'new social partnerships' that involve institutions from different sectors of the community (business, government, civil society) that come together in addressing common purposes that involve the realisation both of social ends and of commercial ends. The Copenhagen Centre has defined these new social partnerships as 'People and organisations from some combination of public, business and civil constituencies who engage in voluntary, mutually beneficial, innovative relationships to address common societal aims through combining their resources and competences' (Nelson and Zadek 2000).

These new social partnerships are often marked out as distinct from other forms of partnerships:

- IBM outsources its catering because it does not see this as a core competence that it has or wishes to develop.

- The United Nations spends upwards of US$4 billion in purchasing goods and services from business, often through complex, long-term relationships.

- The French utilities giant, Suez Lyonnais des Eaux, engages with Brazilian community groups in designing a mechanism of delivering water to low-income areas in a commercially viable and politically sensitive manner because it recognises its lack of competences in realising this challenge.

- The British retail chain, Sainsbury, works with other companies, NGOs, labour organisations and the UK government through the Ethical Trading Initiative on the issue of labour standards in global supply chains because it recognises the potential gains from different competences, shared learning and distinct reputations and credibility.

These partnership cases appear different. The first two (IBM and the United Nations) are familiar, whereas the second two (Suez Lyonnais des Eaux and Sainsbury) are novel, innovative and experimental. However, there is an underlying pattern that links the unfamiliar with the traditional. They are similar in that the actors are consciously seeking opportunities that enable relationship blends that allow them to lever the maximum effectiveness and value of their own (perceived) core competences and capacities. The implications of this similarity are that an analysis of their rationale and process can usefully draw on existing language and insights into how and why individuals and institutions collaborate.

This does not mean, however, that the two types of partnership are the same. Certainly, the latter two differ from the former two in that they involve actors that embrace non-commercial interests, and this means that social goals are explicit in the partnership process. Indeed, this difference has complex ramifications that go beyond the simple fact of non-commercial interests and actors. Centrally is that it raises basic governance questions. At a micro level, it introduces a significant ambiguity into the matter of the purpose of business, which raises basic issues concerning, for example, the fiduciary duties and competences of company directors. At meso and macro levels it poses the challenge of how social policy in its broadest sense is to be defined in the future if it will increasingly require a complementary business case to be in place for it to be effectively implemented.

◢ Describing partnerships

Numerous frameworks have been developed in recent years in search of the best way to look at partnerships, particularly new social partnerships. Most of them embody a broadly similar set of underlying categories or building blocks. Some of these building blocks were drawn together during the research undertaken for the report, *Partnership Alchemy* (Nelson and Zadek 2000), and included:

- **Context**, with a focus on general drivers and specific triggers

- **Purpose**, collective and specific, and its evolution over time

- **Participants**, in terms of organisations and individuals and their respective roles and relationships

- **Organisation**, legal form, structure, governance, etc.

- **Outcomes**, both actual and expected

Understanding how partnerships work is constantly flagged as being the key to understanding whether and to what extent they work. Partnerships are, after all, not a thing but a process. The *Partnership Alchemy* study identified a number of dynamic pathways that were consistently raised in various forms in different studies as being critical determinants of effectiveness and efficiency:[1]

- Acknowledgement by all the participants as to what **drivers** and **triggers** have brought individuals and organisations to the table and an ability to understand and reappraise on an ongoing basis the **shifting context** and its influence on the partnership

- Clarity and openness about individual expectations and agendas, with mutual agreement on a **common purpose** and **agenda**—in short, synergy between desired participant benefits and societal benefits

- Mutual agreement on the **scope** and **complexity** of the partnership's intended locations and levels of action, variety of functions, range of desired outcomes and time-scales

- An individual or institution(s) capable of playing a **leadership** role, acting as inspirer, mediator and/or facilitator between the partnership participants and, in many cases, between the partnership and its ultimate beneficiaries

- Understanding the **resources, skills** and **capacities** that are needed to meet the partnership's objectives and how to optimise both the quality and the quantity of resources, skills and capacities that each partner brings to the initiative

- Appropriate **organisational** and **legal** structure to meet the common objectives of the partnership

- **Transparency, representation** and **accountability** both within the partnership and externally

- **Communication** strategies and systems that facilitate clarity of language, ensure regular dialogue and feedback, provide forums for problem-solving and conflict resolution, generate a shared vision and celebrate success

1 These categories and pathways have been used in a recent report on the role of business in tackling HIV–AIDS (see PWBLF 2000).

- Methodologies for **measurement** and **evaluation** of partnership processes and outcomes against common and individual agendas

- Flexibility and willingness to allow **adaptation** of the partnership's purpose, participants or process in response to evaluation or changes in the external context

◢ Analysing partnerships[2]

It is critically important to move beyond the broad descriptors provided above to defining in analytical terms the dynamic elements of partnerships. Once again many approaches have been proposed. Below are a few of the key parameters that would need to appear in any assessment with illustrations of how they relate to different analytic models.

Building enablers

The business excellence model, created by the European Foundation for Quality Management, is used by many companies, particularly in Europe, and by an increasing number of not-for-profit organisations. This model has traditionally been a nine-segment analysis of enablers of business performance and spheres of performance (Fig. 12.1). Business in the Community (BiTC) in the UK has used the business excellence model as the basis of assessment for its prestigious annual awards for excellence awarded for partnerships with community and business involvement. Some of the criteria are under-specified, in particular that relating to 'impact on society' (see Fig. 12.1), but the underlying idea of enablers and results is helpful in framing our understanding of how partnerships work.

Innovation

The UK-based 'Innovation through Partnership' (ITP) initiative[3] has built on the business excellence model in exploring the innovation effects of partnerships. This has involved various propositions and methodological actions.

- Potential benefits from partnerships are often long-term and indirect and most partners (including business) are not able to recognise and realise these potential benefits (this forms the **core proposition**)

---

2 This section draws from an unpublished paper prepared for the Knowledge and Resources Group of the Business Partners in Development (BPD) initiative convened by Civicus, the Prince of Wales Business Leaders Forum and the World Bank.

3 This involves the UK government Department of Trade and Industry, Business in the Community, the Local Futures Group and the Institute of Social and Ethical AccountAbility (www.partnership-innovation.org and www.accountability.org.uk).

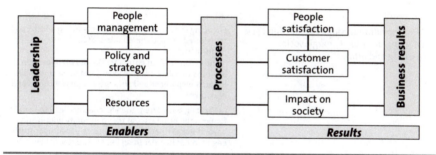

Figure 12.1 **The business excellence model**

- Many of the benefits are usefully understood as developments in the capacities of people and organisations, both those directly involved in the partnership (**impacts**) and those involved in the wider community of businesses, civil society and public-sector organisations (**outcomes**)

- One way to understand this broader, potential innovation effect is to consider impact on the 'enablers' in the business excellence model.

ITP's proposition and approach therefore seeks to capture the learning, knowledge and innovation effects, as summarised in Figure 12.2.

Knowledge

Innovation does appear to be a critical dimension, and it is the learning and knowledge effects that can translate such innovation into longer-term change within the organisations involved. This suggests the need for some way of thinking about learning and knowledge. Knowledge management is a 'hip' subject at the moment, with all manner of models being promoted as 'the way to look at the subject'. One of the first models circulating in the business community was developed by Skandia, in Sweden— the intellectual capital model. This is set out schematically in Figure 12.3, helping to identify the elements of knowledge that need to be better understood in terms of being impacted by partnerships.

Accountability

One of the most contentious dimensions of partnerships concerns the matter of accountability. New social partnerships are portrayed as having at heart public interests as well as commercial and other institutional interests and yet they rarely have a clearly defined mechanism for ensuring stakeholder accountability. All too often the issue of accountability pervades debate about partnerships, even to the extent of crowding out substantive issues such as social and environmental impact.

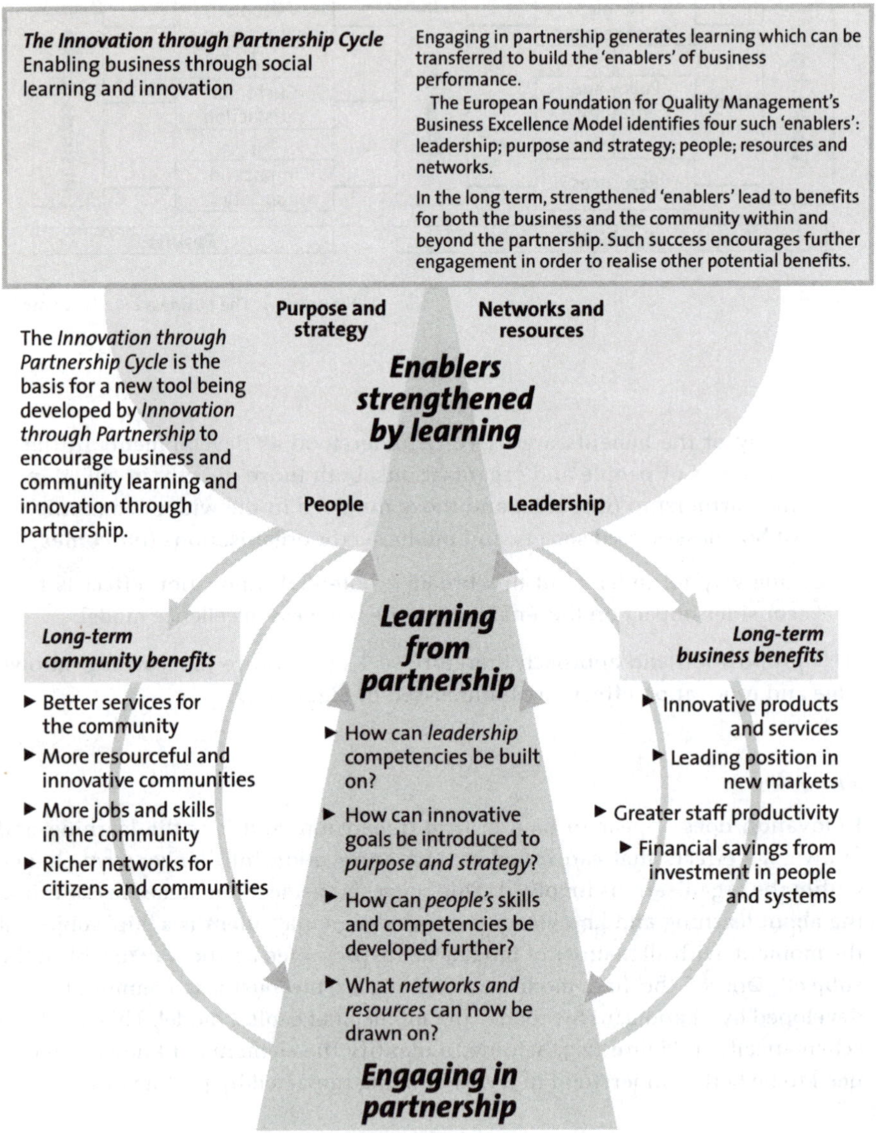

The Innovation through Partnership Cycle
Enabling business through social learning and innovation

Engaging in partnership generates learning which can be transferred to build the 'enablers' of business performance.

The European Foundation for Quality Management's Business Excellence Model identifies four such 'enablers': leadership; purpose and strategy; people; resources and networks.

In the long term, strengthened 'enablers' lead to benefits for both the business and the community within and beyond the partnership. Such success encourages further engagement in order to realise other potential benefits.

The *Innovation through Partnership Cycle* is the basis for a new tool being developed by *Innovation through Partnership* to encourage business and community learning and innovation through partnership.

Purpose and strategy

Networks and resources

Enablers strengthened by learning

People

Leadership

Learning from partnership

Long-term community benefits

► Better services for the community
► More resourceful and innovative communities
► More jobs and skills in the community
► Richer networks for citizens and communities

► How can *leadership* competencies be built on?
► How can innovative goals be introduced to *purpose and strategy*?
► How can *people's* skills and competencies be developed further?
► What *networks and resources* can now be drawn on?

Long-term business benefits

► Innovative products and services
► Leading position in new markets
► Greater staff productivity
► Financial savings from investment in people and systems

Engaging in partnership

Figure 12.2 **The Innovation through Partnership initiative**

Source: ISEA 2000

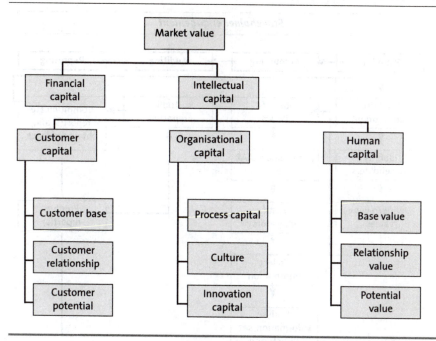

Figure 12.3 **The intellectual capital model**

Developments in social accounting are beginning to offer up basic frameworks that allow accountability to be framed, managed and assessed where traditional structures such as voting, ownership and classical approaches to public account-ability are not alone appropriate or possible. The Institute for Social and Ethical AccountAbility (ISEA 2000), for example, has developed the AA1000 standard, which is rooted in a model of systematic stakeholder dialogue as a means of creating measures and testing policy and practice (Fig. 12.4).

Strategy

Businesses, of course, not only measure and manage financial matters, even in the crudest cases of these being their only real interest. In recent years, non-finan-cial considerations have increasingly emerged in leading-edge planning, manage-ment and assessment tools. A very good example of this is the balanced scorecard. Even the classic balanced scorecard builds in qualitative perspectives, including the views of some stakeholders and a linkage to the whole learning side of the equation of business development.

There are an increasing number of companies trying to build social and environmental elements into their balanced scorecards. This is not necessarily difficult in principle, as Figure 12.5 shows. Although it does not solve all issues, what it does do is build the analytical framework into an existing and much-used (as least within business) strategy tool, which may have value in itself.

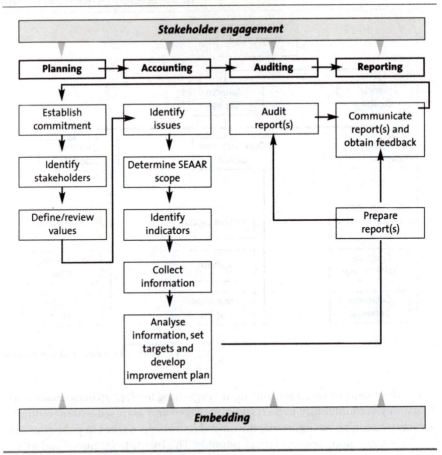

Figure 12.4 **Accountability management (AA 1000)**

Effectiveness

There is an extraordinary mythology about the way companies work out the 'business case' for doing things. The adage 'if you can't measure it, you can't man-age it' has been taken literally to mean that business always does financial sums to work out whether to do things (the 'super-rationale' model). Without wishing to car-icature the point, this is very often not the case. For example, the financial costs and benefits of building a factory are often subjected to rigorous financial analysis, whereas the vast majority of business decisions are not subjected to this kind of analysis (e.g. witness the way in which Internet stocks have been valued).

The most favoured measures have changed over the years. In the 1970s, earn-ings per share and price–equity multiples emerged as lead indicators of financial performance, whereas the 1990s saw the emergence of economic value added

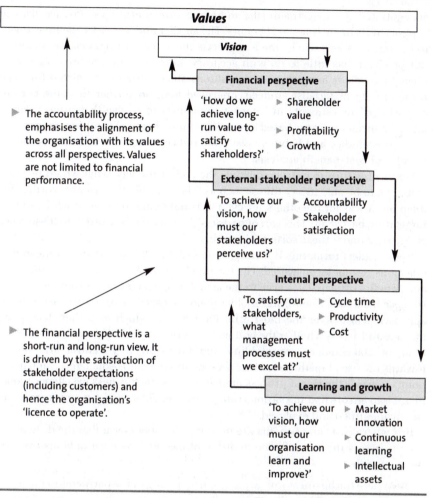

Figure 12.5 **Adjusted balanced scorecard**

Source: Lisa Curtis, Renaissance Worldwide

(EVA) as a favoured formula (Zadek 2000). It must be said that the emerging evidence regarding the use of hard-core financial measures such as EVA is of patchy usefulness. Although EVA can in theory be cascaded down the organisation, it is in practice poorly understood and applied at the level of the business unit. Furthermore, EVA is an outcome measure and therefore cannot usefully drive organisational behaviour. As Marcos Ampuero and his colleagues conclude: 'EVA must exist within a larger universe—a universe that often includes non-financial measures' (Ampuero *et al.* 1999: 48)

A business case is therefore constructed differently depending on what type of investment is being considered. At the simplest level, the larger and more concentrated the investment, the more pressure there is to produce data in support of its likely financial benefits. The smaller and less risky the investment to the business as a whole, the less precise the associated financial predictions. But precision has little to do with accuracy. Research into the financial consequences of major mergers and acquisitions shows that the predicted financial results rarely materialise. Indeed, one need look no further than the current explosion of investments in Internet companies to realise that projections of likely financial returns is based as much on the alchemy of intuition, judgement, perhaps prejudice and habit, or just plain old copying, as it is on the scientific calculus of cost–benefit analysis.

Let us now turn to partnerships. At the end of the day, what would be great would be to be able to say things such as 'The partnership was not worth it for them but it was for the others', or even 'It is not going to be worthwhile, so let's forget it' or, best of all, 'This sort of partnership will (not) be worth it to these types of partners under these sorts of situations'.

In its crudest form, this is a Holy Grail wish-list. But this does not mean that questions cannot be answered. The (relatively) easiest cases are where the costs and benefits principally accrue to the actual people and organisations involved. In these instances, a solid, stakeholder dialogue-based planning and assessment approach will deliver the most effective ways in which to gather data, plan, manage and assess whether the bottom line is red or black. This makes the whole issue of stakeholder accountability and inclusion very central and points towards the use of methods such as AA1000 to systematise dialogue. Similarly it points towards the use of process models such as the business excellence model in order to ensure that the various categories of enablers and outcomes are being clearly identified and explored.

It is where costs and benefits are indirect and longer-term that the difficulties arise to assess the net outcome to different parties. The most obvious cases of these might be:

- Where the business unit actually participating in the partnership incurs the (business-related) costs but the business as a whole or indeed the wider business community derives most of the benefits
- For civil-society and public-sector organisations where the wider community of organisations derives most of the gain through, for example, replication of the approach (or its abandonment if it does not seem to work)

This is the externalities problem. It may often be the positive externalities (i.e. things that happen outside the sphere of the partnership itself) that actually make the partnership worthwhile. For business it may be a product innovation or new approaches to marketing, training and leadership. Often, it may involve gains that accrues to the business (or indeed the sector) as a whole and yet are 'paid for' through the efforts of one (or a few) business unit(s). For civil-society and public-sector organisations it may be a way of developing approaches for addressing deeply rooted human rights or other problems that can then be used elsewhere.

It is in these more complex areas that some of the other elements of methods and tools described above may come in use. The partnership scorecard being developed through the Innovation through Partnership initiative may be helpful, as would be taking into account cutting-edge work on knowledge management and social learning. Similarly, the use of a suitably adjusted balanced scorecard might be useful in more effectively predicting, realising and making the best use of potential benefits right across an organisation, sector or community.

◢ Adding it up

The aspects described above can be grouped into three broad spheres:

- Direct development impacts and institutional benefits
- Learning, and indirect and strategic effects
- Cost–benefit analysis

The first sphere—direct development impacts and institutional benefits—is the one we know best. It addresses the question, 'What happened within the narrow bounds of the partnership?' Here we find that the traditional set of project assessment tools is helpful (e.g. LogFrame, participative assessment techniques, etc.). These tools have received several decades of thought from the development and other communities. There is no need to reinvent and rename these tools, and there is also no need to be overly restrictive in defining which technique to use, as this will vary between contexts and over time.

The second sphere—learning, and indirect and strategic effects—is much trickier and yet is probably where a great deal of the potential value of partnerships in practice lies. This sphere concerns:

- Evolution in the networks within which the organisation operates, which both reflects and reinforces the shift in knowledge and learning (actual and potential) and the overall capacity to act differently in the future

- Specifically, shifts in knowledge among partners and others as to 'how things can be done'

- Innovation in the partners' governance and organisational capacity (e.g. in the enablers, such as policies, procedures and incentives)

- As a specific and critical subset of the above, how the pattern of leadership within the partner organisations has changed, and how this reflects and impacts on the organisations' value orientation and focus

- Specifically, how the partners individually and collectively evolve their understanding and practice of their accountability to key stakeholders

■ How this evolution translates into strategic implications for partners and how this translation is modelled in their decision-making processes beyond the partnership

The classical tools used to assess development projects are not so helpful here. The business community is very focused on the more effective management and measurement of learning and knowledge, so that the tools on offer 'from this neck of the woods' offer considerable potential (as I hope the previous section illustrates).

The third and final sphere—cost–benefit analysis—asks the Holy Grail question, 'Was it worth it and could it have been more effectively and efficiently achieved in some other way?' The earlier discussion highlighted the complexity of the business case even as it relates to purely commercially oriented investments. But that does not mean that the business case is not alive and kicking. High-level strategic business decisions are made with much qualitative and quantitative data, but the key is that such decisions are made by the right people at the right time. The essence of the balanced scorecard approach, for example, is not precision, but materiality, linkage and usability by senior managers, who are accustomed to applying their knowledge in relative information-vacuums. Similarly, the good programme officer of a development agency will know far more about the cost–benefit relationship of an initiative than he or she is able to express in a simple, quantitative model.

What this suggests is that achieving the highest quality cost–benefit analysis requires that the best available information be delivered to the preferred decision-making points in the partnership and partnership organisations where the best knowledge, skills and experience can be applied to the matter. What this may mean, in turn, is that the partnership framework should be 'attachable' to existing strategy tools that are already part of key processes involving the right people, rather than seeking to reproduce this essentially qualitative process with mechanical calculus.

◢ Partnership-based governance

There is a shift taking place in our understanding and practice of governance, underpinned in part by the emergence of new social partnerships (Nelson and Zadek 1999). Traditional reliance on structured representation and the rule of law is giving way to a more fluid pattern of participation. This is characterised by communication-based forms of accountability and partnership-based forms of governance.

These shifts in the structure, process and scope of governance are emerging from deeply rooted changes in the global economy and associated shifts in organisational, technological and political processes. These changes are still in their early stages and will continue to impact on governance as they evolve.

New social partnerships are a core element of this process—both influencing it and in turn being driven by it. At the local level, the partnership approach is increasingly becoming embedded in designing and implementing public-interest programmes and policies. At national and international levels there has been a sharp growth in the active participation of business and civil society organisations in policy formulation. This has ranged from the development of voluntary guidelines and codes of conduct, to regulatory design. Just as business and civil society organisations are having a growing influence on public policy and public service delivery, companies are increasingly extending their own corporate strategies beyond statutory compliance in response to the views of consumers and civil society organisations. Similarly, although with perhaps less visibility, the business community is taking a more active role in the evolution of policy and practice within civil society organisations. In part this is a result of greater interaction, trust and intimacy between these two groups and in part a result of shifts in conditionality of funding, particularly in public contracts for infrastructure development, service delivery and management.

Governance structures are changing fundamentally at all levels of society—locally, nationally and globally. The way this transition develops will have critical implications for the ability of communities and countries to address the challenges of economic competitiveness, social cohesion and sustainable development.

With these changes comes a range of dilemmas associated with such new forms of partnership. In particular:

- Will citizen participation be enhanced or undermined by the growth in governance forms embodied in these new social partnerships? Can the capacity of civil society institutions be developed to enable them to play an effective role in these new forms of governance? How will these institutions evolve to ensure that they remain representative and indeed strengthen their degree of citizen representation?

- What are the implications for the state? It is not accurate to assert a 'reduced' role and yet it is clear that the state's structure of intervention is going through a radical transformation. Can the institutions of government rise to the challenge of handling increasingly complex, cross-sectoral relationships through the development of a more diversified, responsive culture and more integrated approaches to working? Can the growing and more explicit roles of business be balanced with the continued need for governments to regulate business activities?

- Will the business community engage in broader societal processes with combined social and financial purposes? Can business develop its values to support a new understanding of how social and environmental responsibility and accountability can form the foundations for long-term market competitiveness and for contributing to meeting social aims (Zadek 2001)?

The emerging forms of governance therefore present both a potential threat to participative democracy and a real opportunity to strengthen meaningful citizen involvement in decision-making and service delivery. The challenge is to ensure a form of 'civil governance' that effectively manages human affairs while enabling citizens to take an active role in designing the policies, institutions and programmes that shape the quality of their own lives. New social partnerships need to be measured against this yardstick in determining their underlying contribution to societal improvement as well as measuring their specific tangible outputs and outcomes.

Linked to this, the future of new social partnerships depends critically on whether they prove capable of delivering societal benefits that cannot be achieved more effectively through other means. To be effective they will need to demonstrate clear added-value at the:

- Local level, in building sustainable livelihoods and improving quality of life, in ways that actively and practically engage local communities and beneficiary groups

- Strategic level, in helping national and international government bodies to create an enabling environment for more proactive and innovative approaches to addressing socioeconomic problems

New social partnerships can be effective at both the local and the strategic level, but will not necessarily be so. The conditions under which they can be successful have been highlighted above, as have the pitfalls and dangers that partnerships represent in terms of micro-level effectiveness and meso-level and macro-level aspects of societal governance. The challenge is to increase the likelihood that the positive dynamics will prevail.

PATTERNS OF STAKEHOLDER PARTNERSHIP BUILDING

Jörg Andriof
Corporate Citizenship Unit,
Warwick Business School, UK

◢ Towards strategic partnering

The focus of strategy needs to be much broader than the traditional product–market approach of Adam Smith's day. Strategy now engages managers in considering a complex array of factors, of which the social context in which the company operates is an integral part. Furthermore, it requires the value-generating function of the company to be thought of as constituting a set of relationships—with employees, customers, suppliers and community interests as well as shareholders—which can add or subtract value and from which the company derives its ability to go on creating value.

Partnerships between individuals within societies or even across societies are not a new phenomenon within the globalising world, nor indeed a unique phenomenon within Europe. However, the dynamic political, social, economical and ecological environment and the interconnectedness of each of its elements provides a compulsion towards what is known as stakeholder partnership building. This process of change is not a radical one, nor is it a revolution, nor indeed is it limited specifically to certain spheres of our societal life; rather, it is endemic. Although in some areas stakeholder partnerships are already emerging, others are unsuspecting with regard to the value that such engagements can add to the quality of life and to societies' prosperity (Nelson and Zadek 2000).

A definition of the word 'partner', by *The Oxford Compendium* (9th edn, 2000), is that a partner is a person who shares or takes part with another, especially in a business firm with shared risk and profits, and 'partnership' is the state of being a partner or partners. *Webster's Dictionary* states that 'partner' is from the 14th century (Middle English *partener*, alternative of *parcener* [joint heir, *OED*], Anglo-French *coparcener*) and that 'partnership' dates from 1576. The word derives from the Latin term *partionarius*, which describes individuals and/or groups that are linked because they have a stake in something with which they are involved (Mackensen 1985). Since then, the concept of partnership has developed on three levels. First, the oldest notion of partnerships concerns the relationship between individuals, such as marriage and friendship. Second, there is the legal connotation of partnership as the basis for the formation of commercial organisations. Partnerships between various individuals, groups or institutions of the wider society make up the third level, which depicts the area of stakeholder partnerships. The three sectors that come together are business, government and civil society. Pluralistic societies such as Germany have a long-standing history of engaging various entities of society for problem-solving and the search for consensus.

Aristotle (384–322 BC) saw in human nature individuals who live in a community in which everyone is interconnected. In his *Politics*, Aristotle called this *zoon politicon* (Blackwell 1997): people living in overlapping spheres pertaining to family, community and state. A good government of the state as well as of the economy is based on a realistic recognition and integration of this underlying political principle. Aristotle considers monarchy, aristocracy and democracy as good forms of governance (Blackwell 1997). However, on the basis of its centralism, monarchy and aristocracy did not typically allow for social partnerships until the 19th century.

The philosophical ideas for social partnerships developed further in the 18th century around the notion of the social contract. The idea of the social contract focuses on a community or group of rational, self-interested individuals who are presumed to consent to the terms of a hypothetical agreement because it is in their rational interest to do so (Cooper and Argyris 1998). The concept of a social contract or covenant goes back to Socrates and the Greek Sophists and even earlier. The Old Testament refers to a covenant between God and every living thing, a covenant that spans all generations (Genesis 9). Social contract is associated with political theory as a device for understanding the role of government within a society. The use of social contract in political theory reached its apex in the Enlightenment writings of John Locke, Thomas Hobbes and Jean-Jacques Rousseau (Donaldson and Dunfee 1999).

In his treatise on the social contract, Rousseau envisions a moral community in which natural freedom and equality is transferred to civil society, based on the consent of the governed and reflected in the general will of the people (Donaldson 1989). More recently, Rawls (1971) used the idea of social contract as the foundation for his influential book, *A Theory of Justice*. In 1986, Gauthier, in *Morals by Agreement*, develops a rational choice argument, namely that self-interested parties will want to participate in a social contract recognising certain principles of co-operation. Gauthier recognises the implications of his work for socioeconomic life by stating that 'market interactions are a network of contractual arrangements, and that this network is itself founded on an overall social contract, expressive of the two-sided instrumentality that constitutes society from the standpoint of economic man [*sic*]' (1986: 318). An integration of these principles in society would initiate the change from the pursuit of social justice to some sort of communitarianism (Etzioni 1995).

At the end of the 18th century, England had a strong and divided class structure; France, after its 1789 Revolution, began to integrate social responsibility into governance—the early beginnings of social partnerships in Europe. Germany at this time carefully observed the radical changes in its neighbourhood. The German monarchy was afraid of losing its power. Revolutions and tumults were aimed at changing the government system. Governments became less able to handle the impact on society of the Industrial Revolution and the consequent new economic conditions. It was at the end of the 19th century that the first stakeholder partnerships were institutionalised and the social welfare state was born. Bismarck, the (Iron) Chancellor of Prussia, is often seen as the father of this development (Keeley 1988).

After the Second World War and the end of Hitler's dictatorship, Europe was politically divided into Eastern and Western bloc countries. Whereas in the West the free-market system succeeded, communism was the ultimate objective of the East. However, the Eastern bloc countries evolved into a totalitarian system, which provided little ground for social partnerships based on individualism. Western countries, predominately Germany, France and Sweden, developed the free-market system into a social market system (Keeley 1988). Within this context, many of the currently existing institutionalised forms of social partnerships emerged. Unions (not necessarily trade unions) are strong in Europe—codetermination of employee representatives in companies' decision-making, citizen initiatives and movements, non-governmental organisations (NGOs), professional association, the European Union (EU), lobbyists, charities and foundations are only a few general examples of the expression of this. In 1989, the Berlin Wall came down through peaceful revolution, representing another milestone on the way towards stakeholder partnerships.

However, not only was the political system in Europe going through a process of radical change, the whole world changed and is still changing. Seeking to apprehend world structures is akin to catching reality in flight. Huntington (1997) called it 'the clash of civilisation'. Others discuss postmodernism, reflexive modernity or risk society. Giddens (1999) and Beck (1992) talk about the production of risks that influence society rather than traditional natural risks that can be controlled. One needs to be able to manage the possible negative impacts of risks rather than merely striving for the achievement of market efficiency. Stakeholder partnership building might be a way of navigating social risk and achieving sustainability.

Nowadays, participants in stakeholder partnerships come together specifically to achieve social benefits through joint action. This is accomplished in part by enabling individual partners to pursue their own interests, which may include the direct or indirect commercial interest of participating companies, as well as the interests of other partners. Partnerships seek to explore new approaches to addressing social and economic problems and opportunities, often changing and challenging traditional rules and patterns of interaction between different actors and thereby establishing new methods of working and taking the fullest advantage of available resources and competences.

Participants are drawn from two or more of the following:

- Public bodies at the local, national or international level
- Private-sector entities, ranging from individual companies to business associations
- Civil society, ranging from local community initiatives to trade unions, academic institutions and national and international NGOs

Partnership participation is voluntary in the sense that it is based on an active decision by each partner to engage in co-operation, rather than being forced by the imperative of statutory compliance. However, some partners may be pressured to join the stakeholder partnership for reasons of crisis management, conflict avoidance or peer pressure rather than by an entirely self-motivated desire to participate. There is a resource contribution and associated risks or costs borne on the part of each partner, and each partner benefits in some defined way.

Thus, stakeholder partnerships may be seen to be, in effect, a collaboration between individuals and/or organisations from some combination of public, business and civil constituencies who engage in voluntary, mutually beneficial, innovative relationships to address common social aims through combining their resources and competences.

Establishing and sustaining mutually beneficial stakeholder partnerships is rarely simple, especially with non-traditional allies. Some of the operational challenges include bridging diversity, assessing value-added aspects, attracting and sustaining business interest and addressing power. Stakeholder partnerships also raise dilemmas with regard to more strategic issues such as learning from experience, maintaining dynamism and innovation and the role of the state and traditional partners, because partnerships raise questions of accountability and representation. Some of these operational and strategic challenges are at the centre of analysis of stakeholder partnership building.

Engaging with stakeholders

Stakeholder groups can be assessed against strategic aims according to three sets of criteria—influence, impact and alignment (Harrison and St John 1996). Each of these is measurable, to a greater or lesser degree. Clearly, the higher the potential for increasing business economic fortunes and the higher the business impact on stakeholder groups, the more important it is to maintain a constructive dialogue. The easier the dialogue becomes, the greater the alignment of values between the company and the stakeholder group (Scholes and Clutterbuck 1998).

However, managing stakeholder audiences as if they were discrete and unconnected is no longer a viable strategy. The company needs to develop systems and approaches that enable it to prioritise stakeholders, to align itself closely with stakeholders, to integrate the messages to and from stakeholders and to build bridges between itself and the stakeholders rather than to attempt to buffer impacts from stakeholders on the company.

Stakeholder research has concentrated primarily on classifying individual stakeholder relationships and influential strategies. The first such analysis was probably Vogel's (1978) work, focusing as it did on such strategies as proxy resolutions and boycotts. In recent years, stockholder resolutions (Davis and Thompson 1994), boycotts (Paul and Lydenberg 1992) and modified vendettas (Corlett 1989; Shipp 1987) have all been subject to theoretical treatment. Researchers have performed empirical studies on many of these same stakeholder influence strategies. In these empirical studies scholars have generally considered the effectiveness of the strategies, or the market's reaction to such strategies, and have included examinations of boycotts (Garrett 1987; Pruitt *et al.* 1988), divestitures (Davidson *et al.* 1995) and letter-writing campaigns (Smith and Cooper-Martin 1997).

Frooman (1999) goes beyond particular influence strategies. His stakeholder influence theory suggests the existence of four types of stakeholder influence and four types of resource relationship. It argues, further, that the balance of power implicit in the relationship determines which of the types of strategy a stakeholder will use. However, this approach cannot explain how a firm reacts to its stakeholders.

Each firm faces a different set of stakeholders, and these stakeholders aggregate into unique patterns of influence. Thus, firms do not respond to each stakeholder individually but rather must respond to the simultaneous demands of multiple stakeholders. Rowley (1997) contributes to stakeholder research by providing a mechanism for describing this simultaneous influence of multiple stakeholders and for predicting firms' responses. He placed four responses of firms within a two-by-two matrix, looking at the density of the stakeholder network in relation to the centrality of the focal organisation. The bedrock of this work is Oliver's (1991) effort to converge institutional and resource-dependence theory.

However, recent developments have weakened conventional boundaries between internal and external stakeholders as they relate to management principles and systems. As a consequence, stakeholders require more, and different, management attention than they have traditionally received. These ideas lay a foundation for understanding why more and more organisations are embracing a stakeholder management approach.

The instrumental perspective is that stakeholder management activities can lead to other outcomes, which in turn can lead to higher profitability or increased firm value. Examples of instrumental outcomes include:

- Improved predictability of changes in the external environment, resulting from better communication with external stakeholders (which may also lead to greater control)

- Higher percentages of successful innovations, resulting from the involvement of stakeholders in product and service design teams

- Fewer incidents of damaging moves by stakeholders (e.g. strikes, boycotts, bad press), resulting from improved relationships and greater trust (Moss Kanter 1999; Svendsen 1998)

Stakeholders provide a lens for viewing and interpreting important trends in the operating environment.[1] Therefore, 'proactive stakeholder engagement is simply the right thing to do' (Harrison and St John 1996: 49). One of the key factors that determines the priority of a particular stakeholder is the influence of that stakeholder on the uncertainty facing the firm. In addition, it is important to understand the role of strategic choice in determining the nature of the interdependence that exists between a stakeholder and a firm. Strategic decisions at all levels influence the importance of various stakeholders.

When environments are more complex and uncertain, webs of interdependences are created among stakeholders. In such environments, bridging (also called boundary-spanning) techniques are needed that build on interdependences rather than buffering them (Harrison and St John 1996; see Fig. 13.1). As Pfeffer and Salancik argue, 'The typical solution to problems of interdependence and uncertainty involves increasing the mutual control over each other's activities' (1978: 43). Joint ventures with competitors, co-operative product-development

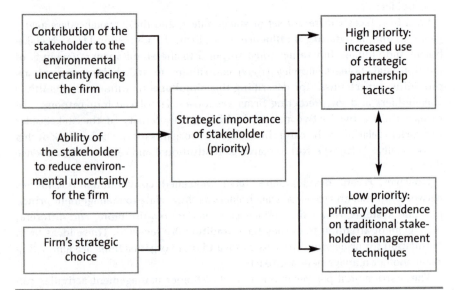

Figure 13.1 **The strategic importance of stakeholders**

Source: Harrison and St John 1996

1 In the following discussion, the term 'environment' is taken to mean the overall environment (business, social, political, etc.) in which the firm operates.

efforts involving suppliers and customers and industry-level lobbying efforts are examples of partnering techniques that bring the firm into closer alliance with its critical stakeholders. Research suggests that strategic alliances are a device for reducing the uncertainties that arise from unpredictable demand and the pressures that come from high levels of interdependences among organisations (Burgers *et al.* 1993).

Harrison and St John (1996) postulate that firms should consider proactive partnering techniques not only to increase control in the face of environmental uncertainty but also to create organisational flexibility. Partnering activities allow firms to build bridges with their stakeholders in the pursuit of common goals, whereas traditional stakeholder management techniques (buffering) simply facilitate the satisfaction of stakeholder needs and/or demands.

The potential benefits of bridges between partners may be illustrated using the case of relationships with customers as an example. Firms with a traditional buffering posture towards customers focus on arm's-length information-gathering about needs and expected demand for new products and compliance with current quality and service expectations, all in an effort to buffer the firm from uncertainty and customer complaints. With bridging techniques, a firm might choose to create stronger linkages with customers by involving them directly in the firm's product development programmes, in its continuous improvement programmes and in its production planning and scheduling. Bridge-building increases interdependence rather than buffering the firm from stakeholders. However, empirical research is needed to describe the process of building stakeholder partnerships.

◢ A framework for analysing stakeholder partnership building

Three theory areas—business and society, stakeholder theory and strategic relationships—form the conceptual foundations and key issues that are used to construct a framework with which stakeholder partnership building is analysed. From each theoretical area a key message can be gained that reflects the theoretical development and its likely future direction. The unfolding trends in business and society make it clear that organisations have moved from a reactive compliance-oriented management of social issues to a more proactive engagement in corporate citizenship-related challenges. Research and the focus within stakeholder theory development have moved away from considering stakeholders as environmental constraints towards engaging them as political partners that are seen as a valuable resource for a firm's long-term survival. Strategic relationship literature clearly indicates a transition from a buffered dependence on stakeholders towards a bridging dynamic interdependence between a firm and its surroundings as well as with its influential stakeholders.

For this research, partnerships are defined as trust-based collaborations between individuals and/or social institutions, each having different objectives that can be achieved only through the various parties' working together. The basis for successful partnerships is an agreement about rules for co-operation. A higher degree of consensus means less need for regulated partnering because of the minimised conflict potential.

Key issues in the analysis of stakeholder partnership building are (Table 13.1):

- The purpose of the partnership
- The power relationships between the various partners
- The pact between the partners
- The process of partnership development

Partnership development		
Conceptual foundations	*Key messages derived from theory development*	*Key issues of stakeholder partnership building*
Business and society	From reactive compliance to proactive engagement	Purpose
Stakeholder theory	From environmental constraints to political partners	Power relationships
Strategic relationships	From dependence to dynamic interdependence	Pact

Table 13.1 **A framework for analysing stakeholder partnership building**

First, the purpose of stakeholder partnership building is linked to corporate social responsibility and corporate social performance. As Schwartz and Gibb (1999) propose, social responsibility is moving beyond mere legal compliance to active stakeholder engagement to manage social risk.

The second defining variable in this management process concerns power relationships (Freeman 1994). Power, together with legitimacy, is the underlying rationale of stakeholder theory (Argenti and Campbell 1997).

Third, the legitimacy of a stakeholder partnership is characterised by the pact within the partnership (Dussauge and Garrette 1999) and can be described by means of strategic relationship concepts (Astley and Fombrun 1983). The relational view of the firm is the basis for stakeholder engagements (Dyer and Singh 1998).

Last, the process of partnership development draws on all three bodies of literature. This key issue of stakeholder partnership building focuses on the sequence of events over time, embedded in the social risk management context (Pettigrew 1985).

Table 13.1 summarises the key messages and issues that establish the framework for analysing stakeholder partnership building, to which I turn in the next section.

◢ Analysing stakeholder partnership building

The classic Ford Pinto case, the Bhopal disaster in India and the more recent Brent Spar affair involving Shell are but three examples where stakeholders have played a leading role in firms' strategic development (Harrison and St John 1994). Business in consensual societies (e.g. Japan and Germany) has tended to take a broad view of stakeholders—at least with regard to owners, employees and customers (Huse and Eide 1996). In Scandinavia and the Netherlands business has been especially sensitive to environmental stewardship (Polonsky 1995). In less consensual societies and more individualistic economies (e.g. the USA and 1980s Britain) the balance of stakeholders has tended to give primacy to owners and shareholders, with mixed results (Näsi 1995).

In 1996, two years after Jürgen Dormann became chief executive officer (CEO) of Hoechst, he announced that the company's performance would now be measured through shareholder value. In 1997, John Browne, CEO of British Petroleum (BP), underlined in a policy statement that BP, as part of society, wants to contribute to the positive development of that society. These two firms seem to be moving from different performance orientations and stakeholder management history to a similar practice of managing social risk. In the 1990s, both companies faced critical incidents because, in my view, they were detached from the societies in which they operated. Hoechst, having its operations in Germany, faced a series of chemical accidents and changed from a chemical to a life-sciences company. BP's operations in Colombia faced accusations of human rights abuses and environmental damage (*Guardian* 1998). The company changed from being a technology-driven to a society-driven company (Andriof 2000; BP 1998). Hoechst and BP built stakeholder partnerships that enabled the companies to manage their induced social risk, to become part of society and to become sustainable companies with the prospect of long-term prosperity (Andriof 2000).

Stakeholder research has focused primarily on stakeholder identification, salience and influence strategies to develop a stakeholder theory relevant to the firm. Stakeholder partnerships are a phenomenon for which only little empirical evidence and theoretical constructs exist. In this chapter I seek to amplify existing stakeholder research by presenting a longitudinal comparative process-oriented analysis of stakeholder partnerships with Hoechst and BP in order to provide insight into how firms build partnerships with stakeholders. In each case, two stakeholder partnerships are studied—one with NGOs and one with communities. The two companies studied here represent stakeholder partnership building within different regional and industrial contexts of social risk management.

Through a qualitative case-study analysis—interviews, archival data, observations, field visits and various publications—I investigate stakeholder partnerships on a macro-organisational level by considering them at the social level as well as at the level of the individual. The research focuses on four elements:

- The purpose—the means and ends—of stakeholder partnerships
- The pact—the covenant between the collaborating partners
- The power relationship—the base and the balance between the partners
- The development process—the evolution of stakeholder partnerships

The research question is:

- How do firms build stakeholder partnerships?

The descriptive, process-oriented analysis of stakeholder partnership building is embedded in the context of social risk issues such as sustainable development, human rights, environmental damage and community development. The purpose of this study is to describe stakeholder partnerships emerging in different contexts, to analyse the process of stakeholder partnership building and to interpret differences and similarities of stakeholder partnership building processes depending on the context of managing social risk in different industries and different parts of the world. The proposed underlying rationale is that firms are able to manage social risk by gaining access to knowledge and by building up the required competences through stakeholder partnership building. My aim is to demystify the rhetoric of stakeholder capitalism (Hutton 1999; Plender 1998) and to work out the perspective firms need to take in order to consider stakeholders as an environmental driving force for strategy.

Research inferences are summarised in terms of the four Ps of stakeholder partnership building: the purpose of partnerships, the pact between partners, the power relationships within partnerships and the processes of the evolution of partnerships. This descriptive research defines variables of stakeholder partnership building that can be tested and applied to a wider population and within different contexts.

Element 1: the purpose of partnerships

The purpose of partnerships is the first defining element of partnerships. It is the outcome that is intended for the partnership and guides stakeholder partnership building actions. For this analysis, the purpose of stakeholder partnership building is defined as the internal function of a partnership. Moreover, it is the synergy potential that describes the level of intent to participate in a stakeholder engagement. Each of the four stakeholder partnerships studied here served one of the following different purposes:

- Acquiring knowledge
- Co-financing of social investment

- Combining of competences
- Improvement of communications

The study here may be regarded as an analysis of the means and ends of stakeholder partnership building. Five variables are applied to describe the four different purposes:

- Strategic objective
- Context
- Content
- Joint interest
- Source of benefits

Purpose 1: acquiring knowledge

The function of acquiring knowledge is the process of coming into possession of concrete or abstract information that adds value to the given partner. Within stakeholder partnerships, business and stakeholders gain knowledge from each other. The partners require the acquired knowledge to accomplish their strategic targets.

Case study 1: BP and IAG

BP aimed to adapt its policy to consider the natural—and its social as well as political—environment. The target of the NGOs within IAG (Inter-Agency Group) was to develop guidelines for the excavation industry in less developed countries. Hence, the strategic objectives were similar. Based on this similarity, BP and the NGOs had a joint interest in improving the human rights records of Colombia and in particular in BPX's operating environment.[2] However, business policy issues formed the context of the partnership. Consequently, the content of the partnership—the actions of BP and IAG—consisted of conversations that composed a dialogue. The source of benefits for both partners was the potential to exchange knowledge. Therefore, the purpose of the partnership between BP and IAG was to acquire each other's knowledge to assist in achieving the strategic objective of changing business policy.

Purpose 2: co-financing of social investment

The co-financing of social investment is the process by which two or more partners provide resources for a joint investment. Within the context of stakeholder partnership building, the notion of resources for co-financing social investments is broad and comprises, in addition to the primary financial resources, managerial resources.

2   BPX is BP's exploration subsidiary.

Case study 2: BPX and its surrounding communities

For the partnership between BPX and its communities it was crucial to transfer the ownership of social development projects to the communities that were involved and affected. Co-financed social investment was an effective approach for social impact management. Both the company and the communities were convinced that social impact management was the key to sustainable development. On that basis, BPX and its communities not only had a similar strategic objective but also a joint interest in social development. Consequently, the partnership's context was social investment. Because these investments are managed on a project-by-project basis, various community development projects represented the content of the co-operation. Enhancement of social investment efficiency was the consequent source of benefits for both partners. Co-financing of social investments as the purpose of the partnership was considered as the means to the end of managing social impact for sustainable community development.

Purpose 3: combining of competences

The combining of competence is the process of joining competences for a common purpose or in a common action. Competences are defined in terms of the quality of being adequately or well qualified, physically and intellectually, to fulfil a set target or achieve an objective. Competence is the product of the compounding of resources and skills.

Case study 3: Hoechst and the Öko-Institut

The combining of competences, therefore, requires similar strategic objectives, which was the case in the partnership between Hoechst and the Öko-Institut. It was not only the objective of developing a product assessment tool that the partners shared; in addition, they pursued the joint interest of promoting sustainable development. The developed tool for measuring product sustainability was designed to be strategic in nature. Hence, the context of the partnership was a strategy for sustainable development. However, a specific project formed the content of the partnership between Hoechst and the Öko-Institut: the development of the product assessment tool. The source of benefit was the building of joint competences not only to fulfil the project task but also to build new internal competences in each partner institution. Consequently, the purpose of the partnership was to combine competence so as to develop a strategy tool for product assessment to promote sustainable development.

Purpose 4: improvement of communications

Improvement of communications is the process of improving the quantity and quality of communication between a sender and a recipient of information. Communication is a connection that allows access between persons or places. Within the context of stakeholder partnership building, improvement of communication is the enhancement of information exchange between business and stakeholders as well as the active participation of stakeholders in this process.

Case study 4: Hoechst and its surrounding communities

Hoechst's intention to become an open company (its strategic objective) and the aim of the communities in which it operates to gain access to information (their strategic objective) were similar to a certain extent because both partners aimed to exchange information with each other. This exchange of information was seen as an effective approach to social conflict management—Hoechst's and the communities' joint interest. Communication was the context of this partnership, and the rules for communicating with each other were the content. Community communication was the source of benefit for both partners.

Analysis

With regard to the five variables being applied to describe the elements of stakeholder partnership building (strategic objective, context, content, joint interest and source of benefits) there is only one similarity between the four functions described above in terms of the purpose for such partnership building. The strategic objectives of the partners within each partnership were equivalent. However, from case to case, the partnerships pursued different strategic objectives. All other variables are different. The distinctions between the partnerships cannot be linked to firm-specific features such as policy, processes or social capital. Hence, there is no evidence that the context—BP's and Hoechst's navigating of social risk—caused the differences between the purposes of partnerships. However, based on the fact that each variable that describes the partnership purposes is different in content, with the exception of the strategic objectives that are similar within but also different between the partnerships, there is evidence that the purpose of partnerships is partnership-specific.

Element 2: partnership pacts

The second defining element is the partnership pact. A pact may be defined as a written or an unwritten agreement between at least two partners from government, society or business. For the purpose of this analysis, the pact involved in stakeholder partnership building is defined as the agreement between the involved partners that is aimed at serving the purpose of the stakeholder partnership. Stakeholder engagement is the core activity of such a pact. Each analysed stakeholder partnership represents a different pact. The four types of stakeholder partnership described below may be regarded as being pacts based on something halfway between a handshake and a contract. These pacts may be described as consisting of:

- Dialogue
- A joint venture
- A joint project
- An alliance

Five variables are applied to describe the four different pacts:

- Basis for the pact
- Degree of choice of partner
- Structure
- Basis of the agreement
- Level of independence

Pact 1: dialogue

Dialogue was originally understood to be a literary construct in the form of a conversation between two people—in other words, the lines spoken by characters in drama or fiction. In the context of stakeholder partnership building, dialogue is the conversation between business and at least one of its stakeholders. Through dialogue it is possible to exchange information and acquire knowledge.

Case study 1: BP and IAG

The basis of the pact between BP and IAG was based on mutual assurance. BP needed the approval of IAG, and IAG in turn had to ensure that it would maintain its integrity. The agreement behind the partnership did not involve actions, only conversations. The structure of the dialogue was very informal. For instance, meetings were not planned, and no rules for conversations were fixed. Because only a few NGOs are experts in developing areas, the possibilities for partner selection was limited. The agreement between BP and IAG was an unwritten memorandum of understanding—a verbal agreement. However, at all times, the partners were able to maintain their independence. The pact between BP and IAG was an exclusive agreement for policy dialogue.

Pact 2: a joint venture

Joint ventures are ventures undertaken by a partnership or conglomerate that are designed to share risk or expertise. Joint ventures may well prove to be a useful, and indeed necessary, way to enter some new markets, especially for multi-national firms.

Case study 2: BPX and its surrounding communities

In terms of integrating its business into Colombia, the only way in which BPX could achieve effective social investment was through joint ventures with the affected communities, this being the only way to mitigate social risks. Hence, the basis of the pact between BPX and its communities in Colombia lay in the field of social expectations. The company's only partners were the surrounding communities and local authorities of its operating sites in Casanare. Therefore, partnership selection was predetermined. The structure of the pact between BPX and its community was formal. Regular meetings were held and every investment project was renegotiated. For each social investment project an agreement was signed. Within joint ventures, clearly equal positions are usually taken by the participants. However, BPX and its community partners considered a formal pact structure and a separate signed agreement for each investment project as the only way to maintain their independence and integrity. Consequently, a joint venture for making social investments was the basis of the pact for the partnership between BPX and its surrounding communities in order to achieve sustainable social development.

Pact 3: a joint project

Joint projects are combined, planned undertakings between at least two involved partners. It is a partnership in which a task is carried out by each of the involved partners. Often, resources, skills or competences are combined to achieve the joint project objective. Any agreement between the partners is limited to the project task. In the context of stakeholder partnership building, a joint project is defined by a partnership between a company and at least one of its stakeholders for the accomplishment of a joint task.

Case study 3: Hoechst and the Öko-Institut
Within the partnership between Hoechst and the Öko-Institut, the task in question was the development of a product assessment tool for sustainable development. However, because the history of the two partners was conflict-loaded, mutual trust had to be built to establish the basis for the partnership pact. The Öko-Institut was not the only competent critic or agency able to assist Hoechst in developing the product assessment tool. However, it was the only stakeholder that was willing to engage in the joint project with the company. Therefore, partnership selection was predetermined. Since the rules of the agreement were based on the differing competences that the partners were able to contribute to the joint project, the structure of the partnership pact was informal. Hoechst and the Öko-Institut maintained their independence by a verbal agreement for the duration of the joint project.

Pact 4: alliance

An alliance is the state of being allied to another (or others) or of being in a confederation with others. It is a connection based on common interest. An alliance is an organisation of people involved in a pact or treaty. It is often a formal agreement establishing an association between nations or other groups to achieve a particular aim. Alliances are a lesser form of participation when compared with joint ventures, which may or may not involve equal participation. With regard to stakeholder partnership building, an alliance is defined as a formal agreement between a company and at least one of its stakeholders to establish an association with a particular aim.

Case study 4: Hoechst and its surrounding communities

The aim of the pact between Hoechst and its surrounding communities was the improvement of communication. Because Hoechst's managers and community representatives already had personal contact with these communities they established the basis of the pact for the partnership. In addition, because the only possible partners in this pact were Hoechst's surrounding communities, partnership selection was predetermined. The community discussion group had a very formal structure. Rules were negotiated and formed a codified but unsigned pact agreement. On this basis, Hoechst and the involved community representatives were able to maintain their independence within the alliance when participating in the community discussion group (CDG).

Analysis

With regard to the five variables that have been applied to describe partnership pacts (basis for the pact, degree of choice of partner, structure, basis of the agreement and level of independence), there is only one similarity between the four diverse stakeholder partnerships studied. Each partnership pact was designed to maintain each partner's independence. However, there were also partial similarities with regard to stakeholder partner selection, structure and agreement. The only stringent difference was in terms of the basis for the partnership pacts. No links between the differences or similarities of the stakeholder partnership pact variables and the context of BP's and Hoechst's risk management approach could be established. Hence, there is no evidence that the pacts studied were dependent on the social risk management context. Consequently, the four different pacts analysed are partnership-specific.

Element 3: power relationships in partnerships

Power relationships constitute the third defining element of partnerships. The preferred linguistic usage of the word 'relationship' pertains to human relations. It defines a state of connectedness between people, where mutual dealings between people, parties or countries are involved. In the context of stakeholder partnership building, power relationships are an important consideration. To have power is to possess a controlling influence. Thus power relationships can cause one partner to be dependent on another if the partner holding the most power chooses to exercise that power. When power relationships are balanced, they lead to interdependence or independence.

Each partnership studied here is characterised by a different power relationship. They may be regarded as being characterised by:

- Cyclic reputation interdependence
- Balanced commitment interdependence
- Balanced competence interdependence
- Regulated knowledge interdependence

The interpretation of power relationships used here draws directly from Nelson and Zadek's book, *Partnership Alchemy*, from the section on 'harnessing power for partnerships' (2000: 39-52). Five variables are applied to describe the four different types of power relationship:

- Source of power
- Balance mechanisms in place
- Level of dominance (by any one partner)
- Consequences of type of relationship
- Propensity to use power

Power relationship 1: cyclic reputation interdependence

Such a relationship is one where the power within the stakeholder partnership is characterised by recurring unilateral dependence of the involved partners. The partners' growth and loss of reputation determines the cycle of the dependence. However, over time the power relationship is balanced and the partners are interdependent. Therefore, the source of power is reputation.

Case study 1: BP and IAG

In such relationships, the source of power is reputation, as was the case in the partnership between BP and IAG. Because an organisation's reputation depends on the effect of incidents such as public relations initiatives or crises, the power balance mechanism can be seen to be incident-driven. Hence, the dominant partner in the partnership of BP and IAG changed cyclically, depending on critical incidents. Because the partnership was long-term rather than designed to manage one specific incident, the result was interdependence between the two partners. However, BP and IAG were aware of how to apply reputation as a source of power and exercised their power to gain access to each other's knowledge. Consequently, the power relationship of this business–NGO policy dialogue was one of cyclic reputation interdependence.

Power relationship 2: balanced commitment interdependence

This type of stakeholder partnership involves financial or other obligations and is characterised by an agreement to share those obligations equally. Interdependence is maintained as long as equality of engagement is obtained.

Case study 2: BPX and its surrounding communities

The commitments between BPX and its surrounding communities were linked to community development projects. If not all involved partners were committed to a specific social investment project, then projects failed, were inefficient or not put into practice at all, as the commitment of every partner was needed to achieve the project objective. Hence, the source of power within this stakeholder partnership rested in commitments to community development projects. The partners' search to meet social expectations formed the power balance mechanism. When all partners were committed to meeting the same social expectation, the power relationship was balanced. The consequence for the power relationship of the partnership between BPX and its communities was interdependence. This balanced commitment interdependence assisted the partners by transferring the ownership of the social investment project to the involved communities.

Power relationship 3: balanced competence interdependence

This type of stakeholder partnership is characterised by equality in terms of the involved partners' ability—being adequately or well qualified, physically and intellectually—to achieve partnership objectives. Interdependence is maintained as long as the involved partners contribute high-quality competence as required to fulfil the partnership task and establish a competence equilibrium. In this way a reciprocal dependence is achieved.

Case study 3: Hoechst and the Öko-Institut
In the case of the partnership between Hoechst and the Öko-Institut, the partners were required to combine their competence so as to achieve influence. Consequently, competence became the source of power in this stakeholder partnership. However, Hoechst and the Öko-Institut tried to avoid exercising their power because to achieve the joint project task each partner needed the other's competence. This mutual need for competence established a power balance mechanism that ultimately led to a balanced dominance between Hoechst and the Öko-Institut and, as consequence, led to interdependence. Both partners were aware of the balanced competence interdependence and applied a power relationship to maintain autonomy.

Power relationship 4: regulated knowledge interdependence

This type of stakeholder partnership is characterised by controlled or governed use of knowledge of the other involved partners. The use of knowledge can be regulated formally or informally. Interdependence is based on the regulation of the application of knowledge.

Case study 4: Hoechst and its surrounding communities
In the case of the CDG between Hoechst and its surrounding communities, knowledge was the source of power. The company could have used its specialist knowledge to mislead or confuse the community representatives. Similarly, the community representatives could have used their knowledge about how to use the public for their own purposes, in order to manipulate or control the company. Therefore, a power balance mechanism needed to be established that would regulate the use of Hoechst's and community representatives' knowledge. The definition of rules for the CDG provided the solution that also led to a regulated

dominance of the involved partners (see also details of case study 4 on page 230). As a consequence of the use of rules, interdependence was created. Hoechst and its surrounding communities applied this regulated knowledge interdependence as an assurance during discussions. The power relationship limited the misuse of the partnership.

Analysis

With regard to the five variables that have been applied to describe the power relationships in partnerships (source of power, balance mechanisms in place, level of dominance, consequences of type of relationship and propensity to use power), there is only one similarity between the four case studies. The consequence of the power relationships in all stakeholder partnerships was interdependence between the involved partners. However, because of the various sources of power, power balance mechanisms, dominance and power application, the power relationships are different in terms of at least one defining feature. There is no evidence that the similarities or differences of the power relationships are driven by the firm-specific context of BP's and Hoechst's management of social risk. Consequently, because all partnerships are different in nature, it can be assumed that the power relationships in partnerships are partnership-specific rather than firm-specific.

Element 4: processes of partnership developments

The process of partnership development is the fourth defining element of partnerships. A process is a sequence of individual and collective events, actions and activities unfolding over time and in a set context. It is a particular course of action intended to achieve certain results. Development is a process in which something passes by degrees to a more advanced or mature stage. A positive development is an act of improving by expanding, enlarging or refining. For the purposes of this analysis, the process of partnership development is defined as the course of action by which a stakeholder partnership passes by degrees to a more advanced or mature stage, unfolding over time and context. The advancement can be measured by the fulfilment of the partnership objectives. Each analysed stakeholder partnership can be seen to develop in a different way, by:

- Incremental adaptation
- Stepwise strategising
- Life-cycle learning
- Spiralling trust building

This interpretation of the four diverse developmental processes is the result of an analysis of stakeholder partnerships over time. Five variables are applied to describe the four different processes:

- Direction of change
- Evolution of the partnership
- Time-horizon of the partnership
- Actions of the partnership
- Durability of the partnership

Development process 1: incremental adaptation

Incremental adaptation is a process of partnership development characterised by gradually increasing, by regular degrees, adjustments to the specific context of the relationship environment. It is a uniform, linear process by which the involved partners adapt to each other.

Case study 1: BP and IAG

For the partnership between BP and IAG, this adjustment was crucial to provide the partners with the ability to acquire each other's knowledge. However, it was not clear in which direction this partnership would develop. Nor was it possible to plan its development. The direction of BP and IAG's partnership emerged over time. Every conversation enhanced the partnership quality by regular degrees. There were no sudden drops or increases in quality. Hence, it was an incremental evolution born from the aim of building a long-term partnership. BP and IAG's behaviour was oriented towards this long-term time-horizon. The actions of the partnership were driven by adaptation. The company and the NGOs had to adjust their behaviour not only to the changed environment but also to meet the expectations of the partner. However, this was no guarantee of endurance. The durability of the partnership was uncertain, since the co-operation depended on each partner's reputation and was incident-driven.

Development process 2: stepwise strategising

Stepwise strategising is characterised by a sequence of events, actions and activities that puts a strategy into practice. Each successive process element is determined by the preceding steps; the process advances one step at a time. Hence, the process can be depicted as a staircase. Every step is a process element, and the height of the step is the extent to which the strategy is put into practice. A strategy is an elaborate and systematic plan for interacting with the environment to achieve set goals.

Case study 2: BPX and its surrounding communities

BPX had a social development plan, and the communities had a community development plan. These were brought together to set up a strategy. Therefore, the partnership between BPX and its surrounding communities was planned but was embedded in a long-term perspective; there was therefore a distant time-horizon for this co-operation. However, since the strategy comprised various projects over a long period of time, every project was renegotiated before the partners started to put it into practice. Consequently, strategising was the primary action of the partnership, leading to stepwise evolution. The durability of the partnership was dependent on various factors such as political issues and the life-span of BPX's operations in Colombia.

Process development 3: life-cycle learning

Life-cycle learning is characterised by a series of stages through which a partner-ship passes between the primary stage recurs. Learning, the cognitive process of acquiring skill or knowledge, is the driver of this type of development. Partners begin to co-operate with different competences, learning from each other, build-ing new and joint competences and, finally, entering a mature stage where further learning with regard to the partnership objective would not add significant value.

Case study 3: Hoechst and the Öko-Institut
The objective of the partnership between Hoechst and the Öko-Institut was to develop a product assessment tool. Since this joint project was specifically designed to fulfil a defined task, the direction of partnership development was planned and its time-horizon bounded. The partners constructed the project in stages. Whereas at the beginning learning from each other was important, later on competences were developed and applied until the project objective was accomplished. Hence, it was a life-cycle learning partnership. Because the time-horizon was bounded, the durability of the joint project was limited from the outset. However, new projects are under way between Hoechst and the Öko-Institut and new life-cycle learning is beginning.

Development process 4: spiralling trust building

Spiralling trust building is a process of partnership building whereby the faith of the partners in each other is built up on a recurring basis. It is a process of constant renewal, but each phase of renewal covers different issues. Conse-quently, since the partnership is progressing over time, it can be portrayed as a spiral rather than as a circle.

Case study 4: Hoechst and its surrounding communities
Trust is something held by someone for the benefit of another. For the partner-ship between Hoechst and its surrounding communities, trust building was certainly at the centre of the activities of the CDG. However, because none of the partners knew how to set up a discussion group, and because the issues that were covered by the CDG changed depending on Hoechst's business practice and critical incidents, the direction of the partnership development could not be planned and therefore tended to emerge gradually. The discussion of each social conflict issue covered by the CDG was associated with a trust-building circle. However, because the issues discussed by the CDG changed over time, the CDG renewed itself by beginning a new trust-building circle with each new discussion

round. Since one discussion led to the next, the circles of trust building were connected and led to a spiralling evolution of the partnership, emphasising a long-term time-horizon. With this spiralling trust-building development, the CDG created a certain amount of durability for which the replication of the CDG provides some evidence.

Analysis

With regard to the five variables that have been applied to describe the processes of partnership developments (direction of change, evolution of the partnership, time-horizon of the partnership, actions of the partnership and durability of the partnership), there are no stringent similarities between the four diverse partnership development processes. Two process directions were planned and two emerged as the process progressed. Three partnerships were long-term-oriented, whereas one was bounded from the beginning. The evolution, developmental actions and durability of the partnerships were fundamentally different from each other. However, no evidence could be found in the firm-specific context of BP's and Hoechst's social risk management that could explain the similarities and differences. Consequently, it can be assumed that the analysed processes of partnership development are partnership-specific rather than firm-specific.

◢ Four patterns of stakeholder partnership building

This research has sought to locate stakeholder partnership building within the context of managing social risk. Two companies were studied and two stakeholder partnerships for each company were analysed. BP was engaged in a partnership with IAG, a group of development NGOs, in the United Kingdom, and BPX, BP's exploration subsidiary, was in partnership with its surrounding communities in Colombia. Hoechst, in Germany, was involved in a partnership with the Öko-Institut, a 'green' NGO, and also with its surrounding communities. A diversity of cases was deliberately chosen to increase the variance between the cases and thus to enhance the validity of the data collected and analysed.

To answer the leading research question of how firms build stakeholder partnerships, the characteristics of partnerships were identified. These were categorised in terms of the purposes, pacts, power relations and processes of partnership development. To analyse each element of stakeholder partnerships with regard to the four partnerships analysed for this research, five variables were identified to enable description of and differentiation among and between the elements of 'partnership alchemy' (Nelson and Zadek 2000). Each of the four analysed stakeholder partnerships represents a different purpose, pact, power relation and process of partnership development. These four characteristics are the defining elements of partnerships and may be called the four Ps of stakeholder partnership building. In turn, each of these four elements may be broken down into a further four characteristics. Since each analysed stakeholder partnership represents a different set of characteristics of partnership building, together they form four distinctive types of partnership alchemy. The columns of Table 13.2 show the four Ps of stakeholder partnership building. The rows represent the four different case-study partnerships and, therefore, four patterns of stakeholder partnership building.

Case study	Purpose	Pact	Power relations	Process of development
1	▶ Acquiring knowledge	▶ Dialogue	▶ Cyclic reputation interdependence	▶ Incremental adaptation
2	▶ Co-financing of social investment	▶ Joint venture	▶ Balanced commitment interdependence	▶ Stepwise strategising
3	▶ Combining of competence	▶ Joint project	▶ Balanced competence interdependence	▶ Life-cycle learning
4	▶ Improvement of communication	▶ Alliance	▶ Regulated knowledge interdependence	▶ Spiralling trust-building

Note: case study 1: BP and IAG; case study 2: BP and its surrounding communities; case study 3: Hoechst and the Öko-Institut; case study 4: Hoechst and its surrounding communities

Table 13.2 **The four Ps of stakeholder partnership building**

◢ Roadmap for further research

This analysis of stakeholder partnership building could be continued and extended in several ways to add further substance to the research findings. Three roads for further research can be approached from three different research directions to achieve, respectively, descriptive, explanatory or prescriptive research outcomes.

The research project described in this chapter was empirically descriptive. In this chapter I have described the four Ps of partnership building, their four characteristics and their five descriptive variables. To continue this research it would be interesting to describe the links between the four analysed patterns of partnership building and the performance of the four case-study partnerships. Performance can be seen in terms of social or financial outcomes. To take this research further, performance causalities could be tested to explain whether links between partnership building patterns and partnership performance exist and, if so, to what extent these patterns affect performance. Furthermore, explanations about context and partnership-specific causalities would contribute to an understanding of the variance between partnerships and the effects of this on performance. Finally, prescriptive research could incorporate the context, partnership-building patterns and performance of partnerships into a framework to determine the boundaries of stakeholder partnership building.

Further descriptive research to analyse partnerships between business and stakeholders other than NGOs and communities would extend this research, as would an analysis of partnerships that focus on issues other than social issues. Partnerships from companies that operate in other industries or other countries might also add further substance to this research. Since the case-study partnerships analysed in this chapter were driven by critical incidents, it would be interesting to compare them with cases that were not embedded in such social dramas. A comparison of good and bad performing partnerships would add to our knowledge as well. Further partnership elements or further partnership-building patterns might be discovered as a result of such research. Explanatory and prescriptive research directions follow a similar road to that followed in the research described in this chapter.

As well as continuing and extending this research project, which has emphasised the macro level of stakeholder partnership building, one could follow a third research road towards a micro perspective of partnership building. This would involve focusing on issues such as the perceptions, motivations or learning of individual people involved in stakeholder partnerships.

A COMPARATIVE STUDY OF STAKEHOLDER ENGAGEMENT APPROACHES IN SOCIAL AUDITING*

Simon S. Gao
**Napier University
Business School, UK**

Jane J. Zhang
**Glasgow Caledonian
University, UK**

Researchers have devoted a considerable amount of attention to corporate social and environmental reporting (CSER) over the past 20 years (for a review, see Gray *et al.* 1995), focusing in particular on the impact of CSER on an organisation's social and environment performance (e.g. Herremans and Akathaporn 1993). The investigation of CSER has recently extended to the links of CSER with corporate social responsibility and accountability. Such links provide researchers the potential to explore the applicability of social auditing concepts to the attainment of an organisation's social objectives and the promotion of accountability and transparency. Social auditing is a (generally voluntary) activity that recognises an obligation incumbent on organisations to give an account of their social performance to their legitimate stakeholders (Zhang *et al.* 2000). It is regarded as a process that an organisation undertakes when assessing and reporting on its social performance in terms of accountability and stakeholder involvement.

There has been considerable interest in recent years in stakeholder theory. In the past two years, over 200 articles on stakeholder theory have appeared in philosophical and business journals (Gibson 2000). These articles have generally concluded that organisations should consider the interests of stakeholders and stakeholder engagement as these provide a net gain to the organisation, helping the organisation to achieve better performance. The notion that stakeholder

* The authors gratefully acknowledge the helpful comments of the two anonymous referees, and participants at the Accounting and Finance Research Conference, Napier University, December 2000.

interests are key strategic assets in an organisation (Useem 1996) has provided a foundation for the establishment and development of stakeholder engagement in the organisation. According to AA 1000 (AccountAbility Standard 1000; ISEA 1999), developed by the Institute of Social and Ethical AccountAbility (ISEA) in 1999, stakeholder engagement is not about organisations abdicating their responsibilities for the results of their activities but rather about using leadership to build relationships with stakeholders and hence about improving their overall performance and accountability. However, the notion does not suggest the ways an organisation can build relationships with stakeholders. There is little research in the literature into approaches adopted by an organisation to engage stakeholders in the areas such as CSER and social auditing.

Social auditing has attracted an unprecedented level of practical interest since the 1990s as it encourages and helps an organisation to monitor and improve its social performance. Correspondingly, social auditing has also attracted considerable attention in the literature (e.g. Cotton *et al.* 2000; Owen *et al.* 2000; Dawson 1998; Dennis *et al.* 1998; Sillanpää 1998; Gray *et al.* 1995, Gray *et al.* 1997). Over the past decade, social auditing research has been dominated by the normative approach, which attempts to determine why organisations ought to adopt social auditing. Little research has been done to analyse how social auditing has been practised by organisations and to what extent stakeholder engagement has been actualised in the social auditing process. Moreover, much of the research involves a single case study, which offers little insight into the common characteristics of the social auditing process.

The purpose of this chapter is to investigate how organisations engage stakeholders in social auditing through a comparative analysis of social auditing processes and reports from five different organisations. The organisations in this study include the Agency for Personal Service Overseas (APSO, Ireland), The Co-operative Bank (UK), BT (British Telecom, UK), Shared Earth (UK) and Vancouver City Savings Credit Union (VanCity, Canada). These cover a representative spread of organisations, from a government-sponsored public agency (APSO), a telecommunications company (BT), financial services firms (The Co-operative Bank and VanCity) to a charity (Shared Earth). As there are only a limited number of organisations that have adopted social auditing and published social accounts or social audit reports, the selection of cases was straightforward, being based mainly on the criteria of having a widespread selection of sectors and countries in addition to the availability of recent social audit reports or accounts in (for our sake) English.

Although social auditing is generally an organisational-based process, this study has found that the organisations in this study adopt more or less the same social auditing process and take similar stakeholder engagement approaches in social auditing. The whole process of social auditing was predominately driven by the management of the organisations and there was very limited meaningful stakeholder engagement. Although the findings of this study are tentative in view of the limited number of cases investigated, the findings echo the arguments of other studies (e.g. Owen *et al.* 2000).

The remainder of this chapter is organised as follows. In the next section we will discuss stakeholder engagement. We will then move on to a general consideration of social auditing. In the penultimate section we will provide a comparison of stakeholder engagement in social auditing across the case-study organisations. In the final section we outline our conclusions.

◢ Stakeholder engagement

Freeman (1984: 46) defines a stakeholder as 'any group or individual who can affect or is affected by the achievement of the organisation's objectives'. This definition suggests a two-way relationship between the organisation and its stakeholders. Each element of this relationship represents a foundation for a model of stakeholder engagement.

First, if stakeholders can influence the achievement of an organisation's objectives, it follows that the organisation's performance can be affected by the activities and involvement of its stakeholders. This link legitimates stakeholder engagement with a view to achieving the best possible performance by the organisation. Second, if stakeholders are affected by the achievement of an organisation's objectives, it follows that the activities of the organisation will have an impact on the wellbeing of its stakeholders. This link legitimates stakeholders' right for information regarding the activities and performance of an organisation and how their wellbeing and interests are affected by the organisation. In turn, this requires the organisation to respect and consider wide and diverse interests of stakeholders in setting up its objectives and planning its activities.

Both orientations expect stakeholder engagement in an organisation's decision-making process. Stakeholder engagement focuses on improving the accountability and performance of an organisation. The past 20 years have witnessed stakeholder theory becoming a large and multifaceted area of management research and a mainstay of management theory (e.g. Donaldson and Preston 1995; Harrison and Freeman 1999; Mitchell *et al.* 1997). This is because in order to manage an organisation effectively it is vital for the management group of the organisation to identify its stakeholders and prioritise them according to their relative importance in terms of the organisation's objectives and performance. It is also important for the management to understand stakeholders' expectations and to assess the consequences of these expectations on the organisation. Johnson and Scholes (1993: 172) note that it is a very important part of any strategic analysis to understand stakeholders and how they are likely to influence the organisation's strategy. However, as noted by Greenley and Foxall (1997), relatively little consideration has so far been given to studying the approaches that organisations use to address the interests of their stakeholder groups.

It is well argued by stakeholder theory that, as most of the activities of an organisation are embedded in a network of stakeholder relationships, the organisation needs to build such a network which is fully understood by stakeholders and which has real meaning for the stakeholders. The building-up of this network requires the identification of stakeholders and their interests. The heart of the problem with stakeholder theory has been the identification or differentiation of the 'stake', or 'interest', of each stakeholder in an organisation. As observed by Harrison and Freeman (1999), very little research has been done so far to help identify which stakeholders really count to managers or share a powerful stake or interest in an organisation. On the one hand, this is mainly a result of the lack of theory or models capable of quantifying the social wellbeing of stakeholders in terms of monetary (market) value. On the other hand, in contemporary organisations, the reality is likely to be very different from many assumptions underpinning stakeholder theory. For example, in reality, a stakeholder group is not a segregated group with its own distinctive interests that can be separated from the interests of other stakeholders. An individual can be labelled variously in terms of different stakeholders—he or she may be all at once a shareholder, a customer, an employee and a member of the local community. It will be difficult for a supermarket group with millions of individual shareholders who are also customers to separate the interests of shareholders from those of its customers. In such a case, the employees themselves may also be the customers and shareholders. Consequently, a critical issue in the management of a supermarket group is whether managers can successfully balance the competing and interrelated interests of various stakeholder groups and individuals. Thus organisations have complex relationships with stakeholder groups (e.g. shareholders, employees, customers and clients and the public) and each stakeholder group will differ in terms of its 'stake', level of trust and requirements for accountability. Therefore, in the development of an organisation's stakeholder engagement model, different levels and forms of stakeholder engagement must be taken into account.

Moreover, it is extremely difficult to measure the quality of stakeholder engagement in an organisation. First, this is because stakeholder engagement can mean different things in different contexts. In one type of engagement an organisation may present an agenda to its stakeholders and ask (e.g. through a questionnaire survey or interviews) for their views on how that agenda may be improved. A dialogue is another type of engagement. However, a dialogue may merely be a form of information-gathering that does not allow feedback or interactive two-way communications. The quality of this type of engagement is obviously low.

Second, the quality of engagement is generally associated with the number of stakeholders participating in the process. For most organisations it will not be possible to create a dialogue with all its stakeholders, particularly individuals, and engage all of them in the process of decision-making and performance measuring. Such engagement generally requires the selection (or election) of stakeholder representatives and the differentiation of stakeholders and their interests,[1] which is always problematic in practice.

---

1 We believe it is wrong to assume that the management of organisations should have overall control over the selection of stakeholder representatives and the selection process. This is an important issue that needs to be addressed in social auditing and stakeholder engagement, but it is beyond the scope of this chapter.

Third, stakeholders themselves may not be interested in engaging with the organisation. Further, they will not care about the quality of such engagement if they cannot directly see the benefits of doing this. In fact, such benefits, especially long-term benefits, cannot easily be observed. Fourth, different issues need to be addressed through different levels of engagement. It will not be effective to compare these different levels of engagement with reference to the same qualitative criteria. We argue that real, meaningful stakeholder engagement should be a genuine process of sharing views, between the stakeholders and the management of an organisation, for the purpose of improving the performance of the organisation and for improving the organisation's accountability.

Table 14.1 provides a simple association between the level of engagement, the engagement approach and the number of stakeholders that can effectively participate in the social auditing process. This suggests that the number of stakeholders directly engaged in the process decreases with increasing quality of engagement; hence real, meaningful stakeholder engagements may exclude many individual stakeholders. To achieve meaningful stakeholder engagement, selection of stakeholder representatives will be essential. This requires an organisation to have a stakeholder-driven management philosophy, system and structure. Based on current best practice, ISEA has launched its first standard, AA 1000, which provides both a framework that organisations can use to understand and improve stakeholder engagement and a means for the organisations to judge the effective-

Level of engagement	Stakeholders are merely given information (Passive)	Stakeholders are consulted (Listening)	Stakeholders engage in dialogue with company (Two-way process)	Management is driven by stakeholders (Proactive)
Stakeholder engagement approach	▸ Inform stakeholders via public media ▸ Publish reports ▸ Policy and product documents	▸ Listen to stakeholders through formal meetings or suggestion boxes ▸ Hear stakeholders' views through questionnaires and interviews ▸ Have a complaint process	▸ Hold focus-group discussions ▸ Provide feedback to stakeholders ▸ Use stakeholder-driven performance measures and reports	▸ Set up a stakeholder council ▸ Allow stakeholder representatives in management ▸ Ask for stakeholder verification of social report
Number of stakeholder participants	▸ Mass stakeholders and wide society	▸ Selected stakeholders	▸ Limited number of key stakeholders	▸ Very limited number of key stakeholders (e.g. stakeholder representatives)

Table 14.1 **The quality of stakeholder engagement**

ness of social auditing practice. According to AA 1000, meaningful engagement needs to:

- Allow stakeholders to assist in the identification of other stakeholders.
- Ensure that stakeholders trust the social and ethical accountant (internal or external) that is collecting and processing the findings of the engagement.
- Be a dialogue, not a one-way information feed.
- Be between parties with sufficient preparation and briefing to have well-informed opinions and decisions.
- Involve stakeholders in defining the terms of the engagement. The terms will include, but are not limited to, the issues covered, the methods and techniques of engagement used, the questions asked, the means of analysing responses to questions and the stakeholder feedback process.
- Allow stakeholders to voice their views without restriction and without fear of penalty or discipline. However, stakeholders must be aware that if their opinions are taken seriously and acted on, this will have consequences on them and other stakeholder groups.
- Include a public disclosure and feedback process that offers other stakeholders information that is valuable in assessing the engagement and allows them to comment upon it (ISEA 1999: 21).

◢ Social auditing

Social auditing and social accounting are relatively new concepts.[2] The term 'social auditing' was first used in the 1950s. Much earlier work took the form of external investigations to assess the impact of large corporations on their workforce, consumers and the community. This investigative trend of social auditing continued into the 1980s, examining the impact of plant closures and of investment or relocation decisions and, increasingly, uncovering the (un)ethical behaviour and environmental impact of business corporations. In the 1990s, more broad developments of social auditing emerged, driven by increased pressures on organisations to demonstrate social and ethical performance and accountability. It has moved on to focus on the process, rather than on the benchmarks, that an organisation should follow to account for its performance, including a dialogue with its stakeholders and external verification and disclosure.

By definition, social auditing is a (generally voluntary) activity that recognises an obligation incumbent on organisations to give an account of their social performance to their legitimate stakeholders (Zhang *et al.* 2000). It is a process

2 Social auditing is sometimes a synonym for social accounting (e.g. Gray *et al.* 1997). In this chapter, 'social auditing' is used as a generic term that refers to the process that an organisation undertakes when assessing and reporting on its social performance and stakeholder involvement.

that an organisation undertakes when assessing and reporting on its social performance, focusing in particular on stakeholder involvement and accountability (Cotton *et al.* 2000). Social auditing attempts to provide a mechanism for decision-makers to evaluate ethical and social planning and to facilitate stakeholder engagement in the social and ethical decision-making process of an organisation. Increasing numbers of corporations have now accepted the notion of 'social responsibility' (e.g. The Body Shop International, BT, The Co-operative Bank) and have begun to publish social accounts and social audit reports. These kinds of reports or accounts have attracted widespread publicity (Gray *et al.* 1997).

Working with Traidcraft, the New Economics Foundation (NEF) developed their first social auditing model in 1993. This model has now been used by, among others, The Body Shop International, Shared Earth, BT, and Black Country Housing Association and Traidcraft in the UK, Ben & Jerry's in the USA, Sbn Bank in Denmark and APSO in Ireland. Other social auditing programmes have also been developed in Italy, South Africa, Scandinavia (a process called the 'ethical accounting statement'), Belgium, Mexico and the Philippines.

Social auditing is seen as a way of managing 'competing interests and pressures from stakeholders' (NEF 1996). The NEF (1996) categorises areas that can be measured by means of social auditing, including: core aims of the organisation, generally reflected in a mission statement, and specific stakeholder aims, identified during a consultation process with identified stakeholder groups. Gray *et al.* (1997) provide a classification of approaches to social auditing based on the complexity and system of the approaches and, more pertinently, their likely desirability to a conventional business organisation. Their classification is shown in Table 14.2.

Different approaches to social auditing have been proposed in the literature (e.g. Gray *et al.* 1997; Hill *et al.* 1998; Sillanpää 1998). Gray *et al.* (1997) suggest the 'polyvocal citizenship perspective' (PCP) approach to social auditing. Hill *et al.* (1998) and Sillanpää (1998) advocate a dialogue-based approach, but Hill *et al.* (1998) place more emphasis on informal dialogue and consultation processes. Sillanpää (1998: 1446) argues that 'a dialogue-driven approach is needed to nurture empowered stakeholder relationships'. Sillanpää believes that it is possible to link processes of stakeholder dialogue and inclusion with management systems designed to secure continuous improvement in product quality, human resource and safety management as well as individual learning and development. Hill *et al.* consider the active involvement of stakeholder groups as central to the operation of the social auditing exercise.

The objectives of social auditing should be to encourage dialogue and sharing of information in order to cope with the tensions of competing interests among stakeholders and increasing demand from stakeholders on services provided. However, the PCP and the dialogue approaches require the issue of identification of 'stakeholders' or 'citizens' to be addressed, particularly the issue of their representation. Zadek (1998) notices that there is a convergence of standards (models and frameworks) taking place in the practice of social and ethical accounting, auditing and reporting. He proposes eight quality principles for the development of social auditing:

Company-preferred approach

► Existing corporate reporting of both voluntary and mandatory data

► Existing corporate public relations and advertising or education data

► Collation of the above into a single 'social accounting' document—a 'silent account'

► 'One-off' experiments with approaches to social accounting

Systematic corporate social accounts

► Stakeholder reporting

► Description of the characteristics of the stakeholder relationship(s)

► Accountability reporting

► Reporting of the voices of the stakeholders

External 'social audits'

► Single-issue reporting (e.g. to consumers, environmentalists, etc.)

► Systematic social audits

► One-off reporting (e.g. investigative journalism)

Table 14.2 **Classification of approaches to social auditing**

Source: Gray *et al.* 1997

▪ Inclusivity

▪ Comparability

▪ Completeness

▪ Regularity and evolution

▪ Embeddedness

▪ External verification

▪ Communication

▪ Continuous improvement

Social auditing is a dynamic process that an organisation follows to account for and improve its performance, consisting of planning, accounting, auditing and reporting, embedding and stakeholder engagement (see AA 1000 [ISEA 1999]). It would be a mistake to consider social auditing as only the disclosure of an organisation's social performance. Reporting on social performance is not only a matter of disclosure; it is also a process of communication between the organisation and key stakeholders. Reporting is a way in which stakeholders can see whether the organisation 'listened' to their concerns and, over time, whether it has responded in practical terms. Consequently, reporting is a part of an integrated communication, dialogue, learning and decision-making process and is not the end-point in a retrospective process.

Although the role of social auditing should be examined in the context of business nature, organisational structure and groupings, the purpose of social auditing is to make an organisation more transparent and accountable (Zadek and Raynard 1995). In recent years, social auditing has been adopted by fair-trade companies, community and co-operative enterprises, the private sector, the voluntary sector and government agencies. Why did these organisations employ social auditing? In the case of APSO, it believed social auditing was the most appropriate model because:

- It focuses on the qualitative aspect of the work of the organisation.
- It identifies and consults all the stakeholders.
- Stakeholders define the performance indicators
- It is transparent.
- It will be published.
- All staff members will be involved—it is not for management only; every staff member is actively involved in the process.
- It facilitates change—all are involved in learning.
- It relates to all aspects of the organisation (APSO 1998: 6).

According to Simon Zadek (1998) of the NEF, 90% of the *Fortune* 500 companies already have codes of conduct covering a range of social and environmental issues. However, very little is known about how organisations engage stakeholders in the social auditing process.

◢ A comparison of stakeholder engagement approaches in social auditing: case studies

In this chapter, five organisations adopting social auditing were selected for a comparative study with a view to identifying how organisations engage stakeholders in social auditing. In view of the limited number of organisations formally undertaking social audit, the study of these five different organisations from three countries is expected to present a genuine picture of the current practice of social auditing and the extent of stakeholder engagement in the social auditing process. In a recent study (Zhang *et al.* 2000) six social auditing models were compared through an analysis of social auditing reports and social accounts from Beechwood College, The Body Shop, Traidcraft, Liverpool Housing Trust's Directions, The Co-operative Bank and APSO. The focus in that study was on the social auditing process, mainly in UK organisations; the focus of this chapter is on stakeholder engagement in social auditing. The cases studied in this chapter include the Agency for Personal Service Overseas (APSO, Ireland), British

Telecom (BT, UK), The Co-operative Bank (UK), Shared Earth (UK) and Vancouver City Savings Credit Union (VanCity, Canada), covering, as already stated in the introductory text of this chapter, different types of business: a government-sponsored public agency, a telecommunications firm, financial services firms, and a charity.

Agency for Personal Service Overseas

APSO is a state-sponsored body that was established in the Republic of Ireland in 1973 and incorporated in 1974. It promotes and sponsors temporary personal service in the developing countries of the world for their economic and social development, in the interest of justice and peace among nations. The mission of APSO is to contribute to sustainable improvement in the living conditions of poor communities in developing countries by enhancing human resources, skills and local capacities in the interests of development, peace and justice (APSO 1998). In 1998, APSO published its first social accounting report, *Social Accounts 1996*, with a view to obtaining the views and perceptions of stakeholders on the quality and effectiveness of the service it delivered.

A core principle of APSO's social auditing methodology was to include the input from all types of stakeholders into the process of identifying the criteria against which the organisation's performance would be measured. In the social auditing process, the social accounting team identified seven stakeholder groups. Each stakeholder group was asked to identify all APSO's stakeholders, and these were checked off against the list of seven put together by the social accountant team.[3] Moreover, each stakeholder group was invited to map each stakeholder relationship with APSO and with other stakeholders. During the process, stakeholders were asked to consider APSO's mission statement and a list of APSO's values and to decide which were the key criteria by which they would judge APSO. In the social auditing process, structured questionnaires were used to obtain the views of five groups of stakeholders on a common set of issues covering APSO's development objectives. Also, each questionnaire contained a further set of questions that referred only to issues raised by the recipient stakeholder group. The contents of the questionnaires was regarded as confidential and were sent in sealed envelopes to the Equality Studies Department at University College Dublin for analysis by a member of the research staff. The statistical results were later passed on to the social accounting team at APSO.

British Telecom

BT, based in the UK, is one of the largest providers of telecommunications in the world, with over 2 million individual shareholders and a turnover of £18.2 billion

3   Note that the concept of 'social accountants' was used in APSO's social accounts. Although there is no explanation of this term, it seems in this case to refer to the members of the social accounting team.

for the financial year ending 31 March 1999. According to BT's mission statement, its intention is to generate shareholder value by seizing opportunities in the communications market worldwide, building on its current business and focusing on high-growth segments while playing its part in the community and achieving the highest standards of integrity, customer satisfaction and employee motivation. In 1999, BT published its first social report.

In the social auditing process, stakeholder consultation comprised a series of 12 focus-group discussions and 18 one-to-one interviews with representatives of some of the organisation's key stakeholder groups (employees, customers, institutional investors, private shareholders, opinion leaders, the community and experts in the field of social reporting). The process of stakeholder consultation was largely carried out by the independent research organisation MORI. Throughout, the primary goal was to identify those factors that were considered by stakeholders to be the most significant social impacts and effects of BT. Taking advantage of its business as the provider of telephone services, BT used the telephone to survey thousands of customers every month; the data was then built into its social auditing process.

The Co-operative Bank

The Co-operative Bank, a UK-based bank with a history of 128 years, has adopted co-operation and partnership principles in managing its business and relationships with stakeholders. It produced its first partnership report in 1998.

The Co-operative Bank's social auditing model is based on the partnership approach that commits the Bank to delivering benefits to all its partners in a socially responsible and ecologically sustainable manner.[4] It recognised the 'interdependence' of partners as well as the conflict of interests among different stakeholder groups. The Bank's approach to this conflict was to try to achieve the best balance possible, which was regarded as the most critical aspect of making the partnership approach work in practice. In the social auditing process, a partnership ballot was used to gather data and assess stakeholders' opinions on specific issues.

The process taken by The Co-operative Bank in its social auditing model was first to establish a partnership development team, the responsibility of which is to undertake a detailed assessment of the Bank's performance in relation to each of the seven stakeholder groups. From this assessment the team carries out research to determine: the areas of priority for each partner, the relationship of

4 The Partnership approach evolved over a ten-year period with three key developments associated with the publication of the 'Mission Statement', 'Ethical Policy' and 'Ecological Mission Statement' of The Co-operative Bank in 1998. A central theme of the 'Mission Statement' is the principle of inclusion (i.e. The Co-operative Bank should take account of the interests of all parties affected by its activities, not just shareholders). The 'Ethical Policy', which was developed in close consultation with its customers, sets out clearly who the Bank will and will not do business with. The 'Ecological Mission Statement' aims at maintaining the minimum conditions for an ecologically sustainable society.

that partner with the Bank, and degree to which the Bank delivers value in a socially responsible and ecologically sustainable manner. Finally, The Co-operative Bank focuses on three areas of assessment: value deliverance, social responsibility and ecological sustainability. Following the assessment of performance in relation to each area, it sets new goals for the next reporting year, with managers taking personal responsibility for performance in their given area.

Shared Earth

Shared Earth started in 1986 as a small partnership shop based in York, UK, selling clothing, jewellery and crafts from developing countries as well as a wide range of recycled stationery and various related products such as books, music, candles and aromatherapy oils. It now has a number of shops across the UK. As a relatively small organisation with about 50 members of staff,[5] Shared Earth used an external auditor, the NEF, to design its social auditing process. It generally follows the conventional method of social auditing by identifying stakeholder groups, surveying stakeholder opinion on various social and ethical issues and then reporting on the results through social accounts.

Vancouver City Savings Credit Union

VanCity is a member-owned credit union based in Vancouver city, Canada. The mission statement states that, 'through strong financial performance, we serve as a catalyst for the self-reliance and economic wellbeing of our membership and community' (1997). To improve the Union's transparency and accountability VanCity has employed social accounting since 1992. In 1997, with the help of external social auditors, particularly those from the NEF, VanCity published its first externally verified social report.

VanCity believed that producing and releasing a social report was a learning process and would enhance its dialogue with stakeholders and provide another means to help the organisation improve its financial and social performance (VanCity 1997: 2). In the social auditing process, randomly selected stakeholder representatives from members, staff, community organisations and credit unions were consulted through focus groups. In addition, stakeholder perceptions were drawn from past survey results, tracking studies, internal documents and interviews with VanCity managers. One-to-one management interviews were conducted to determine the extent to which there were systems in place to support, train and guide VanCity staff to make socially and environmentally responsible decisions in the course of their work. Indicators and benchmarks for measuring and evaluating the organisation's social and environmental performance were developed following management and stakeholder consultations,

---

5   In 1995, Shared Earth turned the office and wholesale part of its business into a limited company, but its shops remained a partnership. In this chapter we treat these two entities as a single organisation.

internal document reviews and a review of social norms and industry best practice.

VanCity's social auditing process aims to explore the company's behaviour towards its social impact on key stakeholders in relation to the organisation's values and objectives and those of its stakeholders. The social auditing approach adopted by VanCity involves policy reviews, development of performance indicators, internal management system reviews, stakeholder dialogue processes (including focus groups, surveys, and interviews), publication of a report summarising information and commitments arising from the audit process and an external verification process. The external verification process involves monitoring all or some stages of the audit process and testing data and qualitative information presented in the published report.

◢ **Stakeholder engagement approaches in social auditing**

In this chapter, by analysing social accounts and reports and social auditing processes, we have examined how each main stakeholder group in the five case-study organisations was engaged in social auditing. Although most stakeholder engagement approaches were explicitly disclosed by the organisations in their accounts and reports, it is possible that some approaches were not disclosed, as organisations use their discretion over whether to disclose information that might be seen as being inappropriate for the organisations. Presently, social auditing is not a statutory obligation for organisations, nor is the approach encoded in any kind of regulations in the case-study countries.

Table 14.3 provides a comparison of stakeholder engagement approaches used in social auditing. Although different organisations have different stakeholder groups, the approaches to stakeholder engagement in the social auditing process have much in common. The most common methods were the use of surveys and focus groups, primarily used by the management of the organisations, to gather information from stakeholders. There is no evidence that these approaches were used by the management to actively engage stakeholders in the organisations' decision-making.

Obviously, the survey and focus-group approaches have limitations. The survey approach may, on the one hand, have a low response rate, as shown in The Co-operative Bank and VanCity cases. In both cases only a small number of individual stakeholders responded to the surveys. On the other hand, survey results may be influenced by the design of the survey and thus may be misleading, as stakeholders did not take part in defining issues or in developing the survey. Owen *et al.* (2000) argue that the results of a questionnaire survey may easily be used to add colourful histograms to social reports, illustrating percentages of responses that are either supportive or otherwise of predetermined survey

Organisations	Stakeholder group	Stakeholder engagement approach
Agency for Personal Services Overseas (APSO, Ireland)	▶ Partner organisations overseas	▶ Interviews; also the field officer submits a list of programmes and an evaluation of these
	▶ Development workers	▶ Focus-group discussions facilitated by an outside consultant and the social accounts consultant; a questionnaire
	▶ APSO field staff	▶ A full meeting with all staff, and further discussion and the interviews forming the questionnaire
	▶ 'Sending' agencies	▶ Consultative meetings
	▶ Dublin office staff	▶ Staff meetings (compile the questionnaire)
	▶ Irish government (sponsor)	▶ Meeting with representatives and a follow-up meeting
	▶ Suppliers (contractors, consultants, banks, travel agents, trainers, Comhlamh, etc.)	▶ Not involved
British Telecommunications plc (BT, UK)	▶ Shareholders	▶ Regular meetings with institutional shareholders; annual reports; a website; freephone help-line; AGM
	▶ Customers	▶ Consumer liaison panels; telephone and mail surveys; interviews
	▶ Employees	▶ Internal survey; intranet; publications
	▶ The community	▶ Research; external survey
The Co-operative Bank (UK)	▶ Shareholders	▶ AGM
	▶ Customers	▶ The partnership ballot; external survey of personal customers such as MORI's Financial Services survey; questionnaires to corporate customers
	▶ Staff and their families	▶ Staff survey, focus-group research by external consultants
	▶ Suppliers	▶ Focus group and interview to identify priorities, then telephone interviews (conducted by researchers from an external consulting firm)
	▶ Local communities	▶ Case studies
	▶ National and international society	▶ Interviews
	▶ Past and future generations of co-operators	▶ Not involved

Table 14.3 **A comparison of stakeholder engagement approaches in social auditing** *(continued opposite)*

Source: authors' survey

Organisations	Stakeholder group	Stakeholder engagement approach
Shared Earth (UK)	▶ Customers	▶ Customer survey; a record of customer complaints
	▶ Staff	▶ Questionnaire survey by an independent consultant; internal records
	▶ Suppliers	▶ Not involved
	▶ Environment	▶ Not applicable
	▶ Community involvement	▶ Not involved
Vancouver City Savings Credit Union (VanCity, Canada)	▶ Members	▶ Member service surveys; tracking of member comments; focus group with specific member segments; internal interviews; document reviews
	▶ Staff	▶ Past employee opinion surveys; exit interviews; survey of branch staff; focus groups; internal interviews; document reviews
	▶ Credit unions	▶ Focus group; internal interviews; document review; external interviews; published documents
	▶ Community	▶ Focus groups; internal interviews; review of documents
	▶ Environment	▶ Not applicable
	▶ Suppliers	▶ Not involved
	▶ Business alliances	▶ Not involved
	▶ VanCity Enterprises Ltd (a subsidiary of VanCity)	▶ Focus groups; internal interviews; review of documents
	▶ VanCity Community Foundation (an arm's-length affiliate of VanCity)	▶ Focus groups; internal interviews reviews of documents

Notes: ▶ APSO is a state-sponsored organisation promoting and sponsoring temporary personal service in developing countries.
▶ BT is a multinational corporation providing telecommunications services.
▶ The Co-operative Bank is a bank with a sole equity shareholder, The Co-operative Wholesale Society.
▶ Shared Earth is a UK-based retailer and wholesaler of clothing, jewellery and crafts, 'recycled' stationery and related products.
▶ VanCity is a member-owned credit union providing financial services.
▶ Comhlamh is a returned volunteer organisation.

Table 14.3 (continued)

statements. This form of communication with stakeholders will negate the effectiveness of social auditing in improving accountability and enhancing transparency.

The major problems of the focus-group approach lie in the limited number of participants in the process and the difficulty of organising them due to availability of individuals and appropriate meeting places. Also, focus groups can be misled by management to specifically focus on a predetermined area. In most cases, focus groups were arranged by management to address a particular concern on behalf of management or a major stakeholder group. For example, in The Co-operative Bank, the major consultative exercise with customers was in the area of ethical policy.

All the cases studied in this chapter show no evidence that management attempted to use social auditing to balance competing interests among stakeholders. Although the partnership approach taken by The Co-operative Bank recognised there is a conflict of interests among different stakeholder groups, the issue and solutions to the conflict were not addressed in the social auditing process. Competing interests were not an issue for stakeholder consultation. There is no evidence from the case studies that stakeholders were able to engage in a real debate over this issue. There were no follow-up or feedback processes.

Moreover, the social auditing systems in the organisations under study were designed mainly from the management perspective with the assistance of external social auditing consultants. Stakeholders did not participate in the design and development of the social auditing systems. This implies that stakeholder voices and real meaningful stakeholder engagement were limited. No organisation in this study has established a stakeholder-focused management system. The whole process of social auditing has been predominately driven by the management of the organisations and by external professional consultants. Very limited meaningful engagement, as defined in AA 1000 (ISEA 1999), exists in social auditing in these organisations.

Clearly, this raises questions about the motivation of organisations in adopting social auditing and the effectiveness of stakeholder engagement. We share Owen *et al.*'s (2000) concern over the potential for 'managerial capture' in the social auditing process. Managerial capture is the potential of management to take control of the whole process (including the degree of stakeholder inclusion) by strategically collecting and disseminating only the information it deems appropriate to advance the corporate image, rather than being truly transparent and accountable to the society it serves. Managerial capture can result not only in a myopic and limited number of stakeholders being included but also in overinflated promises of accountability to an all-encompassing and essentially meaningless set of 'stakeholders'.

We argue that a real, meaningful stakeholder engagement approach should be one that provides a mechanism both for the stakeholders and for the organisation to share each other's views for the purpose of improving the organisation's performance and accountability. It should be a two-way system of both contributing to and gaining from the performance of the organisation and accountability. However, in our opinion, current discussions on the subject have devoted too much time to the contribution side. Obviously, if stakeholders do not know the potential benefits they could capture from the process, they will not show enthusiasm for the process. Management-driven social auditing serves management interests only; hence, such auditing lacks support from stakeholders.

As Owen *et al.* (2000) highlight, without real change to corporate governance structures, social auditing could be monopolised by consultants and/or corporate management so that it amounts to little more than a skilfully controlled public relations exercise. Unfortunately, there are no appropriate strategies or mechanisms to enable stakeholders to be proactive in driving social auditing. No doubt, stakeholders' competences (enthusiasm, skills and resources) will also play a key role in facilitating meaningful stakeholder engagement. Therefore, the issue of building up stakeholder competences should be taken into account in developing social auditing. However, this issue has, to the best of our knowledge, been entirely ignored in current discussions of social auditing.

◢ Conclusions

The comparative study presented in this chapter has yielded a number of important findings with implications for organisation managers and academics alike. As we move into the new millennium with increasing demand for stakeholder engagement and organisation democracy and more pressure on organisations to demonstrate social and ethical performance and accountability, there will no doubt be more organisations applying social auditing. It is interesting and encouraging to see that social auditing has gradually been accepted by organisations, at least from the management perspective, to engage stakeholders in assessing some parts of organisations' performance. The cases in this study show that stakeholders' views were selectively considered by the management of the organisations, especially in developing the organisations' social audit reports and social accounts.

In conclusion, the results of this study indicate that the organisations follow more or less the same social auditing process and take similar approaches to stakeholder engagement in social auditing. The most common approaches are the use of surveys and focus-group meetings; both have their limitations. There is no evidence that the management attempted to use social auditing to balance competing interests among stakeholders. There were no follow-up or feedback processes. The social auditing systems were designed mainly from the management perspective, with the assistance of external consultants. Stakeholders did not participate in the design and development of the social auditing systems. The whole process of social auditing was predominately driven by the management of the organisations and by external professional consultants. We believe that the results of this study, although conclusions should be tentatively made in view of the limited number of cases investigated, lead to a better understanding of current social auditing practice and the extent of stakeholder engagement in social auditing.

CORPORATE CITIZENSHIP
What gets recorded?
What gets rewarded?

Kimberly S. Davenport   *Patsy Lewellyn*
BellSouth Corporation, USA   University of South Carolina Aiken, USA

Stories of corporate citizenship practices abound (see McIntosh *et al.* 1998; Tichy *et al.* 1999); theories of corporate citizenship are in the making (Altman and Davenport 1998; Davenport 1998; Waddock 1999; Wood and Logsdon 1999). However, as far as we are aware, there is as yet no substantial research bridge between theory and practice, no assessment of the gap between desired and current states of corporate citizenship. This chapter reports an initial effort to build such a bridge via a large-scale study of citizenship media reports (what gets recorded) and citizenship awards (what gets rewarded).

By using earlier work (Davenport 1998) on the 20 principles of corporate citizenship as the framework, we conducted a content analysis of ten years of citizenship-related awards and five years of media stories of corporate citizenship. In addition, a comparison was made of media reports of citizenship—in a sense, the public's view of what is important—with the types of behaviour that are formally recognised and rewarded in awards programmes. The criteria used to make the awards were identified and mapped onto the 20 principles. We then compared the award-winning companies' practices and programmes with data on types of company behaviour most frequently cited in media reports.

Among the results reported in this chapter we found that 2 of the 20 principles (responsible human resource management and a family-friendly work environment) were the most cited in media records, with more than 400 citations each. Responsible human resource management was also the most frequently used reward criterion for corporate citizenship. The reward results also show which companies are most frequently acknowledged for their citizenship behaviour. An intriguing example of the findings is the discovery that a group of companies has been the subject of numerous media reports but has never won an award; another group is composed of frequent award-winners who almost never receive positive press for their citizenship efforts.

The results of the study reported in this chapter provide an initial barometer of how corporate citizenship is actually being practised among US companies. The chapter concludes with recommendations for future research to continue bridging the gap between theory and practice in corporate citizenship.

◢ Background: research framework

The framework for assessing corporate citizenship performance was based on earlier research (Davenport 1998, 2000) which explored how social auditing may be used as a methodology for measuring corporate citizenship. The participants in that study consisted of 61 experts representing five corporate stakeholder groups: the community, consumers, employees, investors and suppliers. A two-round Delphi methodology was used to first elicit a comprehensive set of answers to the study's research questions and then an agreed-on, consolidated view representing the group's collective judgements. When asked what constitutes a good corporate citizen, participants consistently ventured beyond their own narrow stakeholder perspectives, ultimately defining corporate citizenship as follows: 'Good corporate citizens strive to conduct all business dealings in an ethical manner, make a concerted effort to balance the needs of all stakeholders while working to protect the environment.'

Study participants universally agreed on three attributes as indicative of good corporate citizenship:

- **Ethical business behaviour.** The company is guided by rigorous ethical standards in all its business dealings.

- **Stakeholder commitment.** The company is managed for the benefit of all stakeholders: the community, consumers, employees, investors, suppliers, etc.

- **Environmental commitment.** The company moderates its overall environmental impact through programmes such as recycling, waste and emission abatement and through impact assessment via environmental audits.

To support these three attributes, participants identified 20 principles of corporate citizenship as criteria for guiding and assessing an organisation's performance. These are shown in Box 15.1.

▶ *Ethical business behaviour*

   The company . . .

   1. Engages in fair and honest business practices in its relationships with stakeholders
   2. Sets high standards of behaviour for all employees
   3. Exercises ethical oversight at the executive and board levels

▶ *Stakeholder commitment*

   The company . . .

   4. Is well managed for all stakeholders
   5. Initiates and engages in genuine dialogue with stakeholders
   6. Values and implements disclosure

▶ *Community commitment*

   The company . . .

   7. Fosters a reciprocal relationship between the corporation and the community
   8. Invests in the communities in which it operates

▶ *Consumer commitment*

   The company . . .

   9. Respects the rights of consumers
   10. Offers quality products and services
   11. Provides information that is truthful and useful

▶ *Employee commitment*

   The company . . .

   12. Provides a family-friendly work environment
   13. Engages in responsible human-resource management
   14. Provides an equitable reward and wage system for employees
   15. Engages in open and flexible communications with employees
   16. Invests in employee development

▶ *Investor commitment*

   The company . . .

   17. Strives for a competitive return on investment

▶ *Supplier commitment*

   The company . . .

   18. Engages in fair-trading practices with suppliers

▶ *Environmental commitment*

   The company . . .

   19. Demonstrates a commitment to the environment
   20. Demonstrates a commitment to sustainable development

Box 15.1 **The 20 principles of corporate citizenship**

Source: Davenport 1998

◢ Results

What gets recorded

Research methodology

Based on the key concepts of the 20 principles, 109 keyword search terms and phrases were developed to search the Business for Social Responsibility (BSR) database (for a list of the search terms, see the Appendix on page 275). BSR is a trade association, the mission of which is to promote socially responsible business practices.[1] Since 1996, BSR has reviewed, on average, 125 publications weekly to provide a newsclip service for its members. Popular press and academic journals are included in the review, such as (as cited in this chapter):

- *American Benefactor*
- *Business and the Environment*
- *Business Week*
- *Environmental News Network*
- *Financial Times*
- *Fortune*
- *Harvard Business Review*
- *HRfocus*
- *Human Resource Executive*
- *Management Review*
- *New York Times*
- *Training and Development*
- *Wall Street Journal*
- *Washington Post*
- *Welfare to Work Partnership Newsletter*

These publications are reviewed for information on the following topics:

- Community economic development
- Community involvement
- Environment
- Ethics
- General corporate social responsibility
- Governance
- Human rights

---

1   www.bsr.org

- Marketplace (consumer issues)
- Social audits and accountability
- Workplace (employee issues)

A search with the 109 keywords and phrases listed in the Appendix resulted in 2,290 citations from the BSR database.[2] The citations were evaluated and mapped onto the 20 principles of corporate citizenship. Two researchers conducted the content analysis, cross-checking each other's coding to ensure inter-rater reliability.

Findings: the eight most-cited principles

The frequencies of citation of corporate citizenship behaviour in the surveyed publications are depicted in Table 15.1. Eight of the 20 principles received more than 100 citations in the database, representing together 85.7% (1,961) of all 2,290 citations studied.

The eight most frequently cited principles included four related to employee practices (principles 12–15), two on community involvement (principles 7 and 8) and one each for environmental concerns (principle 19) and supplier relations (principle 18). The four principles related to employee issues accounted for almost half (47.8%) of all the media citations. Paying attention to workplace issues appears to be the primary way that companies practise good corporate citizenship, at least as reported in the press.

This is in contrast to the two most important types of behaviour characterising good corporate citizens (according to Delphi stakeholder representatives [Davenport 1998]), which relate to ethical business behaviour. A possible explanation for this difference between media citations and stakeholder opinion is that the two ethics principles represent a more abstract statement of citizenship behaviour, whereas the eight principles most frequently appearing in the media are more concrete statements of actual corporate practices and policies with respect to particular stakeholders. Thus they are more easily documented and reported.

Principle 13: the company engages in responsible
human resource management.
The most frequently cited principle, with 441 citations, was principle 13. This principle may be restated as:

> The company demonstrates an honest, long-term commitment to all its employees in its hiring, training, promotion, and layoff policies and to minority and female staff in programmes dedicated to helping them advance (Davenport 1998: 242).

2 Sources that reflected multiple principles were included multiple times, so the 2,290 citations represent the number of times that individual principles appeared in the source text. A source that contained multiple keywords but reflected only one principle was counted only once.

Principle	Citations	
The company . . .	Number	Percentage*
1 Engages in fair and honest business practices in its relationships with stakeholders	3	0.1
2 Sets high standards of behaviour for all employees	41	1.8
3 Exercises ethical oversight at the executive and board levels	17	0.7
4 Is well managed for all stakeholders	2	0.1
5 Initiates and engages in genuine dialogue with stakeholders	7	0.3
6 Values and implements disclosure	3	0.1
7 Fosters a reciprocal relationship between the corporation and community	192	8.4
8 Invests in the communities in which it operates	264	11.5
9 Respects the rights of consumers	19	0.8
10 Offers quality products and services	42	1.8
11 Provides information that is truthful and useful	45	2.0
12 Provides a family-friendly work environment	409	17.9
13 Engages in responsible human-resource management	441	19.3
14 Provides an equitable reward and wage system for employees	120	5.2
15 Engages in open and flexible communications with employees	123	5.4
16 Invests in employee development	87	3.8
17 Strives for a competitive return on investment	37	1.6
18 Engages in fair trading practices with suppliers	132	5.8
19 Demonstrates a commitment to the environment	280	12.2
20 Demonstrates a commitment to sustainable development	26	1.1

* The number of citations as a percentage of the total number of citations (2,290). Figures do not sum to 100 owing to rounding errors.

Table 15.1 **Citations per corporate citizenship principle, 1995–99**

The practice that was most frequently reported relative to this principle was the creation of programming and infrastructure to promote minorities and women.

IBM was frequently mentioned for its diversity efforts. It was one of several leading companies (including Pacific Telesis Group, Price Waterhouse, the Rouse Company and Wisconsin Electric Power) in an Equal Employment Opportunity Commission (EEOC) study profiling companies that successfully incorporate workplace discrimination prevention and resolution into their overall business plans and go 'above and beyond the requirements of the law' with regard to anti-discrimination practices (*Human Resource Executive*, March 1998: 13).

Texaco was also frequently cited for its efforts following the US$140 million settlement of a racial discrimination case in 1997. For example, the company was cited in *The New York Times* (2 November 1997: BU1) for:

- Increasing its purchasing from minority-owned companies and encouraging its suppliers to do the same
- Setting five-year goals to expand minority employee representation
- Tying portions of executives' bonuses to their success in hiring and promoting minorities
- Enrolling 20,000 employees in diversity workshops
- Placing more advertising in minority-oriented magazines
- Sponsoring minority-focused events

Principle 12: the company provides a family-friendly work environment.
The second most frequently cited principle was principle 12, with 409 citations. This principle may also be stated as:

> The company develops policies and programmes, such as day care and flex time, that support its employees' efforts to balance work and personal lives. Of particular importance are flexible benefit options, coverage for domestic partners, eldercare support, and family-leave-time (Davenport 1998: 241).

Again IBM was among the best-practice notables. In a *Business Week* editorial (7 October 1996: 170), IBM was commended for providing health benefits to the domestic partners of company employees. Other companies noted for their efforts on this issue were Harley Davidson, Charles Schwab, Coors Brewing, Dow Chemical, Walt Disney, Time Warner and Microsoft. *The Washington Post* (8 September 1998: A01) reported on the efforts of Hewlett-Packard, Target, NationsBank, Orlando Regional Healthcare Systems and American Bankers Insurance Group to build schools near their work locations for employees' children, which resulted in more successful recruitment and retention. Also, the SAS Institute is a best-practice example of principle 12, with its 35-hour work-week policy. *The Financial Times* (9 November 1998: 12) reports that the SAS Institute offers its employees:

> (1) evening exercise classes; (2) nursery school and daycare, which end at 5 PM to further encourage employees to leave work early; (3) an on-site medical centre; (4) a fitness centre; and (5) a high school for employees' children and members of the community. The company has a three percent turnover rate in an industry where the average company rate is 16 percent.

Principle 19: the company demonstrates a commitment to the environment.
Principle 19, with 280 citations, was the third most frequently mentioned practice. It is defined as:

> The company strives to moderate its overall environmental impact through programmes such as recycling, waste and emissions abatement, and environmental audits (Davenport 1998: 238).

Xerox was cited most frequently for its efforts in this area. For example, its asset recycling management programme saved the firm over US$50 million in costs in 1991, according to *Environmental News Network* (13 October 1997). Ford Motor Company and Saturn have also received substantial positive press coverage for creating recycling programmes to take back plastics from old cars.

Principle 8: the company invests in the communities in which it operates.
In fourth place was principle 8, with 264 citations. This principle is defined as:

> The company devotes money, time, and technical support to the needs-
> driven programmes that are based on community assessment (Daven-
> port 1998: 240).

IBM, Pfizer and Merck were the most frequently cited companies for this prin-ciple. All three companies were on the *American Benefactor's* (Summer 1998: 30) list of the 25 most generous companies in the USA. The selection guidelines include:

- Overall size of philanthropic commitment

- Innovative and effective programmes (i.e. the best programmes have found ways to identify and meet community needs)

Principle 7: the company fosters a reciprocal relationship between the corporation and the community.
Principle 7 received 192 citations, making it the fifth most-cited principle. It is defined as:

> The company develops, publicises, and implements policies and pro-
> grammes that encourage its employees to fully participate in the public
> life of the communities that the company operates in (Davenport 1998:
> 239).

A particular emphasis is placed on the company's partnering with other organ-isations to accomplish things in the community.

Burger King was frequently cited in the press for two efforts relative to this principle. One is its partnership with Cascade Engineering to form a coalition of companies in Michigan to train and hire welfare-to-work recipients (*Welfare to Work Partnership Newsletter*, 3 April 1998). In addition, Burger King has been at the forefront of companies that locate in and hire from low-income communities.

Principle 18: the company engages in fair-trading practices with suppliers.
Citation of principle 18 was sixth in frequency, with 132 citations. This principle is defined as:

> The company encourages reciprocity in its relationships with suppliers
> by treating them as valued long-term partners in enterprise and enlist-
> ing their talents, loyalty, and ideas (Davenport 1998: 244).

The automobile industry has become very progressive in recent years in embracing principle 18, in particular Ford, Chrysler and General Motors. *Fortune* magazine (27 April 1998: S1) highlighted the efforts of these three companies (among others) and their alliance with the National Minority Supplier Development Council (NMSDC) to purchase goods and services from minority-owned businesses. NMSDC estimated that in 1998 corporations purchased US$35 billion dollars' worth of goods and services from minority-owned businesses.

Principle 15: the company engages in
open and flexible communications with employees.
Coming in seventh place, with 123 citations, was principle 15, which is defined as:

> The company enlists employees in improving the work environment and solving problems by establishing a real dialogue in which employee opinions are welcomed and valued (Davenport 1998: 243).

Hewlett-Packard is often cited (*HRfocus*, July 1997: 1) as one of the leading companies utilising empowerment strategies, including such practices as: profit and power sharing, maintaining stable leadership, avoiding lay-offs and emphasising innovation at all levels.

Eastman Kodak is also well known in this regard. It is often cited among those companies that try to foster 'corporate creativity'. One of the more unique ways that Eastman Kodak tries to encourage innovation is by offering employees a humour room, with books, videos and toys (*Training and Development*, May 1998: 50).

Principle 14: the company provides an
equitable reward and wage system for employees.
Finally, we have principle 14, which received 120 citations. This principle is defined as:

> The company pays an equitable, competitive wage to all its employees, including profit sharing, bonuses, and other incentives (Davenport 1998: 43).

Intel Corporation was most frequently cited for its employee incentive system. As reported in *The New York Times* (12 February 1997: C-8), Intel paid out US$214 million under the Employee Cash Bonus Programme in 1996, amounting to a thirteenth month of pay for employees. In addition, Intel employees received almost US$600 million in profit sharing and retirement benefits that year.

What gets rewarded

In addition to examining media reports of corporate citizenship behaviour, we wanted to see what types of citizenship behaviour were most rewarded and what principles such behaviour represented. We report on our results in this section.

Research methodology

To determine how companies are recognised for being good corporate citizens, we examined 15 awards programmes dealing with corporate citizenship (see Box

15.2). The data consisted of 2,031 citations recognising the 15 awards throughout the 1990s. A two-phase analysis consisted of:

- An analysis of award criteria mapped over the 20 principles (Davenport 1998)
- Calculation of frequencies, by company, for each award given in the 1990s

The findings therefore describe what types of corporate citizenship behaviour were rewarded in the USA during the 1990s and which companies were recognised for good corporate citizenship.

Findings

The types of citizenship behaviour rewarded in the 1990s are reported in Table 15.2, which also shows the principles that are reflected in the criteria for each award. The number of awards programmes using each given principle as a criterion is reported in Table 15.3, in descending order of frequency.

Overall, citizenship awards in the 1990s recognised corporate behaviour relative to employees, community, suppliers and stockholders, with emphasis on the treatment of employees. Of the 20 principles (Davenport 1998), all were articulated as criteria in at least one award except the following:

- Principle 5: the company initiates and engages in genuine dialogue with stakeholders.
- Principle 9: the company respects the rights of consumers.
- Principle 14: the company provides an equitable reward and wage system for employees.

1	American Business Ethics Award
2	Black Enterprise Best Places for Blacks to Work
3	Business Enterprise Award
4	*Business Ethics* Award for Corporate Social Responsibility
5	Council on Economic Priorities (CEP) Corporate Conscience Awards
6	Colorado Ethics in Business
7	Corporate Achievement in River Conservation
8	Excellence in Corporate Community Service
9	*Fortune*'s Most Admired
10	*Industry Week*'s Best Managed
11	National Association for the Advancement of Colored People (NAACP) Image Award
12	National Torch Award for Marketplace Ethics (Better Business Bureau [BBB])
13	Opportunity 2000 Award
14	Ron Brown Award for Corporate Leadership
15	Working Mother Best Companies

Box 15.2 **Awards recognising corporate citizenship**

Principle*	Award†											
	1	2	3	4	5	6	7	9	10	12	13	14
1	✓					✓				✓		
2	✓					✓				✓		
3	✓			✓					✓			
4			✓	✓								
6	✓			✓								
7						✓						✓
8	✓				✓				✓			✓
10	✓								✓			
11	✓									✓		
12												✓
13		✓			✓			✓	✓		✓	✓
15					✓							✓
16												✓
17								✓	✓			
18					✓				✓			
19					✓		✓					✓

* Principles 5, 9, 14 and 20 are not covered by the criteria of the awards studied. A full description of each principle may be found in Box 15.1 on page 258.
† There are no award criteria available for awards 8, 11 and 15. A full description of awards may be found in Box 15.2 on page 265.

Table 15.2 **Corporate citizenship principles awarded**

◼ Principle 20: the company demonstrates a commitment to sustainable development

The fact that there are some principles for which there are no awards is not difficult to explain. Most important, and relevant to principle 20, is the existence of a separate group of environmental awards that were not included in this study. Awards programmes of the World Resources Institute, the National Wildlife Federation and a number of other organisations focus exclusively on environmental protection.

A second explanation is that an award is established because some constituency group believes such behaviour is important. Constituencies and rewarded behaviours can change over time, so that unrewarded corporate citizenship behaviour (and principles) may simply be awaiting a champion to establish an award for them. Principle 5, for example, appears to have no specific constituency, although the idea it expresses is embedded into most stakeholder relations awards. This principle, focusing on corporate dialogue with stakeholders, is not yet specifically addressed by any award. Interestingly, some professional groups and business associations, such as the Institute for Social and Ethical Account-Ability (ISEA) and Business for Social Responsibility (BSR), are very concerned with helping companies learn to balance the competing needs of stakeholders and with developing composite measures to address more general principles. Either ISEA or BSR (or both) could well become the champion(s) for a 'stakeholder dialogue' award.

A third explanation is that some principles are simply harder to operationalise. Principle 9 (respect the rights of consumers), for example makes sense as a principle of corporate citizenship but is hardly the subject of agreed-on criteria or even categories of behaviour. Principle 14 (provide an equitable reward and wage system for employees) is also subject to widely varying interpretations and to the political necessities of labour–management negotiations. An inability to operationalise the desired behaviour makes it difficult for awards judges to distinguish excellent from good performance.

◢ Reported compared with awarded behaviours: how do the principles fare?

We have examined in the foregoing sections those types of corporate behaviour (and the principles of corporate citizenship they represent) that are most reported in the business press and those that are rewarded by contemporary corporate citizenship awards. One question of interest is whether the same corporate citizenship principles that were heavily reported in the press were also recognised and rewarded through the formal acknowledgement of an award. In Table 15.4 we report the rank orders of relative significance of the principles as reflected in the criteria of awards and in media reports of cited behaviour.

In Table 15.4(a), the 20 principles are listed according to their 'recorded' ranking; in Table 15.4(b), they are listed according to their 'rewarded' ranking first, and then by their 'recorded' ranking within each 'rewarded' category. If one examines the top six in each ranking, the following is suggested:

- Three of the principles appear among the top six in both groups:
  - Principle 8: invest in the community
  - Principle 13: use responsible human resource management
  - Principle 19: show environmental commitment

- The top six recorded principles address virtually every traditional stakeholder group except investors; company citizenship behaviour with respect to employees (principles 12 and 13), community (principles 7 and 8), suppliers (principle 18) and the environment (principle 19) are all represented by a relatively high volume of mentions in the press.

Principle* The company . . .	Frequency[†]	Percentage of award programmes[‡]
13 Engages in responsible human-resource management	6	50
8 Invests in the communities in which it operates	4	33
1 Engages in fair and honest business practices in its relationships with stakeholders	3	25
2 Sets high standards of behaviour for all employees	3	25
3 Exercises ethical oversight at the executive and board levels	3	25
19 Demonstrates a commitment to the environment	3	25
4 Is well managed for all stakeholders	2	17
6 Values and implements disclosure	2	17
7 Fosters a reciprocal relationship between the corporation and the community	2	17
10 Offers quality products and services	2	17
11 Provides information that is truthful and useful	2	17
15 Engages in open and flexible communication with employees	2	17
17 Strives for a competitive return on investment	2	17
18 Engages in fair-trading practices with suppliers	2	17
12 Provides a family-friendly work environment	1	8
16 Invests in employee development	1	8

* Principles 5, 9, 14 and 20 are not covered by the awards studied (see Box 15.1 on page 258).

‡ The number of awards in which the principle appears as a reward criterion.

† There are no award criteria available for awards 8, 11 and 15. The percentage is therefore calculated as the frequency as a percentage of the total number of remaining awards (12). For a description of the awards, see Box 15.2 on page 265.

Table 15.3 **Principles most frequently rewarded**

Principle

a) *The company . . .*	Recorded	Rewarded
13 Engages in responsible human-resource management	1	1
12 Provides a family-friendly work environment	2	5
19 Demonstrates a commitment to the environment	3	3
8 Invests in the communities in which it operates	4	2
7 Fosters a reciprocal relationship between the corporation and the community	5	4
18 Engages in fair-trading practices with suppliers	6	4
15 Engages in open and flexible communications with employees	7	4
14 Provides an equitable reward and wage system for employees	8	0
16 Invests in employee development	9	5
11 Provides information that is truthful and useful	10	4
10 Offers quality products and services	11	4
2 Sets high standards of behaviour for all employees	12	3
20 Demonstrates a commitment to sustainable development	13	0
9 Respects the rights of consumers	14	0
3 Exercises ethical oversight at the executive and board levels	15	3
5 Initiates and engages in genuine dialogue with stakeholders	16	0
17 Strives for a competitive return on investment	17	4
1 Engages in fair and honest business practices in its relationships with stakeholders	18	3
6 Values and implements disclosure	18	4
4 Is well managed for all stakeholders	19	4

b) *The company . . .*		
13 Engages in responsible human-resource management	1	1
8 Invests in the communities in which it operates	4	2
19 Demonstrates a commitment to the environment	3	3
2 Sets high standards of behaviour for all employees	12	3
3 Exercises ethical oversight at the executive and board levels	15	3
1 Engages in fair and honest business practices in its relationships with stakeholders	18	3
7 Fosters a reciprocal relationship between the corporation and the community	5	4
18 Engages in fair-trading practices with suppliers	6	4

Table 15.4 **Reported versus rewarded behaviour: (a) in recorded order; (b) in rewarded order** *(continued over)*

Source: authors' survey

Principle

b [continued]) *The company* . . .	*Recorded*	*Rewarded*
15 Engages in open and flexible communications with employees	7	4
11 Provides information that is truthful and useful	10	4
10 Offers quality products and services	11	4
17 Strives for a competitive return on investment	17	4
6 Values and implements disclosure	18	4
4 Is well managed for all stakeholders	19	4
12 Provides a family-friendly work environment	2	5
16 Invests in employee development	9	5
14 Provides an equitable reward and wage system for employees	8	0
20 Demonstrates a commitment to sustainable development	13	0
9 Respects the rights of consumers	14	0
5 Initiates and engages in genuine dialogue with stakeholders	16	0

Table 15.4 (continued)

▨ In comparison to the recorded principles, the top six rewarded principles, although including concerns of employees, community and the environment, are much more heavily focused on general ethical guidelines.

Company comparisons

A final question of interest in this study concerns the companies themselves. For
the most frequently cited companies, we wanted to see whether there was any
consistency between the frequency of media reports of corporate citizenship and
the receipt of awards. Table 15.5 shows the breakdown of the most frequently
cited companies for these dimensions.

Recorded and rewarded companies

Table 15.5 includes the top 19 companies whose citizenship practices are
recorded in the press and the top 20 companies that have received citizenship
awards. Of these, only five companies are in both categories—AT&T, Hewlett-
Packard, IBM, Xerox and DuPont. Interestingly, these are all market leaders and
they are all relatively old companies that are operating in a new universe—they
face different technologies, antitrust break-ups and serious challenges to their
industry leadership. Citizenship behaviour may, for such companies, represent a
new market differentiation measure or it may simply be the culmination of their
long experience in managing stakeholder relations effectively.

	The company receives media citations	The company does not receive media citations
The company receives citizenship awards	► AT&T ► Hewlett-Packard ► IBM ► Xerox ► DuPont	► 3M ► Coca-Cola ► Corning ► Gannett ► General Electric ► General Mills ► Herman Miller ► Motorola ► Sara Lee ► Amoco Oil ► Dow Chemical ► Eli Lilly ► Johnson & Johnson ► Merck ► Procter & Gamble
The company does not receive citizenship awards	► British Petroleum ► Mobil Oil ► Shell Oil ► Chrysler ► Ford ► General Motors ► Natural Gas Vehicles Co. ► Nissan ► Eastman Kodak ► Intel ► Levi Strauss ► Marriott ► Music for Little People ► Sears	*[Empty cell]**

* Companies that would appear in the fourth cell (i.e. companies with no awards and no media coverage) are by definition excluded from our database.

Disclaimer: Please read text titled 'Unexpected results' on page 273 to suggest possible reasons for misplacement of companies within this table.

Table 15.5 **Comparison of top-cited and top-awarded companies**

Source: authors' survey

Rewarded but not recorded companies

A fairly large number of companies receive significant recognition via citizenship awards programmes but receive little press coverage for their actions. Nine of the 15 companies in this category are primarily consumer goods companies, including 3M, Coca-Cola, Corning, Gannett, General Electric, General Mills, Herman Miller, Motorola and Sara Lee. One oil company (Amoco) and one chemical company (Dow Chemical) are in the rewarded-not-recorded cell, along with four companies that are pharmaceutical and/or consumer products firms: Eli Lilly, Johnson & Johnson, Merck and Procter & Gamble.

There are a variety of reasons why 'good citizen' companies do not get reported even though they may practise examples of citizen-like behaviour. Some are 'off the beaten path' of news and media gossip and do not ordinarily catch the attention of press writers. Still others are motivated by values for privacy and feel that their efforts in stakeholder relations, ethics, philanthropy and so on would be cheapened by publicity.

Some companies, for a variety of reasons, simply do not want to have attention drawn to them. Press attention is a two-edged sword—some companies may become media darlings for a while, but there can be a severe backlash effect as well. Companies that are aware of this press power may simply be reluctant to expose their citizenship programmes and policies to publicity and criticism. A major retailer, for example, was reluctant to join a trade association with a social mission because the company's executives did not want any additional visibility and exposure to stakeholder criticisms. The clothing and shoe companies that have been experimenting with ways to avoid using child labour in developing countries are also publicity-shy, primarily, because they are 'experimenting' with 'innovative' offshore labour practice with few established guidelines and so they will make mistakes and do not want to be tarnished for trying to do the right thing.

Recorded but not rewarded companies

Equally interesting, perhaps, is the large number of companies that receive major press coverage for citizenship but do not have comparable visibility in awards programmes. Industry trends are even more apparent here. Three major oil companies (British Petroleum, Mobil Oil and Shell Oil) and five automobile makers (Chrysler, Ford, General Motors, Natural Gas Vehicles Co. and Nissan) were in this group during the study period of 1990–99. In addition, consumer goods and retail sales or service companies are well represented, by Eastman Kodak, Intel, Levi Strauss, Marriott, Music for Little People and Sears.

Why would companies receive a lot of press attention for citizenship but no awards? It is possible that companies such as these simply do not apply for awards programmes or do not follow through on nominations and thus are not eligible. The simple answer to this puzzle, however, may lie in corporate public relations budgets. It may be that the companies with the most media citations for citizenship behaviour, but few or no awards, are simply the ones with the best publicity machines (though we must stress that we are not making this claim for any of the companies listed in this category in Table 15.5). It would be interesting to compare companies' public relations and advertising budgets with the 'productivity' factor of citations and awards.

Unexpected results

There are some large and well-known companies noticeably missing from Table 15.5, and others that might appear on the surface to be placed in the wrong cell. For example, Merck, Johnson & Johnson and Procter & Gamble have all experienced massive press coverage for their rapid responses to the river blindness threat, the Tylenol poisonings and the Rely tampon crisis, respectively. One would expect these companies to be among the most cited and the most awarded, and the reason they are not is simply that the media database for this study begins in 1996, whereas the notable events occurred in the 1980s. These companies are still receiving awards for their good behaviour, but the press does not appear to be interested.

There do appear to be some industry groupings in this table, and there are good reasons why industry may make a difference. We do not report the detailed data here, but we will provide a couple of examples to illustrate why the groupings in Table 15.5 are what they are. Consider, for example, that all of the major automobile companies seem to perform well on supplier relations. General Motors has been criticised severely in the past for its overly aggressive demands on suppliers (Wood 1994: 158). General Motors, then, decided to develop a high-profile 'good supplier relations' programme and appeared to be intent on spreading the news through press releases, interviews and media citations. So, once General Motors began to achieve success in being recognised for 'good supplier relations', the other major companies in the industry were perhaps pushed to do the same, from competitive pressures or from pique over the putative blots to their own reputations.

Another industry-based explanation has to do with an industry's natural patterns of involvement with particular stakeholders and issues. The computer software industry, for example, does not have 'strategic suppliers' in the same way that the automobile industry does. One could not expect Microsoft, say, to tout its supplier relations in the press as the automobile companies do, because their value chain does not contain the kind of suppliers that would be considered relevant and newsworthy.

◢ Conclusions and recommendations for future research

Corporate citizenship is often thought of as philanthropy and voluntary community involvement. The results of our study suggest that community relations is one (and not the most important) among several powerful threads of citizenship behaviour. In press reports of citizenship behaviour, all major stakeholder groups are heavily represented (except for investors)—employees, customers, suppliers, communities and the environment. In citizenship awards programmes, general principles of ethical business conduct receive heavy emphasis, along with employee practice, community relations and environmental protection.

Employee principles and issues are the most reported and the most rewarded of the 20 principles. Principle 13 (the company engages in responsible human-resource management) was ranked first both in terms of frequency of reporting and in terms of number of awards received. Only two of the awards focus exclusively on employee relations criteria; however, 8 of the 15 awards include employee criteria, among other things. In addition, four of the top eight principles receiving media citations were employee-focused. Were the award-givers disproportionately focused on human relations functions? It is important to remember that awards reflect specific constituency expectations, and employees are a large, powerful and relatively well-organised constituency group for business. It is reasonable that employee interests would receive heavy attention in reports of and awards for corporate citizenship.

Overall, most of the 20 principles are receiving recognition in various awards programmes. Some of the principles that the Delphi study and the factor analysis articulated may actually be embedded in other principles that tend to result in more visible types of behaviour that are recordable and rewardable. For example, principle 14 (the company provides an equitable reward and wage system for employees) is likely to be embedded in the more general principle 13 (the company engages in responsible human-resource management). We might predict that the relative importance of attention and corporate behaviour to different stakeholder groups is subject to change over time. Shareholders, employees, the environment, suppliers—it would be interesting and fruitful to track trends in attention to various stakeholder interests in the press and in awards.

Indeed, the next wave of corporate citizenship awards could be composite, focused on the big picture of citizenship rather than on specific components of citizenship. A number of organisations, including ISEA (Wheeler and Sillanpää 1997: 156) and social investing firms such as Kinder Lydenberg Domini (Kinder *et al.* 1993: xvii), are working toward developing criteria and scaling for evaluating a wide range of types of citizenship behaviour.

Several interrelated trends will no doubt impact on the emerging link between theory and practice of corporate citizenship. Increasing interest in social accountability, expanding the scope of information made available to the public, will result in new measurements and new standards. It is possible that legislation requiring non-financial performance accountability will become more widespread. As non-financial performance information becomes more available and more consistently reported, management is likely to become less worried about public scrutiny, and constituency groups are likely to voice more coherent opinions about their definitions of good corporate citizenship. Transparency may indeed be the best path toward improving corporate citizenship behaviour for the benefit of all.

◢ Appendix.
Search terms: principles of corporate citizenship

Keyword(s)	Additional keyword(s)
Principles 1–3: ethical business behaviour	
Board	Accountability
Board	Independent
Board	Performance
Ethical	Behaviour
Ethical	Board
Ethical	Business
Ethical	Code
Ethical	Conduct
Ethical	Employee
Ethical	Governance
Ethical	Guidelines
Ethical	Policies
Ethical	Policy
Ethical	Stakeholder
Ethical	Stakeholders
Ethical	Standards
Ethics	Behaviour
Ethics	Board
Ethics	Business
Ethics	Code
Ethics	Conduct
Ethics	Employee
Ethics	Governance
Ethics	Guidelines
Ethics	Oversight
Ethics	Policies
Ethics	Policy
Ethics	Stakeholder
Ethics	Stakeholders
Ethics	Standards
Family	Friendly
Independent	Directors

Keyword(s)	Additional keyword(s)
Principles 4–6: stakeholder commitment	
Stakeholder	Innovative
Stakeholder	Best practice
Stakeholder	Leadership
Stakeholder	Commitment
Stakeholder	Benefit
Stakeholder	Manage
Stakeholder	Dialogue
Stakeholder	Partner(ship)
Stakeholder	Disclosure
Stakeholder	Report(s)
Stakeholder	Gain
Stakeholder	Information

Keyword(s)	Additional keyword(s)

Principles 7 and 8: community commitment

Community	Innovative
Community	Best practice
Community	Leadership
Community	Partnership
Community	Communication
Community	Investment
Community	Volunteerism
Community	Involvement

Principles 9–11: consumer commitment

Consumer(s)	Innovative
Consumer(s)	Best Practice
Consumer(s)	Leadership
Consumer(s)	Rights
Consumer(s)	Privacy
Consumer(s)	Innovative, best practice, leadership
Marketplace	
Advertising	
Packaging	
Labelling	
Product safety	
Product disclosure	

Principles 12–16: employee commitment

Employee(s)	Innovative
Employee(s)	Best practice
Employee(s)	Leadership
Family	
Day care	
Workplace	Flexibility
Workplace	Balance
Employee	Development
Downsizing	
Employee training	
Workplace	Diversity
Workplace	Profit
Workplace	Fair
Workplace	Profit sharing
Workplace	Bonus
Workplace	Communication
Workplace	Team
Workplace	Partnership
Compensation	Performance
Employee	Profit
Workplace	Standards

Keyword(s)	Additional keyword(s)

Principle 17: investor commitment

Keyword(s)	Additional keyword(s)
Investor(s)	
Investment	Innovative
Invest	Best practice
Invest	Leadership
Socially responsible investing	
Competitive return	

Principle 18: supplier commitment

Keyword(s)	Additional keyword(s)
Supplier(s)	Innovative
Supplier(s)	Best practice
Supplier(s)	Leader
Supplier(s)	Fair trade
Supplier(s)	Reciprocity
Supplier(s)	Innovative
Supplier(s)	Relationship
Supplier(s)	Partner(ship)

Principle 19 and 20: environmental commitment

Keyword(s)	Additional keyword(s)
Environment	Innovative
Environment	Best practice
Environment	Leader
Environment	Commitment
Environment	Audit
Environment	Impact
Environment	Quality of life
Sustainable development	
Recycling	
Gas	Emissions

Note: For a description of all 20 principles, see Box 15.1 on page 258.

16

PROCESSES IN SOCIAL AND ETHICAL ACCOUNTABILITY
External reporting mechanisms*

Leigh Holland
De Montfort
University, UK

Jane Gibbon
Newcastle Business School,
University of Northumbria, UK

Together with an increase in individual reporting initiatives from companies there has been an increase in the development of reporting guidelines and standards offered to improve the quality and quantity of what is reported. For instance, Ranganathan (1999) lists 49 initiatives that include elements of reporting, and the Fédération des Experts Comptables Européens (FEE) has 50 environmental reporting guidelines issued by national and international bodies. These approaches seek to offer guidance to both the beginner and the more experienced reporter but they are often unclear about how useful they may be in a particular context or set of circumstances.

The corporate reporter is faced with an array of potential standards, without a review of the usefulness of each of these frameworks to the reporting organisation. Whatever the motivation to report, by not choosing the most appropriate mechanism some of the benefits of reporting will be lost and the message(s) that the organisation wishes to send may be diluted or obscured. It may be argued that demands for information from stakeholders ought to determine the reporting approach taken, but in practice this is rarely the case and reporting practitioners will largely manage the information flow from the organisation. The four recent reporting developments discussed in this chapter are:

- The Global Reporting Initiative (GRI), of the Coalition for Environmentally Responsible Economies (CERES 1999), which provides sustainability reporting guidelines

---

* The authors would like to thank Elizabeth Crawford BA for help with the 'Making Values Count' section.

- A discussion paper on a proposed framework for environmental reporting, from the FEE (1999)

- AccountAbility Standard 1000 (AA 1000), of the Institute of Social and Ethical AccountAbility (ISEA 1999)

- The research report on 'Making Values Count', from the Association of Chartered Certified Accountants (ACCA; Gonella *et al.* 1998)

These are all independent attempts to improve reporting standards in order to encourage companies to take up the reporting challenge. However, companies will need guidance as to the appropriateness of each of the developments. Hence, in an attempt to combine the needs of the reporting enterprise with the requirements of the report users (CTC 1998), in this chapter we offer guidance to reporters to enable them to make a choice over which reporting mechanism to use and to begin the process of social and ethical accounting. The choice offered here is limited to four current initiatives because they appear to offer a range of reporting options that may be required by most business organisations, whatever industrial sector they belong to or at what developmental stage they are at. This does not, of course, preclude the use of other frameworks.

Some initial considerations

A widespread critique of current and suggested reporting practices exist (see e.g. Gray *et al.* 1997; Hibbitt 1999), yet business does not appear to be engaging with this debate. It is therefore important to examine how companies are likely to proceed. The variability of individual reports and the plethora of standards and guidelines demonstrate that corporate social reporting practice is developing in a relatively unstructured way. Although a critique of developments informs progress, it must be recognised that organisations will largely determine for themselves the direction(s) they are to take.

What follows is a form of guidance that may aid in the structuring of a reporting response yet at the same time enable a dialogue between reporters and those who wish to critique the methods employed.

Why report?

Organisations report their activities in order to be accountable to their constituents—their stakeholders, or those agencies that fall within the organisation's sphere of influence. Accountability requires that the company acts responsibly and accounts for its actions or inaction in some form of report provided for its stakeholders. In practice there is a balance between what a company wishes to report and what is demanded of it. The motivation to provide an account of an organisation's actions will be driven both by internal factors and by external factors. This will include the actual or perceived improvement in the company's image and the positive effect on the bottom line through improved market share or better cost control because of improved performance, both of which will have a positive impact on shareholder value. It may also result in a reduction in the risk associated with organisations, particularly for those organisations whose business activities are perceived to be environmentally or socially damaging.

The motivation to report will be a reflection of the organisation's internal value system and ethical stance. These are dynamic and therefore the rationale for reporting may change as internal and external influences change. For instance, an organisation may reposition itself following pressures exerted by its stakeholders or by changes in legislation, or following management or policy changes.

◢ Where to report?

Companies may report their activities in a number of places. The publication of certain financial information is required by statute to be published in an 'annual report', which may also be the location of non-statutory information such as environmental performance indicators. However, many companies are using a separate report as the main communication medium for environmental, social and ethical information. This has been the case for many UK, US and European companies that have begun this process by issuing environmental reports over the past ten years. This has also been stimulated by schemes that motivate 'best practice' by offering awards—the ACCA Environmental Reporting Awards Scheme in the UK and its European counterpart, the European Environmental Reporting Award, are examples of such schemes. However, it is important to consider how this type of information is published and promoted, as it may affect the ability to reach the required audience.

◢ What type of report?

Organisations need to consider the type and format of report they wish to produce. There may be legislative or mandatory pressures—the US Toxic Releases Inventory or the European Eco-management and Audit Scheme (EMAS) each require standard reports (Gray *et al.* 1996). Other initiatives have developed from the desire to report on specific elements of performance. Recent examples of elements reported on include (Gonella *et al.* 1998: iv):

- Capital valuation, indicating how various forms of capital (including environmental and human capital) are managed (example company: Skandia)

- Corporate community involvement reporting, answering the question, 'What are the community involvement policies of the organisation?' (example companies: Diageo, BP)

- Ethical accounting, reporting a wide range of issues through which shared values may be identified (examples companies: Sbn Bank, The Body Shop International)

- Social auditing, providing an external examination of an organisation's social performance (example companies: Vancouver City Credit Union, Traidcraft)

- Social balance, giving a financial analysis across stakeholder groups (example companies: UNIPOL, Co-op Italia)

- Statement of principles and values, an evolving statement of responsibilities (example company: Shell International)

- Sustainability reporting, an attempt to reflect the integration of social, ethical, environmental and economic performance (example company: Wessex Water [see Adams 1999])

This list demonstrates the variety of reporting initiatives taken by organisations. It also shows the range of issues selected by individual companies to report on.

◢ What to report?

The above examples raise the issue of what aspects an organisation may choose to report. Businesses may wish to present an overview of their performance to add to a general understanding of their activities. They may want to provide a detailed review of particular topics or areas, or they could explore the inter-relationships between spheres of activity (i.e. economic, environmental or social). As their reporting becomes more complex, organisations may also need to consider how they define their boundaries—they may wish to move away from simple entity reporting to considering relationships with supply chains or to developing fluid boundaries to incorporate some or all of their stakeholders (Dey *et al.* 1995). The company must not underestimate the importance of stakeholder feedback (Wheeler and Sillanpää 1997) once the reporting process has begun.

◢ Who requires guidance?

Because the information contained in company reports is derived from a number of sources, the reporting team could include members from different disciplinary backgrounds such as those with a financial background (accountants) or with experience in environmental science. There may be an environmental management team to call on, or the company may use its public relations or communications department. If social and ethical performance is a strategic issue, board-level representation will influence both the development and the mechanism for reporting.

◢ A model for positioning the organisation

The model illustrated in Figure 16.1 echoes the work carried out by the United Nations Environment Programme (UNEP) and SustainAbility in which they attempt to position individual organisational reporting efforts on a continuum towards full sustainability reporting. It is unlikely that any organisation has managed to attain the fifth (the highest) position, but the model is designed to act as a motivational force. In the context of this chapter, it can also be used to position the frameworks that are to be examined here (see fourth and fifth [the highest] levels of Fig. 16.1).

This may help preparers select the most appropriate framework for their organisation, their desired outcomes and their relative commitment to the reporting process. A discussion of the four guidelines now follows.

Global Reporting Initiative (GRI): sustainability reporting guidelines

Launched in draft form during March 1999 at a major international symposium in the UK, the GRI guidelines (CERES 1999) were issued for public comment and testing until the end of 1999. They will be re-issued, after consultation, in June 2000. The GRI guidelines were produced with input from a range of stakeholders and provide a framework stressing the links between environmental, economic and social performance, described as 'sustainability'. They examine sustainability at the enterprise level and identify some of the aspects that may be reported in a standardised format. The structure of the guidelines includes:

■ Preamble

■ Reporting principles (underlying characteristics)

■ Report content

■ Appendices

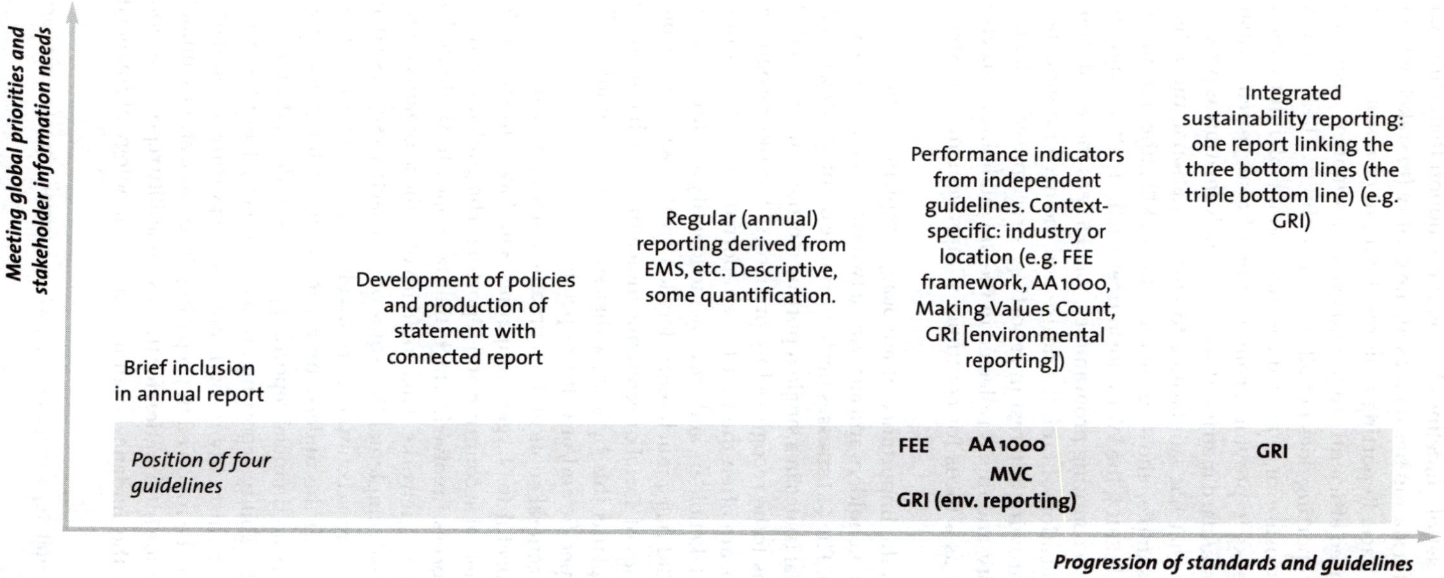

AA1000, AccountAbility Standard 1000; EMS, environmental management system; FEE, Fédération des Experts Comptables Européens; GRI, Global Reporting Initiative; MVC, Making Values Count

Figure 16.1 **A model of reporting requirements: a continuum towards full sustainability**

Sources: CERES 1999; FEE 1999; Gonella *et al.* 1998; ISEA 1999; Gray *et al.* 1996

The rationale behind this set of guidelines lies with the notion that, although the quantity of disclosed information has increased, the quality (to stakeholders) of disclosures has not kept pace. Reporting requires the input of resources, but these resources need to be used efficiently to provide value for money. Also, lack of uniformity in corporate reporting does not allow comparability. These factors may prevent adequate disclosure or may reduce the amount of information disclosed. Hence, the GRI seeks to provide a combination of a suggested format and a set of indicators with standard metrics. It sees this amalgamation as providing a reporting framework that has similarities to current national and international initiatives: for example, those promoted by CERES, the European Chemical Industry Council (CEFIC), the World Resources Institute (WRI) and the Danish statutory and green accounting programmes.[1] CERES sees these independent programmes as an indication of both the desire and the need for guidance on reporting matters. The growing interest in reporting is recognised as both a challenge and an opportunity, and this is reflected in the GRI guidelines. It is also hoped that the GRI will act as a focus for continuous improvement of sustainability reporting.

The GRI guidelines stress the importance of advocacy—explaining the organisation's position to all its stakeholders and allowing a two-way dialogue between enterprise and stakeholders. The GRI stresses the importance of integrating social, economic and environmental issues in a single reporting mechanism, a point that is either omitted or remains to be recognised by preparers. The GRI recognises that environmental impacts are often the first to be reported on, as these often have more resonance with stakeholders and are easier to identify and understand. The indicator guidance in GRI has a much more detailed breakdown of environmental indicators than it does of social or economic indicators, which it tends to combine. The guidance explains this by saying that social and economic indicators tend to be location-specific and/or culture-specific.

Despite the statement of general applicability contained in the guidelines, they would appear to be most useful for larger companies who have already made some progress in environmental accounting and reporting. The guidelines stress that there is a learning process involved, which the GRI hopes to facilitate by building on other reporting frameworks. This could involve those organisations currently reporting and already implementing some of the practices suggested in the guidelines. Similarly, where accountants are involved in the reporting process, they will be familiar with the underlying assumptions in the guidelines, which are devolved largely from financial reporting practice. Indeed, the qualitative characteristics of sustainability reporting are taken directly from the work of FEE (see below) and so are instantly recognisable to a reporting accountant. Accountants will also largely be involved in preparing the organisation's annual report, which itself will provide information for the sustainability report's section on company profile. Hence the guidance often uses the terminology of financial

---

1 In the Danish Environmental Reporting Act, 1996, where environmental reports are called 'Green Accounts'.

reporting, allowing accountants to become progressively more involved in sustainability reporting.

Another set of guidance rules which is specifically referred to is the ISO 14000 series, produced by the International Organization for Standardization (ISO). The terminology used in the guidelines is similar to that used in this series. Links are made between the two: for instance, 'impacts' (GRI) are equated with 'aspects' (ISO). The GRI hierarchy of performance reporting elements (from general categories, through specific issues, to precise measures reflected in indicators) is also a reflection of what is contained in ISO 14000. It is likely, therefore, that any organisation that has a formal environmental management system that in some way follows ISO 14000 (either by accreditation or informal constitution) will also recognise and be able to apply the GRI guidelines.

The guidelines are designed to bring out the linkages between the economic, social and environmental performances of the organisation so that these links can be integrated into a set of reports that examine the extent to which the organisation is moving towards sustainability. This may be helpful to organisations that have begun to examine their performance in each of these three spheres but that have yet to make the underlying connections. In this way it is hoped that the guidelines will help to integrate the information of a range of activities and begin to provide the methodology for this. In the revised version (June 2000 [CERES 2000]) of the guidelines, the term 'sustainability' is downplayed, and consideration is given to the economic, environmental and social aspects themselves. This has been done in order to avoid excluding organisations that may feel that reporting for sustainability is beyond them. Hence, it may encourage greater uptake of the guidelines and provide the incentive for organisations to reconsider the links between the economic, social and environmental spheres.

Most organisations that begin sustainability reporting start with some form of environmental report, and this is reflected in the guidelines, in which the information on environmental impacts and aspects is far more detailed. There is an emphasis on eco-efficiency (economic–ecological efficiency); a detailed example is given of how to calculate how eco-efficient an operation may be. The guidance recognises that social and economic impacts may be less general and relate more to location and culture, but they hope to deliver these in terms of a wider set of indicators. This may be unhelpful to organisations that have already developed a strategy for environmental reporting and that wish to progress—there is a danger that organisations will become disengaged from the process as they wait for future developments.

Organisations looking for specific industrial or sector guidance will not be provided for by the guidelines, although the revised guidance will be somewhat more context-specific, while retaining cultural and national neutrality. Similarly, the report is expected to be at the level of the enterprise—the guidance is not aimed at a lower level of resolution (e.g. the facility or product level). Hence new reporters are faced with the prospect of developing a reporting strategy for the whole organisation rather than 'practising' at the level of, say, a business unit. This may make the task of reporting appear overwhelming.

The requirement to produce an integrated sustainability report—combining aspects of environmental, social and economic performance—may also seem an unobtainable goal. This is recognised in the revision, where it acknowledges that an incremental approach may be more appropriate, so the elements of sustainability begin to be accounted for and reported separately at first, while maintaining the need for recognition that there are interlinking aspects

An organisation that has not reviewed who its stakeholders are may find the lack of guidance on this issue unhelpful. Part 5 of the guidelines gives some generic suggestions on stakeholder identification, but it does assume that identification and scoping has already taken place. There is a danger that some of the less obvious stakeholders—for instance, future generations or other species—may be omitted in any reporting considerations. This assumption of prior knowledge appears elsewhere in the guidelines, and clarification from other sources may be needed if these areas are to be incorporated into a reporting strategy. Examples of this include an indicator of 'habitat improvement' and the suggested use of life-cycle analysis in part 8. Independent review of the report is encouraged, but the scope or extent of the review, and who should carry it out, is not covered.

An organisation's accountability function will only be credible where enhanced communication with stakeholders takes place, and the guidelines provide a framework for effective dialogue. In this way the guidelines are helpful in promoting management's role in enabling two-way dialogue with all the organisation's stakeholders and in developing a motivation to widen stakeholder awareness and participation. A two-way dialogue will also require more reliable information, and such a dialogue is encouraged in the framework provided by the guidelines.

Towards a generally accepted framework for environmental reporting

The FEE's discussion paper on moving towards a generally accepted framework for environmental reporting (FEE 1999) is perhaps the closest to a set of accounting guidelines yet achieved because it uses the language and framework already employed within accounting standards. Of the four models discussed it is most likely to appeal to those accountants who are responsible for implementing some form of reporting strategy. The framework uses a hierarchy of impacts to determine how elements of environmental performance should be reported.

In order to illustrate how the framework approaches environmental reporting, air quality has been chosen as an example of an environmental impact. This can then be utilised as a reference to discuss how such an impact would be included in an environmental report. Hence the hierarchy of environmental impacts is:

- Category: what is the concern? Example answer: urban air quality.
- Aspect: name a specific issue within the concern? Example answer: production of carbon dioxide.

■ Indicator: how is the specific aspect measured? Example answer: in metric tonnes.

The qualitative characteristics can then be identified and related to the category of 'air quality', as indicated in Table 16.1.

The framework is therefore designed to allow the information in an environmental report to conform to recognised and accepted characteristics, making the report both comparable and understandable. Although not purporting to represent social or ethical matters within the reporting framework, it may be most useful for organisations undertaking their first attempt at reporting.

AccountAbility Standard 1000:
social and ethical accounting, auditing and reporting

This standard for reporting social and ethical performance is produced by the Institute for Social and Ethical AccountAbility (ISEA 1999). Recognising that many organisations are becoming increasingly globalised, the standard encourages quality and consistency in reporting and stresses the need to consider the pressure from stakeholders for improved performance and disclosure, through improving stakeholder relationships.

Using a managerialist approach to organisational disclosure, AA 1000 suggests that improved reporting results in increasing accountability, legitimacy and governance. This in turn results in the benefits of increased consumer loyalty and employee innovation and enhances reputation, improves risk awareness and management processes. A proactive reporting strategy will also enable improved responses to new legislation and allow greater management development in the areas of financial valuation of intangible assets (e.g. ethical reputation) and in adding value to non-core activities such as community involvement.

The approach of AA 1000 is one of strengthening stakeholder dialogue and emphasising the organisation's values with respect to its social and ethical behaviour. It defines this as an organisation's responsibility to those humans (other species are not mentioned) with a legitimate interest in the organisation's activities. Hence the management of the organisation has a role in promoting the values throughout the organisation (through processes, products, services, etc.) while also responding to stakeholder views. Figure 16.2 represents the reporting process in outline.

The standard embraces the concept of sustainability, which it sees as informed by the ethical values of an organisation, which stem from the organisation's willingness to recognise and discharge its obligation to be held accountable for its actions. The standard recognises that society is faced with choices when attempting to move closer to a sustainable system, and it requires information from those organisations that have substantial impacts on those decisions.

The type of reporting promoted by the standard allows the organisation to learn about its own performance by recognising the impacts it has on others and its surroundings. It will also allow recognition of the rights and expectations of

Qualitative characteristic	Example
Relevance Information must be attention-directing, knowledge-building and opinion-forming.	If an environmental report produces a set of figures revealing tonnes of CO_2 produced, is this measurement relevant to those stakeholders who most need to know (i.e. the local community who will be concerned with local pollution levels) and the regulatory authorities (who will be concerned with breaches of permit)? Does the measure relate to the overall category: i.e. is CO_2 content actually a constituent of air quality and is it significant to falling air quality levels?
Reliability There must be a reliable description; users must understand the terminology.	Users must understand the terminology. For instance, a statement may say: 'Urban air quality, when deteriorating, can affect human health and wellbeing, and be damaging to infrastructure and local wildlife. Urban air quality is likely to be adversely affected by the amount of pollution particles carried in it—pollution such as gases, particulates, smoke—from activities carried out by local businesses. Air quality will be a combination of human activities and prevailing weather conditions and topographical features.'
There must be an emphasis on substance over form.	What is the context of the disclosure? Legal requirements may require CO_2 levels to be measured but the benchmark against which performance is measured must also be disclosed. There may be other means of disclosing CO_2 levels that have more resonance, and there may be independent bodies that promote measures that relate to the overall category—for instance, the World Health Organisation may relate CO_2 levels with incidents of childhood asthma, which may have more bearing for the local community.
The neutrality of the information must be preserved: it must not influence the direction of a decision or an opinion.	CO_2 levels may be presented as maximum and minimum levels rather than an average for the period.
The completeness of the information must be presented.	Have all relevant pieces of information been included in the report? Is there enough detail to contextualise the aspect? The business may produce CO_2 indirectly, say through its employees' transport and travel processes. The disclosure may wish to suggest ways in which attempts to mitigate this indirect CO_2 production are promoted (by reducing car transport or by ensuring fleet vehicles are fitted with catalytic converters, for example).
Information may be disclosed with prudence and precaution, which recognises the uncertainty surrounding the assessment of environmental impacts.	Does the organisation know the effects of CO_2 in the urban setting at different levels? What future legislative measures are likely and how proactive is the business in meeting new targets? How will this affect general business practice? What is the management strategy in respect of CO_2 levels produced now and those expected in the future?

Table 16.1 **Qualitative characteristics of information** (continued opposite)

Qualitative characteristic	Example
Comprehensibility This relates to the use of suitable language, in particular considering technical language.	The description of the effects of CO_2 levels should be in terms that a reasonably broadly educated reader will be familiar with. Overly scientific language should be avoided. Does the business understand its stakeholders well enough to present comprehensible information?
Comparability This allows stakeholders to judge performance both over time and between organisations.	Are the indicators of CO_2 emissions selected by the business consistent both with previous reports and with other sectoral businesses? Independently produced indicators may be relevant, as they may be seen to have greater acceptability and wider use.
Timeliness The reporting period should be the most appropriate to incorporate all the categories of impact that the business wishes or needs to report.	Data should be recorded in the context of the ecological cycle to which it relates, and to management strategy, which aims to produce continuous improvement.
Verifiability Independent verifiers, clear in their scope, are able to follow an audit trail.	The reader can see that independent verifiers are able to follow an audit trail from CO_2 production, through measurement and recording, to treatment and emission.

Table 16.1 *(continued)*

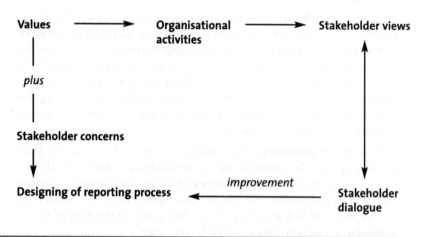

Figure 16.2 **AA 1000's reporting process**

Source: ISEA 1999

stakeholders to improved performance and to information. This should then encourage better decision-making and a programme of continuous improvement in performance to respond to these joint demands.

Embedded in the standard are the qualitative characteristics of information described in the accountants' conceptual framework and the FEE document discussed above. Indeed, the involvement of the accounting bodies in the development of the standard mean that accounting principles are utilised throughout, and this makes it suitable to be implemented by a reporting entity where accountants are a part of the reporting team.

The standard has three categories of principles. These cover:

- The scope and nature of the accounting process
- The value and credibility of the information
- Support for the ongoing management of the process

The process of reporting passes through a feedback loop of planning, designing and implementing systems, collating and producing the report, external verification and disclosure. In further detail, the process is as follows.

- **Review the values and objectives of the organisation.** The stress here is on the organisation itself, not on its stakeholders, and therefore it may be criticised for attempting to impose values on society. What the organisation must attempt is to reconcile its values and its objectives so that there is internal consistency. A commitment to stakeholder dialogue will improve the synergy between stakeholder and organisational values. Values and objectives can be formally documented through published mission or value statements or by making strategic plans available; they will also be implicitly visible by the behaviour exhibited by the organisation.

- **Identify the stakeholders.** The standard requires that key (i.e. direct) stakeholders be identified and their relationship to the organisation be established. The standard also requires that the organisation explain its policies regarding the maintenance of this relationship. There is no direct guidance on stakeholder identification, and it may be that the organisation analyses its stakeholders along traditional lines (e.g. customers, suppliers and employees) and does not examine the scope for identifying less obvious stakeholders.

- **Satisfy the stakeholders.** The standard is quite clear that the stakeholder is the starting point for any reporting strategy. Following this, the organisation must determine the scope of the report it wishes to produce such that its stakeholders will be satisfied by the content—both in terms of completeness and in terms of materiality. Hence the organisation is at this point managing its stakeholder dialogue.

- **Identify the issues.** The organisation is now required to review the range of potential issues that it may wish to include in the final report. This should include the mechanisms it wishes to use to facilitate stakeholder dialogue. This may be an important stage because there is the potential to recognise the wider accountability issues involved in social and ethical reporting, but this point is not stressed in the standard.

- **Decide on the indicators.** The organisation needs to decide on suitable indicators to measure social and ethical performance and establish a management information system that will allow these to be monitored. A clear link can be made to the financial information system if economic information and social information are to be integrated. If the information is to have value, senior management commitment and a recognition of the importance of integrated systems may be required.

- **Collect and collate the data.** The organisation needs to consider third-party information—that generated by the stakeholders—and how this may be incorporated into the report. This will be important in both recognising the importance of stakeholder input and reflecting on the importance of two-way stakeholder dialogue. This stage will also allow the setting of targets that will themselves aid monitoring and feedback.

- **Prepare and verify the report.** The preparation and verification of the report precedes its publication. The content of the report as stated by the standard is as follows, in suggested order of appearance:

  - Descriptions of performance
  - Disclosure of measures taken
  - Data on accountability
  - Stakeholder commentary
  - Measurement of performance against organisational values
  - Links with financial and environmental information

  Such suggested content would provide a certain amount of comprehensive coverage of the issues from an organisational perspective.

As with the guidelines proposed by GRI, there is ample reference to the ISO 14000 series of environmental management standards, and any organisation that has considered or implemented an environmental management system will be familiar with the terminology of the standard. It is firmly rooted in the organisation and its management, and this may be an attractive position for many organisations because it maintains the primacy of the organisation's management.

Making Values Count: a quality scoring framework

Based on a framework of eight principles—completeness, comparability, inclusivity, regularity and evolution, embeddedness, disclosure, external verification, and continuous improvement—the quality scoring framework focuses on a means of assessing quality in reporting practices (Gonella *et al.* 1998). The aim is not solely to introduce a standardised reporting framework, but rather to provide a framework that organisations can use to assess the quality of any process that yields information on the social and ethical performance of an organisation, whether or not a report has been published.

For processes that have culminated in publication, the scoring takes place through an examination of the published report and focuses on whether it reports accurately and fully on the quality of the process undertaken, such as the extent of stakeholder dialogue and whether or not the process has been verified.

Where there is no published report, the quality scoring framework can be used as a self-assessment or training tool. When this occurs, the scoring is achieved through a direct examination of the process. The framework's scoring system is based on eight principles. Each principle has seven criteria. The extent to which each criterion is fulfilled results in a score between 0 and 4. As a result, any process can be rated as being at one of the five possible developmental stages.

The number of principles is realistic. They allow for a sufficient number of areas to be covered, but are not so numerous that they repeat themselves or become confusing. The framework provides a comprehensive range of 'building blocks' that can be developed as are considered appropriate by different types of business. For example, the 'stakeholder map' could be adapted to any type of industry, as could 'new targets' and 'benchmarks'. The comparability section, which includes the criterion 'statutory norm indicators', is particularly useful, as it requires that the reports or processes use accurate, relevant and legitimate indicators.

The eight principles of the framework are somewhat general, and the way in which the scoring process operates ensures that one poor score will not necessarily hinder the overall score. For example, if it is genuinely impossible to meet a criterion, then that criterion is awarded a potential score. This ensures that organisations from any industry at any stage in the reporting process can benefit from the quality scoring framework, whether as a training or self-assessment tool or as a reporting framework. However, to external readers, a difference must be drawn between those scores actually granted and those that are a 'best guess'.

The scoring system

The assignment of scores is relatively easy once the assessor is familiar with the report or process in question and the requirements of the quality scoring framework. A 'harsh but fair' approach is required in order to gain useful results, as to award scores too generously yields little insight into the strengths and weaknesses of current systems. The information provided in Making Values Count is sufficient to allow an attempt at a scoring process.

In agreement with Making Values Count the 'rating is necessary to build an accurate and full picture of the quality of the social reporting process' (Gonella et al. 1998: 55). By awarding scores, comparisons are made easier, between individual companies, industries and reporting periods. As the quality scoring framework can be used by any sort of organisation or as a self-assessment tool, this is particularly useful. By assigning the qualitative data with a quantitative value, a clear picture of an organisation's current position can be attained very quickly. The scores also provide useful summaries and make assessment of an organisation's progress a simple task. This is particularly useful for non-experts attempting to analyse reports, as the numerical values are easy to interpret and provide a more straightforward perspective than large amounts of technical, qualitative data. In this respect the framework is easy to read as the qualitative indicators provide summary views.

The quality scoring framework as a self-assessment tool

In order to use the quality scoring framework as a self-assessment tool it is concluded that some degree of scoring would be useful. This is because it is in considering the reasons for the scores that the organisation will gain the most benefit from the process. The challenge is to distinguish between acceptable reasons for differences in scores (Gonella *et al.* 1998). To simply award a score and then walk away will deliver little if any benefit. Organisations may need to analyse the reasons for their weaker scores and act on their findings, to increase the quality of their reports.

If the framework is intended for use as a self-assessment tool, it is essential that the assessor is rigorous when assigning scores, as it would be fairly easy to score highly by not applying the criteria and principles thoroughly. For example, again considering the 'stakeholder map' criterion, it would be very easy to award a high score to an organisation that had prepared a report that merely mentions the term 'stakeholder'. In actual fact, the award of a high score requires that the report include a 'comprehensive map of all stakeholders including silent stakeholders' (Gonella *et al.* 1998: 38-39).

Owing to the subjective nature of the scoring criteria of the framework it is important that if it is to be used as an ongoing self-assessment tool the same person or group must undertake each consecutive assessment. This is essential, as the individual will interpret each set of results with the same group of biases and assumptions regarding the specific criteria and therefore will be capable of identifying from these results significant changes in the organisation's performance over time. Hence, management needs to make a commitment to this process, both in terms of personnel and in terms of resources.

The fact that the framework can be used as a self-assessment tool is in itself beneficial. Organisations may attempt to use the framework as a training tool or self-assessment model, which may be considered to be less intimidating than attempting to produce a social report. If they then progress to the production of a report it is likely to be of a very high quality, as the eight principles will already have been incorporated into the organisation's activities.

General observations

A high score on the quality scoring framework appears to represent an extremely high standard of social performance, or at least excellent disclosure of underlying performance. The quality scoring framework is probably used to its best potential when all three of its intended uses (as a training tool, self-assessment model and reporting framework) are applied. This could occur at any stage of an organisation's social performance, as training and self-assessment are likely to be ongoing. As a training tool, the principles could form the basics of a training programme, being used to brainstorm and increase understanding of the concept of social performance. The process could develop to one of self-assessment and eventually to a reporting framework.

The quality scoring framework seems to offer most potential for attempting to fill the gap created by a lack of accepted reporting frameworks. The style, which is widely applicable, gives it extra credibility as it can actually be used as a whole process. The scoring system is easy and allows for a variety of comparisons to be made. However, to apply the quality scoring framework at any level requires a great deal of commitment. If organisations see social reporting only as a public relations tool, then they are unlikely to attempt to use this framework.

The quality scoring framework may be linked with reporting awards schemes (as mentioned earlier) to improve motivation. External benchmarking may also be a useful development to enable organisations to make comparisons within their industry sector. Although it is appreciated that the diversity of industries would make specific comparisons impossible, it may be possible to derive general standards: for example, for chemical industries to gain proportionate improvements or to minimise the use of certain substances. In labour-intensive industries, indicators such as staff turnover or job satisfaction may be useful.

An area that is missing from the quality scoring framework is supplier relationships. As the category of companies likely to be producing social reports (global and/or blue-chip companies, etc.) are likely to have a huge influence on their suppliers, the incorporation of having an 'ethical supplier list' may be a useful addition. This may evolve through the stakeholder mapping exercise, as large organisations often recognise suppliers as important stakeholders.

Another important stakeholder is the employee group, and under the embeddedness principle communication of issues to staff is missing. Although stakeholder dialogue features heavily in the quality scoring framework, staff possibly represent a key stakeholder group, and the organisation should perhaps consider their reporting needs.

◢ Conclusions

Organisations considering reporting and requiring guidance need to first answer the 'Why?', 'Where?', 'What type?' and 'What to?' of reporting. Clear answers to these questions will then enable a decision as to whether any of the four frameworks reviewed are suitable for their particular organisation. Overcoming the mismatch between the mechanism an organisation uses to frame its report and the requirements of the stakeholders will result in the achievement of greater accountability.

Once the organisation has decided on the reporting framework to use and has started to produce reports, the reporting cycle, using feedback from all users of the published report, especially stakeholders, will be another way of developing future accountability mechanisms.

Dialogue also needs to (and is) occur(ing) between reporting organisations and those who critique the reporting mechanism, thus developing the process of accountability and improving the reporting frameworks available.

BIBLIOGRAPHY

Abbott, T. (1999) 'Question without Notice. Newcastle: Closure of BHP Steelworks', *Hansard (Australian House of Representatives)*, 29 September 1999: 10,905.

Ackoff, R.L. (1999) 'On Learning and the Systems that Facilitate it', *Reflections* 1.1 (repr. from the Center for Quality of Management, Cambridge, MA): 14-24.

Adams, C. (2000) 'Ethical Reporting: Past and Future', *Management Accounting*, February 2000: 49-50.

Adams, R. (1999) 'Seen to be Right', *Accountancy Age*, 11 February 1999: 24-25.

Albert, S., and D. Whetten (1985) 'Organisational Identity', in L.L. Cummings and B.M. Staw (eds.), *Research in Organisational Behaviour. Vol. 7* (Greenwich, CT: JAI Press): 263-95.

Albert, S., B. Ashforth and J. Dutton (2000) 'Organisational Identity and Identification: Charting New Waters and Building New Bridges', *Academy of Management Review* 25.1: 13-17.

ALI (American Law Institute) (1994) 'The Objective and Conduct of the Corporation', *Principles of Corporate Governance: Analysis and Recommendations* 1.2 (Washington, DC: ALI): 55-76.

Alperson, M. (1995) *Corporate Giving Strategies that Add Business Value* (New York: The Conference Board).

Altman, B.W. (1997) *Corporate Community Relations in the 1990s: A Study in Transformation* (doctoral dissertation; Boston, MA: Department of Organization Behavior, Boston University).

Altman, B.W. (1998a) 'Corporate Community Relations in the 1990s: A Study in Transformation', *Business and Society* 37.2 (June 1998): 221-27.

Altman, B.W. (1998b) 'Transformed Corporate Community Relations: A Management Tool for Achieving Corporate Citizenship', *Business and Society Review* 102–103: 43-51.

Altman, B., and K. Davenport (1998) *New Frontiers in Corporate Citizenship Research: The Theory/Practice Link* (San Diego, CA: Academy of Management).

Altman, B.W., and D. Vidaver-Cohen (2000) 'A Framework for Understanding Corporate Citizenship', *Business and Society Review* 105.1 (Spring 2000): 1-8.

Ampuero, M., J. Goranson and J. Scott (1999) 'Solving the Measurement Puzzle: How EVA and the Balanced Scorecard Fit Together', in Ernst & Young Centre for Business Innovation (1999) 'Measuring Business Performance', *Perspectives on Business Innovation* 2: 45-52.

Andriof, J. (2000) *Managing Social Risk through Stakeholder Partnership Building* (PhD thesis; Coventry, UK: Warwick Business School).

Andriof, J., and C. Marsden (1999) 'Corporate Citizenship: What is it and how to assess it?', *Personalführung* 8: 34-41.

Andriof, J., and C. Marsden (2000) 'Corporate Citizenship: What is it and how to assess it?', http://users.wbs.warwick.ac.uk/ccu/Publications/DGPF.html, 22 June 2000.

Annan, K. (1997) *Renewing the United Nations* (Report of the Secretary-General; New York: United Nations; www.un.org/reform/track2/part1.htm; accessed 1 June 2000).

Annan, K. (1999) 'Address to World Economic Forum, Davos Switzerland, January 31 1999', reprinted in *Vital Speeches*, 15 February 1999: 1-5.

Annan, K. (2000a) 'A Compact for the New Century', www.un.org/partners/business/davos.htm, 5 June 2000.

Annan, K. (2000b) 'Executive Summary and Conclusion, High-Level Meeting in the Global Compact', www.un.org/partners/business/gcevent/press/summary.htm.

Anshen, M. (1980) *Corporate Strategies for Social Performance* (New York: Macmillan).

Apple, R.W., Jr (1997) 'Money, Politics, and its Suckers', *New York Times*, 8 February 1997.

APSO (Agency for Personal Service Overseas) (1998) *Social Account 1996* (Dublin: APSO).

Argenti, J., and A. Campbell (1997) 'Stakeholders: The Case Against/The Case in Favour', *Long Range Planning* 30.3: 442-50.

Argyris, C. (1993) *Knowledge for Action: A Guide to Overcoming Barriers to Organizational Change* (San Francisco: Jossey–Bass).

Argyris, C. (2000) *Flawed Advice and the Management Trap: How managers can know when they're getting good advice and when they're not* (New York: Oxford University Press).

Argyris, C., and D. Schön (1974) *Theory in Practice* (San Francisco: Jossey–Bass).

Astley, W.G., and C.J. Fombrun (1983) 'Collective Strategy: Social Ecology of Organisational Environments', *Academy of Management Review* 8.4: 576-87.

ATK/GBPC (A.T. Kearney/Global Business Policy Council) (2000) 'Globalisation Ledger', www.atkearney.com/ATK/Publications.

Badaracco, J. (1998) 'The Discipline of Building Character', *Harvard Business Review*, March/April 1998; repr. in *Harvard Business Review on Leadership* (Boston, MA: Harvard Business School Publishing): 89-114.

Bai, M. (1999) 'Can pistols get smarter?' *Newsweek*, 2 August 1999: 41.

Banfield, E.C. (1958) *The Moral Basis of a Backward Society* (Glencoe, IL: The Free Press).

Barnard, C.I. (1938) *The Functions of the Executive* (Cambridge, MA: Harvard University Press).

Bartram, P. (2000) 'The Corporate World through Ethical Eyes', *Accountancy Age*, 24 February 2000: 24-26.

Bass, B. (1998) 'The Ethics of Transformational Leadership', in J.B. Ciulla (ed.), *Ethics: The Heart of Leadership* (Westport, CT: Praeger): 169-92.

Bateman, T.S., and D.W. Organ (1983) 'Job Satisfaction and the Good Soldier: The Relationship between Affect and Employee "Citizenship"', *Academy of Management Journal* 26.4: 587-95.

Bebeau, M.J., and M.M. Brabeck (1987) 'Integrating Care and Justice Issues in Professional Moral Education: A Gender Perspective', *Journal of Moral Education* 16: 189-202.

Beck, U. (1992) *Risk Society: Towards a New Modernity* (London: Sage).

Beesley, M., and T. Evans (1978) *Corporate Social Responsibility: A Reassessment* (Andover, UK: Croom Helm).

Belanger, J., C. Berggren, T. Bjorkman and C. Kohler (eds.) (1999) *Being Local Worldwide: ABB and the Challenge of Global Management* (Ithaca, NY: Cornell University Press [ILR Press]).

Bell, D. (1974) *The Coming of Post Industrial Society: A Venture in Social Forecasting* (London: Heinemann).

Bellamy, C. (2000) 'Public, Private and Civil Society', www.unicef.org/, 5 May 2000.

Bennett, A.L. (1984) *International Organisations* (Englewood Cliffs, NJ: Prentice–Hall).

Benning, A. (1999) *Managing Organizational Identity in a Faith-Based Social Services Agency* (unpublished doctoral dissertation; Boston, MA: Department of Strategy and Policy, Boston University).

Birch, D. (ed.) (1999a) *Corporate Citizenship: Awakening the Possibilities. The Proceedings of the First National Conference on Corporate Citizenship, Melbourne 19–20 November 1998* (Melbourne: Corporate Citizenship Research Unit, Deakin University).

Birch, D. (ed.) (1999b) 'Achieving Social Coalition: Some Key Principles of Partnership', *Achieving Social Coalition*, seminar proceedings, 3 June 1999, Melbourne: 10-24.

Birch, D., and M. Glazebrook (2000a) 'Doing Business, Doing Culture: Corporate Citizenship and Community', in S. Rees and S. Wright (eds.), *Human Rights, Corporate Responsibility: A Dialogue* (London: Pluto Press): 41-52.

Birch, D., and M. Glazebrook (2000b) 'Stakeholder Relations: Corporate and Community Perspectives from Australia', *AccountAbility Quarterly* 12: 25-28.

Bird, F.B., and J.A. Waters (1989) 'The Moral Muteness of Managers', *California Management Review*, Fall 1989: 73-88.

Blackwell (1997) *Blackwell Encyclopedic Dictionary of Business Ethics* (Oxford, UK: Basil Blackwell).

Blau, P. (1964) *Exchange and Power in Social Life* (New York: John Wiley).

Blum, W.J., and H. Kalven (1970) *The Uneasy Case for Progressive Taxation* (Chicago, IL: University of Chicago Press, first published 1953).

Bolino, M.C. (1999) 'Citizenship and Impression Management: Good Soldiers or Good Actors?', *Academy of Management Review* 24.1: 82-98.

Bourne, G. (1999) 'Achieving Social Coalition' (paper presented at a seminar, 6 June, Melbourne).

Bovens, M. (1998) 'The Corporate Republic: Complex Organisations and Citizenship', in E.A. Christodoulidis (ed.), *Communitarianism and Citizenship* (Aldershot, UK: Ashgate Publishing): 158-76.

Bowen, H.R. (1953) *Social Responsibilities of the Businessman* (New York: Harper).

BP (British Petroleum) (1998) *What we stand for . . . Our Business Policies* (London: BP).

Brocklehurst, E., and V. Mangnall (1999) 'ANZ Criticised over Children's Account Changes', Australian Associated Press, Sydney, 3 February 1999.

Brown, C.C. (1979) *Beyond the Bottom Line* (New York: Macmillan)

BT (British Telecom) (1999) *An Issue of Responsibility: Social Report* (London: BT).

Buchholz, R.A. (1989) *Fundamental Concepts and Problems in Business Ethics* (Englewood Cliffs, NJ: Prentice–Hall).

Burgers, W.P., C.W.L. Hill and W.C. Kim (1993) 'A Theory of Global Strategic Alliances: The Case of the Global Auto Industry', *Strategic Management Journal* 14: 419-32.

Burke, E.M. (1999) *Corporate Community Relations: The Principle of the Neighbour of Choice* (Westport, CT: Praeger).

Burns, J.M. (1978) *Leadership* (New York: Harper Torchbooks).

Cadman, A. (2000) 'Taxation Laws Amendment Bill, Second Reading (No. 10) 1999', *Hansard (Australian House of Representatives)*, 12 April 2000: 15,090-99.

Calton, J., and L. Lad (1995) 'Social Contracting as a Trust-Building Process of Network', *Business Ethics Quarterly* 5.2: 271-95.

Calton, J., and N. Kurland (1996) 'A Theory of Stakeholder Enabling: Giving Voice to an Emerging Postmodern Praxis of Organisational Discourse', in D. Boje, R. Gephart, T. Joseph and T. Thatchenkery (eds.), *Postmodern Management and Organizational Theory* (Thousand Oaks, CA: Sage): 154-77.

Capowski, G. (1994) 'Anatomy of a Leader: Where are the leaders of tomorrow?', *Management Review* 12; cited in R.L. Daft, *Management* (New York: Dryden Press, 2000, 5th edn): 503.

Carroll, A.B. (1979) 'A Three-Dimensional Conceptual Model of Corporate Performance', *Academy of Management Review* 4.4 (October 1979): 497-505.

Carroll, A.B. (1987) 'In Search of the Moral Manager', *Business Horizons*, March/April 1987: 7-15.

Carroll, A.B. (1991) 'The Pyramid of Corporate Social Responsibility: Toward the Moral Management of Organizational Stakeholders', *Business Horizons* 34.4 (July/August 1991): 39-48.

Carroll, A.B. (1995) 'Stakeholder Thinking in Three Models of Management Morality: A Perspective with Strategic Implications', in J. Näsi (ed.), *Understanding Stakeholder Thinking* (Helsinki: LSR Publications): 47-74.

Carroll, A.B. (1998) 'The Four Faces of Corporate Citizenship', *Business and Society Review* 100–101: 1-7.

Carroll, A.B., and A.K. Buchholtz (2000) *Business and Society: Ethics and Stakeholder Management* (Cincinnati, OH: South-Western College Publishing, 4th edn).

Castells, M. (1996) *The Rise of the Network Society* (Oxford, UK: Basil Blackwell).

Castells, M. (1998a) *The Information Age: Economy, Society and Culture—The Rise of the Network Society* (Oxford, UK: Basil Blackwell).

Castells, M. (1998b) *The Information Age: Economy, Society and Culture—The Power of Identity* (Oxford, UK: Basil Blackwell).

Castells, M. (1998c) *The Information Age: Economy, Society and Culture—End of Millennium* (Oxford, UK: Basil Blackwell).

CCBE (Clarkson Centre for Business Ethics) (1999) *Principles of Stakeholder Management* (Toronto: University of Toronto).

CCCR (Centre for Corporate Community Relations) (1999) *1999 Community Relations Index* (research report; Chestnut Hill, MA: CCCR, Boston College).

CCP (Canadian Centre for Philanthropy) (2000) 'Investors Agree on Corporate Citizenship', *Inter Sector* 5.1 (www.ccp.ca/imagine/publications/inter-sector/issue5-2/investorsagree. html, accessed 4 April 2001).

CCPA (Centre for Corporate Public Affairs) (2000) *Corporate Community Involvement: Establishing a Business Case* (Melbourne: CCPA and the Business Council of Australia).

CEP (Council on Economic Priorities) (2000) 'Social Accountability 8000', www.cepnyc.org/cepaa.htm, 14 June 2000.

CERES (Coalition for Environmentally Responsible Economies) (1999) 'Global Reporting Initiative', www.ceres.org/reporting/globalreporting.html.

CERES (Coalition for Environmentally Responsible Economies) (2000) 'Global Reporting Initiative', www.ceres.org/reporting/globalreporting.html.

Chamberlain, N.W. (1982) *Social Strategy and Corporate Structure* (New York: Macmillan).

Chapman, E., and S.L. O'Neil (2000) *Leadership: Essential Steps Every Manager Needs to Know* (Upper Saddle River, NJ: Prentice–Hall, 3rd edn).

Charkham, J. (1995) *Keeping Good Company: A Study of Corporate Governance in Five Countries* (New York/Oxford,UK: Oxford University Press).

Chowdhury, N. (1999) 'Dell Cracks China', *Fortune*, 12 June 1999: 120ff.

Ciulla, J.B. (ed.) (1998) *Ethics: The Heart of Leadership* (Westport, CT: Praeger).

Clarkson, M.B.E. (1995) 'A Stakeholder Framework for Analyzing and Evaluating Corporate Social Performance', *Academy of Management Review* 20.1: 92-117.

Clemenger Report (1998) *What Ordinary Australians Think of Big Business and What Needs to Change?* (Sydney: Clemenger).

CoF (Council on Foundations) (1996) *Measuring the Value of Corporate Citizenship* (Washington, DC: CoF).

Cohen, J. (2000) 'UN–Business Partnership Cases', *Socially Responsible Business E-mail Listserv*, jcohen@unausa.org.

Cohen, J.R., L.W. Pant and D.J. Sharp (1998) 'The Effect of Gender and Academic Discipline Diversity on the Ethical Evaluations, Ethical Intentions, and Ethical Orientation of Potential Public Accounting Recruits', *Accounting Horizons* 12.3: 250-70.

Cohen, R. (1998) 'High claims in spill betray depth of Nigerian poverty', *New York Times*, 20 September 1998.

Collins, J.C., and J.I. Porras (1997) *Built to Last: Successful Habits of Visionary Companies* (New York: HarperBusiness).

Cooper, C.L., and C. Argyris (1998) *The Concise Blackwell Encyclopaedia of Management* (Oxford, UK: Basil Blackwell).

Co-operative Bank (1998a) *Mission Statement* (Manchester, UK: The Co-operative Bank).

Co-operative Bank (1998b) *Ethical Policy* (Manchester, UK: The Co-operative Bank).

Co-operative Bank (1998c) *Ecological Mission Statement* (Manchester, UK: The Co-operative Bank).

Co-operative Bank (1998d) *Partnership Report* (Manchester, UK: The Co-operative Bank).

Corlett, J.A. (1989) 'The "Modified Vendetta Sanction" as a Method of Corporate Collective Punishment', *Journal of Business Ethics* 8: 937-42.

Cornell, A. (1998) 'Rural branch closures threaten banks' image', *The Australian Financial Review*, 8 May 1998: 62.

Corporate Watch (2000a) 'Citizens Compact on the United Nations and Corporations', www.corpwatch.org/trac/globalization/un/citizenscompact.html, 1 February 2000.

Corporate Watch (2000b) 'Corporatization of the United Nations', www.corpwatch.org/trac/globalization/un/, 21 February 2000, 16 June 2000.

Cotton, P., I.A.M. Fraser and W.Y. Hill (2000) 'The Social Audit Agenda: Primary Health Care in a Stakeholder Society', *International Journal of Auditing* 4.1: 3-28.

Covey, S.R. (1989) *The Seven Habits of Highly Effective People* (New York: Simon & Schuster).

CTC (Centre for Tomorrow's Company) (1998) *Sooner, Sharper, Simpler: A Lean Vision of an Inclusive Annual Report* (London: CTC).

D'Andrea Tyson, L. (1999) 'Old Economic Logic in the New Economy', *California Management Review* 41.4: 8-16.

D'Aveni, R. (1994) *Hyper-Competition: Managing the Dynamics of Strategic Maneuvering* (New York: Free Press).

Dalai Lama and H. Cutler (1998) *The Art of Happiness* (New York: Penguin Books).

Daniels, J.D., and L.H. Radebaugh (1995) *International Business: Environments and Operations* (Reading, MA: Addison-Wesley).

Davenport, K.S. (1998) *Corporate Citizenship: A Stakeholder Approach for Defining Corporate Social Performance and Identifying Measures for Assessing It* (PhD dissertation; Santa Barbara, CA: The Fielding Institute).

Davenport, K.S. (2000) 'Corporate Citizenship: A Stakeholder Approach for Defining Corporate Social Performance and Identifying Measures for Assessing It' (dissertation abstract), *Business and Society* 3.2 (June 2000): 210-19.

Davenport, K.S., J.M. Logsdon, P.G. Lewellyn and D.J. Wood (1999) 'Business Citizenship: Theory and Practice' (symposium presented at the Academy of Management annual meeting, Chicago, IL, August 1999).

Davidson, W.N., D.L. Worrell and A. El-Jelly (1995) 'Influencing Managers to change Unpopular Corporate Behaviour through Boycotts and Divestitures: A Stock Market Test', *Business and Society* 34: 171-96.

Davis, G.F., and T.A. Thompson (1994). 'A Social Movement Perspective on Corporate Control', *Administrative Science Quarterly* 39: 141-73.

Davis, J.H., F.D. Schoorman and L. Donalson (1997) 'Toward a Stewardship Theory of Management', *Academy of Management Review* 22.1: 20-47.

Davis, K. (1973) 'The Case for and against Business Assumption of Social Responsibilities', *Academy of Management Journal* 16.2 (June 1973): 312-22.

Dawson, E. (1998) 'The Relevance of Social Audit for Oxfam GB', *Journal of Business Ethics* 17.13: 1457-69.

De Alvarez, L.P.S. (1980) 'Introduction', in N. Machiavelli, *The Prince* (trans. L.P.S. de Alvarez; Prospect Heights, IL: Waveland Press, first published 1513): i-xxxiv.

De George, R.T. (1993) *Competing with Integrity in International Business* (New York: Oxford University Press).

De Waal, F. (1996) *Good Natured: The Origins of Right and Wrong in Humans and Other Animals* (Cambridge, MA: Harvard University Press).

Dennis, B., C.P. Neck and M. Goldsby (1998) 'Body Shop International: An Exploration of Corporate Social Responsibility', *Management Decision* 36.10: 649-53.

Dey, C., R. Evans and R. Gray (1995) 'Towards Social Information Systems and Bookkeeping: A Note on Developing the Mechanisms for Social Accounting and Audit', *Journal of Applied Accounting Research* 2.3 (December 1995): 38-63.

Dion, M. (1993) 'Institutionalising Environmental Ethics into the Corporation', *Research in Philosophy and Technology* 13: 301-18.

Dion, M. (1994) *L'éthique de l'entreprise* (Montreal: Fides).

Dion, M. (1995) 'La composition des conseils d'administration et de leurs principaux comités: Une question d'éthique', *Revue Organisation* 5.1 (Autumn 1995): 75-84.

Dion, M. (1996) 'Organisational Culture as Matrix of Corporate Ethics', *International Journal of Organisational Analysis* 4.4 (October 1996): 329-51.

Dion, M. (1998a) 'A Typology of Corporate Environmental Policies', *Environmental Ethics* 20.2 (Summer 1998): 151-62.

Dion, M. (1998b) *Investissements éthiques et régie d'entreprise. Entre la mondialisation et la mythologie* (Montreal: Médiaspaul).

Dion, M. (2000) 'Valeurs et croyances organisationnelles dans les codes d'éthique des entreprises manufacturières', *Revue Organisations et Territoires* 9.1 (Winter 2000): 47-54.

Dion, M. (2001a) *Le héros, le leader et le messie: Trois figures symboliques du milieu des affaires des sociétés occidentales* (Montreal: Fides, forthcoming).

Dion, M. (2001b) 'The Ethical Leadership in Organisations: A Philosophical and Cross-Cultural Perspective' (forthcoming).

Dion, M., and L. Marquis (2001) 'Les codes d'éthique des entreprises manufacturières et leurs mécanismes de renforcement interne', *Revue Organisations et Territoires*, Spring 2001.

Dion, M., and R. Lescarbeau (1994) 'Les entreprises manufacturières sans code d'éthique: État des préoccupations des dirigeants', *Ethica* 6.1 (Spring 1994): 89-103.

Dion, M., and R. Lescarbeau (1995) 'Les codes d'éthique des entreprises manufacturières au Québec: État des perceptions des dirigeants', *Ethica* 7.1: 113-44.

Dion, M., and W.Z. Ibrahim (1995) 'Joint Ventures between Canadian Companies and Malaysian Business Corporations: An Ethical Outlook', *Journal of Oriental and African Studies* 7: 57-67.

Dodd, E.M., Jr (1932) 'For whom are corporate managers trustees?', *Harvard Law Review* 45: 1145-63.

Donaldson, T. (1989) *The Ethics of International Business* (New York: Oxford University Press).

Donaldson, T., and T.W. Dunfee (1999) *Ties that Bind: A Social Contracts Approach to Business Ethics* (Cambridge, MA: Harvard Business School Press).

Donaldson, T., and L.E. Preston (1995) 'The Stakeholder Theory of the Corporation: Concepts, Evidence, and Implications', *Academy of Management Review* 20.1 (January 1995): 65-91.

Drath, W.H., and C.J. Palus (1994) *Making Common Sense: Leadership as Meaning-Making in a Community of Practice* (Greensboro, NC: Centre for Creative Leadership).

Drucker, P.F. (1946) *The Concept of the Corporation* (New York/Toronto: The New American Library, 2nd edn 1964).

Drucker, P.F. (1993) *Post-capitalist Society* (New York: Harper Business; Oxford, UK: Butterworth–Heinemann).

Dunning, J. (1993a) *The Globalisation of Business: The Challenge of the 1990s* (London/New York: Routledge).

Dunning, J. (1993b) *Globalisation: The Challenge for National Economic Regimes* (Dublin: The Economic and Social Research Institute).

Dussauge, P., and B. Garrette (1999) *Co-operative Strategy: Competing Successfully through Strategic Alliances* (New York: John Wiley).

Dworkin, R. (1978) *Taking Rights Seriously* (Cambridge, MA: Harvard University Press, 2nd edn).

Dyer, J.H., and H. Singh (1998) 'The Relational View: Co-operative Strategy and Sources of Interorganisational Competitive Advantage', *Strategic Management Journal* 23.4: 660-79.

Eastman, K.K. (1994) 'In the Eyes of the Beholder: An Attributional Approach to Ingratiation and Organisational Citizenship Behaviour', *Academy of Management Journal* 37: 1379-91.

Eccleston, R. (1998) 'The Need for Charity', *The Australian*, 28 April 1998: 10.

Economist (1998) 'Oil industry: The Decade's Worst Stocks', *The Economist*, 5 December 1998: 87-88.

Economist (1999a) 'Cheap Oil: The Next Shock?', *The Economist*, 6 March 1999: 21-23.

Economist (1999b) 'Oil: Why Big is still Beautiful', *The Economist*, 3 April 1999: 57-58.

Economist (1999c) 'Economic Indicators: Oil Supplies', *The Economist*, 3 July 1999: 104.

Economist (1999d) 'Go Global, Sue Local', *The Economist*, 14 August 1999: 54.

Economist (1999e) 'Finance and Economics: Exaggeration', *The Economist*, 30 October 1999: 87.

Economist (1999f) 'The Revolutionary Spirit: Jack Welch, GE and Creative Destruction', *The Economist*, 18 September 1999: 17-18, 23-26.

Elfstrom, G. (1991) *Moral Issues and Multinational Corporations* (London: Macmillan).

Elias, D. (1999) 'Insurers in Push for Ecology', *The Age*, 16 October 1999: 1.

Elkington, J. (1997) *Cannibals with Forks: The Triple Bottom Line of Twentieth Century Business* (Oxford, UK: Capstone Publishing).

Elkington, J. (2000) 'Sustainable Profits: Triple Bottom Line Strategies for Business and Markets', presented at *From Sustainable Development to Dow Jones* conference, Melbourne, 17 May 2000.

Elkington, J., and S. Fennell (1998) 'Partners for Sustainability', *Greener Management International* 24 (Winter 1998): 48-60.

Enderle, G., and G. Peters (1998) *A Strange Affair? The Emerging Relationship between NGOs and Transnational Companies* (Notre Dame, IN: University of Notre Dame Press; London: Price Waterhouse).

EPA v. Caltex (*Environmental Protection Authority vs Caltex Refining Co Pty Ltd*) (1993) High Court of Australia, 178 CLR 477 F.C. 93/058.

Ericsson (2000) 'Ericsson response launches pilot project for disaster preparedness and response in disaster-prone countries', www.ericssonresponse.com/eps/article_display. cfm?section=8&ID=21, 4 May 2000.

Etzioni, A. (1995) *The Spirit of Community: Rights, Responsibilities and the Communitarian Agenda* (London: Fontana).

Evan, W.M., and R.E. Freeman (1988) 'A Stakeholder Theory of the Modern Corporation: Kantian Capitalism', in T. Beauchamp and N. Bowie (eds.), *Ethical Theory and Business* (Englewood Cliffs, NJ: Prentice–Hall).

Evans, S. (1998) 'Corporates must "Give for Profit"', *Australian Financial Review*, 6 November 1998: 4.

Fahr, J., P.M. Podsakoff and D.W. Organ (1990) 'Accounting for Organisational Citizenship Behaviour: Leader Fairness and Task Scope versus Satisfaction', *Journal of Management* 16.4: 705-22.

FEE (Fédération des Experts Comptables Européens) (1999) 'Towards a Generally Accepted Framework for Environmental Reporting' (discussion paper; Brussels: FEE, January 1999).

Fisher, D., and W.R. Torbert (1995) *Personal and Organizational Transformations: The True Challenge of Continual Quality Improvement* (London: McGraw–Hill).

Fombrun, C.J. (1996) *Reputation* (Boston, MA: Harvard Business School Press).

Fombrun, C.J. (1997) 'Three Pillars of Corporate Citizenship: Ethics, Social Benefit, Profitability', in N.M. Tichy, R. Andrew, R. McGill and L. St Clair (eds.), *Corporate Global Citizenship Doing Business in the Public Eye* (San Francisco: The New Lexington Press): 27-61.

Fox, C. (2000a) 'Be Part of Debate: BCA', *Australian Financial Review*, 4 April 2000: 70.9

Fox, C. (2000b) 'Good deeds still seen as bad business', *Australian Financial Review*, 15 February 2000: 62.

FPA (Foundation for Public Affairs) (1999) *Corporate Public Affairs: The State of Corporate Public Affairs Survey* (Washington, DC: FPA).

Frederick, W.C. (1986) 'Toward CSR3: Why Ethical Analysis is Indispensable and Unavoidable in Corporate Affairs', *California Management Review* 28.2: 126-41.

Frederick, W.C. (1995) *Values, Nature, and Culture in the American Corporation* (New York: Oxford University Press).

Frederick, W.C., and J. Weber (1987) 'The Values of Corporate Managers and their Critics', in W.C. Frederick and L.E. Preston (eds.), *Research in Corporate Social Performance and Policy. Vol. 9* (Greenwich, CT: JAI Press): 131-52.

Frederick, W.C., J.E. Post and K. Davis (1992) *Business and Society: Corporate Strategy, Public Policy, Ethics* (New York: McGraw–Hill).

Freeman, D. (1999) 'Bloomberg Financial Services News E-mail', dfreeman@bloomberg.net, 26 August 1999.

Freeman, R.E. (1984) *Strategic Management: A Stakeholder Approach* (Boston, MA: Pitman).

Freeman, R.E. (1994) 'The Politics of Stakeholder Theory: Some Further Directions', *Business Ethics Quarterly* 4: 409-21.

Freeman, R.E., and D.R. Gilbert, Jr (1988) *Corporate Strategy and the Search for Ethics* (Englewood Cliffs, NJ: Prentice–Hall).

French, H. (2000) *Vanishing Borders: Protecting the Planet in the Age of Globalisation* (New York: W.W. Norton).

Friedman, M. (1962) *Capitalism and Freedom* (Chicago, IL: University of Chicago Press).

Friedman, M. (1970) 'The Social Responsibility of Business is to Increase its Profits', *New York Times Magazine* 32–33 (13 September 1970): 32-33, 122, 124, 126.

Fritzsche, D.J. (1997) *Business Ethics: A Global and Managerial Perspective* (New York: McGraw–Hill).

Frooman, J. (1999) 'Stakeholder Influence Strategies', *Academy of Management Review* 42.2: 191-201.

Gadamer, H.-G. (1976) *Vérité et méthode: Les grandes lignes d'une herméneutique philosophique* (Paris: Seuil).

Galbraith, J.K. (1973) 'On the Economic Image of Corporate Enterprise', in R. Nader and M.J. Green (eds.), *Corporate Power in America* (New York: Grossman Publishers, 2nd edn 1977): 3-9.

Gandz, J., and N. Hayes (1988) 'Teaching Business Ethics', *Journal of Business Ethics* 7: 657-69.

Gardner, H. (1983) *Frames of Mind* (New York: Basic Books).

Garrett, D.E. (1987) 'The Effectiveness of Marketing Policy Boycotts', *Journal of Marketing* 51: 46-57.

Gauthier, D. (1986) *Morals by Agreement* (New York: Oxford University Press).

Gibson, K. (2000) 'The Moral Basis of Stakeholder Theory', *Journal of Business Ethics* 26.3: 245-57.

Giddens, A. (1990) *The Consequences of Modernity* (Cambridge, UK: Polity Press).

Giddens, A. (1991) 'Structuration Theory: Past, Present and Future', in C.G.A. Bryant and D. Jary (eds.), *Giddens' Theory of Structuration: A Critical Appraisal* (London: Routledge): 201-21.

Giddens, A. (1999) 'Risk: Reith Lectures 1999—Runaway World', http://news2.thls.bbc.co.uk/hi/english/ static/events/reith_99/week2/week2.htm.

Gilligan, C. (1982) *In a Different Voice: Psychological Theory and Women's Development* (Cambridge, MA: Harvard University Press).

Gilpin, K.N. (1998) 'What's Behind the Gush of Deals?', *New York Times*, 29 November 1998.

Gladwin, T.N., J.J. Kennedy and T.S. Krause (1995) 'Shifting Paradigms for Sustainable Development: Implications for Management Theory and Research', *Academy of Management Review* 20.4: 874-907.

Glazebrook, M. (1999) 'Corporate Citizenship and Action Research: An Australian Perspective', in D. Windsor (ed.), *International Association for Business and Society* (Tenth Anniversary Conference Proceedings, Paris, 25 June 1999): 120-25.

Glazebrook, M. (2000) *Exchange as a Determinant of Corporate Citizenship Outcome* (unpublished PhD dissertation, Corporate Citizenship Research Unit, Deakin University, Burwood, Australia).

Goleman, D. (1995) *Emotional Intelligence* (New York: Bantam Books).

Goleman, D. (1998) *Working with Emotional Intelligence* (New York: Bantam Books).

Gonella, C., A. Pilling and S. Zadek (1998) *Making Values Count* (research report 57 from the Association of Chartered Certified Accountants; London, Certified Accountants Educational Trust).

Goodpaster, K.E. (1991) 'Business Ethics and Stakeholder Analysis', *Business Ethics Quarterly* 1.1: 53-73.

Graham, J. (1991) 'An Essay on Organisational Citizenship Behaviour', *Employee Responsibilities and Rights Journal* 4.2: 249-70.

Grattan, M. (1998) 'PM ups the ante on goodwill', *Australian Financial Review*, 6 November 1998: 4.

Gray, R., R. Kouhy and S. Lavers (1995) 'Corporate Social and Environmental Reporting: A Review of the Literature and a Longitudinal Study of UK Disclosure', *Accounting, Auditing and Accountability Journal* 8.2: 47-77.

Gray, R., C. Dey, D. Owen, R. Evans and S. Zadek (1997) 'Struggling with the Praxis of Social Accounting: Stakeholders, Accountability, Audits and Procedures', *Accounting, Auditing and Accountability Journal* 10.3: 325-64.

Gray, R., D. Owen and C. Adams (1996) *Accounting and Accountability: Changes and Challenges in Corporate, Social and Environmental Reporting* (Hemel Hempstead, UK: Prentice–Hall Europe).

Greanias, G.C., and D. Windsor (eds.) (1982) *The Changing Boardroom: Making Policy and Profits in an Age of Corporate Citizenship* (Houston, TX: Gulf Publishing).

Greenley, G.E., and G.R. Foxall (1997) 'Multiple Stakeholder Orientation in UK Companies and the Implications for Company Performance', *Journal of Management Studies* 34.2: 259-84.

Greenspan, A. (1998) 'Is There a New Economy?', *California Management Review* 41.1: 74-85.

Guardian (1998) 'BP in Colombia: A Tale of Death, Pollution and Deforestation', *The Guardian*, 15 August 1998.

Guéhenno, J.M. (1985) *The End of the Nation State* (Minneapolis: University of Minnesota Press).

Halal, W.E. (1986) *The New Capitalism* (New York: John Wiley).

Halal, W.E. (1994) 'From Hierarchy to Enterprise: Internal markets are the new foundation of management', *Academy of Management Executive* 8.4: 69-83.

Hamel, G. (1998) 'The Challenge Today: Changing the Rules of the Game', *Business Strategy Review* 9.2 (Summer 1998): 19-26.

Handy, C. (1997) *The Hungry Spirit. Beyond Capitalism: A Quest for Purpose in the Modern World* (London: Arrow Books).

Harrison, J.S., and R.E. Freeman (1999) 'Stakeholders, Social Responsibility, and Performance: Empirical Evidence and Theoretical Perspectives', *Academy of Management Journal* 42.5: 479-85.

Harrison, J.S., and C.H. St John (1994) *Strategic Management of Organizations and Stakeholders: Theory and Cases* (St Paul, MN: West Publishing).

Harrison, J.S., and C.H. St John (1996) 'Managing and Partnering with External Stakeholders', *Academy of Management Executive* 10.2: 46-60.

Hartcher, P. (1997) 'Companies take lesson in giving', *Australian Financial Review*, 24 November 1997: 1-10.

Hawken, P., A. Lovins and L. Lovins (1999) *Natural Capitalism* (London: Earthscan Publications).

Heggen, B. (1999) 'Gambling on Lawsuits', *The Advertiser*, 12 June 1999: 15.

Heidegger, M. (1962) *Being and Time* (New York: Harper & Row).

Heidegger, M. (1971) *Poetry, Language and Thought* (New York: Harper & Row).

Heifetz, R.A., and D.L. Laurie (1998) 'The Work of Leadership', *Harvard Business Review*, January/February 1997; repr. in *Harvard Business Review on Leadership* (Boston, MA: Harvard Business School Publishing): 171-97.

Held, D., A. McGrew, D. Goldblatt and and J. Perraton (1999) *Global Transformations: Politics, Economics and Culture* (Cambridge, UK: Polity Press).

Henry Mintzberg, H. (1998) 'The Manager's Job: Folklore or Fact', *Harvard Business Review*, July/August 1975; repr. in *Harvard Business Review on Leadership* (Boston, MA: Harvard Business School Publishing): 1-36.

Herremans, I.M., and P. Akathaporn (1993) 'An Investigation of Corporate Social Responsibility Reputation and Economic Performance', *Accounting, Organization and Society* 18.7/8: 587-604.

Hibbitt, C. (1999) 'Sustainability Reporting Guidelines: A Commentary. Searching for the Lion's Tracks not the Lion', Global Reporting Initiative Exposure Draft, www.limperginstituut.nl.

Hicks, L. (1996) 'Caterpillar Flunks Corporate Citizenship Test', *The York Dispatch* (8 May 1996); repr. in *UAW CAT Update* 1.2 (August 1996).

Hill, W.Y., I.A.M. Fraser and P. Cotton (1998) 'Patients' Voices, Rights and Responsibilities on Implementing Social Audit in Primary Health Care', *Journal of Business Ethics* 17.13: 1481-97.

Himmelfarb, G. (1999) *One Nation, Two Cultures* (New York: Knopf).

Hirst, P., and G. Thompson (1996) *Globalisation in Question: The International Economy and the Possibilities of Governance* (Cambridge, UK: Polity Press).

Hobbes, T. (1996) *Leviathan* (New York: Oxford University Press).

Hoffman, W.M., A.E. Lange and D.A. Fedo (1986) *Ethics and Multinational Enterprise* (Boston, MA: University Press of America).

Hollander, E. (1998) 'Ethical Challenges in the Leader–Follower Relationship', in J.B. Ciulla (ed.), *Ethics: The Heart of Leadership* (Westport, CT: Praeger): 49-61.

Horne, B. (2000) 'Grievance Debate. Telstra: Rural and Regional Australia', *Hansard (Australian House of Representatives)*, 13 March 2000: 14, 155-57.

Houston Chronicle (2000) 'Customers pay sugar subsidy of $1.9 billion', *Houston Chronicle*, 10 June 2000: 3C.

Howard, J. (1998) Press conference transcript, Parliament House, Canberra, 4 February.

Howard, J. (1999) 'The Australian Way', Federation Address, The Queensland Chamber of Commerce and Industry, 28 January 1999, www.pm.gov.au/media/pressrel/2000/federation0106.htm.

Huntington, S.P. (1996) *The Clash of Civilisations and the Remaking of World Order* (New York: Simon & Schuster).

Huntington, S.P. (1997) *Der Kampf der Kulturen (The Clash of Civilisations): Die Neugestaltung der Weltpolitik im 21 Jahrhundert* (Vienna: Europaverlag Munich).

Huse, M., and D. Eide (1996) 'Stakeholder Management and the Avoidance of Corporate Control', *Business and Society* 35.2: 211-43.

Hutton, W. (1995) *The State We Are In* (London: Jonathan Cape).

Hutton, W. (1997) 'Six Stakeholder Propositions', *Business Strategy Review* 4: 7-10.

Hutton, W. (1999) *The Stakeholding Society: Writings on Politics and Economics* (ed. D. Goldblatt; Cambridge, UK: Polity Press).

ICC (International Chamber of Commerce) (1996) *Extortion and Bribery in International Business Transactions* (Paris: ICC).

ICC/UN (International Chamber of Commerce/United Nations) (2000) 'Origins of a Partnership', www.iccwbo.org/home/icc_and_united_nations/icc_and_un.asp, 14 May 2000.

Interfaith Center on Corporate Responsibility (1995) *Principles for Global Corporate Responsibility* (New York: Interfaith Center on Corporate Responsibility).

Interfaith Declaration (1993) *Interfaith Declaration: A Code of Ethics on International Business for Christians, Muslims and Jews* (London: British–North American Association).

ISEA (Institute of Social and Ethical AccountAbility) (1999) *Draft Standards in Social and Ethical Accounting, Auditing and Reporting* (AA1000; London: ISEA, February 1999).

ISEA (Institute of Social and Ethical AccountAbility) (2000) *Innovation through Partnership* (London: ISEA).

Ivanovich, D. (2000) 'OK for African oil project expected, but its impact on two impoverished nations debated', *Houston Chronicle*, 6 June 2000: 1C, 5C.

Jackall, R. (1988) *Moral Mazes: The World of Corporate Managers* (New York: Oxford University Press).

Johnson, G., and K. Scholes (1993) *Exploring Corporate Strategy: Text and Cases* (Hemel Hempstead, UK: Prentice–Hall International).

Johnson, H.L. (1979) *Disclosure of Corporate Social Performance: Survey Evaluation and Prospects* (New York/London: Praeger).

Jones, T. (1983) 'An Integrating Framework for Research in Business and Society: A Step toward the Elusive Paradigm?', *Academy of Management Review* 8.4: 559-64.

Kahn, J. (2000) 'Multinationals Sign UN Pact on Rights and Environment', *New York Times*, 27 July 2000: A1.

Kaltenheuser, S. (1998) 'Tenth Annual Business Ethics Awards', *Business Ethics*, November/December 1998: 11.

Kant, I. (1983) *Foundations of the Metaphysics of Morals* (Indianapolis, IN: Bobbs–Merrill and Library of Liberal Arts).

Kanter, R.M. (1995) *World Class: Thriving Locally in the Global Economy* (New York: Simon & Schuster).

Kanungo, R.N., and J. Conger (1993) 'Promoting Altruism as a Corporate Goal', *Academy of Management Review* 7.3: 37-48.

Katz, D., and R.L. Kahn (1966) *The Social Psychology of Organisations* (New York: John Wiley).

Keeley, M. (1988) *A Social-Contract Theory of Organizations* (Notre Dame, IN: University of Notre Dame Press).

Kegan, R. (1982) *The Evolving Self: Problem and Process in Human Development* (Cambridge, MA: Harvard University Press).

Kegan, R. (1994) *In over our Heads: The Mental Demands of Modern Life* (Cambridge, MA: Harvard University Press).

Kell, G., and J.G. Ruggie (1999) 'Global Markets and Social Legitimacy: The Case of the "Global Compact"', www.icfconsulting.com/gc/UNWeb.nsf/content/gkjr.htm, 10 May 2000.

Kinder, P., S. Lydenburg and A. Domini (1993) *Investing for Good* (New York: HarperCollins).

Kinsley, M. (1987) 'Companies as Citizens: Should they have a conscience?', *Wall Street Journal*, 19 February 1987: 29.

Koechlin, D., and K. Muller (eds.) (1993) *Green Business Opportunities: The Profit Principle* (London: Financial Times/Pitman Publishing).

Kohlberg, L. (1976) 'Moral Stages and Moralization: The Cognitive-Developmental Approach', in T. Lickona, G. Geis and L. Kohlberg (eds.), *Moral Development and Behavior: Theory, Research, and Social Issues* (New York: Holt, Rinehart & Winston).

Korten, D.C. (1995) *When Corporations Rule the World* (West Hartford, CT: Kumarian Press; San Francisco: Berrett–Koehler).

Kotchian, A.C. (1977) 'The Payoff: Lockheed's 70-Day Mission to Tokyo', *Saturday Review*, 9 July 1977: 7-12.

Kotter, J. (1998) 'What Leaders Really Do', *Harvard Business Review*, May/June 1990; repr. in *Harvard Business Review on Leadership* (Boston, MA: Harvard Business School Publishing): 37-60.

Krasner, S.D. (1999) *Sovereignty: Organized Hypocrisy* (Princeton, NJ: Princeton University Press).

Kymlicka, W., and W. Norman (1995) 'Return of the Citizen: A Survey of Recent Work on Citizenship Theory', in R. Beiner (ed.), *Theorizing Citizenship* (Albany, NY: State University of New York): 283-322.

Labaton, S. (1999) 'US set to clear a merger between Exxon and Mobil', *New York Times*, 27 November 1999.

Lampedusa, G.T. (1991) *The Leopard* (New York: Pantheon Books).

Le Journal Les Affaires (1999) *Les 500 Plus Grandes Entreprises au Québec* (Montreal: Groupe Transcontinental).

Lefebvre, M., and J.B. Singh (1992) 'The Content and Focus of Canadian Corporate Codes of Ethics', *Journal of Business Ethics* 11.10 (October 1992): 799-808.

Letts, J.S. (1982) 'Is There Really a Model Board?', in G.C. Greanias and D. Windsor (eds.), *The Changing Boardroom: Making Policy and Profits in an Age of Corporate Citizenship* (Houston, TX: Gulf Publishing): 116-27.

Levitt, T. (1983) 'The Globalisation of Markets', *Harvard Business Review*, May/June 1983: 92-102.

Lewis, C.S. (1955) *The Abolition of Man* (New York: Macmillan, first published 1947).

Lewis, N.A. (1999) 'Rules regulating oil industry are mired in debate on ethics', *New York Times*, 27 June 1999.

Lindahl, G. (2000) 'New Role for Global Business: Multinational firms must make protecting human rights a priority', *Time, Europe* 155.4 (31 January 2000): 31-32.

Lindblom, C.E. (1977) *Politics and Markets* (New York: Basic Books).

Locke, J. (1966) *Quelques pensées sur l'éducation* (Paris: Vrin).

Logan, D., D. Roy and L. Regelbrugge (1997) *Global Corporate Citizenship* (Tokyo: The Hitachi Foundation).

Lydenberg, S.D., A.L. Marlin, S.O. Strub and the Council on Economic Priorities (1986) *Rating America's Corporate Conscience: A Provocative Guide to the Companies behind the Products You Buy Every Day* (Reading, MA: Addison–Wesley).

Macdonald, R. (1995) *Valeurs de l'entreprise québécoise* (Montreal: Guérin universitaire).

Machiavelli, N. (1513) *The Prince* (Oxford, UK: Oxford University Press, repr. 1984).

Machiavelli, N. (1980) *The Prince* (trans. L.P.S. de Alvarez; Prospect Heights, IL: Waveland Press, first published 1513).

Mackensen, L. (1985) *Ursprung der Wörter: Etymologisches Wörterbuch der Deutschen Sprache* (Munich: Südwest Verlag).

MacKenzie, S.B., P.M. Podsakoff and R. Fetter (1991) 'Organisational Citizenship Behaviour and Objective Productivity as Determinants of Managerial Evaluations of Salespersons' Performance', *Organisational Behaviour and Human Decision Processes* 50.1: 123-50.

Marsden, C., and J. Andriof (1997) 'Understanding Corporate Citizenship' (unpublished paper; Coventry, UK: University of Warwick).

Marsden, C., and J. Andriof (1998) 'Towards an Understanding of Corporate Citizenship and How to Influence it', *Citizenship Studies* 2.2: 329-52.

Marshall, T.H. (1965) 'Citizenship and Social Class', *Class, Citizenship, and Social Development* (Garden City, NY: Anchor Books).

Mason, G. (1999) 'Wyllie's a Winner', *Australian Sunday Times*, 14 November 1999: 65.

Maturana, H.R., and F.J. Varela (1998) *The Tree of Knowledge: The Biological Roots of Human Understanding* (Boston, MA: Shambala Press).

McCoy, C.S. (1985) *Management of Values: The Ethical Difference in Corporate Policy and Performance* (New York: Harper & Row).

McIntosh, M., D. Leipziger, K. Jones and G. Coleman (1998) *Corporate Citizenship: Successful Strategies for Responsible Companies* (London: Financial Times/Pitman Publishing).

Meralin, Y., and J. McGee (1998) 'Information Competences and Knowledge Creation at the Corporate Centre', in G. Hamel, C.K. Prahalad, H. Thomas and D. O'Neal (eds.), *Strategic Flexibility: Managing in a Turbulent Environment* (New York: John Wiley): 196-217.

Miles, R.H. (1986) *Managing the Corporate Social Environment: A Grounded Theory* (Englewood Cliffs, NJ: Prentice–Hall).

Mill, J.S. (1956) On Liberty (Indianapolis, IN: Bobbs–Merrill/The Liberal Arts Press).

Miller, A.S. (1968) *The Supreme Court and American Capitalism* (New York: Free Press).

Mitchell, N.J. (1989) *The Generous Corporation: A Political Analysis of Economic Power* (New Haven, CT: Yale University Press).

Mitchell, N.J. (1997) *The Conspicuous Corporation: Business, Public Policy, and Representative Democracy* (Ann Arbor, MI: University of Michigan Press).

Mitchell, R., B. Agle and D. Wood (1997) 'Toward a Theory of Stakeholder Identification and Salience: Defining the Principle of Who and What Really Counts', *Academy of Management Review* 22.4: 853-86.

Moldoveanu, M., L.S. Paine and R.J. Crawford (1999a) *Royal Dutch/Shell Nigeria A* (publication N9-399-126; Cambridge, MA: Harvard Business School).

Moldoveanu, M., L.S. Paine and R.J. Crawford (1999b) *Royal Dutch/Shell Nigeria B* (publication N9-399-127; Cambridge, MA: Harvard Business School).

Monks, R., and N. Minow (1995) *Corporate Governance* (Cambridge, MA: Basil Blackwell).

Moon, J. (1995) 'The Firm as Citizen? Social Responsibility of Business in Australia', *Australian Journal of Political Science* 30.1: 1-17.

Moorman, R.H. (1991) 'The Relationship between Organisational Justice and Organisational Citizenship Behaviours: Do fairness perceptions influence employee citizenship?', *Journal of Applied Psychology* 76.4: 845-55.

Moorman, R.H., and G.L. Blakely (1995) 'Individualism–Collectivism as an Individual Difference Predictor of Organisational Citizenship Behaviour', *Journal of Organisational Behaviour* 16.1: 127-42.

Moorman, R.H., G.L. Blakely and B.P. Niehoff (1998) 'Does Perceived Organisational Support Mediate the Relationship between Procedural Justice and Organisational Citizenship Behaviour?', *Academy of Management Journal* 41.3: 351-57.

Moss Kanter, R. (1999) 'From Spare Change to Real Change: The Social Sector as Beta Site for Business Innovation', *Harvard Business Review*, March/April 1999: 122-32.

Mundt, J., and F. Houston (1996) 'Externalities and the Calculation of Exchange Outcomes', *Journal of Macromarketing* 16.1: 73-82.

Myerson, A.R. (1998) 'For oil workers, merger is just another word for more layoffs', *New York Times*, 30 November 1998.

Myerson, A.R., and A. Salpukas (1998a) 'Mobil and Exxon discussions reflect a global competition', *New York Times*, 27 November 1998.

Myerson, A.R., and A. Salpukas (1998b) 'Exxon and Mobil announce $80 billion deal to create world's largest company', *New York Times*, 2 December 1998.

Nader, R., and M.J. Green (eds.) (1973) *Corporate Power in America* (New York: Grossman Publishers, 2nd edn 1977).

Nagel, I.H., and W.M. Swenson (1993) 'The Federal Sentencing Guidelines for Corporations: Their Development, Theoretical Underpinnings and Some Thoughts about their Future', *Washington University Law Quarterly* 71: 205-58.

Näsi, J. (1995) *Understanding Stakeholder Thinking* (Helsinki: LSR Publications).

NEF (New Economics Foundation) (1996) *Value-Based Organisation: Organising NGOs for Value-Based Effectiveness* (London: NEF).

Nelson, J., and S. Zadek (2000) *Partnership Alchemy: New Social Partnerships in Europe* (Copenhagen: Copenhagen Business School).

NGOTOBI (Non-Governmental Organisation Taskforce on Business and Industry) (2000) *United Nations Commission on Sustainable Development Caucus Meeting* (New York: United Nations, 3 May 2000).

Nielsen, R.P. (1984) 'Arendt's Action Philosophy and the Manager as Eichmann, Richard III, Faust, or Institution Citizen', *California Management Review* 26.3: 191-201.

Nunan, R. (1988) 'The Libertarian Conception of Corporate Property: A Critique of Milton Friedman's Views on the Social Responsibility of Business', *Journal of Business Ethics* 7.12 (December 1988): 891-906.

O'Reilly, C.A., and J. Chatman (1986) 'Organisational Commitment and Psychological Attachment: The Effects of Compliance, Identification, and Internalisation on Prosocial Behaviour', *Journal of Applied Psychology* 71.3: 492-99.

Oberman, W.D. (2000) Book Review of Mitchell, *The Conspicuous Corporation* (1997), *Business and Society* 39.2 (June 2000): 239-44.

OECD (Organisation for Economic Co-operation and Development) (1976) *Declaration and Decisions on International Investment and Multinational Enterprises* (Paris: OECD).

OECD (Organisation for Economic Co-operation and Development) (1997a) *The OECD Guidelines for Multinational Enterprises* (contains OECD 1976 document, revisions and commentaries; Paris: OECD).

OECD (Organisation for Economic Co-operation and Development) (1997b) *Convention on Combating Bribery of Foreign Public Officials in International Business Transactions* (Paris: OECD).

Oehl, T.P. (1993) 'Thoughts about the Changeability of Corporate Cultures', in D. Koechlin and K. Muller (eds.), *Green Business Opportunities: The Profit Principle* (London: Financial Times/Pitman Publishing): 207-25.

Ohmae, K. (1991) *The Borderless World: Power and Strategy in the Interlinked Economy* (London: Harper Business, rev. edn 1999).

Ohmae, K. (1995) *The End of the Nation-State* (New York: Free Press).

Oliver, C. (1991) 'Strategic Responses to Institutional Processes', *Academy of Management Review* 16.1: 145-79.

Organ, D.W. (1977) 'A Reappraisal and Reinterpretation of the Satisfaction-Causes-Performance Hypothesis', *Academy of Management Review* 2.1: 46-53.

Organ, D.W. (1988) *Organisational Citizenship Behaviour: The Good Soldier Syndrome* (Lexington, MA: Lexington Books).

Organ, D.W., and M.A. Konovsky (1989) 'Cognitive versus Affective Determinants of Organisational Citizenship Behaviour', *Journal of Applied Psychology* 74.1: 157-64.

Organ, D.W., and K. Ryan (1995) 'A Meta-analytic Review of Attitudinal and Disposition Predictors of Organizational Citizenship Behaviour', *Personnel Psychology* 48.4: 775-800.

Orts, E.W. (1992) 'Beyond Shareholders: Interpreting Corporate Constituency Statutes', *George Washington Law Review* 61.4 (November 1992): 1-135.

Owen, D.L., T.A. Swift, C. Humphrey and M. Bowerman (2000) 'The New Social Audits: Accountability, Managerial Capture or the Agenda of Social Champions?', *European Accounting Review* 9.1: 81-98.

Paine, L.S. (1994) 'Managing for Organizational Integrity', *Harvard Business Review*, March/April 1994: 106-17.

Painter, J. (1998) 'Business altruism develops a mean streak', *The Age*, 2 June 1998: 1.

Parry, G. (1991) 'Paths to Citizenship', in U. Vogel and M. Moran (eds.), *The Frontiers of Citizenship* (New York: St Martin's Press): 166-201.

Paul, K., and S.D. Lydenberg (1992) 'Applications of Corporate Social Monitoring Systems', *Journal of Business Ethics* 11: 1-10.

Perkins, F. (1994) *Practical Cost Benefit Analysis* (Melbourne: Macmillan).

Pettigrew, A.M. (1985) 'Contextualist Research: A Natural Way to Link Theory and Practice', in E.E. Lawler III, A.M. Mohrman Jr, S.A. Mohrman, G.E. Ledford Jr and T.G. Cummings (eds.), *Doing Research that is Useful for Theory and Practice* (San Francisco: Jossey-Bass): 222-73.

Pfeffer, J., and G.R. Salancik (1978) *The External Control of Organisations* (New York: Harper & Row).

Piaget, J. (1969) *The Psychology of the Child* (New York: Wiley).

Piore, M.J. (1995) *Beyond Individualism* (Cambridge, MA: Harvard University Press).

Piper, T.R. (1993) 'Rediscovery of Purpose: The Genesis of Leadership, Ethics, and Corporate Responsibility Initiative', in T.R. Piper, M.C. Gentile and S.D. Parks (eds.), *Can Ethics Be Taught?* (Boston, MA: Harvard Business School): 1-12.

Plender, J. (1998) 'Giving People a Stake in the Future', *Long Range Planning* 31.2: 211-17.

Pocock, J.G.A. (1995) 'The Ideal of Citizenship since Classical Times', in R. Beiner (ed.), *Theorizing Citizenship* (Albany, NY: State University of New York): 29-52.

Podsakoff, P.M., and S.B. MacKenzie (1997) 'Impact of Organisational Citizenship Behaviour on Organisational Performance: A Review and Suggestions for Future Research', *Human Performance* 10.1: 133-51.

Podsakoff, P.M., S.B. MacKenzie, R.H. Moorman and R. Fetter (1990) 'Transformational Leadership Behaviours and their Effects on Followers' Trust in Leader, Satisfaction, and Organisational Citizenship Behaviours', *Leadership Quarterly* 1.2: 107-42.

Podsakoff, P.M., M. Ahearne and S.B. MacKenzie (1997) 'Organisational Citizenship Behaviour and the Quantity and Quality of Work Group Performance', *Journal of Applied Psychology* 82.2: 262-70.

Pojman, L.P. (ed.) (2000a) *The Moral Life: An Introductory Reader in Ethics and Literature* (Oxford, UK: Oxford University Press).

Pojman, L.P. (2000b) 'On the Nature and Purpose of Morality', in L.P. Pojman (ed.), *The Moral Life: An Introductory Reader in Ethics and Literature* (Oxford, UK: Oxford University Press): 1-4.

Polonsky, M.J. (1995) 'Incorporating the Natural Environment in Corporate Strategy: A Stakeholder Approach', *Journal of Business Strategy* 12.2: 151-68.

Post, J.E. (2000a) *Meeting the Challenge of Global Corporate Citizenship* (policy paper series; Chestnut Hill, MA: Centre for Corporate Community Relations, Boston College).

Post, J.E. (2000b) 'Moving from Geographic to Virtual Communities: Global Corporate Citizenship in a dot.com World', *Business and Society Review* 105.1: 27-46.

Post, J.E., and J.J. Griffin (1997) *The State of Corporate Public Affairs: Final Report* (Washington, DC: Foundation for Public Affairs).

Post, J.E., L. Preston and S. Sachs (2002a) *Redefining the Corporation: Stakeholder Management and Organizational Wealth* (Palo Alto, CA: Stanford University Press).

Post, J.E., A.T. Lawrence and J. Weber (2002b) *Business and Society: Corporate Strategy, Public Policy, Ethics* (New York: McGraw-Hill, 10th edn).

Powers, C.W., and D. Vogel (1980) *Ethics in the Education of Business Managers* (Hastings-on-Hudson, NY: The Hastings Centre).

Pratt, M.G., and P. Foreman (2000) 'Classifying Managerial Responses to Multiple Organisational Identities', *Academy of Management Review* 25.1: 18-42.

Preston, L.E., and D. Mihalko (1999) 'Corporate Responsibility: Comparative Analysis of Current Documents', in The Clarkson Centre for Business Ethics, *Principles of Stakeholder Management* (Toronto: Joseph L. Rotman School of Management, University of Toronto): 21-59.

Preston, L.E., and J.E. Post (1975) *Private Management and Public Policy: The Principle of Public Responsibility* (Englewood Cliffs, NJ: Prentice–Hall).

Pretorius v. Venture Stores (1991) Federal Court of Australia, Nos G102, 103 and 105, Fed. no 58.

Pruitt, S.W., K.C. Wei and R.E. White (1988) 'The Impact of Union-Sponsored Boycotts on the Stock Prices of Target Firms', *Journal of Labor Research* 9: 285-89.

Putnam, R.D. (1993) *Making Democracy Work: Civic Traditions in Modern Italy* (Princeton, NJ: Princeton University Press).

Putnam, R.W. (1996) 'Creating Reflexive Dialogue', in S. Toulmin and B. Gustavsen (eds.), *Beyond Theory: Changing Organisations through Participation* (Philadelphia, PA: John Benjamins North America).

PWBLF (Prince of Wales Business Leaders Forum) (2000) *The Response to HIV/AIDS: Impact and Lessons Learnt* (London: PWBLF).

Quinn, D.P., and R.V. Shapiro (1991) 'Business Political Power: The Case of Taxation', *American Political Science Review* 85.3 (September 1991): 851-74.

Raelin, J.A. (2000) *Work-Based Learning: The New Frontier of Management Development* (Upper Saddle, NJ: Prentice– Hall).

Ranganathan, J. (1999) 'Signs of Sustainability: Measuring Corporate Environmental and Social Performance', in M. Bennett and P. James with L. Klinkers (eds.), *Sustainable Measures: Evaluation and Reporting of Environmental and Social Performance* (Sheffield, UK: Greenleaf Publishing): 475-95.

Rawls, J. (1971) *A Theory of Justice* (Cambridge, MA: Belknap Press).

Rawls, J. (1993) *Political Liberalism* (New York: Columbia University Press).

Rawls, J. (1999) *The Law of Peoples* (Cambridge, MA: Harvard University Press).

Reder, A (1995) *Seventy Five Best Business Practices for Socially Responsible Companies* (New York: G.P. Putnam).

Regelbrugge, L. (ed.) (1999) *Promoting Corporate Citizenship: Opportunities for Business and Civil Society Engagement* (Washington, DC: CIVICUS).

Reich, R. (1998) 'The New Meaning of Corporate Social Responsibility', *California Management Review* 40.2: 8-17.

Reich, R.B. (1996) 'Pink Slips, Profits, and Paychecks: Corporate Citizenship in an Era of Smaller Government' (address at George Washington University School of Business and Public Management, 6 February 1996).

Robinson, S.L., and E.W. Morrison (1995) 'Psychological Contracts and OCB: The Effect of Unfulfilled Obligations on Civic Virtue Behaviour', *Journal of Organisational Behaviour* 16.2: 289-98.

Rowley, T.J. (1997) 'Moving Beyond Dyadic Ties: A Network Theory of Stakeholder Influences', *Academy of Management Review* 22.4: 887-910.

Sahlman, W.A. (1999) 'The new economy is stronger than you think', *Harvard Business Review* 77.6 (November/December 1999): 99-106.

Salpukas, A. (1994) 'Lucio Noto: From Brooklyn, Around the World, to Mobil's Top Job', *New York Times*, 6 February 1994.

Salpukas, A. (1998) 'Exxon–Mobil union raises questions on varying styles', *New York Times*, 2 December 1998.

Schein, E.H. (1992) 'Organisational Culture and Leadership' (San Francisco: Jossey–Bass).

Scholes, E., and D. Clutterbuck (1998) 'Communication with Stakeholders: An Integrated Approach', *Long Range Planning* 31.2: 227-38.

Scholte, J.A. (1993) *International Relations of Social Change* (Buckingham, UK: Open University Press).

Schön, D.A. (1983) *The Reflective Practitioner: How Professionals Think in Action* (New York: Basic Books).

Schopenhauer, A. (1966) *Le monde comme volonté et comme représentation* (Paris: PUF).

Schopenhauer, A. (1978) *Le fondement de la moralité* (Paris: Aubier & Montaigne).

Schwartz, P., and B. Gibb (1999) *When good companies do bad things: Responsibility and Risk in an Age of Globalisation* (New York: John Wiley).

Schwarzkopf, H.N. (1998) 'Ethical Leadership in the 21st Century', *Imprimis*, March 1998: 5.

Senge, P.M. (1990) *The Fifth Discipline: The Art and Practice of the Learning Organisation* (New York/London: Currency Doubleday).

Sérieyx, H. (1993) *Le Big Bang des organisations* (Paris: Calmann-Lévy).

Sethi, S.P. (1975) 'Dimensions of Corporate Social Responsibility', *Californian Management Review* 17.3: 58-64.

Sethi, S.P. (1994) *Multinational Corporations and the Impact of Public Advocacy on Corporate Strategy: Nestlé and the Infant Formula Controversy* (Norwell, MA: Kluwer).

Sheikh, S. (1996) *Corporate Social Responsibilities: Law and Practice* (London: Cavendish Publishing).

Shipp, S. (1987) 'Modified Vendettas as a Method of Punishing Corporations', *Journal of Business Ethics* 6: 603-12.

Sillanpää, M. (1998) 'The Body Shop Values Report: Towards Integrated Stakeholder Auditing', *Journal of Business Ethics* 17.13: 1443-56.

Simon, H. (1947) *Administrative Behaviour* (New York: Macmillan).

Sims, H., Jr, and D.A. Gioia (1986) *The Thinking Organization: Dynamics of Organizational Social Cognition* (San Francisco: Jossey–Bass).

Skarlicki, D.P., and G.P. Latham (1996) 'Increasing Citizenship Behaviour within a Labour Union: A Test of Organisational Justice Theory', *Journal of Applied Psychology* 81.1: 161-69.

Smith, A. (1937) *An Inquiry into the Nature of the Wealth of Nations* (New York: The Modern Library).

Smith, A. (1976) *The Wealth of Nations* (ed. R.H. Campbell and A.S. Skinner; Oxford, UK: Clarendon Press).

Smith, C.A., D.W. Organ and J.P. Near (1983) 'Organisational Citizenship Behaviour: Its Nature and Antecedents', *Journal of Applied Psychology* 68.4: 653-63.

Smith, N.C., and E. Cooper-Martin (1997) 'Ethics and Target Marketing: The Role of Product Harm and Consumer Vulnerability', *Journal of Marketing* 61: 1-20.

Solomon, R.C. (1984) *Morality and the Good Life* (New York: McGraw–Hill).

Svendsen, A. (1998) *The Stakeholder Strategy: Profiting from Collaborative Business Relationships* (New York: Barrett–Koehler).

Swanson, D.L. (1995) 'Addressing a Theoretical Problem by Reorienting the Corporate Social Performance Model', *Academy of Management Review* 20.1: 43-64.

Swanson, D.L. (1999) 'Toward an Integrative Theory of Business and Society: A Research Strategy for Corporate Social Performance', *Academy of Management Review* 24.3: 596-21.

Sweeney, J. (1995) 'The Moral Expertise of Auditors: An Exploratory Analysis', *Research on Accounting Ethics* 1: 213-34.

Taylor, L. (1999) 'Business on the give and take', *Australian Financial Review*, 7 December 1999: 18-19.

TCB (The Conference Board) (1999) *The Expanding Parameters of Global Corporate Citizenship* (report 1246; New York: TCB).

Teal, T. (1998) 'The Human Side of Management', *Harvard Business Review*, November/December 1996; repr. in *Harvard Business Review on Leadership* (Boston, MA: Harvard Business School Publishing): 149-69.

Thurow, L. (1966) *The Future of Capitalism: How Today's Economic Forces Shape Tomorrow's World* (St Leonard's, NSW, Australia: Allen & Unwin).

Tichy, N.M., A.R. McGill and L. St Clair (eds.) (1997) *Corporate Global Citizenship: Doing Business in the Public Eye* (San Francisco: New Lexington Press).

Tillich, P. (1952) *The Courage to Be* (New Haven, CT: Yale University Press).

Torbert, W.R. (1991) *The Power of Balance: Transforming Self, Society, and Scientific Inquiry* (Newbury Park, CA: Sage).

Transparency International (1999) *1999 Corruption Perceptions Index* (Berlin: Transparency International).

Tully, S. (1993) 'The Real Key to Creating Wealth', *Fortune*, 20 September 1993: 38-40, 44-45, 48, 50.

Turner, D., and M. Crawford, (1998) *Change Power: Capabilities that Drive Corporate Renewal* (Sydney: Woods Lane).

UNDESA (United Nations Department of Economic and Social Affairs) (1999) *Business and the United Nations: Partners in Sustainable Development, Industry and Technology* (New York: United Nations).

UNDP (United Nations Development Programme) (2000) 'UNDP Today', www.undp.org/toppages/discover/pdf/intrundp.pdf, 23 May 2000.

UNDPI (United Nations Department of Public Information) (1995) *A Guide to Information at the United Nations* (New York: United Nations).

UNDPI (United Nations Department of Public Information) (1998) *Image and Reality: Questions and Answers about the United Nations* (New York: United Nations).

UNEP (United Nations Environment Programme) (1995) *Insurance Industry Initiative for the Environment* (Geneva: UNEP).

UNEP (United Nations Environment Programme) (2000) 'UNEP Financial Institutions Initiative on the Environment', www.unep.ch/etu/finserv/fimenu.htm, 23 May 2000.

United Nations (2000a) 'The United Nations and Civil Society', www.un.org/partners/civil_society/home.htm, 15 May 2000.

United Nations (2000b) 'Global Compact, Executive Summary and Conclusion: High-Level Meeting on the Global Compact Held on July 26 2000, United Nations Headquarters', www.unglobalcompact.org, 27 July 2000.

UNJIU (United Nations Joint Inspection Unit) (2000) *Report on Private Sector Involvement and Co-operation with the United Nations System* (Geneva: UNJIU).

UNOPS (United Nations Office for Project Services) (2000a) *The UN and Business: A Partnership for the New Millennium* (conference announcement, 31 May 2000; New York: United Nations).

UNOPS (United Nations Office for Project Services) (2000b) 'The UN and Business: A Partnership for the New Millennium', www.unops.org.my/partnerships/toolbar/unops/unops.htm, 14 May 2000.

UNSG/PWBLF (United Nations Staff College/Prince of Wales Business Leaders Forum) (2000) *The UN and Business: Building Partnerships that Last* (conference workshop, 31 May 2000; New York: United Nations).

USDC (US Department of Commerce) (1989) *Statistical Abstract of the United States* (Washington, DC: USDC, Bureau of the Census).

USDC (US Department of Commerce) (1999) *Statistical Abstract of the United States* (Washington, DC: USDC, Bureau of the Census).

Useem, M. (1996) 'Stakeholders as a Strategic Asset', *California Management Review* 39.1: 827.

Van Dyne, L., J. Graham and R.M. Dienesch (1994) 'Organisational Citizenship Behaviour: Construct Redefinition, Measurement, and Validation', *Academy of Management Journal* 37.1: 765-802.

Van Dyne, L., L.L. Cummings and J. McLean Parks (1995) 'Extra Role Behaviours: In Pursuit of Construct and Definitional Clarity (a Bridge over Muddied Waters)', in L.L. Cummings and B.M. Staw (eds.), *Research in Organizational Behaviour* (Greenwich, CT: JAI Press) 17: 215-85.

VanCity (Vancouver City Savings Credit Union) (1997) *Mission Statement* (Vancouver: VanCity).

VanCity (Vancouver City Savings Credit Union) (1997) *VanCity's Social Report 1997* (Vancouver: VanCity).

Venkatraman, N. (1998) 'Competing in the Knowledge Economy: Real Strategies for Virtual Organizing', in *Proceedings of Learning Forum on Competing in the Knowledge Economy* (Boston, MA: Systems Research Centre, Boston University): 15-24.

Vernon, R. (1998) *In the Hurricane's Eye: The Troubled Prospects of Multinational Enterprises* (Cambridge, MA/London: Harvard University Press).

Vidal, D.J. (1999) *The Link between Corporate Citizenship and Financial Performance* (report 1234; New York: The Conference Board).

Vogel, D. (1978) *Lobbying the Corporation: Citizen Challenges to Business Authority* (New York: Basic Books).

Von Weizsäcker, E., A. Lovins and L.H. Lovins (1997) *Factor Four: Doubling Wealth, Halving Resource Use. The New Report to the Club of Rome* (London: Earthscan Publications).

Waddock, S. (1999) *Global Corporate Citizenship: Implications of a Pluralistic World for Changing Management Education* (Chicago, IL: Academy of Management).

Waddock, S. (2001) *Leading Corporate Citizens: Meeting the Business and Society Challenge* (Homewood, IL: Irwin; Burr Ridge, IL: McGraw–Hill Irwin).

Waddock, S.A., and S.B. Graves (1997a) 'The Corporate Social Performance–Financial Performance Link', *Strategic Management Journal* 18.4: 303-19.

Waddock, S.A., and S.B. Graves (1997b) 'Quality of Management and Quality of Stakeholder Relations: Are they synonymous?', *Business and Society* 36.3 (September 1997): 250-79.

Wallis, S. (1999) 'Chairman's Address to Shareholders', Coles Myer Annual General Meeting, Australian Stock Exchange Announcements, 18 November 1999.

Walz, S.M., and B.P. Niehoff (2000) 'Organisational Citizenship Behaviours and their Effect on Organisational Effectiveness', *Journal of Hospitality and Tourism Research* 24.3: 301-19.

Wartick, S.L., and P.L. Cochran (1985) 'The Evolution of the Corporate Social Performance Model', *Academy of Management Review* 10.4: 758-69.

Wartick, S.L., and D. J. Wood (1998) *International Business and Society* (Malden, MA/ Oxford, UK: Basil Blackwell Publishers).

Waters, M. (1995) *Globalisation* (London: Routledge).

Wayne, S.J., L.M. Shore and R.C. Liden (1997) 'Perceived Organisational Support and Leader–Member Exchange: A Social Exchange Perspective', *Academy of Management Journal* 40.1: 82-111.

Weber, M. (1958) *The Protestant Ethic and the Spirit of Capitalism* (trans. T. Parsons; New York: Scribner).

Weick, K.E. (1999) 'Educating for the Unknowable: The Infamous Real World' (talk presented at the Academy of Management Annual Meeting, Chicago, IL, 1999).

Welch, S.D. (1990) *A Feminist Ethic of Risk* (Minneapolis, MN: Fortress Press).

Welford, R. (1995) *Environmental Strategy and Sustainable Development: The Corporate Challenge for the Twenty-first Century* (London: Routledge).

Wenger, E. (1998) *Communities of Practice, Learning, Meaning, and Identity* (New York: Cambridge University Press).

Werhane, P.H. (1985) *Persons, Rights, and Corporations* (Englewood Cliffs, NJ: Prentice–Hall).

Wheeler, D., and M. Sillanpää (1997) *The Stakeholder Corporation: A Blueprint for Maximising Stakeholder Value* (London: Pitman).

WHO (World Health Organisation) (1999) WHO Press Release E-mail Listserv, padeyg@who.ch, 8 October 1999.

Wilber, K. (1995) *Sex, Ecology, Spirituality: The Spirit of Evolution* (Boston, MA: Shambala Press).

Wilber, K. (1996) *A Brief History of Everything* (Boston, MA: Shambala Press).1

Wilson, J.Q. (1989) 'Adam Smith on Business Ethics', *California Management Review* 32.1 (Autumn 1989): 59-71.

Wilson, J.Q. (1993) *The Moral Sense* (New York: Free Press).

Wolfensohn, J. (1998) 'A Battle for Corporate Honesty', *The Economist*, 19 November 1998: 38.

Wood, D.J. (1991) 'Corporate Social Performance Revisited', *Academy of Management Review* 16.4 (October 1991): 691-718.

Wood, D.J. (1994) *Business and Society* (New York: HarperCollins).

Wood, D.J. (1996) 'Organisational Citizenship', in N. Nicholson (ed.), *The International Encyclopedia of Organisational Behaviour* (Oxford, UK: Basil Blackwell).

Wood, D.J., and J.M. Logsdon (1999) *Toward a Theory of Business Citizenship: Ruffin Lectures on Business Ethics* (Charlottesville, VA: University of Virginia).

Wood, D.J., and J.M. Logsdon (2001) 'Global Business Citizenship: From Individuals to Organisations', *Business Ethics Quarterly*, forthcoming.

Wood, D.J., K. Davenport, L. Blockson and H.J. Van Buren III (1997) *Field Mapping: Business School Approaches to Corporate Involvement in Community Economic Development* (a report to the Ford Foundation, Asset Development Unit, New York).

Wood, D.J., K. Davenport, L. Blockson and H.J. Van Buren III (1998) 'With Liberty and Justice for All: The Business School's Role in Community Economic Development', in J. Weber and D. Windsor (eds.), *Proceedings of the International Association for Business and Society*, Destin, FL.

Wood, L. (1999) 'Bountiful BHP cuts its social dividend', *The Age*, 5 May 1999:1.

Workcover Authority v. BHP (*WorkCover Authority of New South Wales [Inspector Chad-wick] v. BHP Steel [AIS] Pty Limited*) (2000) NSWIRComm 75, 18 May, New South Wales Industrial Relations Tribunal.

WRDEL (*Webster's Reference Dictionary of the English Language*) (1982) 'Citizenship', in *Webster's Reference Dictionary of the English Language* (Springfield, MA: Merriam-Webster): 183.

WRI (World Resources Institute) (1999) *Beyond Grey Pinstripes: Preparing MBAs for Social and Environmental Stewardship* (Washington, DC: WRI).

Wriston, W. (1997) *The Twilight of Sovereignty* (New York: Charles Scribner's Sons).

Yancey, K.B. (2000) 'Omni turning off porn at some hotels', *USA Today*, 4 February 2000: 4D.

YLJ (*Yale Law Journal*) (1982) 'Constitutional Rights of the Corporate Person', *Yale Law Journal* 91.8 (July 1982): 1641-58.

Zadek, S. (1998) 'Balancing Performance, Ethics, and Accountability', *Journal of Business Ethics* 17.13: 1421-41.

Zadek, S. (2000) *Doing Well by Doing Good: The Business Case for Corporate Citizenship* (New York: The Conference Board).

Zadek, S. (2001) *The Civil Corporation* (London: Earthscan Publications).

Zadek, S., and P. Raynard (1995) 'Accounting Works: A Comparative Review of Contemporary Approaches to Social and Ethical Accounting', *Accounting Forum* 19.2–3: 164-75.

Zadek, S., R. Hojengaard and P. Raynard (eds.) (2001) *Perspectives on the New Ecology of Corporate Citizenship* (Copenhagen: The Copenhagen Centre).

Zaleznik, A. (1998) 'Managers and Leaders: Are they different?', *Harvard Business Review*, May/June 1977; repr. in *Harvard Business Review on Leadership* (Boston, MA: Harvard Business School Publishing): 61-88.

Zhang, J., I Fraser and W.Y. Hill (2000) 'A Comparative Study of Social Audit Models and Reports', paper presented at the *11th International Conference of Accounting Academics*, Hong Kong, June 2000.

ABBREVIATIONS

AA 1000	AccountAbility Standard 1000
ABB	Asea Brown Boveri
ACCA	Association of Chartered Certified Accountants
AGM	annual general meeting
AIDS	acquired immuno-deficiency syndrome
ALI	American Law Institute
AOL	America Online
APSO	Agency for Personal Service Overseas (Ireland)
ASEAN	Association of South-East Asian Nations
ATK	A.T. Kearney
BBB	Better Business Bureau
BCA	Business Council of Australia
BHP	Broken Hill Proprietary Company Ltd
BiTC	Business in the Community
BP	British Petroleum
BPA	BP Australia
BPD	Business Partners in Development
BPX	BP's exploration subsidiary
BSR	Business for Social Responsibility
BT	British Telecom
CCBE	Clarkson Centre for Business Ethics (Canada)
CCP	Canadian Centre for Philanthropy
CCPA	Centre for Corporate Public Affairs (Australia)
CDG	community discussion group
CEFIC	European Chemical Industry Council
CEO	chief executive officer
CEP	Council on Economic Priorities
CEPAA	Council on Economic Priorities Accreditation Agency
CERES	Coalition for Environmentally Responsible Economies
CO_2	carbon dioxide
CoF	Council on Foundations
CSER	corporate social and environmental reporting
CSR	corporate social responsibility
CTC	Centre for Tomorrow's Company
EBNSC	European Business Network for Social Cohesion
ECOSOC	Economic and Social Council
EEOC	Equal Employment Opportunity Commission
EMAS	Eco-management and Audit Scheme

EPA	Environmental Protection Agency
EU	European Union
EVA	economic value added
FAQ	frequently asked question
FDI	foreign direct investment
FDIC	Federal Deposit Insurance Corporation (USA)
FEE	Fédération des Experts Comptables Européens
FPA	Foundation for Public Affairs (USA)
GATT	General Agreement on Tariffs and Trade
GBPC	Global Business Policy Council
GRI	Global Reporting Initiative
GSDF	Global Sustainable Development Facility (UNDP)
HIV	human immunodeficiency virus
IAG	Inter-Agency Group
ICC	International Chamber of Commerce
ILO	International Labour Organisation
IMF	International Monetary Fund
IPO	initial public offering
ISEA	Institute for Social and Ethical AccountAbility
ISO	International Organization for Standardization
ISP	Internet service provider
IT	information technology
ITP	Innovation through Partnership (UK)
MNC	multinational corporation
MORI	Market Opinion Research International
MP	member of parliament
MVC	Making Values Count
NAACP	National Association for the Advancement of Colored People
NAFTA	North American Free Trade Agreement
NASA	National Aeronautics and Space Administration (USA)
NEF	New Economics Foundation (UK)
NGO	non-governmental organisation
NGOTOBI	Non-Governmental Organisation Taskforce on Business and Industry (USA)
NIEO	new international economic order
NIOSH	National Institute of Occupational Safety and Health (USA)
NMSDC	National Minority Supplier Development Council (USA)
NSW	New South Wales
OECD	Organisation for Economic Co-operation and Development
OED	*Oxford English Dictionary*
OSHA	Occupational Safety and Health Administration (USA)
PCP	polyvocal citizenship perspective
PM	prime minister
PQMD	Partnership for Quality Medical Donations
PWBLF	Prince of Wales Business Leaders Forum
R&D	research and development
SA 8000	social accountability standard 8000
SEAAR	social and ethical accounting, auditing and reporting
SME	small and medium-sized enterprise
TB	tuberculosis
TCB	The Conference Board (USA)
TNC	transnational corporation
UN	United Nations
UNCSD	UN Commission on Sustainable Development
UNDESA	UN Department of Economic and Social Affairs

UNDP	UN Development Programme
UNDPI	UN Department of Public Information
UNEP	UN Environment Programme
UNICEF	UN Children's Fund
UNIDO	UN Industrial Development Organisation
UNJIU	UN Joint Inspection Unit
UNOPS	UN Office for Project Services
USAID	US Agency for International Development
USDC	US Department of Commerce
WBCSD	World Business Council for Sustainable Development
WEF	World Economic Forum
WHO	World Health Organisation
WRDEL	*Webster's Reference Dictionary of the English Language*
WRI	World Resources Institute
WTO	World Trade Organisation
Y2K	Year 2000
YLJ	*Yale Law Journal*

AUTHOR BIOGRAPHIES

Jörg Andriof joined KPMG Corporate Finance Frankfurt in April 2000. During and after studying business and engineering in Berlin and Leicester, UK, he worked with Daimler-Benz, BMW Rolls-Royce, KPMG Corporate Finance and Corporate Recovery. Jörg received his PhD in industrial and business studies from Warwick Business School, UK, his thesis focusing on the development of a concept for strategic partnering. As a Research Fellow of the Centre for Creativity, Strategy and Change at Warwick Business School, he was one of the founding members of the Corporate Citizenship Unit. At KPMG Corporate Finance in Frankfurt, Jörg works as an advisor for Mergers and Acquisitions. In addition, he is Associated Fellow of Warwick Business School. Jörg's areas of expertise are corporate citizenship, stakeholder management, corporate development and value-based management. He is a member of the editorial board of *The Journal of Corporate Citizenship*.
J.Andriof@Warwick.ac.uk

Shawn L. Berman is Assistant Professor of Strategy and Policy at Boston University, USA. In September 2001 he will join the faculty of the Department of Organizational Analysis and Management at Santa Clara University. His research has appeared in *Academy of Management Journal, Business Ethics Quarterly, Academy of Management Review* and *Business and Society*. His research interests include empirical examinations of firm–stakeholder relationships, issues of inter-organisational trust, and corporate governance.
shberman@bu.edu

David Birch is Professor of Communication and Director of the Corporate Citizenship Research Unit, Deakin University, Australia. He has published widely in communication and cultural policy in Asia and is on the editorial boards of several international journals. He is currently working with a large number of companies and organisations in Australia on corporate citizenship, including BP, Rio Tinto, TXU, Worldvision, the City of Melbourne, Ford, BHP and Ernst & Young.
birchd@deakin.edu.au

Archie B. Carroll is Professor of Management and holder of the Robert W. Scherer Chair of Management and Corporate Public Affairs at the Terry College of Business, University of Georgia, Athens, GA, USA. He is Director of the Non-profit Management and Community Service Programme. He has been on the faculty of the University of Georgia since 1972. Dr Carroll earned his three academic degrees from Florida State University. He has published 13 books and 80 articles on the subjects of corporate social performance, business ethics and strategic management. His most recent book is *Business and Society: Ethics and Stakeholder Management*, co-authored with Ann. K. Buchholtz (South-Western College Publishing, 2000, 4th edn).
acarroll@terry.uga.edu

Jonathan Cohen is the Manager of the Council of Organisations, a group of over a hundred non-governmental organisations, for the United Nations Association of the USA. He is also founding Content Manager of the news link of the UN Global Compact website, and also manages e-mail lists on the UN as well as socially responsible business. He has served as a member of national NGO communities on the UN International Year of Volunteers in 2001, the Five-Year Review of the UN Beijing Women's Conference in 2000, the UN International Year of Older Persons in 1999, and the Universal Declaration of Human Rights 50th Anniversary in 1998. He is a former guest host on UN radio. Mr Cohen has an MA in The Relationship between Non-profit Organisations and Socially Responsible Business from New York University.

jcohen@unausa.org

Kim Davenport is the Manager of Leadership Development for BellSouth Corporation in Atlanta, GA, USA. Her responsibilities include design and delivery of high-potential leadership programmes, mentoring initiatives and BellSouth's human resource strategy. Kim's overall responsibility is to identify the most effective ways to develop leaders to support BellSouth's corporate strategies and objectives. Prior to working for BellSouth, Kim had a ten-year career at AT&T. She has published numerous articles and co-authored a book on total quality management. Her education includes a bachelor's degree in journalism from the University of Kentucky, a master's degree in organisational development from the American University, and a PhD in human and organisational systems from The Fielding Institute. She is currently enrolled in the Gestalt Institute of Cleveland's Organisation Systems and Development programme.

kim.davenport@bellsouth.com

Michel Dion is Full Professor of Applied Ethics at the Université de Sherbrooke, Canada, and focuses his research on business and environmental ethics. He is the director-founder of the Southeast-Asia North America Consortium on Trade and Human Rights. He is the director of a research group on governmental ethics, working now on deregulation processes and corporate social responsibility. A lawyer and an ethicist, he has published in various academic journals in Canada, USA, UK, France, Netherlands, Greece, Poland and India. His major books are: *Relations d'affaires et croyances religieuses* (GGC, 2001); *Le paradoxe humain* (GGC, 2000); *Investissements éthiques et régie d'entreprise* (Médiaspaul, 1998); *L'éthique de l 'entreprise* (Fides, 1994); and *L'éthique ou le profit* (Fides, 1992). He edited *L'éthique gouvernementale* (Fides, 1997), and is currently editing the forthcoming book, *Responsabilité sociale de l'entreprise et déréglementation* (Guerin, 2001).

m.dion@courrier.usherb.ca

Simon Gao is Professor of Accounting and Finance at Napier University, Edinburgh. He received his PhD in accounting and finance from Erasmus University, Rotterdam. He is a guest professor at Southwestern University of Finance and Economics, China. He has previously taught at Glasgow Caledonian University, Staffordshire University, UK, University of Central Lancashire, UK, and Shaanxi Institute of Technology. He has authored *International Leasing: Financial and Accounting Applications* (University of Central Lancashire Publications, 1994), *International Leasing: Strategy and Decision* (Ashgate Publishing, 1999), and co-edited *Perspectives on Accounting and Finance in China* (with John Blake; Routledge, 1995). He has written over 20 articles on leasing in Eastern Europe, lease accounting, Chinese accounting, environmental accounting, and public-sector risk management. His current research interests include social and environmental reporting, derivatives disclosure and risk management.

s.gao@napier.ac.uk

Jane Gibbon is Senior Lecturer in the School of Accounting, Finance and Information Systems at Newcastle Business School, UK. She teaches management accounting and her subject specialism is social and environmental accounting. She has developed internal and external courses on social and environmental reporting. Her current research interests are corporate sustainability reporting, ethics and gender issues, and she has published papers in these areas. She is on the editorial board of *The Journal of Applied Accounting Research*. Jane is currently completing an MA in environmental philosophy.
jane.gibbon@unn.ac.uk

Mark Glazebrook is the Co-ordinator of the Corporate Citizenship Research Unit, Deakin University, Australia. Based on an intensive analysis of Australian business practices, his field-based doctoral research titled *Exchange as a Determinant of Corporate Citizenship Outcome* maps the key organisational processes and milestones that businesses such as BP go through as they attempt to develop corporate citizenship as a central part of their business. This analysis is then contrasted with similar research undertaken within the non-government and government sectors. From the findings of this research, Mark is modelling how business can more effectively interpret the strengths and weaknesses of contemporary corporate citizenship practice as the basis for developing sustainable business solutions.
ccr-unit@deakin.edu.au

Leigh Holland is Principal Lecturer in the Faculty of Business and Law at De Montfort University, UK, where she teaches financial accounting on both undergraduate and post-graduate degrees. Her teaching includes specialist courses on accounting for sustainable development, which also reflects her research interest in corporate sustainability reporting. This has generated publications and conference presentations. Leigh is a member of of the Cuban Financial Reform Group and the Editor of *The Journal of Applied Accounting Research*. She has an MA in environmental management.
lhacc@dmu.ac.uk

Patsy Lewellyn is the John M. Olin Professor of Enterprise Development at the University of South Carolina Aiken, SC, USA. She received a BA in economics from Hendrix College and an MBA and DBA in quantitive analysis and information systems from Louisiana Technical University. She is a certified public accountant. She is the first American to have been certified as an Associate Member of the Institute for Social and Ethical AccountAbility, the organisation for social accountability professionals. Prior to entering academia in 1983, her professional experience included public and private accounting, and she served as the Executive Director of the Arkansas State Board of Public Accountancy. She teaches accounting information systems, auditing and financial accounting. Her current research interests focus on trends in non-financial performance measurement and reporting. Her work has recently appeared in *The Journal of Business Ethics, Business and Society Review, Business and Society* and *Accountability Quarterly*.
lewellyn@aiken.sc.edu

Jeanne M. Logsdon, is Regents' Professor of Management at the University of New Mexico, USA. She received her PhD in management from the University of California–Berkeley in 1981. Her research interests include global business citizenship, collaboration, environmental management, stakeholder theory and business ethics. Her articles have appeared in numerous scholarly journals, and she is co-author of *Research in Stakeholder Theory 1997–98*. She is editor of *Business and Society* and has held elected office in several major professional associations.
jlogsdon@unm.edu

Malcolm McIntosh is the Director of the Corporate Citizenship Unit at Warwick Business School, University of Warwick, UK. He is interested in the development of the idea of corporate citizenship and facilitating learning on the issue of business and society. At Warwick he runs courses on the MBA and MPA (public administration) programmes, as well co-ordinating open programmes on accountability. He is General Editor of *The Journal of Corporate Citizenship* and, as co-ordinator of the Global Compact Learning Forum, works closely with the United Nations, the United Nations Environment Programme, the International Labour Office and the United Nations Office of High Commissioner for Human Rights, as well advising many large companies and the UK Foreign Office and Department for International Development. He graduated in education from the University of London, and has a master's and a doctorate from the Department of Peace Studies at the University of Bradford. He lives in the ancient city of Bath in the West of England with his family.

Malcolm.McIntosh@warwick.ac.uk

Brian P. Niehoff is the Head of the Department of Management and the Mark R. Truitt Professor of Entrepreneurial Studies at Kansas State University College of Business Administration, USA. He received his PhD in organisational behaviour from Indiana University in 1988. He teaches both undergraduate and masters' courses in organisational behaviour, organisational training and development, and entrepreneurship. He has published his research in such journals as *Academy of Management Journal, Organizational Behavior and Human Decision Processes* and *Journal of Organizational Behavior*. His research focuses on the antecedents and consequences of organisational citizenship behaviours, including how organisational leaders and employee perceptions of workplace justice influence such behaviours. He has also conducted numerous training programmes with organisations in Kansas and the surrounding areas.

niehoff@ksu.edu

James E. Post, Professor of Management at Boston University, has written extensively on corporate responsibility, public affairs management and business ethics. His forthcoming book, with Lee E. Preston and Sybille Sachs, is *Redefining the Corporation: Stakeholder Management and Organizational Wealth* (Stanford University Press, 2002). He is also co-author, with Anne T. Lawrence and James Weber, of *Business and Society: Corporate Strategy, Public Policy, Ethics* (McGraw–Hill, 10th edn, 2002). His current research addresses the relationship of corporate citizenship strategies to business strategies among companies with global brand identities. This work is being conducted in North America, Europe and Australia.

jepost@bu.edu

Alejo José G. Sison, PhD, teaches ethics and human resource management at the University of Navarre, Spain, where he is also Executive Secretary of the Institute for Enterprise and Humanism. Previously, he worked at IESE (Barcelona) and at the University of Asia and the Pacific (Manila). In 1997, he was appointed Fulbright Senior Research Fellow and Visiting Scholar at Harvard University, USA. Since then, he has also received fellowships from the 21st Century Trust Foundation (London), the Academic Council on the United Nations System (Yale University), the American Society of International Law (Washington, DC) and the Salzburg Seminar. His research deals with the issues at the juncture of ethics with economics and politics.

ajsison@unav.es

Diane L. Swanson is an Associate Professor of Management and Faculty Fellow in the College of Business Administration at Kansas State University, USA, where she teaches undergraduate and graduate courses in business, government and society, and legal and social issues in business. Her research on corporate social performance, government regulation, organisational dynamics and ethics of leadership has been published in several outlets, including *Academy of Management Review, Behavioral Science, Human Relations, The Journal of Business Ethics, Companion to Business Ethics, Business and Society* and *Systems Research and Behavioral Science*. Dr Swanson has served as Book Review Editor for *The International Journal of Organizational Analysis* since 1993. She received her PhD in strategy, environments and organisation from the University of Pittsburgh in Pennsylvania in 1996.

swanson@ksu.edu

Sandra Waddock is Professor of Management at Boston College's Carroll School of Management, USA and Senior Research Fellow at Boston College's Center for Corporate Citizenship. She received her MBA (1979) and DBA from Boston University (1985) and has published extensively on corporate responsibility, corporate citizenship and inter-sector collaboration in journals such as *The Academy of Management Journal, Strategic Management Journal, The Journal of Corporate Citizenship, Human Relations* and *Business and Society,* among many others. Her book, *Not by Schools Alone,* was published by Praeger in 1995. Her 1997 paper with Sam Graves entitled, 'Quality of Management and Quality of Stakeholder Relations: Are They Synonymous?', in *Business and Society,* won the 1997 Moskowitz Prize. Her latest book is *Leading Corporate Citizens: Vision, Values, Value Added* (McGraw–Hill, 2002). She is Senior Fellow at the Ethics Resource Center in Washington, DC, and a founding faculty member of the Leadership for Change Program at Boston College.
waddock@bc.edu

Duane Windsor (PhD, Harvard University; BA, Rice University) is Lynette S. Autrey Professor of Management in the Jesse H. Jones Graduate School of Management at Rice University, Houston, TX, USA. He has published several books and numerous scholarly papers. His most recent book (with Lee E. Preston, University of Maryland at College Park) is *The Rules of the Game: Policy Regimes for International Business* (Kluwer Academic Publishers, 1997, 2nd edn). His articles include (with Kathleen A. Getz, American University) 'Regional Market Integration and the Development of Global Norms for Enterprise Conduct: The Case of International Bribery', *Business and Society,* December 1999; and 'Multilateral Cooperation to Combat Corruption: Normative Regimes despite Mixed Motives and Diverse Values', *Cornell International Law Journal* (2000).
odw@rice.edu

Donna J. Wood, is Professor of Business Administration at the Katz School, University of Pittsburgh, USA. She received her PhD in sociology from Vanderbilt University. Her research interests focus on global business citizenship, corporate social performance, stakeholder theory and business ethics. Her articles have appeared in numerous scholarly journals. In addition, she has authored or co-authored several books, including *Research in Stakeholder Theory 1997–98* (University of Toronto Press, 2000); *International Business and Society* (Blackwell, 1998); *Strategic Uses of Public Policy* (Ballinger Books, 1986); *Business and Society* (HarperCollins, 1994); and *Research in Teams* (Prentice–Hall, 1991). Dr Wood has spent a year as visiting professor in Berlin, as well as two semesters as visiting professor at the Darden School, University of Virginia. She is past editor of *Business and Society* and has held elected office in several major professional associations.
djwood@katz.pitt.edu

Simon Zadek is Chairperson of the Institute of Social and Ethical AccountAbility. He works with businesses, non-governmental organisations and governments as advisor, external reviewer and trainer. He also works at the governance level of the Global Reporting Initiative, the Global Alliance for Workers and Communities, and the Copenhagen Centre. His recent co-authored publications include *Perspectives on the New Ecology of Corporate Citizenship* (The Copenhagen Centre, 2001); *Conversations with Disbelievers* (Brody & Weiser, 2000); and *Unlocking the Evidence: The New Disability Business Case* (Employers' Forum on Disability, 2001).
www.zadek.net

Jane Zhang is a doctoral research student in the Division of Accounting and Finance at Glasgow Caledonian University, UK. She has a BSc in medicine from Huashan Medical School, China, and an MSc in risk management from Glasgow Caledonian University. Her current research interests are social auditing in the UK National Health Service and long-term-care social insurance. She has presented papers at several conferences on social auditing and long-term-care social insurance.
j.zhang@gcal.ac.uk

INDEX

DATE DUE
